SOCIAL WORK IN CANADA
An Introduction

Education either functions as an instrument which is used to facilitate the integration of generations into the logic of the present system and bring about conformity to it, or it becomes "the practice of freedom," the means by which men and women deal critically and creatively with reality and discover how to participate in the transformation of their world.

– Paulo Freire, *Pedagogy of the Oppressed*

SOCIAL WORK IN CANADA

An Introduction

STEVEN HICK

Carleton University

THOMPSON EDUCATIONAL PUBLISHING, INC.

Toronto

Information on how to obtain copies of this book may be obtained from:

Website:	www.thompsonbooks.com
E-mail:	publisher@thompsonbooks.com
Telephone:	(416) 766-2763
Fax:	(416) 766-0398

National Library of Canada Cataloguing in Publication Data

Hick, Steven F.

Social work in Canada : an introduction

Includes bibliographical references and index.
ISBN 1-55077-124-8

1. Social service—Canada. I. Title

HV1050.H52 2002   361.3'0971   C2001-901210-1

Copy Editing: Elizabeth Phinney
Cover Design: Elan Designs

We acknowledge the support of the Government of Canada through the Book Publishing Industry Development Program for our publishing activities.

Printed in Canada.
1 2 3 4 5   06 05 04 03 02 01

Contents

Preface

There are many books available in Canada that introduce social work to students, but most of these originate in the United States, the United Kingdom and Australia. This book fills a need for an introductory-level book written from a Canadian perspective. It is addressed to students who are new to social work and may be considering a career in the field. Unlike many foreign texts, which tend to emphasize techniques, this book emphasizes the importance of being clear about one's values and worldview before practising social work.

The content of this book falls generally into two parts. The first part (Chapters 1-5) introduces the profession and practice of social work. Chapter 1 introduces the basic concepts and sets the context for looking at the theory and practice of Canadian social work. Chapter 2 surveys the emergence (and some might say unravelling) of income security in Canada. Chapter 3 looks at the historical context of social work practice in Canada, and Chapter 4 examines profession-related and ethical issues. Chapter 5 provides a foundation of direct social work—work with individuals, groups and communities. Chapter 2 (dealing with income security system) is included so that social work students will have a sense of the broader social welfare system in Canada.

The remaining chapters (Chapter 6-13), comprising the second part of the book, present how social work is conceived and practised in various fields with different sectors of society. Chapter 6 focuses on social work with children and youth; Chapter 7, social work and health; Chapter 8, social work with women; Chapter 9, social work and Aboriginal peoples; Chapter 10, anti-racist social work; Chapter 11, social work and sexual diversity; Chapter 12, social work with persons with disabilities; and Chapter 13, international social work practice.

This book does not pretend to provide any "ten-step" recipe that students can simply take away and apply to any particular social work problem. Instead, the book presents a variety of viewpoints and approaches, all of which have something useful to offer when determining an appropriate course of action to rectify a problem.

The author feels, above all, that social work practitioners should possess a broad knowledge and a multifaceted outlook, and always be open to new ideas. Throughout the text, there is emphasis on the need for students to think deeply about issues, particularly controversial ones, before arriving at a recommended course of action.

Steven Hick
Carleton University

Acknowledgments

This book has been over five years in the making. It sprang from discussions between myself and Allan Moscovitch while teaching an introductory social work course at Carleton University. Allan Moscovitch, in particular, played an important role in initiating the work on this book and provided invaluable guidance in its preparation. The book went through several stops and was re-started when Keith Thompson at Thompson Educational Publishing encouraged its completion.

From the beginning, the intention was to give a voice to people from the communities or groups in society who teach directly in the field. A special thanks to Gordon Bruyere for his extensive contribution to the history section of the chapter on Aboriginal peoples; to Shirly Judge for her guidance on the examples in the chapter on social work with women; to Bernice Moreau for the advice on the section dealing with the history of Blacks in Canada; and for the hard work of Emily Cronin, a graduate student who made the instructor's manual a possibility. Special thanks also to Roy Hanes for his chapter on disability, to George Bielmeier for the chapter on sexual diversity, and to Reva Gutnick for her contribution to Chapter 2.

I must express my deep-felt thanks to my family—Vaida, my partner, Justin, my son, and Kristina, my daughter—not only for bearing with my many hours at the keyboard but also for encouraging my writing through their support and lively dinner conversations.

Finally, and once again, a special thanks to Allan Moscovitch, who initiated the project with me and laid much of the groundwork, and to Keith Thompson, for his excellent editorial work and tireless support.

1
Introduction

What This Book Is About

Despite reductions in social expenditures in recent years, government social programs continue to play a significant role in the life of many individuals and families. Every Canadian is eventually touched by a social worker at some point in their life, whether while in hospital or through a child welfare agency, community centre or income security agency.

One hundred years ago private charity was the main recourse for persons in distress (and even then for only a small part of the population). Today, however, public (government-run or government-funded) social programs and services are widespread and affect nearly everyone at some point in his or her life. Nevertheless, while the social services are commonplace, Canadians today in general are not well aware of the history of social welfare in their country or the role it plays in our daily lives.

This book is an effort to redress that imbalance. We hope that you, with the aid of this textbook, will become familiar with the key concepts and issues in social work practice in Canada.

WHAT IS THE WELFARE STATE?

The basic goal of our social welfare system is simple: it is to help people through difficult times until they can rebuild their lives. This may sometimes be long term, as, for example, when persons have a physical or psychiatric disability, a continuing illness or lack the skills required by the labour market and require ongoing help. The kinds of "contingencies" for which the welfare system is designed can be grouped into three interrelated categories: (1) contingencies that threaten economic survival, (2) contingencies that threaten the integrity of the person and (3) contingencies that affect the family. Retirement, unemployment, a drop in income and price changes are examples of contingencies that affect economic survival. Disability, illness, violence, homelessness, addiction, racism, warfare and death are examples of contingencies that affect the integrity of the person. Separation, divorce, the ageing of family members and additional children are events that threaten the survival of the family.

While this book focuses on social work and the provision of social services, it is important to understand that social services are part of a range of activities that fall more generally under the term social welfare. **Social welfare** includes not only the **social services** proper (the provision of

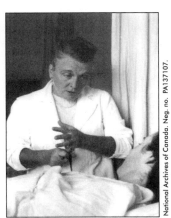

Social welfare is indispensable in a civilized society.

TWO COMPONENTS OF SOCIAL WELFARE

- Social services–personal or community services provided to help individuals and families improve their social well-being.

- Income security–financial or material assistance provided to increase the income or other resources of individuals and families.

Chapter 2 provides an overview of the income security system. The remainder of the chapters focus on social work and the social services proper.

personal or community services to help people improve their well-being–including child care, child protection services, women's shelters, counselling and so forth) but also a range of **income security** provisions–Employment Insurance, Social Assistance, Old Age Security, Workers' Compensation–that provide monetary or other material benefits to supplement income or maintain minimum income levels. Taken together, social services and income security comprise what is known, loosely, as social welfare.

The above distinction between social services and income security is an important one, but, in real life, it is difficult to maintain. This is often a source of confusion for beginning social workers because, frequently, difficulties come in pairs or in even more complex combinations. For example, a man who becomes ill or has an accident may also lose his job and, as a result, his home. A woman who is subjected to violence may be forced to leave her home and may need assistance in obtaining child support as well as personal income support. A man with an addiction may lose his employment and is at risk of becoming homeless, tied up in the prison system and/or the mental health system. Thus, social services are often needed to deal with problems that have their roots in economic insecurity and vice versa. This book deals primarily with the social services and the practice of social work; it does not cover in any depth the complex income security programs in Canada that provide monetary assistance to individuals and families. However, because a basic understanding of the income security system is necessary for effective social work practice, the second chapter in this book provides a quick overview of this vast field.

The range of programs and services available to Canadian citizens is commonly referred to as the welfare state. One might define the **welfare state** as a system whereby the state undertakes to protect the health and well-being of its citizens, especially those in social and financial need. The key elements of the welfare state are the use of state power (government, bureaucracy, the judiciary, political parties) to achieve the desired ends; altering the normal operation of the private marketplace; and the use of grants, taxes, pensions, social services and minimum-income programs, such as welfare and social insurance.

The various services are provided to citizens through social policies developed by the government and specific social programs designed to carry out these social policies. **Social policies** are the overall rules and regulations, laws and other administrative directives, that set the framework and objectives for state social welfare activity. For example, universal medicare is a social policy to which the government of Canada is committed.

Social programs, on the other hand, are specific initiatives that follow on from and implement social welfare policies. Continuing with the medicare example, there are special incentives (programs) to encourage newly accredited physicians to move to outlying areas, thus ensuring greater equality of access to medical services (in line with the commitment to universal medicare for Canadians).

THE PROVISION OF SOCIAL WELFARE

There are several different types of welfare available to Canadians. A key distinction is between public programs and private programs.

Because Canada is a federal state, **public welfare** occurs at the three levels of government: the federal or national government, the provincial and territorial governments and the regional and municipal governments. As well, there are public non-government agencies, such as advisory and appeal boards, which are the creations of government (whether federal, provincial or municipal) but which consist of members who are appointed from the public by government. Government is ultimately responsible for their activities, but they are either completely independent or semi-independent.

There is also **private welfare**. Here we should distinguish between two types of organizations: private non-profit and private for-profit. Non-profit organizations are mandated to provide a service or an activity but not to create a profit. In Canada, such organizations are often registered by law, and rules and regulations govern what steps must be taken if a profit is generated. Many of these agencies are incorporated as non-profit corporations; they receive funds from one or more levels of government and from private sources. At the same time, they can earn money by providing services for other organizations. Take the example of the Children's Aid Societies in Ontario. They receive their principal funding from the provincial government of Ontario, they are registered as non-profit organizations and they have boards of directors composed of private citizens who are elected annually, and they also receive funds from private organizations or individuals. For-profit organizations, on the other hand, are prevalent in certain social service areas, such as nursing homes, home care and child care. These organizations provide services that are often purchased by government on behalf of individuals, but their purpose is to generate a profit for the owner of the organization. With government cutbacks in recent years, more and more welfare services are being provided by non-profit and for-profit private agencies.

All three organizations–public, private non-profit and commercial –are part of the structure of social services in the Canadian welfare state. (Another important source of funding for income security and social services in Canada, but not covered in this text, is industrial welfare. Industrial welfare is available through employment and provides everything from dental and optical plans to legal aid services and pension plans. Only people employed by companies offering these services can access these benefits.)

• Approaching Social Welfare

The idea of providing social services to citizens in need is no longer a controversial one in Canada. Major disputes do arise, however, in determining which groups are in need and to what extent they need state assistance. Different **approaches to social welfare** are represented in these disputes. Generally, there are two such approaches: let's call these the residual view and the institutional view.

Many services are threatened by government spending cuts.

© Dick Hemingway

Homelessness in urban centres is a national problem that requires urgent attention by politicians, social policy makers and social workers.

HOMELESSNESS

Recent estimates of the number of homeless are alarming.

In Canada's largest city, Toronto, emergency shelters for the homeless took in an average of 6,500 persons each night in 1997. About 30,000 different people used Toronto's shelters in 2000.

"Housing Again" is a website dedicated to putting affordable housing back on the public agenda. For information and statistics, go to: http://www.housingagain. web.net

In the **residual view**, social welfare is a limited and temporary response to human need, implemented only when all else fails. It is based on the premise that there are two natural ways through which an individual's needs are met—the family and the market economy. The residual model is based on the idea that government should play only a limited role in the distribution of social welfare. The state should only step in when these normal sources of support fail, and the individual is unable to help him or herself. Residual social welfare is, therefore, highly targeted to those most in need. Additionally, residual social welfare tends to provide benefits at a low level in order to discourage use and not make social welfare appear desirable. Canadian public social welfare programs, from early history to the Depression of the 1930s, can be characterized as residual in nature.

In the **institutional view**, on the other hand, social welfare is a necessary public response in helping people attain a reasonable standard of life and health. Within this view, it is accepted that people cannot always meet all of their needs through family and work. Therefore it is both proper and legitimate in a complex industrial society for society to help people through a set of publicly funded and organized systems of programs and institutions. The institutional model promotes the principle that all citizens are entitled, as a matter of right and unconditionally, to a decent standard of living, and it is the role of the state to ensure this. The institutional model, then, seeks to even out, rather than promote, stratification or status differences that arise in the market.

These views represent different overall approaches to social welfare and capture the political controversy surrounding social welfare today. It is useful to think about and understand this distinction, since each gives a different sense of what social welfare is all about and how extensive it should be–and, more particularly, how much government funding it should receive.

WHAT DO SOCIAL WORKERS DO?

People are often confronted with unforeseen events, such as accidents, illness, incidents of violence and death. People are also faced with economic contingencies, such as unemployment, retirement and homelessness. A whole range of welfare services are available to Canadians to help them deal with such circumstances, and it is within this complex web of social welfare institutions (income security programs and social services) that social workers work or practice.

Those who choose social work as their profession do so for a variety of reasons. They appear to be motivated to make this choice by some combination of humanitarian and egalitarian values, and by a desire to understand how society works. Frequently, a person is motivated to become a social worker following exposure to injustice and oppression. Whatever the combination of factors that leads a person into the profession, social workers require more than just the desire to "do good." Social workers require the necessary values and skills of analysis to be able to approach social situations in a way that is useful. In order to provide assistance, they require knowledge and skills in a variety of areas.

The Canadian Association of Social Workers' *Code of Ethics* (1994; see Appendix A for the full *Code of Ethics*) defines social work practice as including

- the assessment, remediation and prevention of social problems, and the enhancement of social functioning of individuals, families and communities by means of
  - the provision of direct counselling services within an established relationship between a social worker and client;
  - the development, promotion and delivery of human service programs, including that done in collaboration with other professionals; and
  - the development and promotion of social policies aimed at improving social conditions and equality.

The *Code*, in fact, distinguishes between two types of social work: direct social work and indirect social work. **Direct social work** involves providing services (such as individual counselling, group work and community development). Most often people who are doing direct social work will be working for public or publicly funded but privately administered social service agencies and institutions. Some social workers work on their own or in groups in a private practice.

Indirect social work also benefits those in need, but usually those who do indirect social work will do so with governments–formulating,

SOCIAL WORK

The term social work has been credited to Jeffery Brackett, who was a Charity Organization Society volunteer in the early 1900s. He argued for the adoption of the term to differentiate between professionals doing social work and the volunteers who helped at various societies as a recreational or volunteer activity. The inclusion of the word "work" was meant to emphasize this distinction.

EMPLOYMENT SETTINGS

"93% of all [social workers] are employed either in the health and social services or government industries, with 74% in the former and 19% in the latter. There is increasing participation ... in health and social services and a corresponding decrease in their presence in government services. This is at least in part a reflection of government withdrawal from the direct provision of social services.

"Relatively few social workers are employed in private practice offices, but the number almost doubled between 1991 and 1996."

Source: CASSW, *In Critical Demand: Social Work in Canada, Final Report* (September 1998-April 2001). To find out more about this important study, go to: http://www.socialworkincanada.org

WEBSITES

http://www.policyalternatives.ca
http://www.ccsd.ca
http://www.caledoninst.org
http://www.napo-onap.ca

analyzing, developing and evaluating social policies and programs. Others will be involved with social service agencies, advocacy or research groups and organizations whose purpose is to advocate for and with people in need and to conduct research. Examples of such organizations in Canada would be the Canadian Centre for Policy Alternatives, the Canadian Council on Social Development, the Caledon Institute of Social Policy and the National Anti-Poverty Organization (NAPO).

Whether involved directly with citizens or indirectly in research, social workers are above all committed to serving people in need. They are there when circumstances go wrong and people need help. As professionals, social workers approach difficult situations with compassion and a skill set that can help people overcome obstacles and get back on track with their lives.

The traditional notion of the social worker has been that of a caseworker. However, this conception has increasingly changed as practicing social workers have come to realize that their roles are much more complex. Until recently, social work was defined only as an institutional method of helping people improve their social functioning and resolve their problems, probably stemming from its historical roots as a crusade to abolish the moral evils causing poverty. Today, social work in Canada involves not only attending to individual problems but also changing the social environment and empowering people to improve their situation.

APPROACHES TO PRACTICE

The manner in which social workers conceptualize and approach their work is influenced by their own worldviews, life experiences and personal preferences and styles. Throughout this book, the preferred criteria for distinguishing the different approaches to social work practice is the primary location of the cause of the target social work problem. At one end are approaches that emphasize primarily the personal (or internal) factors. At the other end are theories and approaches to social work that view structural (or external) factors as being dominant. Of course, few problems are organized by either internal or external factors alone.

Approaches that locate the problem in the individual. There are a wide variety of approaches within this category. Some approaches locate the problem in the body (such as in traditional medical practice), while others locate the problem in the mind (for example, psychoanalytic approaches such as Gestalt and Transactional Analysis, cognitively based theories and behaviour-based theories). These approaches say very little about how to address issues outside of the individual. On the other hand, other theories within this general school of thought—such as developmentally based theories, task-centred and problem-solving approaches, and generalist approaches—do take into account the importance of broader environmental demands and the changes in social systems involved in the problem. In these approaches, the purpose is to enhance the coping and problem-solving abilities of the client, link people to resources, promote access to human services and contribute to better social policy.

Approaches that locate the problem in social structures. Approaches within this category give emphasis to the wider social factors influencing a particular problem. These factors may include social class, poverty, racial discrimination and patriarchal relations. Approaches within this category include structural social work practice, radical casework, and feminist, anti-racist and Aboriginal approaches. These approaches vary according to their particular emphasis, but they are all based on the belief that structural factors have major significance for many types of social work problems.

In Canada today there are a variety of perspectives and several different approaches or models of social work. The two dominant approaches in Canadian social work (the "generalist" and the "structuralist" approaches) are discussed briefly at the end of Chapter 5 (see page 89). What is important for the beginning social worker to understand is that there is a range of approaches and that there is no single or best body of knowledge to inform one's practice. In order to be effective, the social work practitioner must be prepared to approach daily practice from all angles and to find the one that works for him or her.

DEFINING SOCIAL WORK

A new international definition of social work was adopted at the General Meeting of the International Federation of Social Workers' (IFSW) in Montreal in July 2000 (available on-line at http://www.ifsw.org):

> The social work profession promotes social change, problem solving in human relationships and the empowerment and liberation of people to enhance well-being. Utilizing theories of human behaviour and social systems, social work intervenes at the points where people interact with their environments. Principles of human rights and social justice are fundamental to social work.

The definition emphasizes four concepts: social change, problem solving, person-in-the-environment and empowerment. To begin to understand this complex work it is necessary to explore these four key concepts.

• Social Change Mandate

A **social change mandate** means working in solidarity with those who are disadvantaged or excluded from society so as to eliminate the barriers, inequities and injustices that exist in society. Social workers should be at the forefront of promoting policy and legislation that redistributes wealth in favour of those who are less well-off—that is, promoting equal opportunity for women, gays, lesbians, bisexuals, transgender persons, people with disabilities, Aboriginal peoples and racial and other minorities, and defending past gains made in these areas.

• Problem Solving

Social workers respond to crises and emergencies as well as everyday personal and social problems. Within this process, social workers use **problem-solving techniques** to identify the problem and formulate possible plans of action. A problem is not usually clearly defined when

SOCIAL WORK VALUES

- Humanitarianism
- Egalitarian ideals
- Self-determination
- Mutual respect and dignity of every person
- Privacy
- Human rights
- Fair and non-judgemental
- Co-operation

Public Archives of Canada. Neg. no. PA-118221.

Child welfare continues to be a main focus for social work.

EMPOWERMENT

Elizabeth Whitmore and Maureen Wilson, two Canadian social work faculty members, worked with other social workers at the Universidad Centroamericana in Nicaragua to help redesign their social work program. As part of this, they did workshops on gender equality, which included linking the local with the global.

They worked from a model of international development practice that they called "accompaniment." This practice emphasizes ownership and control by the partners.

The principles of "accompaniment" are outlined in *Seeds of Fire: Social Development in an Era of Globalism,* a book compiled by Wilson and Whitmore.

someone comes to a social service agency. It is therefore crucial for the social worker to explore the person's concerns, to identify the need(s) involved, to identify barriers to meeting need(s) and to carefully determine the goals and possible plans of action. A key characteristic of the problem-solving process is the inclusion of the client at each stage. The process should also teach clients problem-solving skills so that they can better deal with future problems on their own.

• Person-in-the-Environment

A key aspect of effective social work practice is to go beyond the "internal" (psychological) factors and examine the relationship between individuals and their environments. This **person-in-the-environment** approach is partly what distinguishes social work practice from other helping professions. These "environments" extend beyond the immediate family and include interactions with friends, neighbourhoods, schools, religious groups, laws and legislation, other agencies or organizations, places of employment and the economic system. Based on this understanding, intervention may focus on the individual, interactions between people and any given system or structure, or on the system or structure itself.

• "Empowerment" and Social Work

In order for the interventions of social workers to be successful, the clients must believe that the efforts of the social worker will make a difference. This leads to the important concept of empowerment. Being empowered means feeling that you have power and control over the course of your life.

Empowerment is the process of increasing personal, interpersonal or political power so that one can improve one's particular situation. Power can be a personal state of mind, in the sense that one feels that one can make a difference and have control and influence over one's own life. It can also be empowerment within an organization in the sense that one has tangible influence and legal rights. Empowerment, then, involves both a personal perception of being in control and tangible elements of power within the various social structures of society. Social workers seek to empower their clients as a way of helping them to focus on, among other things, access to resources and the structures of power.

"Empowerment-based social work," therefore, has three aspects:

- making power explicit in the client-worker relationship (in order thereby to help equalize the relationship between the client and the worker);

- giving clients experiences in which they themselves are in control (to allow them to see the potential for controlling their lives); and

- always supporting the client's own efforts to gain greater control over their lives as a way of promoting change.

Putting an empowerment perspective into practice can involve techniques that make power relations between the workers and their clients explicit, thereby equalizing the client-worker relationship. Additionally,

Empowering individuals and communities into action.

it may entail giving clients powerful experiences or experiences that put them in a position to exercise power. Offering voluntary work experiences that allow clients to use their skills to help others can often be an empowering experience. Another approach may be to support clients' efforts to change policies or practices that impinge on their lives and the lives of others. Such experiences can help people see the potential for power in their lives.

In other instances, an empowering perspective may involve simply focusing on the strengths of the person, rather than on the "pathology" or what is wrong with the person. In all relationships, it is generally acknowledged that constructive feedback and positive reinforcement is conducive to helping people make positive changes in their lives. It is often more helpful for social workers to guide their client's focus towards the success they have achieved in the past rather than dwelling on how they have been unsuccessful and dysfunctional.

An empowerment perspective is the key to good social work practice. And like other aspects of good practice, it involves not a specific set of skills, but a general orientation on the part of the worker. This orientation is based on helping clients identify their own needs and then helping them to deal with the exigencies of their own particular situation.

CONCLUSION

The complex field known as social welfare includes two major components: income security (or programs that provide financial or material assistance) and social services (which provide personal and community services to help people improve their well-being). Although this book deals with social services, it is important to have an understanding of the entire social welfare field, including the area of income security.

The social services are provided by a large number of public and private agencies and employ social workers in both direct and indirect social work. Key to comprehending the nature of social work practice are four concepts: social change, problem solving, person-in-the-environment and empowerment. Using these basic concepts, professional social workers carry out their work at the individual, group, community and societal levels.

Politicians, and even the general public, do not agree on the extent to which the state should provide income security or social services to people in need. Yet it is within this uncertainty that social worker practitioners face real people with real problems, and increasingly with fewer and fewer resources to do so. To be effective, social workers are more and more using an empowerment process to develop the personal, interpersonal and political power of the people they are helping so that they may gain greater control over their lives and thereby promote change.

REFERENCES

- Canadian Association of Schools of Social Work. 2001. *In Critical Demand: Social Work in Canada, Final Report*. Ottawa. This report is available on-line at: http://www.socialworkincanada.org

- Casavant, Lyne. 1999. Overview. Ottawa: Public Works and Government Services Canada, Political and Social Affairs Division.

- Wilson, Maureen G., and Elizabeth Whitmore. 2000. *Seeds of fire: Social Development in the Era of Globalization*. Halifax, N.S.: Fernwood Press.

CHAPTER 1: INTRODUCTION

Key Concepts

- Social welfare
- Social services
- Income security
- Welfare state
- Social policies
- Social programs
- Public welfare
- Private welfare
- Approaches to social welfare
- Residual view
- Institutional view
- Direct social work
- Indirect social work
- Social change mandate
- Problem-solving techniques
- Person-in-the-environment
- Empowerment

Discussion Questions

1. What are the main components of the social welfare system in Canada?

2. Define and compare the following terms: (1) social policy and social program, and (2) public welfare and private welfare.

3. What is meant by the "residual" and "institutional" approaches to welfare?

4. List and describe the four key concepts contained in the International Federations' definition of social work practice.

5. Define empowerment and outline what a social worker could do to put an empowerment perspective into practice.

Websites

- **Social Work Glossary**
  http://www.socialpolicy.ca

  This site contains Steven Hick's personal collection of over 600 definitions of social welfare terms. It also includes links to publications and on-line course materials.

- **Canadian Council on Social Development (CCSD)**
  http://www.ccsd.ca

  CCSD is one of Canada's most authoritative voices promoting better social and economic security for all Canadians. A national, self-supporting, non-profit organization, the CCSD's main product is information and its main activity is research, focusing on concerns such as income security, employment, poverty, child welfare, pensions and government social policies. Check out the Internet launch pad for a variety of excellent links.

- **Canadian Social Research Links**
  http://www.canadiansocialresearch.net

  This is Gilles Séguin's virtual resource centre for Canadian social program information. His purpose in creating and maintaining this site is to provide a comprehensive, current and balanced collection of links to Canadian social program information for those who formulate Canadian social policies and for those who study and critique them.

- **Critical Social Work journal**
  http://www.criticalsocialwork.com

  An on-line journal with articles on how social work can contribute to social justice. In part the goal of Critical Social Work is to assist in collectively recognizing the current potentials for social justice as well as the future possibilities. They propose that through dialogue there exists the possibility of refining our ideas about the individual and community, clarifying the relationship between interpersonal relations and institutional structures, and identifying actions that promote both individual and community well-being.

2

Income Security and Social Welfare

An Overview

Steven Hick and Reva Gutnick

This chapter focuses on income security in Canada. In addition to detailing the many government programs currently in place, the chapter surveys some of the ideas and debates surrounding income security provisions. It also draws attention to some of the major social issues that the welfare state attempts to address, such as unemployment, poverty and globalization.

There is no question that income security programs are at the core of the welfare state in Canada. However, two myths should be dispelled. The first is that income security programs are used only by the poor. The reality is that every Canadian over the course of their lives is a beneficiary of Canada's income security infrastructure, whether it in the form of a retirement pension, Employment Insurance, Death Benefits, Social Assistance or Family Benefits. The second myth is that income programs serve only to keep the poor from destitution. While it is true that they accomplish this more or less, they also provide the government with key levers over the economy. In the post-World War II period, social welfare spending played a vital role in the macro management of the Canadian economy and labour force.

The level of commitment to social welfare, in Canada or any other country, is derived from what the members of the society in question value as a society, and what they believe the role of government is in their lives. For example, should the risk of unemployment be shared or should those who fall on bad times be left to fend for themselves? What are the long-term costs to society of letting people spiral into hopelessness?

These are a few of the underlying questions that need to be considered, and this chapter attempts to sort through some of the complexities.

INCOME SECURITY AND SOCIAL SERVICES

In this text, we try to maintain a distinction between income security and social services. Of course, as noted in Chapter 1, it is not always easy to distinguish between an income security provision and a social service.

Social services, in our sense of the term, essentially involve providing non-monetary help to persons in need; that is, the work done largely by social workers as outlined in the other chapters of this book. Examples are child welfare (e.g., Children's Aid Societies, which include adoption

National Archives of Canada. Neg. no. C29397.

Income security should be a right of Canadian citizenship.

19

services and foster care), probation services, addiction treatment services, youth drop-in centres, parent-child resource centres and shelters for abused women.

By contrast, the income security system, as we are defining it, has income redistribution or income supplementation as its primary aim. Unlike social services, these programs provide monetary or financial assistance to individuals and families. If all members of a society were able to consistently meet their income needs (through wages from employment, investment income or inheritance), the need for income security programs would be drastically reduced or eliminated. Unfortunately, most people do not have a secure income throughout their lifetime. Without income security programs, all Canadians would be much more vulnerable.

The immediate relief of poverty and severe destitution sparked the earliest government involvement in social welfare. Thus began the acknowledgment of Canadians that their society was responsible for caring for those at risk and in need. It was, however, a very narrow acknowledgment: early social welfare was of a residual nature or meant to serve those in need only when all else had failed. Following World War II and the Great Depression of the 1930s and 1940s, a new consensus developed. Citizens of Canada began to recognize that hard times could strike anyone through no personal fault. This new consensus led to the development of a comprehensive set of income security programs.

Income security programs provide monetary support to individuals or families. They are often called transfers because they "transfer" cash and other benefits from government-funded or government-administered programs to individuals or families. Public income security programs fall into the following four broad categories:

- **Social insurance.** These programs follow the insurance principle of shared risk. Persons contribute to insurance plans with the understanding that not all will necessarily need to access the benefits of the program. Insurance-based programs are generally tied to work. All workers contribute, and only those who contribute become eligible for benefits should the need arise. Employment Insurance, Workers' Compensation and the Canada/Quebec Pension Plan are social insurance programs.

- **Minimum income.** These are programs that provide monetary assistance to those with no other source of income. They are primarily geared towards those deemed to be living in poverty, and the amount of assistance tends to be based on what is considered to be the minimum necessary to have one's basic needs met. Social Assistance, also called welfare or workfare, is a minimum income program.

- **Demogrants.** These are universal flat-rate payments made to individuals or households on the sole basis of demographic characteristics, such as number of children or age, rather than on the basis of proven need (as in minimum income programs) or contributions (as in social insurance programs). The Old Age Security (OAS) paid to all person aged sixty-five and over and the former Family

Allowance program benefitting all families with children under the age of eighteen are demogrants.

- **Income supplementation.** These are programs that, as the name suggests, supplement income that is obtained elsewhere, whether through paid employment or through other income security programs. These programs are not intended to be the primary source of income. These programs may have a broad entitlement, in that they may be available to everyone within a very broad category, or they may be targeted to those most in need. Family Allowance (which was also a universal demogrant), the National Child Benefit and the Guaranteed Income Supplement (GIS) are income supplementation programs.

Government participation in income security covers a broad range: cash benefits for people with disabilities, old age, survivors, occupational injuries and illness, sickness, families and unemployment. However, the above list of direct government cash benefits does not reflect the entire spectrum of income security expenditure.

First, income security is provided through the tax system when governments provide tax breaks or forego the collection of taxes or when income or benefits are taxed differently. While this is not often thought of as income security, it can dramatically affect the income of Canadians. By not collecting taxes from those who have a taxable income, an individual's income is effectively increased. A personal tax exemption for a single parent with income high enough to be taxed provides income for the parent and a foregoing of tax revenue (a tax expenditure) for the state. When the government provides a tax deduction for Registered Retirement Saving Plans (RRSP), it foregoes collecting taxes on the money invested by the individual, which effectively allows a tax break to those with enough money to put some away towards retirement.

Second, income security can be provided by the private sector–both private employers and the voluntary sector. Some countries, such as Norway, the Netherlands and Denmark, have substantial mandatory employer-paid income security programs. Canada does not. Conversely, Canada has comparatively high amounts (3.5 percent of Gross Domestic Product [GDP]) of voluntary sector income security benefits, outstripping all other developed countries except the United States and the United Kingdom (Adema 1999, 15).

Employment-related policies and legislation can also affect the income of Canadians and can therefore be considered a part of our income security framework. These include labour standards and minimum wage legislation, as well as policies that affect the quantity and distribution of employment and employment equity programs. Employment equity and pay equity legislation attempted to address wage discrimination based on gender, ethnicity and disability.

PUBLIC INCOME SECURITY PROGRAMS

Most people know which government expenditure programs are part of the income security network. Recently, Employment Insurance,

Family Allowance office in Charlottetown, PEI (1940s).

Social Assistance, Old Age Security and Child or Family Benefits have been in the headlines. The effectiveness and affordability of these programs is a frequent topic of discussion. The past decade has seen significant changes to our income security programs. Expenditures have been cut, eligibility requirements have been tightened and benefits have been reduced, usually in the name of reducing the government deficit.

In Canada, today, we have the following range of income security programs:

- *Employment Insurance (EI)*. This federally administered program, originally called Unemployment Insurance, dates back to 1940. Since then, EI has undergone numerous changes. It was initially expanded to include more workers but was more recently severely contracted, making fewer workers eligible. EI provides a level of income replacement to workers who are temporarily unemployed and meet strict eligibility conditions. Sickness, maternity and parental benefits are included in this program. Also included in EI are fishing benefits for those whose livelihood depends on the fishing industry. Claimants are eligible for a range of re-skills development programs. EI is paid for through employer and employee contributions.

- *Workers' Compensation*. Workers' Compensation programs are provincially administered benefits designed to protect individuals against income loss due to workplace injury or disease. The program is funded by employers. In return for participation in this program, workers waive their right to sue their employer in the case of a work-related injury or disease. The first Workers' Compensation program was instituted in Ontario in 1914.

- *Social Assistance*. Social Assistance programs have their roots in early municipal and provincial relief programs that were designed to provide minimal support to the "deserving" poor or those deemed unable to work because of age or infirmity. Gradually expanded to include those in need but without resources, Social Assistance has remained a residual program of last resort for those with no other source of income or savings. Social Assistance programs, also called welfare, have remained a provincial responsibility with some funding coming from the federal government. Because the federal government requires only that length of residency must not be a requirement of eligibility, the provinces are free to design their program. As a result, in some provinces, those receiving benefits must work or be in training for employment. Each province is free to determine the level of benefits.

- *Canada Child Tax Benefit/National Child Benefit*. There is a long history in Canada of benefits to families with children. Some of these benefits have been and continue to be delivered through the tax system in the form of tax credits and exemptions, and others have been direct cash transfers. In 1944, a universal benefit called the Family Allowance was instituted, and this benefit went to all families with children regardless of income. Over time, this benefit became targeted towards middle- and low-income families. In 1993,

National Archives of Canada. Neg no. PA168131.

Soup kitchen for the poor in Montreal, Quebec, 1931.

this benefit was eliminated completely. The Canada Child Tax Benefit and the National Child Benefit are the current major child-related benefits supplement for families with children. Application for this benefit is through the tax system, with eligibility determined by family income. An interesting aspect of this federal benefit is that families on Social Assistance receive it in lieu of provincial Social Assistance benefits for their children. The provinces, then, are not responsible for "welfare for children." With the monies saved, the provinces are expected to re-invest in programs to help alleviate child poverty and its effects. In 1998-99, 3.2 million families received benefits totalling $5.7 billion.

- *Canada/Quebec Pension Plan.* C/QPP is a national contributory and earnings-related pension program introduced in 1966. It provides benefits in the case of retirement, death and long-term disability. CPP and QPP are jointly financed by employees and employers with current contributions supporting current beneficiaries. In this sense, the plan is a "pay-as-you-go" system. Any funds not paid out are invested for the purposes of creating a larger reserve fund. The plan comprises Retirement, Disability and Survivors and Orphans Death Benefits. Eligibility for this benefit is at sixty years of age with maximum benefits paid out after age sixty-five. While the pension is earnings related, there is a maximum amount for which claimants are eligible. It should also be noted that periods of low earnings, whether because of caring for young children, illness, unemployment or re-training, are considered exempt from the calculation. This provision is particularly significant for women who often take time out of the labour force to provide "caring labour."

- *Disability.* Severe and prolonged disability resulting in the inability to participate in the labour force qualifies one for a disability pension. This pension consists of both an earnings-related portion and a basic flat-rate portion, which is unrelated to earnings one had while employed. Recipients may also qualify for a supplemental Child Benefit should there be dependants. People with disabilities may be eligible to receive benefits through provincial Social Assistance programs, Workers' Compensation, the Canada/Quebec Pension Plan and, in some cases, through the Veterans' Disability Pension. Because there is no reason to assume that persons with disabilities are unable to work, eligibility for these programs is based upon a determination of ability to work and severity of disability. Tax credits and exemptions play an important income security role for people with disabilities.

- *Survivor and Death Benefits.* In the case of a contributor's death, surviving family members may be eligible for benefits. These benefits are intended to provide support to both the surviving spouse and children.

- *Old Age Security (OAS); Guaranteed Income Supplement (GIS); Spouses Allowance (SPA).* Between 1952 and 1989, all older Canadians received a universal monthly benefit called Old Age Security, an income security program financed and administered by the federal

OLD AGE SECURITY

Old Age Security, Guaranteed Income Supplement, and Spouses Allowance.

1980, $7.0 billion

1984, $11.1 billion

1989, $15.9 billion

1994, $20.4 billion

1999, $23.2 billion

Canada/Quebec Pension Plan, Retirement, Disability, Children's Disability, Survivor's, Orphan's and Death Benefits

- 1980, $1.9 billion
- 1984, $4.1 billion
- 1989, $9.2 billion
- 1994, 15.2 billion
- 1999, $18.6 billion

Source: *Forecasting, Information and Results Measurement, Income Security Programs,* Human Resources Development Canada (Summer 2000).

government. Prior to 1952, this benefit was targeted to the very low-income elderly population. Since 1989, the benefit has again become targeted, with only those who qualify because of low or modest income being eligible for benefits. OAS benefits are quite low in relation to the cost of living. Without another source of income upon retirement, such as C/QPP or Registered Retirement Savings Plans, many seniors would still live in poverty. To further assist those who do not have access to these programs, there are two related programs, the Guaranteed Income Supplement (GIS) and Spouses Allowance (SPA). These benefits supplement the OAS for the low-income elderly. From 1966 until today, the GIS has provided a politically popular add-on to the OAS for those pensioners with little or no other income.

- *Veterans Benefits.* Income security programs for veterans specifically recognize the service of war veterans. A Veterans Disability Pension is available to those who apply to Veterans' Affairs Canada, provided there is a service-related medical condition. Income and assets are not considered as eligibility criteria; the benefit is based solely on the extent of the disability. As is the case with disability benefits, what constitutes a disability and its extent is not easily determined or agreed upon by all interested parties.

- *Occupational Benefits.* In addition to publicly administered benefits, there also exist private benefit plans. These plans may be directly tied to one's workplace and include both retirement plans and other insurance-based benefits such as dental and drug plans, or they may be savings plans with tax supported provisions, such as Registered Retirement Savings Plans. While individuals save and invest this money for future use, the government foregoes the collection of tax on this saved money. The "lost revenue"—revenue not collected by government—amounts to billions of dollars per year.

THE COSTS OF INCOME SECURITY

The expenditures for government-funded income security benefits is extensive, comprising just over one-quarter of all government expenditures. The most recent social security spending figures from Statistics Canada show that, in 1997-98, total expenditures for all levels of government including federal, provincial, territorial and local on social welfare programs were $99.5 billion out of total government expenditures of $372.9 billion. Expenditures for health were $55.5 billion, and for education, $55.3 billion.

Spending on health, education, social services and income security was $210 billion or 56.4 percent of total 1997-98 expenditures. These areas of social spending constitute what the federal government broadly defines as **social security** spending. It does not include mandatory private social benefits provided by employers or voluntary private social benefits provided by charities or tax breaks for social purposes.

Income security receives the largest share of social security funding (47.38 percent) and includes pensions and benefits for the elderly, Employment Insurance, Social Assistance, Child Benefits, and Workers' Compensation. A more detailed breakdown for 1994-95 reveals that the largest expenditure of income security funding went to pensions and benefits for the elderly. Canada and Quebec Pension Plan spending totalled $19.76 billion and Old Age Security expenditure was $20.07 billion for a total of $39.83 billion or 40 percent of the total of income security spending. It is also interesting to note that 59.2 percent of income security spending and 40.8 percent of health expenditures were spent on persons aged sixty-five and over. Therefore, social spending will no doubt increase as the proportion of elderly people in Canada increases.

Canadian social welfare expenditures may appear to be rather generous given these numbers, but in fact they are much less than most other developed countries. A 1995 ranking according to income security expenditures by the Organization for Economic Co-operation and Development (OECD) places Canada eleventh among twelve countries, falling behind only the United States (Adema 1999, 32). Our commitment to social welfare is also revealed if we compare the amount we spend as a percentage of our Gross Domestic Product (GDP). Here again, Canada ranks poorly, falling behind only the United States and Australia. Canadian government income security expenditure is 11.4 percent of our GDP, compared with 22.9 percent for Finland and 21.4 percent for Denmark and Norway—the three highest (Adema 1999, 15).

• Who Benefits?

Regardless of how poorly we might compare with other countries, Canada does spend a large portion of its revenue from taxes on income security. Eventually these tax dollars come back to us in the form of income security benefits. But what is the distribution of income security benefits among different groups in the population? Are the poor the only beneficiaries of income security benefits?

An analysis of who benefits from income security illustrates that all Canadians benefit at different times in their lives. Middle- and lower-income Canadians receive over 30 percent of their total income from government income security programs. In Table 2.1 below, the population is broken down into groups of 20 percent according to their total income. Each group is called a **quintile**. The table reveals that, in 1980, the poorest 20 percent of the population received 46.5 percent of their income from income security programs. In 1996, this number jumped to 59 percent. The middle 20 percent of income earners received 12.8 percent of their income from government programs, up from 6.9 percent in 1980. Income security programs are, without doubt, a key factor in shaping income distribution in Canada. Indeed, these cash benefits are an important source of income for at least 60 percent of the population, and have become even more so since 1980. They also provide some benefits for the other 40 percent as well.

All sectors of Canadian society benefit from income security programs, although different programs benefit income groups to varying

TOTAL GOVERNMENT EXPENDITURES

Federal, Provincial/Territorial and Local Government Expenditure, 1997-98 (Total, $372.9 billion).

• Social Welfare, $99.5 billion
• Education, 55.4 billion
• Health, $55.3 billion

Source: Statistics Canada, Cansim Matrices 3472, 3482 (2000).

Table 2.1: Income Security Payments as a Percentage of Income, All Households, 1980-96

	1980	1984	1990	1996
Lowest Quintile	46.5	56.2	53.2	59
Second Quintile	13.8	21.3	21.5	25.5
Third Quintile	6.9	10.3	10.5	12.8
Fourth Quintile	4.2	6.1	6.3	6.8
Top Quintile	2.3	3	3	3

Source: Statistics Canada, *Income After Tax, Distributions by Size in Canada.* Cat. No. 13-210-XPB.

Table 2.2: Percentage Distribution of Specific Income Security Benefits, All Households, 1995

Pre-Transfer Income Groups (Quintiles)	Child Tax Benefit	Old Age Security	Canada/ Quebec Pension Plan	Employment Insurance	Social Assistance	Other*
Lowest	17.6	49.0	34.0	10.5	73.0	33.5
Second	21.3	25.5	30.7	27.4	16.7	26.6
Middle	26.7	12.5	16.8	23.4	5.6	18.9
Fourth	24.5	7.9	11.7	22.2	2.9	10.9
Highest	9.9	5.1	6.7	16.5	1.8	10.0

Source: Prepared by the Centre for International Statistics at the CCSD based on microdata from Statistics Canada's 1996 *Survey of Consumer Finances* (1995 income).

degrees. As Table 2.2 indicates, different programs affect different sectors of society and different income groups. The Child Tax Benefit is spread across all income categories. Social Assistance is directed towards those who live in poverty with little other income, so it is of benefit to the lowest-income earners. Other programs, such as pension plans and Employment Insurance, provide social insurance funded through individual contributions. Since benefit levels are generally proportionate to earnings, middle-income households usually receive more from these programs than do low-income households.

TAX CUTS AND SOCIAL WELFARE

Of late, it seems that a main area of economic policy discussion, especially at election times, concerns how much each political party is prepared to cut taxes. The debate is premised on the idea that Canadians are overtaxed, and by decreasing taxes, people will spend more, investors will invest more and the economy will grow, resulting in more jobs and more prosperity. However, this underlying premise is questionable. Canadians are not taxed more than residents of most other industrialized countries, and a reduction in taxes does not automatically affect the economy in some magical way.

Revenue Canada reports that Canadians with a taxable income of between $30,000 and $40,000 paid 15 percent of their earnings in income tax in 1996. To determine if this is too high, it is instructive to compare the amount of taxes Canadians pay as a percentage of GDP with that of other countries. In Canada, the equivalent of 35.1 percent of GDP is paid in taxes to all levels of government. According to OECD data from 1994, Canadian taxes as a percentage of GDP is in the low range when compared to other developed countries. The majority of countries have higher tax loads, including Denmark (49.9 percent of GDP), Finland (46.7 percent of GDP) and Norway (41.3 percent of GDP). Canada therefore has a tax load that is lower than that of most other developed nations.

The other argument is that taxes stifle economic growth. Again, evidence from the OECD shows that Canada's economic growth rate was lower than that of the higher tax-load countries, so there would seem to be more to stimulating economic growth than the lowering of taxes. Indeed, some studies suggest that public spending on programs such as income security can have a greater impact on economic growth than tax cuts, since part of the tax cut will flow into savings and an increase in imports.

The role of taxation policy in redistributing wealth on the one hand and fostering economic growth on the other underlies many social welfare policy debates. This is a subject on which every social work practitioner will need to have an informed opinion. Suffice it to say that the currently prevailing view (that tax cuts will automatically lead to economic growth) is at least an oversimplified one.

SELECTIVE AND UNIVERSAL PROGRAMS

In designing an income security program, a government must decide if a benefit will be universal or selective. **Universal benefits** are available to everyone in a specific category, such as "people over age sixty-five" or "children," on the same terms and as a right of citizenship. The idea is that all persons regardless of income and financial situation are equally eligible to receive program benefits.

Selective programs target benefits to those who are determined to be in need or eligible based on a means test (sometimes called an income test) or a needs test. A **means test** determines eligibility based on the income of the prospective recipient. The benefit is reduced according to income level, and there is always a level at which no benefit is granted. A **needs test** determines eligibility based on the income and the need of the prospective recipient. Eligibility criteria define need, which is then compared to the prospective recipient's life situation.

There are advantages and disadvantages to universal and selective programs with implications for both the applicant and society. The main objection to universal programs is their cost. Selective programs are often viewed as more efficient and less costly as the government provides benefits only to those most in need. However, identifying eligible recipients using means or needs tests can be administratively complex

DIMINISHING RETURNS

The income of low- and middle-income Canadians is decreasing.

The income from paid employment for the lowest quintile dropped 31.6% between 1989 and 1998. When total disposable income (which includes income security transfers) is used, this group is still left with a 12.6% decline in income.

Source: Statistics Canada, *Income in Canada* (Ottawa, 2000).

GUARANTEED ANNUAL INCOME

Canadian governments have examined the feasibility of a lifetime guaranteed annual income (GAI) program.

Modern proposals have taken two basic forms. The form favoured by people who place a high value on simplification and work incentives is the negative income tax (NIT). This is a selective payment to persons or households below a certain income level.

The second form is the universal demogrant (UD), a payment to all persons regardless of income and usually favoured by those who see the GAI as a right of citizenship whose purpose is to eliminate poverty and lead to more equal sharing of the economic benefits of society.

Currently, the federal government is reviewing the creation of a lifetime guaranteed annual income program to combat poverty. Whether any GAI plan adopted by the government will work to lessen income inequality in Canada will depend on the form it takes.

and costly. These administrative costs take money out of the system that could be directed towards benefits. Most will agree, however, that some selective programs are necessary for tackling inequality and implementing affirmative action policies.

Supporters of universal social programs maintain that they promote a sense of citizenship and nationhood. They believe that universal programs are necessary for promoting social solidarity. Further, supporters claim that selective programs for the needy tend to be punitive, of poor quality and more susceptible to cutbacks, whereas universal programs enjoy mass public support, are harder to cut, are of higher quality and avoid stigmatizing the recipient. Finally, many believe that universal income security programs fulfil various economic functions, such as economic stabilization, prevention, investment in human resources and development of the labour force.

Over the years, Canada has had a mix of selective and universal programs. Today, however, we have few universal programs as governments have moved away from a focus on citizenship rights and inclusion to an anti-poverty strategy geared towards promoting attachment to the labour force.

Old Age Security (OAS) and Veterans Benefits are currently the only income security programs that have an element of universality. Health care and education are examples of universal service programs, but they are not income security programs. All citizens are equally entitled to accessible, publicly administered health services and primary education regardless of their income. There are no tests to determine eligibility.

In the past, there were a number of universal income security programs available to Canadians. Family Allowance, which was available from 1944-93, is the most commonly cited example. All families with a child under the age of eighteen were entitled to a financial benefit. Because of the progressive tax system, wealthier people paid much of that back through taxation, but it was nevertheless an acknowledgment of citizenship entitlement and the importance and cost of raising children. In 1993, the Family Allowance was redesigned to become a targeted program, the National Child Benefit, now available to low- and middle-income families.

All of Canada's other income security programs offer selective entitlements. Most have complex selection criteria based on income, work history or the willingness to find a job. Employment Insurance is based on an insurance principle with eligibility tied to employment and income levels. Everyone within the broad category of "employee" pays into the program, and in this sense it is comprehensive, but a strict set of criteria determines who is eligible to receive benefits. The level of benefits depends on the earnings and contributions one has made. In recent years, eligibility for Employment Insurance has become more restrictive.

Other selective programs are based solely on how much money one has and whether this is sufficient to meets one's needs. To be eligible for Social Assistance or workfare (as it is known in Ontario), one must pass through a means test proving that income and assets fall below a certain specified maximum level. In provinces with workfare, such as Ontario and Alberta, applicants must also comply with an employment or training placement. The benefit is then calculated by a social worker. Those wishing to access these programs must complete forms and possibly have an interview with a social worker in order to prove that they are in need and do not have the means to meets their needs.

Another example of selective programming is the National Child Benefit. If family income falls below a specified level, benefits are paid through the tax system.

UNEMPLOYMENT AND EMPLOYMENT INSURANCE (EI)

In 1945, the Canadian government issued a statement committing itself to full employment. The government committed to intervening in the economy to create jobs and control job losses. This resulted from the recognition that government could affect unemployment by directly generating economic activity or assisting the private sector. This commitment represented a strong break from former social welfare policy, in which individuals were responsible for their own employment. Although individuals were still responsible for finding their own job, Western governments made a public commitment to avoid the conditions that had prevailed during the Great Depression. Full employment as a policy recognized that unemployment results from the unregulated operation of markets.

In our economy (a capitalist economy), social welfare is largely determined by attachment to the labour force. **Unemployment** is an involuntary loss of wage income. Those counted in the official unemployment statistics are those who cannot find paid employment and are actively looking for a job—persons who have given up the search for a job are not considered to be part of the labour force and are not included in the unemployment statistics. (Many Canadians also confront underemployment. This occurs when the education and training required for the job obtained is less than the education and training completed by the worker who is doing the job.)

The **unemployment rate** in 1999 was 7.6 percent (Statistics Canada, Matrices 3472-3482). This means that 7.6 percent of those who were officially counted as part of the labour force and were actively looking for work could not find a job. The labour force consists of just over 16 million Canadians or 65.6 percent of the adult population. Of this 16 million, 1.2 million cannot find paid employment. The total number of employed Canadians is therefore 14.5 million. Of these, almost 3 million are employed part time (Statistics Canada, Matrix 3472).

Today, Canada has an Employment Insurance (EI) system. Employment Insurance helps unemployed Canadians who are between jobs by providing temporary financial assistance while they look for work or upgrade their skills, while they are pregnant, caring for a newborn or adopted child, or sick. Individuals that have paid into the EI account can qualify for regular benefits of 55 percent of their average weekly insured earnings, to a maximum of $413 per week, provided they have worked

Unemployment insurance dates back to 1940 in Canada.

National Archives of Canada. Neg no. PA125093.

EMPLOYMENT INSURANCE

Employment/Unemployment
Insurance (All Benefits) for
Selected Years, 1974-99

- 1998-99, $12.0 billion
- 1994-95, $15.0 billion
- 1993-94, $17.7 billion
- 1992-93, $19.2 billion
- 1989-90, $11.8 billion
- 1984-85, $10.2 billion
- 1979-90, $4.0 billion
- 1974-75, $2.3 billion

Source: Statistics Canada,
Cansim.

the minimum required number of insurable hours within the last 52 weeks, or since the start of their last claim, whichever is shorter.

Changes to EI eligibility requirements during the 1990s severely cut the number of people who were eligible for benefits. From 1989 to 1998, the percentage of unemployed that actually received benefits dropped from 70 to 30 (CCPA 2000). This increasingly affects women who work less than the required 35 hours per week, due in part to additional family responsibilities. In 1998, 70 percent of employed women were ineligible for EI benefits.

POVERTY AND INEQUALITY

Who is poor in Canada? Official statistics reveal that in 1997 just over 5 million Canadians, or 17.2 percent, live in poverty, including 1.2 million children (Statistics Canada 1999). The human cost of poverty, in terms of isolation, lack of opportunity and being negatively labelled by the larger society, is more difficult to measure. Over the past few decades, the face of poverty has changed. Government programs have effected a significant drop in the number of poor seniors, but the number of single women and children living in poverty has increased.

Canada does not have an official "poverty line." Statistics Canada, however, produces low-income rates for different household sizes and regions, based on a measure they call the **Low Income Cut-off**. This measure is popularly known as LICO. According to Statistics Canada, those who spend more than 55 percent of their earnings on basic needs are living under the LICO. A household that spends 20 percent more than what the average household spends on food, clothing and shelter is below the LICO or in "straightened circumstances." Although LICO is not put forth as an official poverty line, many analysts, including the United Nations, treat it as such. For example, the 2000 LICO for a family of four in a medium-sized city of 100,000-500,000 is $29,356.

There are two conceptions of poverty: absolute poverty and relative poverty. **Absolute poverty** is measured by examining an essential basket of goods and services deemed necessary for physical or medical survival. **Relative poverty** measures low income in comparison to other Canadians. The LICO measure is a relative calculation, as it is based on the percentage of income that individuals and families spend on basic needs or necessities in comparison with the rest of Canadians. Some have called it a "relative necessities" approach.

Another measure of poverty calculates its depth. Poverty rates do not show whether poor people are living in abject poverty or merely a few dollars below the poverty line. To determine this, we need to measure the **poverty gap** or how much additional income would be required to raise an individual or household above the LICO. Statistics Canada refers to this as the **average income deficiency**. The number of people in Canada living at less than 50 percent of the LICO line grew from 143,000 families and 287,000 individuals in 1989 to 277,000 families and 456,000 individuals in 1997 (National Council of Welfare 1999, 54; http://www.ncwcnbes.net).

National Archives of Canada. Neg no. PA136195 (J. Smith).

Statistics Canada's LICOs measure relative poverty.

Table 2.3: 1999 Low Income Cut-offs, 1999					
Family Size	**Population of Community of Residence**				
	500,000 +	**100,000-499,999**	**30,000-99,999**	**Less than 30,000**	**Rural**
1	17,886	15,341	15,235	14,176	12,361
2	22,357	19,176	19,044	17,720	15,450
3	27,805	23,849	23,683	22,037	19,216
4	33,658	28,869	28,669	26,677	23,260
5	37,624	32,272	32,047	29,820	26,002
6	41,590	35,674	35,425	32,962	28,743
7	45,556	39,076	38,803	36,105	31,485

Notes: This table uses the 1992 base. Income refers to total pre-tax, post-transfer household income.

Source: Prepared by the Canadian Council on Social Development using Statistics Canada's Low Income Cut-offs, from *Low Income Cut-offs from 1990 to 1999* (January 2001).

LOW INCOME CUT-OFFS

Low Income Cut-offs are published by Statistics Canada. Families living below these income levels are considered to be living in "straitened circumstances."

The LICOs are more popularly known as Canada's "poverty lines."

For social statistics on poverty, income and welfare, check out: http://ccsd.ca/facts.html

In 1989 the Canadian Parliament passed a resolution vowing to eliminate child poverty by the year 2000. Campaign 2000, a national anti-poverty coalition, recently released *The Report Card on Child Poverty in Canada*, which shows that one in five of Canada's children lives below the Statistics Canada LICO. The Campaign 2000 Report summarizes the deteriorating economic situation of Canada's children since 1989, with an increase in the population of poor children of 402,000 or 43 percent, an increase of 27 percent in the number of families living with less than $20,000 per year, and an increase of 49 percent of poor children in single-parent families.

One might think that, in a country with such wealth and resources, child poverty would not be a large issue. Yet comparing Canadian child poverty to that of other countries is very revealing. Using a fairly conservative measure of poverty to compare child poverty rates and poverty rates for lone mothers across countries, a UNICEF study (*Child Poverty Across Industrialized Nations*) found that Canada has the second-highest rate of single mother poverty (45.3 percent) in the world, falling behind all countries studied except the United States (see p.27). Canada ranked behind countries such as Russia, Slovakia and Taiwan. Canada's poverty rate (11.2 percent) relative to the median for children is fourth worst, falling behind only the United States, Russia and Italy.

The face of child poverty is changing, from the lone mother on welfare to that of the working-poor mother who is holding down at least one job. While just 6.8 percent of poor children lived with mothers who worked full time in 1996, 11.5 percent of all poor children did so in 1998. Single mothers who are taking up the challenge of welfare departments across the country in trading a welfare cheque for a pay stub are not finding that the transition raises them out of poverty.

INCOME INEQUALITY

One way to measure inequality is to look at total income in Canada for each quintile (the income-earning population divided in fifths).

In 1994, the bottom 20% of income earners received only 7.7% of the total income, while the top 20% received 36.8%.

- Bottom, 7.7%
- Second, 13.4%
- Middle, 18.3%
- Fourth, 23.8%
- Top, 36.8%

Source: Taken from statistics prepared by the Centre for International Statistics using Statistics Canada, *Income after Tax, Distributions by Size in Canada* (various years).

The number of women in poverty is increasing faster than that of men. This is sometimes called the feminization of poverty. Almost 19 percent of women live below the LICO, which is the highest rate in two decades. Poverty among lone mothers (45 percent) and unattached women over age 65 (49 percent) is particularly high. (For more on this subject, see Chapter 8, page 154).

Since income security is largely a provincial responsibility, it is informative to compare the poverty rates of provinces. British Columbia has had the biggest decrease in child poverty as it has taken decisive steps to address the issue. Ontario, on the other hand, has had the sharpest increase in child poverty, partly because it has cut social assistance.

• Food Security and Insecurity

With cutbacks in many income security programs, Canadians are increasingly resorting to **food banks and feeding programs** in order to survive. In March 2000, there were over seven hundred food banks in Canada, and emergency food was provided to 726,902 people in that month alone. This is almost double the number of people who used food banks in March of 1989. The number of people using food banks in Canada rose by 1.4 percent over 1999, a time of record prosperity for more affluent Canadians. Over 40 percent of those being helped were under the age of eighteen (Wilson and Steinman 2000, 1).

Of those Canadians using food banks, 81.2 percent relied on income security programs as their income source (62.1 percent Social Assistance, 10 percent Employment Insurance, and 9.1 percent Disability Benefits). Only 13.7 percent were employed, and 5.1 percent reported no income (Wilson and Steinman 2000, 1). As Social Assistance rates decrease and eligibility requirements for EI tighten, it is estimated that food bank usage by Canadians will continue to increase.

Feeding programs provide cooked meals at specified times during the day. They often operate out of shelter or church basements and provide two meals per day. Such programs are operated by volunteers and by those who use the service. For example, The Well in Ottawa does not start providing meals until enough of the crowd volunteer to help. Feeding programs often provide additional services, such as free laundry facilities, a telephone, newspapers, clothing and, in certain instances, access to computers and the Internet. At most times, social workers are available and may even work directly from within the feeding program.

There is difficulty in keeping pace with demand, with 49 percent of food banks reporting that they often run out of food and must turn people away. Many believe that the steady unravelling of the social safety net means that access to basic food is in jeopardy. Hunger in an affluent country such as Canada is unnecessary, and the answer should not be an increase in the number of food banks and feeding programs.

The overall structure of Canada's income security system is at the root of the food security issue. Fundamental changes in benefit levels and eligibility requirements are needed to address the hunger problem. Food security is a basic right and means that all people in the community should have access to good nutritious food at all times.

CANADIAN FEDERALISM AND SOCIAL WELFARE

Canada is organized according to a form of political organization known as **federalism**, a system of government in which a number of smaller states (in this case, provinces and territories) join to form a larger political entity while still retaining a measure of political power.

When Canada was formed in 1867, social welfare was largely a private responsibility of the individual, family and church. Not surprisingly, the *British North America Act* (1867) said little about jurisdiction over income security or social services. The terms, in fact, did not even exist at the time. This omission caused Canada nothing short of political agony as it attempted to determine which level of government had the legislative jurisdiction to fund and deliver social welfare. Political wrangling, informal side-deals between the federal government and the provinces, and non-stop constitutional amendments formed the basis for our income security system. Throughout this process, income security slowly emerged as an area of federal dominance. The provinces, on the other hand, largely prevailed in the delivery of social services. The *Constitution Act* of 1982 in no way changed these arrangements.

The delivery of social services by local and provincial levels of government is consistent with the *Constitution Act* of 1982, and its predecessor, the *British North America Act* (1867), which gave the provinces, rather than the federal government, the responsibility for social services. An important point to note is that, while the provinces were given this responsibility in general, the federal government retained its responsibilities for Aboriginal people, as defined by the *Indian Act*. "Lands and lands reserved for Indians" remained within the jurisdiction of the federal government. The provision of social welfare to Aboriginal people is, therefore, somewhat different than for the rest of the population.

• Reforms to the Social Welfare System

One of the most significant changes to Canada's social welfare system arose with the introduction of the **Canada Health and Social Transfer** (CHST) in 1996. Previous to CHST, federal government contributions to social assistance and social services had been funded through the **Canada Assistance Plan** (CAP), established in 1966. Federal government contributions to health care services and post-secondary education had been funded through Established Programs Financing (EPF) since 1977. Both of these programs were replaced with the CHST. In its first two years, CHST paid the provinces $7 billion less than they would have received under CAP/EPF.

CAP was a 50/50 cost-shared program. Therefore, the federal government shared 50 percent of the cost of eligible Social Assistance and social services spending with the provinces. With CAP, federal transfers rose as provincial social welfare expenditures increased. CAP provided an economic stabilizing function, as federal transfers increased in economic recessions, thereby stimulating the economy through social spending. Conversely, CHST is a fixed per-capita or per-person amount based on the population of the province. Hence, federal transfers are not

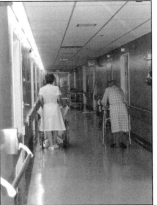

Federal-provincial disputes jeopardize health standards.

THE SOCIAL UNION AGREEMENT

The Social Union Agreement of 1999 between all the provinces (except Quebec) and the federal government established the procedures for changing social policy.

It was agreed that the first priorities should be children in poverty and persons with disabilities. In addition, the provinces and the federal government agreed that they would give one another advance notice prior to the implementation of a major change in a social policy or program that would likely substantially affect another government. The federal government also agreed that it would consult with the provincial and territorial governments at least one year prior to renewal or significant funding changes in the existing social transfers to the provinces and territories, unless otherwise agreed, and will build due-notice provisions into any new social transfers.

The "official" Government of Canada Social Union website provides a good overview of this important social welfare agreement. It can be found at: http://www.socialunion.gc.ca

connected to either the needs of the people or the state of the economy. Many believe that it is the economic stabilizing effect of social spending that has prevented a depression-style drop-off in the Canadian economy since the Great Depression of 1930. With CHST, this stabilizing effect is greatly reduced.

The national standards as set out in CAP are also largely gone in CHST. CAP stipulated that the provinces establish eligibility for Social Assistance based on need as determined by a means test, make services available for all those eligible regardless of when they established residency in the province, establish an appeal procedure and require no community or other work (also known as workfare) in return for social benefits. The regulations associated with CAP were removed except for the ban on residency requirements, and funding regulations associated with Medicare were retained. Many policy analysts fear that, with the removal of national standards, provinces will establish very different benefit levels and eligibility criteria.

Another recent welfare reform is the **Social Union Agreement of 1999** between the Government of Canada and the provinces and territories. According to the federal government, the social union initiative is the umbrella under which governments will concentrate their efforts to renew and modernize Canadian social policy. The objective of the social union agreement is to reform and renew Canada's system of social services and to reassure Canadians that their pan-Canadian social programs are strong and secure. So far, several social welfare initiatives have been established under this framework, such as the National Child Benefit, the national children's agenda for child care, and services for persons with disabilities.

The social union was largely a result of disapproval on the part of provincial governments of the unilateral cancellation of CAP and its replacement with CHST. The provinces wanted to be notified of and participate in formulating any future funding changes. They wanted the federal government to agree that, if it initiated any new social programs, even ones for which it paid the total costs, any province could opt out and take the cash instead with virtually no strings attached. The province would only be required to spend the money in the same general area as the national plan. The provinces also made it clear that they wanted more of a say in the future about how the federal government acted when stepping into provincial jurisdictions.

IDEOLOGY: OR WHY PEOPLE DIFFER ON WHAT TO DO

Canadians differ in their perception and explanation of social issues or problems and on how they believe these issues or problems should be solved. Opposing views are also held of the role of government in solving or alleviating such problems. As discussed in Chapter 1, the two political approaches to social welfare—the residual and institutional—capture the controversy surrounding social welfare today. Indeed, the history of the welfare state is a perpetual controversy over what the boundaries or extent of the welfare state should be.

The residual and institutional views of social welfare are informed by ideas and values that can be lumped together under broad categories of thought called ideologies. The term **ideology** refers to a set of ideas, values, beliefs and attitudes held by a particular person or group that shape our way of thinking. Political ideologies can be categorized along a spectrum, with communism on the far left and fascism on the extreme right. The more left-wing views of the democratic socialists and social democrats hold that social welfare is part of our collective responsibility to our fellow citizens and should be publicly provided within an institutional framework. The more right-wing approach of the neo-conservatives and liberals (although liberals move around from the centre to the right) includes the belief that welfare should be an individual responsibility within a residual model and that private-sector provision should be encouraged.

• Workfare

An example of this ideological difference in action is the introduction of **workfare** by Conservative governments in Ontario and Alberta. Such programs have shifted the determination of eligibility away from proof of financial need to that of compliance with employment requirements. Under workfare, welfare recipients are placed in non-profit and public agencies or in private employment as a condition for receiving assistance. To ensure that placements are made the Ontario government provides municipalities with $1,000 for every placement above its target. Over 30,000 placements had been made by March 2000.

Workfare, a notion originating in the United States, has been strongly criticized by those who advocate on behalf of the poor and the unemployed as being ideologically driven, an attack on citizens who are already the most vulnerable members of society. They argue that workfare is a reversion to the punitive approach of the Victorian-era workhouse, when the "undeserving poor" were obliged to perform meaningless tasks in return for minimal subsistence. For example, critics argue that the program imposes a mandatory employment requirement on single mothers but no corresponding legal obligation on the provincial government to assure access to quality child care.

• Social Welfare Economics

Some of these ideological debates have become part of the general public discourse. This is the case, for example, with the debates among professional economists over the causes of unemployment.

In very broad terms, the **Keynesians** (named after the famous British economist John Maynard Keynes, 1883-1946) believe that governments should emphasize policies that combat unemployment in order to maintain the income of consumers. **Monetarists**, on the other hand, believe that governments should keep inflation in check and not worry so much about unemployment. Those adhering to a more radical **political economy** perspective believe that private ownership creates two classes that are structurally antagonistic, and unemployment results when unions are weakened and can no longer protect the jobs of the working people.

THE SUMMIT OF THE AMERICAS

The Summit of the Americas in Quebec City in April 2001 was met with protest from many Canadians who believe that "free trade" without concern for social and human rights and environmental protection will further increase global poverty and magnify social problems.

Courtesy of Errol Sharp.

Young protester experiences teargas in Quebec City.

CORPORATE POWER

Globalization reflects, in part, the global expansion of large corporations. Of the 40,000 corporations operating in the world today, 200 control a quarter of the world's economic activity. These top 200 have combined revenues ($7.1 trillion) larger than all the economies of the world minus the largest nine. By most measures there corporations are more powerful than most countries in the world.

Source: James Rice and Michael Prince, *Changing Politics of Canadian Social Policy* (2000).

The Keynesians and monetarists not only have different views on unemployment but have fundamentally contrasting views on social spending in general. The monetarists believe that social spending stimulates inflation, undermines labour market flexibility and productivity and distorts the work/leisure trade-off. Keynesians believe that economic efficiency and social equity are compatible; that social spending helps economic recovery, enhances productivity and keeps the labour market flexible. The political economy perspective holds that the operation of economic markets is tied to private ownership and is essentially exploitative; that social spending is a right fought for by the working class. (Some adherents of this latter approach believe that social spending essentially serves to prop up the economic system—a process sometimes referred to as the "legitimating function" of the welfare state.)

Canadian government social policy has alternated between the Keynesian and monetarist approaches since World War II. Needless to say, the political economy perspective has never figured prominently in the social policy of Canadian governments—but it has certainly shaped its many critiques.

GLOBALIZATION AND SOCIAL WELFARE

This chapter has focused exclusively on providing an overview of income security issues in Canada. However, and by way of conclusion, it needs to be stressed that Canada does not exist in isolation from the other nations of the world. This is especially the case in the new era we are now entering, commonly referred to as globalization.

Globalization is essentially a new stage in the global expansion of capitalism. Although risking oversimplification, there are three main characteristics of this period: (1) the economies of individual countries (particularly those within the orbit of Western capitalism) are increasingly interdependent; (2) the most powerful of these Western nations (and their dominant corporations) increasingly have the economic power to dictate how lesser countries should be run; and (3) the fundamental objective is not to make these nations run better or redistribute the wealth of nations but above all to shore up the fortunes of these large, international corporations.

Given this new era of globalization, the traditional concerns of social welfare practitioners in addressing the immediate needs of their clients will need to be broadened to include a concern with the issue of global human rights. What might be called **global social welfare** (a concern with justice, social regulation, social provision and redistribution between nations) is already a part of the activities of various supranational organizations or international governmental organizations of the United Nations. Within this new world context, several new political strategies have emerged: regulating global competition, making international institutions such as the World Trade Organization and G-7 more accountable, empowering the United Nations and its international organizations and strengthening human rights capacity.

Courtesy of Errol Sharp.

Security police move against protesters at Quebec Summit.

The economic pressures of globalization will continue to affect the day-to-day work of Canadian social workers. In many smaller Western nations, and in the developing world, economic restraint and cutbacks to social programs have already been imposed by international agencies such as the World Bank and the International Monetary Fund. Similarly, Canadians and all levels of government will increasingly be under pressure to adjust their social programs to this new world order.

The full implications of globalization for Canada's welfare system remain to be seen. Whatever the eventual outcome, Canadian social workers will need to be more and more aware of developments in the international arena so as to mount an effective response that will both protect their clients and create the conditions that will allow them to do their work effectively.

CONCLUSION

Social welfare is about helping the citizens of Canada face difficulties in their lives—whether they be social or economic. It is a way of sharing the risk of events such as poverty, unemployment, disability and old age among all citizens. Social welfare is also about regulating and stabilizing our economic and social system. A healthy, well-trained and educated workforce is required for our economy to grow. Social welfare programs also help to relieve some of the distress of economic downturns, thereby preventing social unrest and stimulating the economy, by putting money into the hands of those who will spend it. For example, the Baby Bonus or Family Allowance program introduced following World War II gave a $20 monthly amount to every mother with the belief that the mother would spend the money on her children and stimulate the post-war economy.

Canadians do not always agree on whether social welfare programs should be expanded and strengthened or whether they should be reduced. Politicians agree even less. What is clear is that in recent years the welfare state in Canada has been reformed in ways that weaken overall social equality and social justice. Moreover, the economic forces of globalization seem to be leading to a harmonization of our social welfare system with that of the United States, our largest trading partner, and this will mean a serious deterioration in our welfare system.

Emulating the United States is not the only path open to us. Other countries in Europe, notably Denmark and the Netherlands, have continued to support and even expand their social welfare commitments and continue to have good productivity and economic growth. What is certain is that the debate over the future of the welfare system in Canada will be at the forefront of public discourse in the coming years.

REFERENCES

- Adema, W. 1999. *Net Social Expenditure, Organization for Economic Co-operation and Development. Labour Market and Social Policy*. Occasional Papers no. 39 (August). Available on-line at http://www.olis.oecd.org/OLIS/1999DOC.NSF

- Campaign 2000. 2001. *Child Poverty in Canada: Report Card 2000*. Toronto: Campaign 2000. Available at: http://www.campaign2000.ca

- Canadian Centre for Policy Alternatives. 2000 (March). CCPA monitor. Available at: http://www.policyalternatives.ca/publications/articles/article225.html

- National Council of Welfare. 1999. *Poverty Profile*. Ottawa: National Council of Welfare.

- Rice, James, and Michael Prince. 2000. *Changing Politics of Canadian Social Policy*. Toronto: University of Toronto Press.

- Statistics Canada. 1999. *Low Income Cut-offs*. Cat. No. 13-551-X1B.

- UNICEF. 1999. *Poverty across Industrialized Nations*. Innocenti Occasional Papers. Economic and Social Policy Series no. 71.

- Wilson, B., and C. Steinman. 2000. *HungerCount 2000*. Toronto: Canadian Association of Food Banks. Available on-line at http://www.icomm.ca/cafb

REVA GUTNICK, co-author of this chapter, teaches social work at Carleton University. She has a long-standing interest in social policy and social justice issues.

CHAPTER 2: INCOME SECURITY AND SOCIAL WELFARE

Key Concepts

- Social insurance
- Minimum Income
- Demogrants
- Income supplementation
- Social security
- Quintile
- Universal benefits
- Selective programs
- Means test
- Needs test
- Unemployment
- Unemployment rate
- Low Income Cut-off (LICO)
- Absolute poverty
- Relative poverty
- Poverty gap
- Average income deficiency
- Food banks and feeding programs
- Federalism
- Canada Health and Social Transfer (CHST)
- Canada Assistance Plan (CAP)
- Social Union Agreement of 1999
- Ideology
- Workfare
- Keynesianism
- Monetarism
- Political economy
- Globalization
- Global social welfare

Discussion Questions

1. What are the four categories of income security programs?
2. What is the main difference between a social insurance program and a minimum income program?
3. List five income security programs and describe the level of government responsible for it and who is eligible.
4. Who benefits from income security programs?
5. What are the two primary differences between universal and selective programs? Does Canada currently have any universal programs?
6. How did the discontinuation of the Canada Assistance Plan (CAP) affect social welfare programs?
7. What are the Social Union Agreement and the CHST and how have they changed social policy in Canada?

Websites

- **Policy.ca**
  http://www.policy.ca
  Check out the social policy issue area. Policy.ca is a non-partisan resource for the public analysis of Canadian policy issues. It consists of a constantly growing database of on-line public policy resources in sixteen different issue areas. These resources are selected to provide users with a balanced review of both documents and organizations in key Canadian public policy issue areas.

- **Canadian Centre for Policy Alternatives**
  http://www.policyalternatives.ca
  The CCPA is a non-profit research organization, funded primarily through organizational and individual membership. It was founded in 1980 to promote research on economic and social policy issues from a progressive point of view. Check out the "Behind the Numbers" section.

- **Caledon Institute of Social Policy**
  http://www.caledoninst.org
  The Caledon Institute of Social Policy does rigorous, high-quality research and analysis; seeks to inform and influence public opinion and to foster public discussion on poverty and social policy; and develops and promotes concrete, practicable proposals for the reform of social programs at all levels of government.

3
The History of Social Work

The Development of a Profession

In the early twentieth century, social work established itself as a vocation committed to major social reform, social change and the eradication of poverty. Over time, it shifted from a religious and charitable practice to a more systematic, professional one. Along with this, social service shifted from a privately funded and volunteer activity to a publicly funded, paid occupation.

The systematic giving of charity to the poor coincides, more or less, with the upheaval of the Industrial Revolution and, in particular, with the consolidation of the wage-labour system (at the time, capitalism was quickly becoming the dominant economic system). The immediate antecedents of Anglo-Canadian social work can be found in such socioeconomic changes in Britain and the United States in the eighteenth and nineteenth centuries.

Broadly speaking, relief in the nineteenth century was based on the poorhouse or house of industry. In the twentieth century, it shifted to the provision of food and other necessities to people in need in their homes, and later to the provision of cash. From the mid-twentieth century onwards, the state came to play an increasingly important role. Following World War II, Canada's economic surplus grew, as did the expectation that the state would ensure the economic and social security of its citizens. As state provision of social welfare has expanded, so has the social work profession. Most members of this profession are now employed in government-financed social welfare agencies.

We can thus divide the history of social work practice into three more or less distinct phases. These coincide roughly with major social and economic changes taking place at the time. In each phase, certain characteristics predominate.

- The era of moral reform: the pre-industrial phase from the formation of Canada until 1890;

- The era of social reform: the transition from a commercial to an industrial society, from 1890 to 1940; and

- The era of applied social science: the post-war transformation period of rapid economic growth and mass consumption, from 1940 to the present.

This chapter looks at each phase so as to provide a quick overview of the evolution of social work practice in Canada. For a more detailed survey of the history, readers are referred to the various reference sources listed at the end of this chapter.

Lining up to get into the Scott Mission, Toronto, 1953.

National Archives of Canada. Neg no. PA93921.

39

SOCIAL WORK HISTORY

The author's website provides
an overview of the history of
social work and income security.
The site can be found at:
http://ia1.carleton.ca/cush/
contents.html

PHASE 1: THE ERA OF MORAL REFORM—TO 1890

The pre-industrial phase of the development of social work includes the period from the formation of Canada up to the 1890s. **Private charities** developed during this time, offering material relief and lessons in moral ethics. Many were explicitly associated with religious organizations, and it was religiously motivated individuals working through these organizations who became the early social workers. This period saw the rise of the charity movement, epitomized by the Charity Organization Society (COS; see below). The roots of casework and the notion of helping people adjust to their environment can be traced to the COS.

The response to urban poverty in Canada during this phase was the result of two types of religious motivation. The explanation by James Leiby of the development of charitable activity in the United States provides some insight into similar development in English Canada as well:

> The early institutional responses to urban poverty came from people who had religious interests and motives. There were two broad types. One was native, Protestant, and missionary. It expressed a concern of pious and rather well established people for those whom they perceived as strangers and outsiders (and of course unchurched). The other type developed among the immigrant groups as forms of mutual aid and solidarity in a threatening environment (Leiby 1978, 75).

• Early Charity Organization: The Roots of Social Work

In the nineteenth century, public assistance in English Canada was guided largely by the example of England. The early English legislation, the Poor Law, required local parishes to provide relief to the deserving poor (those who were elderly, ill or disabled). Parishes were administrative districts organized by the Church of England. Each had a local council that was responsible for assistance to the poor, known as **poor relief**. The Poor Law of 1601 and its reform in 1832 carefully distinguished two types of indoor relief: one for the elderly and sick who could receive relief in almshouses or poorhouses, and one for the able-bodied poor who were made to work for relief in workhouses, the purpose of which was to make public assistance cruel and demeaning.

Early in the nineteenth century, "relief," where it was available, was provided primarily by private philanthropic societies founded in the territories that would become Canada. Organizations such as the Society for Improving the Condition of the Poor of St. John's (1808), the Society for Promoting Education and Industry among the Indians and Destitute Settlers in Canada (1827), the Kingston Benevolent Society (1821), the Halifax Poor Man's Friend Society and the Montreal Ladies Benevolent Society (1832) were preoccupied with the termination of begging and the value of labour. Relief, rarely given in cash, was usually in return for work. These same organizations, however, resisted the introduction of scientific methods of charity that were advocated from the 1830s onwards (Rooke and Schnell 1983, 46-56).

Following a request for assistance, a charity visitor would be designated to visit and interview the applicant in his or her home. Their role was to promote industry, thrift and virtue among the poor. The visitors were volunteers, generally elite men and women from the upper classes and people from the ranks of the emerging professional and business classes. Their first task was to classify the applicant as either deserving poor or undeserving poor. People designated as **deserving poor** were seen as being of good moral character and only temporarily out of luck due to no fault of their own. The deserving did not ask directly for help and were clean and tidy. The **undeserving poor** were deemed to be lazy and/or morally degenerate. Once an applicant was judged to be deserving, he or she had to appear before a committee of trustees who made the final decision to grant aid. The board granted aid in only about half of the cases determined to be circumstances of destitution. While the work required experience and skill, the early boards resisted proposals to hire full-time visitors.

The early relief provided by these volunteers in numerous charities and church parishes was soon deemed disorganized and inefficient, as there was very little regulation or co-ordination. In Toronto alone there were forty-three different charity organizations by 1894. Over time, the agencies developed their own training programs for volunteers, which, when a shift to a more scientific approach surfaced, formed the basis for the University of Toronto Socials Services Program in 1914.

Proponents of better organization of charitable assistance in England organized the London-based **Charity Organization Society** in 1869 to co-ordinate the efforts of the various charities. The voluntary charity work conducted under the auspices of the COS was possibly the most widespread attempt to help the poor. COS brought some order to the chaos created by the overlapping activity of 640 charitable institutions. Workers in this organization were expected to co-operate with other charities and with the agents of the Poor Law so as to give aid to the deserving poor. The popularity of this voluntary organization partly stemmed from the relief it accorded to local taxpayers. Money could be saved if private charities used unpaid volunteers and members of religious orders (Blyth 1972, 21).

The Protestant Charity Organization Society arrived in Montreal in 1901, following a similar and earlier effort to organize in Toronto. It was primarily directed by businessmen and upper-class women who believed that poverty was the fault of the individual. The COS, which differentiated between the deserving and undeserving poor, believed that indiscriminate material relief would cause pauperism; relief could lure a person from thrift and hard work into a life of dependency and reliance on handouts. The COS tried to control relief provision and, therefore, the poor. They believed that the existence of so many charities was more likely to create poverty than eliminate it. They also believed that neighbourhood-organized charities would promote a sense of community among the poor.

The Charity Organization Society believed that the charity visitors in the homes of the poor could serve as models of the value of hard work and thrift. However, the visitors encountered many difficulties and soon sought out specific training and "scientific methods" to cope with their problems. As these visitors became more familiar with standardized

National Archives of Canada. Neg no. C30937.

Family living in one-room accommodation, 1912.

techniques, they formed the base of what came to be called social "case-work" (Copp 1974, 108-120).

The COS goals were as follows:

1. *Restore people to a life of self-sufficiency, moral rectitude and Christian values.* Visitors were often rigidly moralistic; the COS was notorious for its rigid moralistic stand. Relief was a matter of Christian uplifting.

2. *Restore the bonds of obligation and understanding between the classes.* This was similar to the relationship between feudal lord and serf out of which could come a social and moral contract.

3. *Organize and control charity work, aiming for efficiency and communal relations.*

• The Settlement House Movement

That aspect of social work concerned with community work has its roots in the Canadian **settlement house movement**. The first social settlement house was established in the east end of London in 1884. It was named Toynbee Hall, after an Oxford University student who had settled in London's east end and had died a year previous. The purpose of the settlement house was to bring the youth of the educated middle class and the charitable gentry to live among the urban natives—a kind of mission to the poor. The term derived from the notion of "settling in," whereby a worker would live in the homes of the poor. As its founder Canon Barnett explained, the settlement idea was simple: "to bridge the gap that industrialism had created between rich and poor, to reduce the mutual suspicion and ignorance of one class for the other, and to do something more than give charity.... They would make their settlement an outpost of education and culture" (Davis 1967, 6).

The settlement house workers were more inclined to engage in social reform activities than those of the COS. They tended to advocate for better working conditions, housing, health and education. Many early workers came to the settlement house movement with radical political ideas, but this radicalism faded out after World War I. It is worth noting that during this period women began to be involved more actively in work on social and political issues outside the home (Allen 1971).

While the settlement house movement developed in this period, its influence on the development of social work continued for years to come. Jane Addams was the most prominent of Americans who transported the idea of social settlements to the United States, founding Hull House in Chicago in 1889. The young Mackenzie King, later to become prime minister of Canada, worked at Hull House in the 1890s to learn about the charitable work of Addams and others (Addams 1961, viii; Ferns and Ostry 1976, 37).

The idea of the settlement house spread throughout the United States and Canada early in the twentieth century. Evanglia, the first settlement house in Toronto, was founded in 1902 by Libby Carson and Mary Bell with the support of the Toronto YWCA. Carson had founded several other settlement houses, including Christadora House in New York in 1897.

Several other settlement houses were established in Canada. In Winnipeg, J.S. Woodsworth (who would later would become the independent labour Member of Parliament for Winnipeg, and the first leader of the Co-operative Commonwealth Federation, the forerunner of the present-day New Democratic Party) directed the All People's Mission, which was founded in 1907; in Montreal, the University Settlement House was established in 1909; and in Toronto, the St. Christopher House was founded in 1912, the University Settlement, in 1910, and the Central Neighbourhood House, in 1911. Most large Canadian cities had at least one settlement house by World War I. During the war the radical activist aspects of the settlement movement declined, however.

The first schools of social work in Canada were connected to, or often started by, settlement workers (Davis 1967, 3-25).

PHASE 2: THE ERA OF SOCIAL REFORM—1890 TO 1940

During this period the notion of helping the needy shifted from private philanthropy or charity provided by volunteers to the concept of public welfare funded by government bodies and provided by trained and paid workers. This shift provided the foundation for the birth of social work as an occupation. The perception that a publicly funded response to poverty was needed arose from fears among the middle class that increased poverty might result in mob violence and the spread of illness.

In the late nineteenth century, church members in charities were motivated by a desire for a more socially oriented church, based on a scientific rather than a moral worldview. Recognition grew that skilled and trained workers were required, rather than volunteer, untrained charity visitors.

The notion of **scientific philanthropy** emerged from the ideals of reform and social progress. These were increasingly influenced by scientific practice, that is, being fact-minded and rational. James Leiby summarizes the interaction of ideas of science and philanthropy:

> Faults might lie in a particular line of argument or judgment, but in theory at least, the scientific spirit pointed toward self-correction and consensus. Of course in thinking about philanthropy and social justice there would be partisans of religious and political causes, and they would disagree; probably all of them had some insight into the situation, most likely all of them were to some degree fallible. On what better ground could they meet and agree than that of a "scientific philanthropy"? (Leiby 1978, 91).

According to this new scientific approach to social work, the purpose was to depart from moral judgements of deservingness; the client was seen as having an objective problem and the role of the social worker was to help him or her deal with it. To be effective in this role, it was necessary for the worker to have a scientific understanding of human behaviour and social processes. It was assumed that a thorough gathering of information would lead to an understanding of the causes of the person's problem. Further, it was assumed that once the problem was identified a solution would be objectively found and then applied.

Child waits while mother enquires about housing, 1940.

As large urban areas grew, and the number of people in need grew with them, the large number of poor could no longer be evaluated by a system of charity visitors alone. Charity organization and the founding of children's aid societies led to the replacement of voluntary organization with paid and trained staff. Organizations were forced to hire paid workers to efficiently handle the growing demands. This transformation was common to many cities and districts in Canada, as well as other parts of the world, during the early part of the twentieth century.

There was a moral as well as a pragmatic concern that poverty might lead to social instability. In the latter third of the nineteenth century, people of the middle and upper classes in England became concerned, either for moral or political reasons, with the unequal distribution of wealth and the poor conditions of the working class. They also feared that, with an increase in poverty, the working classes might rise up in mob violence, or that the poor might become diseased and therefore spread illness to all members of society.

These concerns also emerged in Canada as **social survey research** was used to highlight the extent of poverty and inequality in Canadian cities. One of the first social survey research studies was carried out by H.B. Ames in Montreal. Published in 1897 under the title *The City Below the Hill,* it illuminated the conditions of the poorest of Montreal residents. Early studies by other social researcher/reformers, such as J.J. Kelso in Toronto and J.S. Woodsworth in Winnipeg, contributed to the Canadian middle and upper classes' understanding of poverty and what to do about it. Royal Commissions, such as the Dominion Commission on the Relations of Labour and Capital (1889), the Ontario Royal Commission on the Prisons (1890) and the Dominion Board of Inquiry into the Cost of Living (1915), also contributed to increased awareness and a growing interest in social service and social work.

The transition from friendly visitors to paid social workers was not a smooth one. The fact that many workers accepted payment often incurred the criticism of the rich and the opprobrium of the unthinking. A willingness to work for nothing, it was considered, was the hallmark of a sincere charity worker (Woodroofe 1962, 97).

• The Rise of Trained Social Workers

The training of social workers gradually shifted from agency-based volunteer training to a university-based professional education as the more scientific view of human services emerged. This shift occurred simultaneously in countries such as Britain and the United States.

In 1914, the University of Toronto established a Department of Social Services for the scientific study of society. This program was the first in Canada to undertake the task of training social workers. In 1918, McGill University opened up the second English-language social work training program, the School of Social Study and Training. Carl Dawson, its director, was convinced that study and action did not fraternize well in the university. According to Dawson, the study of social phenomena should proceed separately from its application, which should be left to others. A similar program was begun in 1928 at the University of British

National Archives of Canada. Neg no. C85881.

Early welfare activist John Joseph Kelso with children.

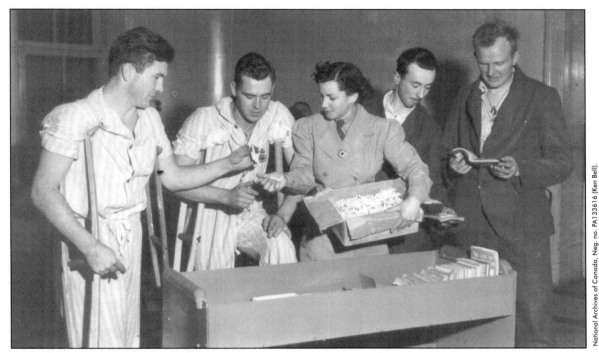

National Archives of Canada, Neg. no. PA133616 (Ken Bell).

Social work officer Mary Wright with the Canadian Red Cross distributes supplies to patients at the Canadian General Hospital in 1944.

Columbia. Several other schools developed after World War II. Training was based on the idea that social work had already evolved a base of knowledge that could be passed on to potential participants.

Originally based on the concept of charity, social work had evolved from a set of rules to guide volunteers in their work as **friendly visitors** of the poor into a philosophy that embodied many of the principles of modern casework and a technique that could be transmitted by education and training from one generation of social workers to another (Woodroofe 1962, 54). Social work in Canada gained a professional prominence in 1927 when the Canadian Association of Social Workers (CASW) was established.

In 1947, the first professional social work degree (Master of Social Work) was offered by the University of Toronto. In 1966, they awarded the first Bachelor of Social Work degree (Armitage 1970).

• Social Casework

The development of modern **casework**—systematic methods of investigation, assessment and decision making—was strongly influenced by Mary Richmond, who worked for the Charity Organization Societies of Baltimore and Philadelphia and for the Russell Sage Foundation. Her 1917 text, *Social Diagnosis,* was used in the training of workers and its contents reflect "the strong influence played by medicine in Miss Richmond's conception of social casework" (Coll 1973, 85-86). Richmond

CHARLOTTE WHITTON

Between 1922 and 1941, Charlotte Whitton led the Canadian Welfare Council, a forerunner to the Canadian Council on Social Development, and followed that by lecturing across North America on social programs. She was Canada's most influential voice on social welfare matters at the time.

She was elected mayor of Ottawa in 1952, 1954, 1960 and 1964 and later served as an alderman until 1972. Not a believer in the role of the state in providing welfare and social services, she would be regarded today as neo-conservative in her outlook on such matters.

Feisty to the end, she is also attributed with the wry remark: "Whatever women do, they must do twice as well as men to be thought half as good. Luckily, this is not difficult."

felt that the casework technique could approach a "scientific understanding of social dynamics and human behaviour" (Pitsula 1979, 39). In *Social Diagnosis,* she described the social work process as follows:

1. Collection of social evidence, data on family history and data pertaining to the problem at hand;

2. Critical examination of the material leading to diagnosis; and,

3. Development of a case plan with the involvement of the client.

Richmond originally used the term *diagnosis* for the construct of assessment, borrowing the term from medicine. Her work became the source of what would later be known as the medical model.

The Social Service Commission in Toronto first introduced the practice of professional casework in Canada. The Commission was appointed by the city in 1911, and employed staff who were paid for their work. It requested that the House of Industry in Toronto hire paid staff to operate their relief program. The distribution of out-of-door relief was co-ordinated according to modern social work principles.

> Distress is relieved with care and sympathy, but the emphasis is not placed on mere relief giving. With each family helped the work includes co-operation with other agencies, diagnosis of need, decision as to remedy, application of remedy, subsequent care and tabulation of results. This is not haphazard "tinkering" with human beings but a real effort to render constructive and progressive service (Social Service Commission Annual Report 1916).

After World War I, the emergent social work profession was called upon to assist with the resettlement of war veterans and with others who were not poor but in need of assistance. In 1918, Charlotte Whitton was chosen as assistant to the Reverend J.G. Shearer at the Social Service Commission and began a period of twenty-five years of intense involvement in social work and in the development of the social services. She subsequently became a successful municipal politician, becoming a local councillor and then mayor of Ottawa. By 1921, the Social Service Commission had become the social welfare division of the Department of Public Health, illustrating the shift from the premise of moral to social reform. In fact, social work became a secular and scientific alternative to moral and religious work. As this replacement occurred over time, religious faith continued to be central to the practice of social work.

The story of the founding of the Canadian Council on Child Welfare, which became the Canadian Welfare Council and is currently the Canadian Council on Social Development, is told in the work of Rooke and Schnell. A group of social reformers who met at the end of World War I encouraged the founding of a children's bureau in Canada, based on the American model. What resulted was a child welfare bureau in the federal Department of Health, and the founding of a private organization of which Charlotte Whitton became secretary. She did this work until the late 1920s while she supported herself by working for a Conservative Member of Parliament. She then became a full-time staff member supported by memberships and funds from contracts.

National Archives of Canada. Neg no. PA137535 (Costongucy).

Charlotte Whitton, Canadian Council on Child Welfare.

As secretary, she initiated the social survey as a method of modernizing and professionalizing the provision of charity, a task she saw as her mission. She believed that the use of scientific methods had to replace the dated methods of charity visiting. At the same time, Whitton disagreed strongly with the new breed of social worker/reformer as espoused by Harry Cassidy and Leonard Marsh. She believed in containing and not expanding the role of the welfare state. In *The Dawn of Ampler Life*, a book she wrote at the behest of the leader of the Conservative Party for whom she worked, she explained how charity was a sensitive task requiring the involvement of private organizations and not the involvement of the state. Writing in 1943, she opposed the development of state social programs in Canada, criticizing the work of Leonard Marsh, who wrote what many consider to be the blueprint for the welfare state in his *Report on Social Security for Canada*, earlier the same year (Whitton 1943, 205-221).

• Psychology and Social Work

Freudian thought played an increasingly important role in social work in the 1920s, in tandem with Richmond's text, *Social Diagnosis*. While the latter provided guidance on procedure, Freud provided insight into the inner workings of the individual. Social work shifted from a concern with the societal context to a concern with a person's psychological make-up as the source of problems. Goldstein's comments on the American situation apply since the American influence was still very strong in Canada: "Freudian theory overshadowed all other approaches to social problems and orientations about behaviour. By the mid-1920s casework teaching staffs at universities taught psychoanalytic principles as a basis for casework practice" (Goldstein 1973, 31).

Freudian ideas led to a change in social work, in a sense supporting a move from a more active to a more passive role for the worker. This was designed to permit social work clients to express themselves. Casework remained the dominant form of social work practice, but social workers began to specialize in such areas as family welfare, hospitals and psychiatry. In the 1930s, what became known as functional social work, in which the casework relationship itself would aid the client, began to emerge. Also during this time, group work and community work emerged as different forms of social work (Goldstein 1973, 31-38).

• Social Gospel, Social Work and Social Action

In this period, the **social gospel movement** had a particular influence on Canadian social work. Movements for a more socially oriented church began to appear within the major Protestant churches in the latter part of the nineteenth century. Within each of the Methodist, Presbyterian, Anglican and Congregationalist churches, there were movements for a more socially oriented message, or social gospel, concerning justice and social action. The social gospel wings of the churches eventually started many of the settlement houses in Canada. The movement had strong roots in the prairies.

J.S. WOODSWORTH

James Shaver Woodsworth was born in Etobicoke, Ontario, in 1874 and moved to Brandon, Manitoba, in 1885. Woodsworth was ordained in 1896 and spent two years as a Methodist circuit preacher.

Having observed industrial capitalism in Canada and Britain and its failure to meet the needs of working people, Woodsworth came to the view that personal salvation could not right social and economic wrongs. While working with immigrant slum dwellers in Winnipeg between 1904 and 1913, he wrote extensively, expounding the "social gospel" in which he called for the Kingdom of God "here and now."

Woodsworth was elected to Parliament in the federal election of 1921 as the member for Winnipeg North Centre. His first resolution was one on unemployment insurance.

In 1907, these main Protestant churches established the Moral and Social Reform League. This was the first organization in the country to advocate for social reform. The League was the forerunner of the Social Service Council of Canada, founded in 1914, with the Rev. J.G. Shearer serving as its first director. The Council remained the main social service advocacy organization in Canada for the next twenty years. The name change indicated the shift from a religious and moral perspective to a more scientific one. Not carried out casually, this move was indicative of larger changes in Canadian society, promoting a reform movement that sought to distance itself from a moral base. Several leading members of Canada's trade union movement were active in the Council. After 1925, the Social Service Council declined in significance and was replaced by the Canadian Association of Social Workers in 1927.

Another noted Canadian figure, J.S. Woodsworth, applied social gospel ideas to his work in social services and later to his political life. He helped develop the work of social workers in Winnipeg, which then spread to other parts of Canada. For example, he created the All People's Mission, which provided a variety of direct social services. Woodsworth also served as secretary of the Social Welfare League. Social gospel reformers such as Woodsworth were greatly influenced by the labour movement, particularly by ideas concerning worker control of enterprises and workers' direct participation in decision making. For these reformers, service to other human beings was considered a form of service to God. In the churches this spirit manifested itself as the social gospel, implying the achievement of justice in this world rather than in the next. Woodsworth and other social gospellers were also at the forefront in the western agrarian populist movements and political parties. Many Canadian historians, such as Ramsey Cook (1985), view social work as the secular replacement of the social gospel movement.

• Social Work and the Depression

The **Great Depression** of the 1930s was a time of mass unemployment and seriously reduced living standards. In 1933, nearly one-quarter of the labour force was unemployed. This period left an indelible mark on Canadian society. For many Canadians, the Depression shattered the idea that market forces should be left unregulated. They came to see unemployment as a socioeconomic problem requiring a national response, rather than as a personal problem to be solved by local charity.

J.S. Woodsworth, an ardent democratic socialist.

One important outcome was a change in the nature of politics in Canada, a change that endures to this day. In the 1920s, J.S. Woodsworth began working with a group called the Ginger Group. When the Depression struck, they joined with various labour and socialist groups in 1933 to found the Co-operative Commonwealth Federation (CCF). The CCF is the precursor of the current New Democratic Party of Canada, a party formed in 1961 when the CCF came together with the union movement to forge a new party committed to advocating on behalf of farmers and working people.

The New Democratic Party's founding convention in 1961 brought the Co-operative Commonwealth Federation together with unions affiliated to the Canadian Labour Congress.

This period saw remarkable growth in the number of social workers. During the Depression of the 1930s, new staff had to be hired to run the expanding social service agencies called on to administer relief to a large percentage of the population. In the year 1941, the census recorded 1,805 social workers in Canada, a 65 percent increase over 1931.

PHASE 3: THE ERA OF APPLIED SOCIAL SCIENCE—1940 TO PRESENT

During the war, the federal and provincial governments began to realize that social services were not a luxury but a vital part of a smoothly functioning economy. They were required to assist the many returning war veterans and their families. The war ended a period of massive unemployment, speeded up industrialization and urbanization, doubled the number of women in the labour force and increased and legitimated government intervention in the economy. In the post-World War II period, a period of rapid economic growth and mass consumption, the career opportunities for social workers began to open up. Education and training programs for prospective social workers increased as well.

Following World War II, the federal Liberal government legislated a series of social welfare measures that were, in retrospect, seemingly intended to forestall the election of the Co-operative Commonwealth

Table 3.1: Key Events of the Post-War Period and the Implications for Social Work

CANADA AND WORLD EVENTS	SOCIAL WELFARE	SOCIAL WORK
1940s		
• War-related state controls • Crown corporations • End of World War II • High labour unrest • International revolutions • Keynsian economics	• Universal Social Legislation • Family Allowance, 1944 • Veterans benefits, 1944 • CMHC, 1945 • White paper on employment, 1945 • Hospital construction • Organization of provincial departments of social services • End of federal grants for relief	• First social work degree (M.S.W.) awarded • Well-paid social work jobs • State regulation • Men in SW administration • Modest growth in employment • First social work unionization • National Committee of Schools of Social Work established
1950s		
• Prosperity • High employment • Cold War purges of left • Low level of unrest • Liberal government	• Expanded social programs • Old age pension for all at 70 (1952) • Means-tested pension at 65 (1952) • *Disabled Persons Act* (1955) • Unemployment Assistance Act (1956) • Allowances for blind disabled • Hospital care coverage (1957)	• Professionalism (CASW) • Private agencies dominant • Volunteerism • *Child Welfare Act* (Ont) (1954)
1960s		
• Grassroots unrest-growth of anti-poverty, Indian, labour, student, peace organizations • Founding of NDP • Quebec separatism • Economic growth & employment	• *General Welfare Assistance Act* (Ont) (1960) • *National Housing Act* (1964) • Canada Pension Plan (1965) • Canada Assistance Plan (1966) • *Medicare Act* (1968)	• State becomes main social work employer • Grassroots advocacy & social action programs • Radical social work • Unionization of public sector • First Bachelor of Social Work awarded in 1966
1970s		
• Fiscal crisis of state • Conservative business strike • US influence rises in Canada • Rise of women's movement • Rise in women's employment	• Cutbacks begin in Health, education, welfare programs • More law and order • Rise of Contracting out • NGOs funding of militant groups	• Community college SSW programs • Contracting out • Co-optation of militancy • Large growth in schools of social work • CASSW begins accreditation of social work degree programs
1980s		
• Monetarist economics • Conservative policies • US-dominance in Canada • Decline in US empire • Cold War tensions • Third World unrest • Waves of refugees • Rise in militancy & popular coalitions	• Major contracting out, cutbacks, workfare • Increases in punitive programs • Women's issues (day care, reproductive choice, pay equity, violence discussed-little concrete progress • Rise of food banks, charities • Rise of free trade (NAFTA) • *Young Offenders Act* (1984)	• Restraint, burnout • Cuts of advocacy programs • Privatization • Short-term training • Unionization of NGO workers
1990s		
• Economic stabilization • Rising militancy of Indians, women, visible minorities, disabled, etc. • Environmental movement strong • Polarization of rich and poor • Popular demands for real social justice • Rising labour militancy at grassroots • Rise of information and communications technology (ICT)	• Attempts to dismantle welfare state, and transfer costs to provinces, cities • Regressive taxes • Cuts in corporate taxes • Free trade • Privatization of universal programs • Cuts to women's, immigrant, Native rights and programs • Move to workfare and privatization (residual model)	• Split between professional vs. union and coalition strategies in SW • Defensive era • Potential for linkages with client groups

Federation. The CCF had achieved considerable popularity during the war with a social reform platform. The Liberals were also concerned with the possibility of a recession, which could cause considerable social unrest. The federal government therefore introduced the Family Allowance, which put more funds into the hands of families, helping to spur more economic growth. In 1951, through constitutional amendment, the federal government introduced a federally financed and administered universal Old Age Pension. Several years later, they introduced benefit programs for persons with disabilities. Many of these programs led to the expansion of employment in the administration of these new services and programs, precipitating a fundamental change in the nature of Canadian social work. Social work opportunities were now shifting from mainly private, voluntary agencies to government departments or government-financed agencies.

The ideas of Freud continued to have a impact on how social workers practised during this period. Debate occurred between the adherents of the Freudian or diagnostic approach and the newer functional approach. In the **diagnostic approach**, the emphasis was on understanding the condition of the individual by reference to causal events in his or her early life. This approach required a skilled worker who could diagnose the problem and establish and carry out a plan for treatment. The **functional approach** was based on the belief in the potential of clients to determine their own direction with the assistance of a skilled worker. The role of the worker was to establish a structured relationship with the client and facilitate a process of change (Goldstein 1973, 38-39).

In the 1960s the profession renewed its interest in poverty as a result of anti-poverty measures instituted by the federal government. Community organizing initiatives sprang up in major cities across the country. In Ontario a second generation of more radical social workers unionized, forming the Federation of Children's Aid Staff in the early 1970s. Several years later this group of unions joined the Canadian Union of Public Employees, which today represents a large number of social workers who are employed by municipalities across the country.

A range of new models of social work practice also appeared in the 1960s and 1970s, such as the generic or integrated approach, the problem-solving approach, the behaviour modification approach and the structural approach. The latter was based, in part, on a critique of approaches to individual and family social work that tended to seek explanations for and solutions to problems within the individual alone and not within the institutions or structures of society.

• The Expansion of Social Services and Social Work

Despite the economic expansion of the post-war years, demands on private organizations for relief grew. The few church and private charities could not keep up. Pressure was brought to bear on the federal government by these organizations and by the Canadian Welfare Council, which presented the case for a national program of support for those who were unemployed but not eligible for Unemployment Insurance. The 1956 *Unemployment Insurance Act* provided federal assistance to the

A man finds warmth in a manhole shelter, 1955.

National Archives of Canada. Neg no. PA93920.

Table 3.2: Numbers of Post-Secondary Institutions Offering Social Services Education, Levels of Accreditation, and Number of Graduates

	College/CEGEP (Quebec)	University (34 total)	Number of Graduates
Bachelors	Not Applicable	31	2,085 (1977)
Masters	Not Applicable	23	705 (1997)
Ph.D.	Not Applicable	8	9 (1996)
Certificate/Diploma	46	Not Applicable	4,540 (1996)

Source: CASSW, *In Critical Demand: Social Work in Canada, Final Report* (Ottawa, 2001).

provinces for the so-called unemployed but employable person who did not have access to other income security programs or employment income. A condition of this assistance was that the province could not impose a residency requirement on an applicant. This federal legislation marked the beginning of the process of modernization of relief administration, which led to the passage of the Canada Assistance Plan in 1966. By offering to share 50 percent of the provincial costs of welfare and social services, the federal government effected key changes in social assistance, transforming it into a publicly financed and administered program. This was accompanied by a rapid expansion of social services in child welfare, child care and other services for people in need.

The period from 1963 to 1973 saw the expansion of income security and social service programs. By the end of this period, Canada had become a welfare state with a public system of health and hospital care, and expanded or new income security programs for children, the unemployed, single parents and persons with disabilities. Public or publicly financed social services, including child welfare and child care, were also expanded, many of which were extended for the first time to meet the needs of Canada's Aboriginal population, including Indians on reserves. Social workers were required to fill a wide range of new positions created by the need to administer these new programs and deliver the expanded social services. The number of persons who identified themselves in the census as social workers rose from 3,495 in 1951 to 30, 535 in 1971, with most of that increase occurring in the decade following 1961. The current number is 85,955.

With the increased demand for trained social work staff to administer and deliver the wide range of new social service and income security programs, there was also an increase in the number of college and university social work programs. The Canadian Association of Schools of Social Work was established in 1967 to oversee professional university-based education programs in Canada, replacing the American Council on Social Work Education. Currently, there are thirty-four universities and forty-six colleges providing social work and social service education.

CONCLUSION

Social work is a profession with a largely twentieth-century history. In the nineteenth century, charities and settlement houses expanded to provide assistance to the large number of people in need. This later led to the desire to put charity on a more systematic footing. Subsequently, in the late nineteenth and early twentieth centuries, charities received public funds to carry out their work. It was this sequence of events that ultimately lead to the formation of the profession of social work–a profession dedicated to helping those in need. The Canadian Association of Social Workers was formed in the 1920s.

The two World Wars (1914-17 and 1939-45) and the Great Depression of the 1930s contributed to the need for an expansion of social services and income security programs and an increased demand for social workers. Later, in the 1960s, federal and provincial funding for social assistance and social services increased substantially as a result of a national funding program (the Canada Assistance Plan). Consequently, the demand for training also increased, resulting in many new social work programs in the community colleges and universities.

Social work practice itself has undergone considerable change. At its inception, casework was the predominant form of social work practice, but since that time both group work and community work have been added. Further, some universities have recognized social administration and policy as an additional arena of practice, rather than simply as a useful background to practice. From the 1920s onwards, social work was strongly affected by the development of the social sciences. Freud's influential ideas about individual psychology tended to lead social work to focus initially on the individual, but later the area of focus was broadened to include a wider range of factors. In the 1930s, a minority in the profession were attracted by radical political ideas and saw social work as a way of address the social ills of society. They supported a broad alliance with the trade union movement and the unionization of social work practitioners as well. From the 1940s, functionalism in social work began to replace the Freudian approach. By the 1970s, there was a proliferation of approaches that included both Freudian and functional but also the generalist, the problem solving, the behavioural and the structural approaches, all testifying to the importance of the field to society and the economy.

REFERENCES

- Addams, Jane. 1961. *Twenty Years at Hull House.* New York: Signet Books.

- Allen, Richard. 1971. *The Social Passion: Religion and Social Reform in Canada, 1914-1928.* Toronto.

- Armitage, A. 1970. *The First University Degree in Social Work.* Ottawa: Canadian Association for Education in Social Service.

- Blyth, J.A. 1972. *The Canadian Social Inheritance.* Toronto: The Copp Clark Publishing Company.

- Coll, B.D. 1973. *Perspectives in Public Welfare: A History.* Washington: U.S. Government Printing Office.

- Cook, R. 1985. *The Regenerators: Social Criticism in Late Victorian English Canada.* Toronto: University of Toronto Press.

- Copp, T. 1974. *The Anatomy of Poverty: The Condition of the Working Class in Montreal, 1897-1929.* Toronto: McClelland and Stewart Limited.

- Davis, Allen F. 1967. *Spearheads for Reform: The Social Settlements and the Progressive Movement, 1890-1914.* New York: Oxford University Press.

- Ferns, H., and B. Ostry. 1976. *The Age of McKenzie King.* Toronto: Lorimer Books.

- Goldstein, H. 1973. *Social Work Practice: A Unitary Approach.* Columbia University of South Carolina Press.

- Guest, D. 1980. *The Emergence of Social Security in Canada.* Vancouver: University of British Columbia Press.

- Leiby, J. 1978. *A History of Social Welfare and Social Work in the United States.* New York: Columbia University Press.

- Pitsula, James. 1979. The Emergence of Social Work in Toronto. *Journal of Canadian Studies* 14, no.1.

- Rooke, Patricia, and R.L. Schnell. 1983. *Discarding the Asylum: From Child Welfare to the Welfare State in English Canada, 1800-1950.* Boston: University Press of America.

- Whitton, Charlotte. 1943. *The Dawn of Ampler Life.* Toronto: Macmillan Company of Canada.

- Woodroofe, K. 1962. *From Charity to Social Work in England and the United States.* Toronto: University of Toronto Press.

CHAPTER 3: THE HISTORY OF SOCIAL WORK

Key Concepts

- Private charities
- Poor relief
- Deserving poor
- Undeserving poor
- Charity Organization Society (COS)
- Settlement house movement
- Scientific philanthropy
- Social survey research
- Casework
- Freudian thought
- Social gospel movement
- Great Depression
- Diagnostic approach
- Functional approach

Discussion Questions

1. What are the historical roots of social work?
2. What are the three phases of the evolution of social work in Canada, and what are the defining characteristics of each phase?
3. What has been the influence of charity organization, the settlement house movement and social reformers on social work in Canada?
4. Describe the influence of the social gospel movement on social work in Canada.
5. What was the effect of the Depression of the 1930s on the development of social work in Canada?
6. How has casework changed since the days of Mary Richmond?
7. What was the influence of Freudian psychology on the way social work was understood and practised? Why has this influence lessened since the 1960s?
8. What is the scientific approach to social work and how did it change the nature of social work practice?

Websites

- **A History of Social Work on-line Timeline**
  http://ia1.carleton.ca/cush/m4/m4contents.stm
  Go and click on Topic 2, A Timeline of the Evolution of Social Work in Canada, for a timeline of the major events in the history of social work.

- **World Wide Web Resources for Social Workers**
  http://www.nyu.edu/socialwork/wwwrsw
  This vast resource for social workers, produced by Dr. Gary Holden at New York University, offers an eclectic collection of material on social welfare with a useful search engine, covering many of the topics in these pages. It is particularly helpful for researching a particular topic or locating an international association. Try clicking on "social work," then "general" and finally "history" for a few interesting history links.

4

Social Work as a Profession

Making a Difference

It was not until the end of World War I that social work began to be recognized as a distinct profession in Canada. Since that time there has been rapid growth in the number of professional social workers. All levels of government, federal, provincial and municipal, now fund and deliver social services and income security programs.

According to available census data, there were 1,056 self-described social workers in 1931, the first year for which data is available. Thirty years later, in 1961, there were 10,854 social workers. As a result of the funding made available after the passage of the Canada Assistance Plan in 1966, there was enormous growth in the number of social workers in the following years. The 1971 census recorded 30,535 social workers. By 1991 the number of workers had doubled to 61,135. Today the combined total of social workers and community and social service workers is 85,955.

Of course, this growth in the number of social workers reflects the expansion of social services and income security programs over this period, particularly in the 1960s when significant new money was put into child welfare and Social Assistance. As the importance of social welfare programs increased, and as more and more people were involved in providing these services, a higher level of organization and a greater degree of professionalization was required from all those involved in the system. Important legislation was passed by provincial legislatures to meet the increasing demands for social services, and provincial associations were created to help train and organize social workers at the local level. Training and professional programs were introduced to accommodate this expansion, and codes of practice were elaborated to ensure quality service.

This chapter examines the state of the social work profession today.

THE CANADIAN ASSOCIATION OF SOCIAL WORKERS

The **Canadian Association of Social Workers** (CASW) was "founded" at the 1924 American National Conference of Social Work, which was held in Toronto. At this meeting, several Canadian social workers discussed the need for a professional association that addressed the specific needs of Canadians. The Association was formally established in 1927, and the first edition of its professional journal, *The Social Worker*, appeared in 1932. Initially, social workers joined the Association

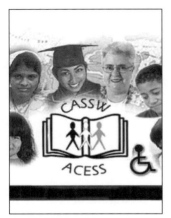

Canadian Association of Schools of Social Work homepage

55

individually. Today, CASW is a federation of ten provincial associations. The Association has jurisdiction over some issues while the provincial associations maintain jurisdiction over others. Because social services are a provincial responsibility in Canada, the provincial associations assume great importance in the development and administration of social work.

Data on the number of members in the Canadian Association of Social Workers gives an indication of the rapid growth of the profession. By 1939, CASW had 600 members. By 1966, it had 3,000 members, and by 1986, there were 9,000 members. Today, there are approximately 14,000 members across the country, all having some formal credentials in social work. CASW supplies members with relevant professional documents, a national journal, activities and events, access to benefits, representation nationally and internationally, and an opportunity to participate in professional development panels and organizations. CASW also influences governments through consultations, position statements and the presentation of briefs. The main benefit of belonging to the CASW is being part of a like-minded group of people who share the same goals and work together to improve their profession.

Employers frequently ask that their employees be members of CASW. Although this is not yet legally mandated, some provinces have introduced legislation that will give the government more control over the title and practice of social workers. Social workers, in turn, have tended to support this move as a way to protect the public and as a way to guarantee a level of professionalism. There are disciplinary bodies in every provincial association, but they can discipline only their members. When membership in professional associations is legally mandated, it will be easier to ensure that professional conduct is guaranteed.

Like the provinces themselves, the associations vary significantly in terms of their level of organization, their activities and their priorities. The box at the end of this chapter describes the main provincial associations and the legal framework within which they operate.

THE CANADIAN ASSOCIATION OF SCHOOLS OF SOCIAL WORK

The **Canadian Association of Schools of Social Work** (CASSW) was established in 1967, replacing the National Committee of Schools of Social Work, which, since 1948, had been the forum for programs offering professional education in social work. The CASSW is a national association of university faculties, schools and departments offering professional education in social work at the undergraduate, graduate and post-graduate levels.

The purpose of CASSW is to advance the standards, effectiveness and relevance of social work education and scholarship in Canada and, in other countries, through participation in international associations. CASSW is responsible for reviewing and approving social work educational programs. It also publishes a quarterly journal entitled the *Canadian Social Work Review* and undertakes research studies, such as women and HIV, anti-racism and a recent study of the social service sector.

The sector analysis of the profession of social work throughout Canada was released in February 2001. *In Critical Demand: Social Work in Canada* (see http://www.socialworkincanada.org for the report) is the most comprehensive examination of the profession ever undertaken. It studied the human resources needs of social work in Canada, including the demand for workers, wage levels and benefits, working conditions, qualifications and experience, turnover rates, opportunities for advancement and job satisfaction, as well as how social education and training is meeting the demand. The *In Critical Demand* report finds that the primary skills required by professional social workers include:

- Direct intervention strategies with individual, families, groups or community services;
- Supervision, management and administrative skills;
- Legislative and policy analysis and development; and
- Advocacy on behalf of individuals, families or the larger community (CASSW 2001, 85).

Many of the statistics provided in this chapter are derived from this important recent study of the profession.

THE INTERNATIONAL FEDERATION OF SOCIAL WORKERS

The **International Federation of Social Workers** (IFSW) is a successor to the International Permanent Secretariat of Social Workers, which was founded in Paris in 1928. In 1950, the International Federation of Social Workers was created, with the goal of becoming an international organization of professional social workers. Today the IFSW represents over half a million social workers in fifty-five different counties. The IFSW seeks to promote social work as a profession, link social workers from around the world and promote the participation of social workers in social policy and planning.

The IFSW has facilitated the development of a series of thirteen International Policy Papers. With these Papers, the IFSW hopes to address some basic concepts from a social work perspective, utilizing the in-depth experiences of various national associations to throw light on some of the broadest issues confronting contemporary society. They also hope to provide social workers globally with practical as well as philosophical guidelines. The titles of these papers are as follows: Advancement of Women, Child Welfare, The Welfare of Elderly People, Health, HIV-AIDS, Human Rights (re-printed in Appendix C of this book), Migration, Peace and Disarmament, The Protection of Personal Information, Refugees, Conditions in Rural Communities, Women's Self-Help and Youth.

A new international definition of social work was adopted at the IFSW General Meeting in Montreal in July 2000. The new definition replaces the IFSW definition of 1982, and recognizes that social work in the twenty-first century is dynamic and evolving and therefore no definition should be regarded as exhaustive. (There is a further discussion of this new definition of social work on page 15.)

IFSW WEBSITE

The IFSW website is also worth a visit: http://www.ifsw.org

Once you are there, you will find general information about the IFSW, it's history and aims, as well as several of their publications.

All thirteen policy papers as well as the IFSW *Code of Ethics* are on-line.

War Child Canada provides aid in the aftermath of Kosovo war.

Courtesy of Steven Hick.

SOCIAL WORK KNOWLEDGE

- human growth and behaviour
- family dynamics
- communication theory
- community development theory
- organizational theory
- theories of the state
- theories of oppression and empowerment
- social treatment interventions
- social action methods
- social research methods, and policy analysis

THE AMBIGUITY OF SOCIAL WORK

The **ambiguity of social work** refers to the fact that the social worker frequently has to balance urgent and practical intervention measures with more difficult ethical and political questions. In the course of their work, social workers are inevitably confronted with situations in which the policy and regulations of the agency conflict with what they, as experienced social workers, see as being in the best interests of their client. As well, the standards and ethics of the profession may be inconsistent with an agency's procedures and practices. Balancing one's beliefs, professional standards and agency rules can be difficult. In this context, the social worker's place of employment can be either a source of empowerment or a source of burnout.

Such **ethical dilemmas** often arise, for example, in income support and child custody cases. Welfare workers interview clients and, based on their assessment, often refer them to particular services for which they qualify. However, part of the mandate of welfare organizations is to save precious money. Therefore, welfare workers must ensure that the client is genuinely in need and eligible for assistance, while representing the client's interests as fairly as possible.

Similarly, in child custody cases (where a child welfare worker is expected to act in the best interest of the child), the social worker may be criticized for leaving a child in the home or for taking the child away from its family prematurely. Such dilemmas are obviously aggravated when there are large caseloads or tight budgets that make it difficult for social workers to provide services in a way that is consistent with their professional *Code of Ethics.*

The working life of a social worker, then, is very much a mix of the "ideal" and the "practical." They have a *Code of Ethics* with high ideals, but the reality is that they must practice within a context of institutions and laws that in many ways limits the capacity of an individual to deliver on such ideals.

In practice, there is no easy answer to such ambiguities and ethical dilemmas. Social workers make judgements based on their knowledge and experience and, in the end, that is all they can be expected to do. Then again, those entering the profession normally do so hoping the journey will, on the whole, be mostly satisfying but knowing full well that it will not always be simple or easy.

Many introductory texts present the delivery of social services in an idealized form, assuming that the professional's relationship with the client will always be governed by an exclusive concern for the client's well-being. Unfortunately, this is not often the reality. While staffed with the most dedicated and hard-working people, many social work agencies may enforce rigid rules and regulations, excessive paperwork and computerized control over the client-social worker relationship. And too often such rigid controls are at direct odds with the needs of the client. Indeed, there are experienced practitioners, quite discouraged by all this, who are convinced that social services simply "paper over" serious cracks in the walls of a fundamentally unjust society (Carniol 2000, 6).

CASW'S CODE OF ETHICS

As mentioned above, the CASW has a **Code of Ethics** to help guide social workers in the course of their work. The *Code*, a set of guiding principles that can lead to the formulation of more specific standards of practice, is reprinted in Appendix B of this book. It is a key document and should be studied carefully by those entering the profession.

The *Code* encompasses the values and principles of human worth, dignity, self-determination and justice upon which social work is based. Its key principles deal with confidentiality, respect for the individual and his or her opinion, and conflicts of interest. The CASW *Code of Ethics* summarizes these values as follows:

> The profession of social work is founded on humanitarian and egalitarian ideals. Social workers believe in the intrinsic worth and dignity of every human being and are committed to the values of acceptance and self-determination.
>
> Social workers are dedicated to the welfare and self-realization of human beings; to the development and disciplined use of scientific knowledge regarding human and societal behaviours; to the development of resources to meet individual, group, national and international needs and aspirations; and to the achievement of social justice for all.
>
> Social workers are pledged to serve [their clients] without discrimination on any grounds of race, ethnicity, language, religion, marital status, gender, sexual orientation, age, abilities, economic status, political affiliation or national ancestry (CASW 1994).

Above all, the *Code of Ethics* demands that a social worker take the best interests of the client as the primary consideration in any intervention. The best interests of client means:

- that the wishes, desires, motivations, and plans of the client are taken by the social worker as the primary consideration in any intervention plan developed by the social worker subject to change only when the client's plans are documented to be unrealistic, unreasonable or potentially harmful to self or others or otherwise determined inappropriate when considered in relation to a mandated requirement,

- that all actions and interventions of the social worker are taken subject to the reasonable belief that the client will benefit from the action, and

- that the social worker will consider the client as an individual, a member of a family unit, a member of a community, a person with a distinct ancestry or culture and will consider those factors in any decision affecting the client (CASW 1994).

Whether dealing with **voluntary clients** (people who have chosen to seek the services of a social worker) or **involuntary clients** (those who are legally obligated to accept services, such as prisoners on parole or children in care), social workers have a responsibility to their clients to address their needs while respecting their dignity and self-worth.

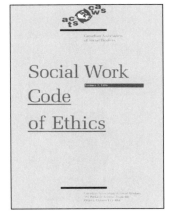

CASW *Social Work Code of Ethics* (1994).

THE ROLES OF THE SOCIAL WORKER

In performing their day-to-day work, a social worker is expected to be knowledgeable and skillful in a variety of roles. The role that is selected and applied should ideally be the role that is most effective with a particular client in the particular circumstances.

A practitioner may be involved in a number of **social worker roles**, depending on the nature of their job and the approach to practice that they use:

- The role of *enabler* involves the worker in helping people to organize to help themselves; for example, helping a community identify problems, to explore and select strategies, to organize and to mobilize to address the problems.

- A *broker* links individuals and groups who need help; for example, linking a woman who is abused by her spouse to a shelter for battered women.

- In the role of *advocate,* the worker provides leadership in advocating on behalf of a person or in challenging an institution's decision not to provide services.

- The *initiator* calls attention to problems or the problems a particular policy or program may cause.

- The role of *mediator* involves participating as a neutral party in a dispute between parties to help them reconcile differences or achieve mutually beneficial agreements.

- As a *negotiator* the social worker is allied with one side in a dispute and tries to achieve agreement by bargaining on his or her client's behalf. The *activist* seeks to change institutions and structures in society, helping to organize people to shift power and resources to oppressed or disadvantaged groups.

- As an *educator* the social worker is providing information and awareness of problem and solutions.

- The social worker is frequently a *co-ordinator*, bringing all the pieces together in an organized manner to accomplish a task.

- As *researcher,* the social worker provides resources for clients and stays abreast of his or her field.

- The *group facilitator* may lead a group activity as part of group therapy, a self-help group or any other type of group.

- The social worker may be engaged as a *public speaker* at schools, service organizations, with police or within related agencies.

Whatever the particular context social workers find themselves in, and whatever roles they are required to fulfil, they must apply themselves at all times in a professional manner, utilizing all the knowledge and skills they have at their disposal and taking into account the specific needs of the client and the remedies currently available.

Some of the roles social workers find themselves in.

EMPLOYMENT OPPORTUNITIES IN SOCIAL WORK

As a career, social work offers many rewarding opportunities to make a difference in the quality of life of other individuals. Social workers work with people who are homeless, dispossessed and unemployed, as well as with people who have mental or physical health concerns; with street youth, splintered families, victims of violence and people who have committed crimes. The job opportunities are plentiful and seemingly unlikely to diminish in the near future. Forty-seven percent of employers estimate that they will have job openings for social work practitioners in the next few years (CASSW 2001, 101).

However, the career opportunities for qualified social workers are much broader than this. As well as working with individuals, families and small groups, many social workers work with organizations and communities to improve social conditions and to plan for better communities. Large-scale government programs that improve life for individuals in society, such as Employment Insurance and Old Age Security, need careful planning and require social workers who are specially trained in social policy matters. Some social workers devote their careers to studying problems as diverse as homelessness, unemployment and family, research that helps us to understand causes and informs us as to what methods might be effective in addressing these issues.

Social workers, then, work in a variety of settings:

- *Health and social services.* Seventy-four percent of social work jobs in health and social service agencies. Most are funded directly or indirectly by municipal, provincial or federal governments. Some jobs are in agencies funded by voluntary donations. Job settings include family and child welfare agencies, hospitals and other health care facilities, group homes and hostels, addiction treatment facilities and social assistance offices, where social workers provide help to individuals, families and small groups.

- *Government services.* A large number of social workers work directly for some level of government (19 percent), although this setting is declining as more and more services are devolved to community agencies. These services include planning and administration of programs, correctional facilities and the justice system.

- *Communities.* Community organizers work out of community health centres, resource centres and other grassroots organizations.

- *Research.* Research is carried out in universities, government departments and in large social agencies and institutions.

- *Self-employment.* A small but growing number of social workers are self-employed, offering services directly to the public for fees or contracting their services to large organizations. The number of private practitioners has increased from 675 in 1991 to 1,460 in 1996 or by 116.3 percent (CASSW 2001, 37).

Obviously, each of these specialties calls for different training and personal qualities. Direct clinical service is emotionally demanding. Community organization requires practical political insight and leadership.

WHERE THE JOBS ARE

- Managers, 14,075 (11.4%)
- Social workers, 37,470 (30.2%)
- Family, marriage and related counsellors, 29,310 (23.7%)
- Probation officers, 4,480 (3.6%)
- Community and social Service workers, 48,485 (39.1%)
- Total, 133,840 (100%)

Source: CASSW, In Critical Demand (2001).

National Archives of Canada. Neg no. PA126556 (W. Doucette).

Physician provides help to Inuit woman in Frobisher Bay, 1951

**IN CRITICAL DEMAND:
SOCIAL WORK IN CANADA**

Five partners recently
(1998-2001) sponsored a
major review of the social work
profession in Canada. The
organizations involved were:
the Canadian Association of
Schools of Social Work
(CASSW), the Canadian
Committee of Deans and
Directors of Schools of Social
Work (CCDDSSW), the
Canadian Association of Social
Workers (CASW), the
regroupement des unités de
formation universitaires en
travail social (RUFUTS), and
Human Resources
Development Canada (HRDC).

To find out more about this
important study and its findings,
go to: http://
www.socialworkincanada.org

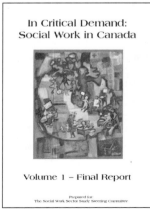

In Critical Demand:
Social Work in Canada

Volume 1 – Final Report

Prepared for:
The Social Work Sector Study Steering Committee

CASSW report on the social
work profession in Canada

Social work research demands scientific rigour and an interest in theoretical issues. Moreover, in the course of a career, a social worker may move from one employment setting to another. In recent years, the employment pattern of social workers has been changing. In the five-year period ending in 1996, as a result of government cutbacks, 19.2 percent fewer social workers were employed in government. On the other hand, there has been an increase in the percentage of social workers employed in institutional health and social services (73.9 percent) and non-institutional social services (25.9 percent).

THE EDUCATION OF SOCIAL WORKERS

Whatever type of work is pursued, some post-secondary education is required in order to practice in the field of social work. A Bachelor of Social Work (B.S.W.) normally requires four years of university study. At least one additional year of graduate study is required for the Master of Social Work (M.S.W.) degree. A Diploma in Social Service Work from a community college also requires several years of training. Those holding a non-social work undergraduate degree normally must complete two years of study for a Master of Social Work degree. Completion of the M.S.W. degree generally ensures greater job mobility and a higher level of earnings (an average of $43,218 per annum). Post-graduate study leading to a doctorate degree in social work is normally pursued by those who wish to teach at a university or those who are involved in high-level research, social policy or large-scale administration.

The first trained Canadian social workers graduated from the University of Toronto's Department of Social Services in 1914. Until the early 1970s, social work schools in Canada were accredited by the American Council of Social Work Education. There are currently thirty-four universities offering social work degrees and forty-six community colleges offering diplomas. Nearly 4,000 students enroll annually in social work degree education, and about 370 faculty are employed to teach them.

Each province has extensive legislation governing social work. Most of this provincial legislation has come into effect over the last thirty years. Manitoba was the first to enact legislation, in 1966, and Ontario was the last, having only recently passed social work legislation. In general, each Act governs who can call themselves a social worker, the qualifications required to use the title and penalties for contravening the regulatory Act or unethical behaviour. For example, in British Columbia, the *Social Workers Act* of 1979 provides for the control of the use of the title Registered Social Worker and stipulates that whoever contravenes these provisions commits an offence and is liable to a fine of not more than $1,000. It also specifies that a Board of Registration be appointed by the Lieutenant Governor in Council to enforce the Act. Similarly, the early Manitoba legislation, the *Manitoba Institute of Registered Social Workers Incorporation Act* (1966), provides for voluntary registration and control of the designation Registered Social Worker. The Board of the Manitoba Institute of Registered Social Workers requires either a B.S.W. or an M.S.W. from an accredited university or college or the equivalent as they determine.

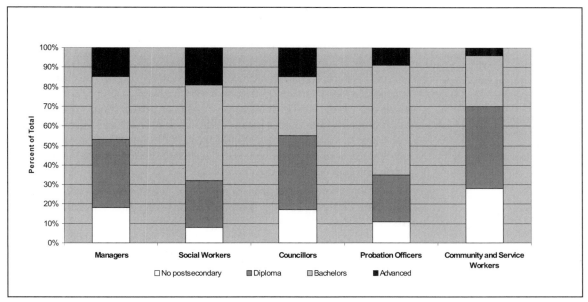

Figure 4.1: Educational Levels of Social Service Occupations Compared with other Employment Sectors. *Source:* CASSW, *In Critical Demand* (2001).

In 1998, the Ontario Government passed Bill 76, the *Social Work and the Social Service Work Act*. The Act stipulates that any practitioner wishing to use the title Social Worker/Registered Social Worker or Social Service Worker/Registered Social Service Worker must be a member of the regulatory College established by the legislation, the College of Social Workers and Social Service Workers of Ontario. The College has full regulatory functions including a complaint review process and disciplinary proceedings that can result in suspension or revocation of license to practice. The new College will be governed by a Council consisting of seven elected social workers, seven elected service workers and seven appointed members of the public to a total of twenty-one members. A Registrar will be the Chief Executive Officer of the College and accountable to the governing Council. The primary duty of the College is to serve and protect the public interest, whereas the professional association advocates for the concerns of its members. The College's website is located at http://www.ocswssw.org. The text of the *Social Work and the Social Services Act* is available at: http://www.e-laws.gov.on.ca.

The websites for the various provincial associations can be found at http://www.casw-acts.ca/ProvOrg.htm. More information can also be found at the end of this chapter.

UNIONIZATION

Today most Canadian social workers are members of **public sector unions**. Indeed, they were part of the wider unionization of the public sector during the 1960s and 1970s, when, for the first time, public sector employees were permitted to join a union. In that period, social workers in both private non-profit and for-profit organizations began to look to

THE SOCIAL WORKER PROFILE

According to the 1996 census, 71.5% of social workers were women (compared with 75% in 1991), 4.6% were Aboriginal (compared with 4% of the overall population) and 7.4% were visible minorities (compared with 11% of the population).

unions for assistance. Of course, there was some debate over whether social workers should join trade unions. Did they not, after all, have their own **professional associations** and were trade unions not traditionally more associated with industrial workers than with people who were professionally trained? This matter was resolved, in the end, by a division of labour. The associations represent social workers in issues pertaining to the development of the profession, the education of its members and in discussions of social issues and social policy. The unions represent them in the areas of pay or working conditions. The professional association and the union in effect complement each other and both have mandates to act as voices for those they represent.

The largest unions representing social workers in Canada are the Canadian Union of Public Employees (CUPE) and the Public Sector Alliance of Canada (PSAC). CUPE members are represented by provincial level divisions and sectors. For example, the membership of CUPE Ontario is broken down into five principal sectors: Municipal, Health Care, School Boards, University and Social Services. Social workers in Children's Aid Societies, Associations for Community Living, Children's Care Centres, Municipal Social Services, Community Agencies (such as women's shelters), and municipal and charitable homes for the aged are all unionized.

Unionization has benefited social workers in ways similar to other unionized workers: they have helped to raise the salaries of social workers, improve working conditions and enhance job security. Pressure from female social workers and from the broader women's movement encouraged the unions to campaign for issues important to women, such as equal pay for work of equal value, child care, maternity leave, sexual harassment protection and pensions. Unions in social work agencies have also played another important role that is less well known and recognized. Labour unions have, throughout history, advocated for improved social programs, income security and social services. Programs such as Employment Insurance and Medicare would not exist today without pressure from the union sector. As these programs come under increasing pressure from funding cuts, the unions are again playing a key role in opposing cutbacks. For example, CUPE is at the forefront is struggling to save universal health care.

SALARIES OF SOCIAL WORKERS

It is probably safe to say that people enter social work more for the selfless rewards of helping other people in need than for earning high incomes from such work. However, having said that, and taking into account the importance of their work for other human beings, one might expect a somewhat higher level of remuneration in the field. Social workers are generally among the lowest-paid service workers. The average earnings of social workers (full-time and part-time) was $33,023 in 1995. Earnings for community and social service workers were only $22,614. This compares with nurses at $32,355 and secondary school teachers at $41,009 (CASSW 2001, 41).

National Archives of Canada. Neg no. PA93697.

Unions represent workers on pay and working conditions.

Two main reasons have been advanced to explain why this is so. First, social workers are paid less because they work with underprivileged people who are themselves not highly respected and have little power. When government cutbacks come, they frequently begin with cuts to services for the disadvantaged–the very people with whom social workers work. Second, the profession has always been seen as female dominated (and since women in general are paid less than men, social work tends to pay less than other male-dominated professions). Unfair as this may be, both explanations are undoubtedly a large part of the reason for the low wages (and, of course, these explanations beg even larger questions).

Social spending cutbacks not only affect the benefits and levels of service, but also the amount that is available to pay for staff delivering the services. Recent government cutbacks in social spending therefore have directly affected the income of social workers. As well, all levels of government are moving towards contracting out the delivery of social services to private-sector contractors (arguing that it will save money). Accordingly, social workers increasing find themselves working for non-unionized, underfunded private agencies. As these services are shifted from unionized public agencies to non-unionized private agencies, the wages of social workers are squeezed.

All this does not help to advance the morale of social workers in the field. With the increasing likelihood of even greater funding cutbacks in the near future, there will be an ever greater need for social workers, their association and their union representatives to be more forceful in demanding just compensation for their efforts.

SOCIAL WORKERS' AVERAGE EARNINGS

- All, $33,023
- Visible Minorities, $31,695
- Aboriginal, $26,509
- Men, $37,486
- Women, $31,618

Source: CASSW, *In Critical Demand* (2001), pp.41, 50. These are figures for full- and part-time workers in 1995.

THE FUTURE OF THE PROFESSION

The profession of social work will face significant challenges in the future. Four factors contribute to these challenges.

- Demographics and therefore service demands are rapidly shifting. The overall population is growing older, common-law and lone-parent families are increasing, as is the proportion of children living in poverty, and immigrant flows are creating cultural shifts.

- There is a devolution of services from direct government delivery to third-party community or private provision.

- There is decreasing financial support and a weakening of public support for the work social workers do and for those they serve.

- There is intensification of the use of technology in the workplace.

Nevertheless, employment opportunities for social workers will continue to be good, according to the recent CASSW report *In Critical Demand* (2001, 8). Employment in the social work and social service sector is expected to grow by 2 percent per year, in line with Canadian population growth projections. The types of jobs will change as services for the elderly, children in dire straits, and recent immigrants become more urgent.

REFERENCES

- Canadian Association of Schools of Social Work. 2001. *In Critical Demand: Social Work in Canada, Final Report*. Ottawa. This report is available on-line at: http://www.socialworkincanada.org

- Canadian Association of Social Workers. 1994. *Code of Ethics*. Ottawa: CASW.

- Carniol, B. 2000. *Case Critical: Challenging Social Services in Canada*. Toronto: Between the Lines.

The profession of social work currently finds itself facing a dilemma: there is an unprecedented demand for the skills and knowledge of social workers, but at the same time there is a devaluation of the social services and of those providing them. Services are rapidly being devolved from direct government delivery to third-party community or private provision. This is causing shifts in the types of jobs and earning of social workers. Social workers are increasingly finding jobs in community-based and non-institutional social services where they earn less, have fewer benefits and have less security than government and hospital social workers.

It seems likely that social service workers in the next period will be expected to do more with less funding, resulting in increased caseloads and a higher level of work-related stress. Moreover, as the use of computer and communications technology for case management and file recording intensifies, workers will need to be aware of the implications of this for judgements about client needs as well as client privacy.

CONCLUSION

Social workers work mainly with the disadvantaged in Canadian society. Increasingly, their task is legally defined or mandated, and their work is guided by professional standards; that is, there are laws, practices and precedents that provide a structure for their work. More often than not, however, situations arise in daily practice for which there are no clear laws or precedents. This is ultimately why values, training and approach are so important.

The task of the social worker is to simultaneously act in the best interests of their clients and adhere to agency policy and procedures. These basic objectives frequently are at odds with each other, and the social worker is left using all of his or her knowledge, experience and skill to resolve the conflict.

Social work is a noble profession, and social workers require a dedication no less than those in the other "helping professions." Above all, social work requires an overriding commitment to the welfare of people, to the development of resources to meet individual, group, national and international needs and aspirations, and to the achievement of social justice for all.

The opportunity to make a difference is the defining characteristic of social work, whether with individuals and small groups or on a larger scale. And, whatever the employment setting, the opportunities to so make a difference are plentiful. To meet the challenges of the future, social workers will need a clear sense of purpose and strong professional identity.

STATUS OF SOCIAL WORK LEGISLATION IN CANADA: A SUMMARY

Alberta College of Social Workers

Title of Act/Regulation: Social Work Professions Act (1995)

Mission and Goals: The mission and goals of the College are to promote, regulate and govern the profession of social work in the Province of Alberta; to advocate for skilled and ethical social work practices; and, to advocate for policies, programs and services that promote the profession and protect the best interests of the public.

Membership: In 1999, the Provincial Legislature passed an amendment to the Social Work Profession Act making it mandatory for people who have a social work education, who work within the scope of social work practice and who work with the public, to be registered. To be considered for Registration you must be actively engaged in social work practice, meet the character and reputation requirements, provide two references from Registered Social Workers who can attest to your social work practice, and complete additional training in social work ethics and standards of practice.

Governing Body: The Alberta College of Social Workers (ACSW) is both the designated regulatory body for the practice of social work in Alberta and the professional association representing the interests of social workers.

Website: http://www.acsw.ab.ca

British Columbia Association of Social Workers and the Board of Registration for Social Workers

Title of Act/Regulation: Social Workers Act, R.S.B.C., c.389, (1979)

Mission and Goals: The mandate of the British Columbia Association of Social Workers (BCASW) is to advocate for the interests and concerns of professional social workers. The Association does not carry a disciplinary role, which is the mandate of the profession's regulatory body, the Board of Registration for Social Workers (BRSW) which provides for the control of the use of the title registered social worker. The Association is currently advocating for new legislation to govern the profession. See regulation update on their website for the most up-to-date information.

Membership: You are eligible to join BCASW if you hold a graduate degree in social work or are a student currently enrolled in a social work degree program. To become a registered social workers with the BRSW you require a bachelor's or master's degree in social work; or a degree or certificate deemed by the Board to be equivalent to a master's degree in social work or post-graduate degree in social work; or to be a "registered social worker" or "professional social worker" in another province where the standards are not less than the minimum standards prescribed under this Act and regulations.

Governing Body: A board of directors of the BCASW comprises seven members and nine regional representatives. The Board of Registration for social workers is composed of not more than 12 or less than 10 members appointed by the Lieutenant Governor in Council including two persons who are not social workers and the remainder are R.S.W.s.

Website: http://www.bcasw.org

Manitoba Association of Social Workers/ Manitoba Institute of Registered Social Workers

Title of Act/Regulation: The Manitoba Institute of Registered Social Workers Incorporation Act (1966)

Mission and Goals: The Manitoba Association of Social Workers (MASW) is the voice of the social work profession, providing peer support, and connecting you with social workers across Canada. The Manitoba Institute of Registered Social Workers (MIRSW) is the regulatory arm of the profession, responsible for certifying members and protecting the public through recognized, ethical standards of practice. It requires registrants to maintain current knowledge through education. It is a disciplinary body to investigate public complaints.

Membership: Membership in the MASW requires a B.S.W., M.S.W., or D.S.W. degree or a Welfare Worker's Certificate from a Manitoba Community College, or its equivalent, and two consecutive years of employment and letters of recommendation.

You are eligible for registration with the MIRSW if you are employed by an agency or are in private practice, possess a B.S.W., M.S.W. or D.S.W. degree from an accredited school of social work, and have practiced social work for a minimum of one year.

Governing Body: The Board of the Manitoba Institute of Registered Social Workers.

Website: http://http://www.geocities.com/masw_mirsw

New Brunswick Association of Social Workers

Title of Act/Regulation: The Act to Incorporate the New Brunswick Association of Social Workers (1988)

Mission and Goals: The New Brunswick Association of Social Workers ensures quality professional social work services to the population of New Brunswick. The Association accomplishes its mission by ensuring all persons practising social work and/or using the title social worker are registered; establishing and enforcing standards of qualification, knowledge, skill and efficiency of practice; investigating complaints against its members; promoting public awareness of the role of social work; and assisting members in the pursuit of social justice and social change.

Membership: To become a regular member you require a bachelor's, master's or doctoral degree in social work or the equivalent from a School of Social Work approved by the Committee; a person who has passed the examination prescribed by the Committee and has sufficient experience; or a person who is a member of an association of social workers approved by the Committee.

Governing Body: The Board of Directors is comprised of an elected executive, one director from each local chapter, the NB Director to the Canadian Association of Social Workers (CASW) board, and one public member appointed by the Minister of Health and Community Services. The Board serves as the governing body of the general membership and administers the affairs of the Association.

Website: http://www.nbasw-atsnb.ca

Newfoundland and Labrador Association of Social Workers

Title of Act/Regulation: Social Workers Association Act (1993)

Mission and Goals: The Act provides for the control of practice of social work and the use of the title social worker or registered social work, or abbreviations of such titles. The NLASW enforces the Act and works to promote excellence in the social work profession.

Membership: A bachelor's, master's or doctoral degree or other equivalent education in social work from an educational institution approved by the committee of examiners and completion of the examination prescribed.

Governing Body: The Board of the Newfoundland and Labrador Association of Social Workers is composed of the president, a president-elect, an at-large executive member, a member who is a member of the Board of CASW, and other members as provided by the bylaws and a member appointed by the Minister. The Board of Directors is empowered to be the regulatory body and the professional association for social workers.

Website: http://www3.nf.sympatico.ca/nlasw

Nova Scotia Association of Social Workers

Title of Act/Regulation: Social Workers Act (1993)

Mission and Goals: The Nova Scotia Association of Social Workers promotes and regulates the practice of social work so its members can provide a high standard of service that respects diversity, promotes social jus-

tice, and enhances the worth, self-determination and potential of individuals, families and communities.

Membership: To become a member everyone must pass an examination. Other requirements include a doctoral or master's degree or a graduate-level diploma in social work from an approved faculty of social work and two years of experience, or a bachelor's degree in social work from an approved faculty of social work and three years of experience, subsequent to the degree.

Governing Body: The Council of the NSASW consists of the president, vice-president, secretary, treasurer, immediate past president, the chair of the Board of Examiners and other members as provided by the bylaws.

The Board of Examiners consists of 7 social workers appointed by the Council who represent the diversity of various fields of social work practice and who reflect the sex, racial, and ethnic composition of the Association, one of whom is teaching at an approved school of social work and 3 persons appointed by the Governor in Council who are not social workers.

Website: http://www.nsasw.org

Ontario Association of Social Workers

Title of Act/Regulation: Social Work and Social Service Work Act, 1998

Mission and Goals: The Social Work and Social Service Work Act, 1998, was proclaimed in law with Bill 76 in 2000. With this legislation, anyone wishing to call him or herself a "social worker" or "social service worker" must belong to the Ontario College of Social Workers and Social Service Workers.

Membership: Applicants may apply for membership in one of two categories: Professional Membership or Student Membership. Applicants for Professional Membership must hold a bachelor's, master's or doctorate degree in social work (BSW, MSW, or PhD/DSW). Applicants for Student Membership must be enrolled in an accredited university social work program.

Governing Body: A 21-member Council comprised of 7 elected social workers and 7 elected social service workers representing five electoral districts across the province, and 7 public members appointed by the Lieutenant Governor, govern the OCSWSSW.

Website: http://www.oasw.org

Ordre professionnel des travailleurs sociaux du Québec

Title of Act/Regulation: Code des professions (1973, Amended 1974, 1975, 1994)

Mission and Goals: The Act provides for control of the use of the title social worker or other title which suggests this designation or an equivalent one, or the use of the initials P.S.W., T.S.P., S.W., T.S.

Membership: To become a member and to use the titles above a person must have a B.S.W. or M.S.W. or equivalent diploma if obtained outside the province.

Governing Body: The governing body consists of a Board of 20 directors elected on a regional basis, and 4 directors appointed by the Office des professions du Québec.

Website (French only): http://www.optsq.org

Prince Edward Island Association of Social Workers

Title of Act/Regulation: Social Work Act (1988)

Mission and Goals: The Act provides for the control of the practice of social work and the use of the title social worker or registered social worker, or abbreviations of such titles.

Membership: To become a member you require a degree from a School of Social Work recognized by the Board; practical training as prescribed; professional competency demonstrated by examination; good standing under any existing legislation; and currency of professional knowledge and skills.

Governing Body: The PEI Social Work Registration Board is composed of 5 members nominated by the PEI Association of Social Workers and appointed by the Minister including 4 registered social workers and members of the Association; and one person to represent the perspective of the general public.

The Prince Edward Island Association of Social Workers executive of the Association consists of a president, vice-president, secretary, treasurer and other members as prescribed by their bylaws.

E-mail: panmure.island@pei.sympatico.ca

Saskatchewan Association of Social Workers

Title of Act/Regulation: An Act respecting Social Workers (1993) a.k.a. The Social Workers Act.

Mission and Goals: The Act provides for the control of title. Sec. 24 states that no person other than a member shall engage in the practice of social work by using the title "social worker." The Saskatchewan Association of Social Workers (SASW) administers the Act.

The association maintains the standards for the profession, promotes the profession, provides a means by which the association through its members may take action on issues of social welfare, disseminates publications and information and encourages studies in field.

Membership: Membership requires a certificate or bachelor's or master's or doctoral degree in social work from a university approved in the bylaws.

Governing Body: The Council of the SASW consists of 7 members elected by the members and a person appointed by the Lieutenant Governor in Council. The officers are Past President, President, President-elect, Secretary, Treasurer and 2 members-at-large.

E-mail: sasw@cableregina.com

The above information is for general interest only and it should not be relied upon as being either comprehensive or current. It was compiled from information found in large part on the CASW website (http://www.casw-acts.ca) and from provincial association websites. For up-to-date information, check with the appropriate provincial association.

For information on the Association of Social Workers of Northern Canada (ASWNC), contact the Association, c/o Aurora College, Box 1008, Inuvik, NT   X0E 0T0.

CHAPTER 4: SOCIAL WORK AS A PROFESSION

Key Concepts

- Canadian Association of Social Workers (CASW)
- Canadian Association of Schools of Social Work (CASSW)
- International Federation of Social Workers (IFSW)
- Ambiguity of social work
- Ethical dilemmas
- Code of Ethics
- Voluntary clients
- Involuntary clients
- Social worker roles
- Public sector unions
- Professional associations

Discussion Questions

1. What are the main associations to which Canadian social workers belong?

2. Define the ambiguity of social work, and its implication for direct practice.

3. Social work has its own code of ethics. What is the purpose of the code, and what are three of the key elements contained in the code?

4. Define and describe the various roles that social workers may take on in the course of their work.

5. Does the composition of the profession (women, Aboriginal and visible minority) reflect the diversity of Canadian society? Why is this important?

6. How are the employment patterns of social workers changing and what are the implications for social workers?

7. What four challenges does the profession of social work in Canada face, and how will they affect the social workers and social work practice?

Websites

- **Canadian Association of Social Workers**
  http://www.casw-acts.ca

  The CASW website contains useful information about how the CASW represents Canadian social workers, information about the profession, and the status of professional legislation in each province.

- **The Canadian Association of Schools of Social Work (CASSW)**
  http://www.cassw-acess.ca

  CASSW-ACESS is a voluntary, national charitable association of university faculties, schools and departments offering professional education in social work at the undergraduate, graduate and post-graduate levels. Check out their research reports, news and school information.

- **International Federation of Social Workers–Code of Ethics**
  http://www.ifsw.org

  "The Ethics of Social Work Principles and Standards" adopted by the IFSW General Meeting, Colombo, Sri Lanka, in 1994 is on-line. Also check out the various policy documents.

- **In Critical Demand: Social Work in Canada**
  http://www.socialworkincanada.org

  A major review and analysis of the profession of social work. The study examined human resource issues such as wages and benefits, working conditions, qualifications and experience, turnover rates, opportunities for advancement, job satisfaction, career and educational paths, portability of credentials, licensing and regulation, training and human resource development programs and unionization.

5

Social Work with Individuals, Groups and Communities

Direct Social Work Practice

Social work practice is the use of social work knowledge and skills to implement society's mandated policies and services in ways that are consistent with social work values. It is the values and principles that social workers work and live by that are at the core of this work. It is what motivates social workers to do what they do.

It is important for all social workers to have a basic understanding of the processes and activities for the three fields of social work commonly defined under the category of direct practice. They are (1) social work with individuals, (2) group work, and (3) community work. The purpose of this chapter is to introduce each of these fields and to discuss the main kinds of activity a social worker is likely to encounter in each field.

The three social work specializations or fields emerged in the 1940s. Today many schools of social work use this breakdown for purposes of social work training. **Social work with individuals** is directed at helping individuals, using counselling and other one-on-one methods. **Group work** aims to assist a group of people in a variety of ways–the group could be a therapy group, a peer group or a family. Assisting a local community to plan, implement and evaluate efforts at health and social welfare can be fostered through **community work**.

Most social workers will find themselves involved in one or another of the three forms of direct practice at different times in their careers. This diversity of fields within which social workers practice requires a multi-skilled and broad-based practitioner. Although one may specialize in one of the three fields, all workers will need a range of basic skills to intervene effectively with individuals, groups and communities.

THREE FIELDS OF DIRECT PRACTICE

Social work practice essentially consists of a series or process of interventive actions. The worker calls upon his or her repertoire of helping knowledge, skills and values and applies them in particular ways in specific situations to achieve planned and purposeful change. While each situation will require a different pattern of interventions, the process or steps are essentially the same.

Often, individual, group and community work overlap.

71

SOCIAL WORK PRACTICE THEORIES

An individual's background knowledge and beliefs about social work (practice theories) obviously affect how that person intervenes in a particular situation.

Social work draws from a wide variety of such practice theories:

- Anti-Racist Practice
- Aboriginal Theory
- Behaviour Therapy
- Cognitive Therapy
- Communication (Communicative-Interactive)
- Crisis Intervention
- Developmental
- Ecological (Life Model)
- Ego-State Therapy
- Existential Therapy
- Feminist Therapy
- Functional
- Generalist Approach
- Gestalt Therapy
- Integrative
- Locality Development
- Mediating
- Narrative Therapy
- Organizational (Remedial-Group)
- Person-Centered Therapy
- Play Therapy
- Psychosocial
- Problem Solving
- Rational-Emotive Therapy
- Social Action
- Social Planning
- Socialization
- Structural Approach
- Task Approach

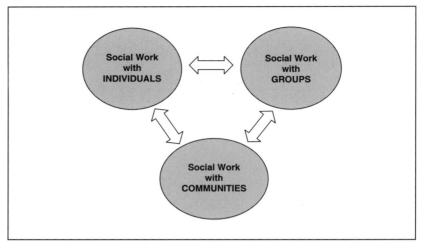

Figure 5.1: Three Fields of Direct Intervention

Social work practice is not a mechanical process to be executed in a rigid, step-like manner. Rather, each case or person must be viewed as being unique. To do otherwise would not be effective social work, as one would miss many of the intricacies and nuances of each new situation. Social work, therefore, involves more than technical knowledge and skills applied in a set series of steps. It is an interplay of action, reflection and more action. A useful analogy is that of a dancer who has the technical skills to dance, who knows the steps and moves involved in a particular dance, but to be truly excellent, must combine and re-combine the moves into new patterns. Social work needs this kind of artful improvising, or the ability to "think on one's feet." It is art as much as it is science.

Regardless of the approach taken to social work, it is important to have a basic understanding of all three fields of direct practice. The above diagram indicates how each field influences the other and reveals that a primary intervention in one field may involve some level of intervention in the others.

SOCIAL WORK WITH INDIVIDUALS

The helping process with individuals is sometimes called social casework, although this term is used infrequently nowadays. A majority of social workers spend their time working with individuals in private or public agencies or in private practice. Even though other types of social work are increasing, the practice of social work with individuals still predominates.

Individual social work is aimed at helping people resolve their problems or situations on a one-to-one basis, that is, helping unemployed people obtain work or training, providing protective services for abused children, providing counselling for mental health, providing parole or probation services, supplying services to the homeless and poor, co-ordinating services for people with AIDS and co-ordinating discharge services for a person being released from hospital. All of us on

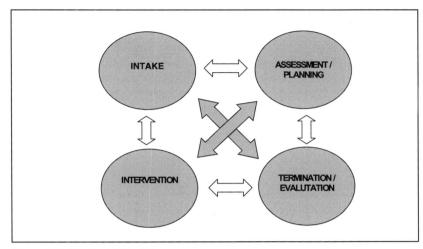

Figure 5.2: The Social Work Process

ACTION-REFLECTION-ACTION

The notion of "action-reflection-action" originates with Paulo Freire in his book *Pedagogy of the Oppressed* (1970). For Freire, becoming conscious of how social, political and economic relations affect one's life and the lives of others, and taking action to challenge those structures, involves the practice of "praxis"–the synthesis of "reflection and action upon the world in order to transform it."

occasion find ourselves with problems that we cannot resolve alone. At times the help of a friend or family member may be enough, but at other times the skilled help of a social worker is necessary. Social work with individuals can take different forms depending on the philosophy and perspective of the social worker. While some workers may address personal problems, others may emphasize the social relations underlying the problem. Still others may address both dimensions simultaneously.

In general, social work practice with individuals involves the following steps. These steps are common to most social work interventions with individuals and families. Although assessment precedes intervention, and intervention precedes termination, the process can be cyclical. For example, during intervention the client and worker may discover new information that in turn raises the need for more planning. In fact, each process is taking place throughout the intervention, but at each step one or more is emphasized. As mentioned previously, the steps are mere guideposts for a process that involves a combining and re-combining of actions into new ways of looking at things–that is, a **praxis** or a process of "action-reflection-action."

• Intake

Intake is usually the first step taken by a worker when a client seeks help. Intake is a process whereby a request for service is made by or for a person, and it is then determined whether and what kind of service is to be provided. The social worker attempts to gather initial information from the client in order to determine what assistance is needed, and whether the agency and worker is the appropriate provider. If it is mutually determined by both the worker and client that the agency can be of service, then some sort of agreement or contract is made. When it is determined that the person's needs cannot be met by the agency, then a referral to a service elsewhere is made or a decision is made that no social work service is required.

THE TERM "CLIENT"

Throughout this text the term *client* is used to denote the person or persons with whom the social worker is working. However, some social work practitioners view the term as a somewhat derogatory one, since it seems to imply that the person is a powerless object of practice. This text certainly does not intend to give this negative connotation to the term but rather sees the client as being involved in a partnership with the social worker in a relation of empowerment. For a further discussion of empowerment, see Chapter 1, page 16.

During the intake phase, the client makes a personal request for help or someone from the community directs the client to a particular social work agency. The social work relationship can be either voluntary or involuntary. The intake step is voluntary when a client willingly seeks help from a social work agency. For example, a parent who recognizes the difficulties of caring for a child may approach a child welfare agency for assistance. By contrast, an involuntary client is ordered to see a social worker or is required to do so by law. For example, a social worker is required by law to assist a child in danger when, for example, the child's situation has been reported as unsafe by a physician, hospital worker, police officer or school teacher. In such cases, families are often uncooperative, especially if allegations of child abuse are reported.

In the intake step, the social worker acknowledges the client's need for help, collects information from the client, assesses the client's problem or situation and, based on the agency's resources, determines if the social work agency can help the client. In essence, when they first meet, both the worker and client want answers to specific questions. The applicant or potential client wants to know: Can I get the help I need here? Can this person help me? How can I get the help I need at this agency or with this person? The worker will ask: Can I help this person or would it be more appropriate for someone else to help? How can I help this person?

• Assessment and Planning

The **assessment and planning** step includes two processes. In the assessment process, the social worker and the client analyze what help is needed based on the client's ideas, thoughts and feelings about the particular problem. Once the assessment is complete, the social worker formulates a plan designed to help the client with the particular problem. The plan is not set in stone but provides an initial course of action.

Many social work textbooks describe a process that involves problem definition, data collection and objective setting. This type of model flows more from a management or bureaucratic approach to social work that stresses technical rationality. In this model, the worker knows best and can rationally plan the optimal course of action. In this section, we are emphasizing a social work process that stresses reflection-action-reflection in which the social worker continually thinks things through while acting on the problem at hand. He or she adapts the intervention based on dialogue and reflection on experiences of and feelings about past actions. Assessment is both a process and a product of understanding on which action is based (Siporin 1975, 219). It involves gathering relevant information and developing an understanding. How a social worker selects information and how he or she analyzes it is accomplished with reference to the assumptions that underlie a particular social work model, and by one's own experience of the world. In order to form a plan in the assessment phase, the social worker also relies on other people who know the client personally. For example, in cases in which a client is provided with social services as a result of an involuntary intervention, the social worker may initially rely on information provided by a teacher, doctor or police officer (or, for example, an elder in a First Nations community).

During assessment and planning, the worker and client identify problems and a set of actions needed to reach the desired goals. The skill set for direct intervention would include the following items:

- *Validating feelings.* The social worker validates the client's feelings by conveying an understanding of them. This builds a rapport and helps the client to identify and sort out a variety of feelings. The social worker must also consider non-verbal emotional responses in developing this understanding.

- *Interview questioning.* Open-ended and closed-ended questions are used in an interview to elaborate information. Open-ended questions give the client the opportunity to discuss aspects of the problem that they see as important in more depth. The questions often begin with "how" or "what." Closed-ended questions give the social worker the opportunity to clarify details of the client's narrative. They are often used late in a session to check for accuracy.

- *Paraphrasing.* Paraphrasing is a basic social work communication skill. With paraphrasing the social worker re-states what the client has said in her or his own words. Social workers use paraphrasing to confirm that the meaning the worker has attached to a client message is indeed the meaning intended by the client. It also provides feedback to the client that the worker has grasped what he or she is saying. Beginning social workers need to be aware that overuse of paraphrasing can give the client the impression of being mimicked.

- *Clarification.* This skill is used to determine if the worker and client are on the same "wavelength." It is often used to probe an issue that is not understood by the social worker. It involves asking for specific details about an event. Clarification often becomes a reciprocal process between the social worker and client as each tries to understand the true meaning of what the other is saying.

- *Summarizing.* This skill is used in attempts to capture or pull together the most important aspects of the problem or situation. It provides focus for the next interview and can assist in planning. Both the feelings and content of the client's message should be used. It is also useful when the social worker believes that it is time to move on to another topic.

- *Information giving.* Without overwhelming people with too much information at one time, the social worker often shares information about resources in the community (e.g., women's shelters) or information that shows that the client is not alone in experiencing the problem. Be sure the client realizes that they can refuse the information, and provide pamphlets or brochures where possible.

- *Interpretation.* This skill enables the social worker to delve into the presented problem and "read between the lines." The worker's insights may help the client develop a deeper understanding of what is really going on, and not just what appears to be happening. It may provide an alternative way of looking at the problem or a new frame of reference. Always check both verbal and non-verbal responses of the client to your interpretation.

CHARACTERISTICS OF EFFECTIVE ASSESSMENT

Regardless of the model or approach one takes, social work assessment has several important characteristics:

- It is ongoing and not a static stage in a linear process.
- It provides the basis for subsequent action.
- It involves mutual dialogue between client and worker.
- It provides an understanding that is developed through an analysis related to both the worker's and client's assumptions, as well as technical knowledge.
- The assessment is related to the specific situation of clients.

INTERVENTIONS WITH THE ELDERLY

The number of elderly persons in Canada is growing rapidly and this will be a major area for social programming in the future.

The age-group 65 and older grew by 11% between 1991 and 1996 (the 75 and older age-group grew by 15%). This is expected to further accelerate as the baby boom generation ages.

Of course, social workers have always been the primary service providers for the elderly. The types of interventions commonly include:

- enhancing health and continuing care
- helping access resources and housing
- addressing isolation by connecting with individuals with larger groups
- working with family members to facilitate intervention planning
- analyzing and confronting gaps in service delivery systems

- *Consensus building.* Consensus building attempts to work out agreement on what should be done to address the problem. It may be easily attained or there may be discrepancies between what a client says they want and their behaviour, or between separate messages given by a client. Confrontation may be used to challenge a client to examine such discrepancies. It should be non-adversarial and respectful and used only when a safe and trusting relationship has developed.

Planning is based on sets of decisions made by the worker and the client that are shaped by the worker's analysis of the information collected in the assessment phase. The planned actions may be at a wide variety of levels: individual, environmental, multi-person, systemic or structural. For example, they might involve therapeutic, educational and social action-oriented approaches. What frequently varies between practice models is the focus of attention. A behaviour therapy approach would tend to focus on changing individual behaviours, whereas a social action or structural approach may focus on changing systems or structures in society in order to shift power relations. In any event, the social worker assesses the client's problem with the client and negotiates a plan with the client that includes:

- the type of actions or interventions;
- the length of the intervention;
- the frequency of their meetings;
- desired effects; and
- the intervention plan (where a contract is made with the client).

The next step, following assessment and planning, is intervention.

• Intervention

The worker, the client or both may undertake the **intervention** stage. The actions taken may be directed at the client, other individuals, groups, communities, institutions, social policies or political and social structures or systems. In other words, intervention can include a wide variety of actions, tactics and techniques that are not always directed at the treatment of the individual alone. For example, where the social worker is using a structural or feminist approach to practice, the intervention will usually include some kind of organizational, community or social action measures.

It is through the process of intervention that the worker and client implement the assessment and plans. The intervention undertaken is directed at meeting the client's needs as determined by the worker and client. In the intervention stage of social work with individuals, the client shares with the social worker any information regarding what progress has been made in resolving the problem or situation. During this step, the social worker:

- establishes a rapport with the client;
- accompanies the client in the intervention;
- provides advice and support to the client;

- adjusts the intervention based on the client's information; and
- helps the client to resolve the problem or situation by providing new knowledge and skills that assist in solving the problem.

The intervention phase should focus on creating a dialogue between the client and worker and perhaps others who are implicated in the situation being addressed. There will always be jumps, hesitations, uncertainties and half-formed ideas. In situations where the uncertainties are large or numerous, it would be advisable to take small cautious steps and then reflect on the experience. This opens up the possibility of enhancing an understanding of the important elements in the situation and altering the course of action.

• Evaluation and Termination

In this final step, **evaluation and termination,** the client and the social worker work together to assist the client to achieve a resolution to the original problem or situation, and to prevent the situation from occurring again. In this step, the social worker evaluates the following elements of the intervention with the client and the social work supervisor:

- the choice of the intervention;
- the length of the intervention;
- the frequency of their meetings;
- the outcomes;
- the need for any follow-up; and
- when to terminate the intervention—in most cases, the decision to terminate the relationship is mutually agreed upon by the client and the social worker.

Evaluation is an ongoing part of the social work process, aimed at determining whether the goals and needs of the client are being met. Evaluation should identify the rationale for the actions chosen, whether or not needs were met, the expected and unexpected effects and alternative courses of action that may need to be taken.

Clients are usually not involved in the evaluation process because it is believed that specific skills are required and evaluation is focused primarily on issues of accountability. Increasingly, however, there is a recognition of the benefits of client participation: clients have an insider's perspective on agency functioning, information can be validated by clients, issues of confidentiality can be discussed, plans and contracts can be adjusted, knowledge and skills can be gained, the client-worker relationship may be strengthened and clients can be empowered.

Finally, in the **termination** stage essential records are organized and stored. The use of records raises concerns about the **confidentiality** of sensitive information: what constitutes the ethical disclosure of information about a client? In addressing this question, social workers are obligated to follow the guidelines of the agency or organization employing them. They must also obey legislation and association policy. The CASW *Code of Ethics* stipulates, at length, the requirements for collecting, recording, storing and accessibility of client records.

RECORD-KEEPING

In general, social workers should ensure that the client is aware that records are kept and what kind of information sharing may be required of the worker, so that the client can make informed decisions. Also, social workers must use information in such a way as to protect a client's privacy and confidentiality.

SOCIAL WORK WITH GROUPS

Social work with groups has its historical roots in informal, recreational groups such as those organized by the YWCA, the YMCA, settlement houses, scouting organizations, and more recently, in self-help groups. Settlement houses are frequently credited with providing the roots for group work. Today, most social agencies do some kind of group work, including recreation, education, socialization and therapy.

When deciding between individual or group intervention, a social worker must consider which method would be most effective. In some cases, group work may be the most appropriate and least costly mode of intervention. Group work may be more appropriate in cases where the problem lies within group systems, such as families or peer groups. In other cases, a problem may be dealt with by a group of people experiencing a similar problem. For example, a group of abused women may be able to relate to one another and share a common experience, thereby overcoming feelings that the abuse was somehow their own fault. Group work may also be appropriate when addressing the problems involved in the development of relationships between people.

It can be more economical to work with people in a group. For example, it may be a more efficient forum for sharing information, delivering education and providing support. A group may also be more effective in working to change the policy of an agency or advocating for particular benefits, as a group generally has a stronger voice than any one individual. The choice of group work or individual work depends largely on the particular situation being addressed. Neither is necessarily more effective than the other.

Social work practice with groups occurs in hospitals, mental health settings, institutions for persons with disabilities (which led to the popularity of self-help groups), prisons, halfway houses for former prisoners (to prepare them for reintegration into the community), residential treatment centres, residential centres for adolescents in trouble with the law, education groups dealing with issues such as child rearing and violence, self-help groups such as Alcoholics Anonymous, abused women's groups, and therapy groups dealing with emotional or personal problems and other settings. Today, almost every social service agency has one or more such groups for their clients.

• Ingredients of Group Work

Group social work involves several key elements: an agency, a group with membership, a group consensus and a contract. An agency has social workers that have an interest in particular issues and the expertise to deal with them in a group situation. The group work experience also requires individuals who need each other in order to work towards the goals they have set for themselves. These members must hold a degree of consensus on the issues with which they will deal. Finally, a contract must exist that outlines an understanding between the potential group members and the social worker (agency) and the terms and frames of reference for the group work experience.

For the purposes of social group work, groups can be classified in a variety of ways. Generally groups are classified according to the purpose that brings the group together. For example, Mesber (Turner 1999, 213) describes two types of groups based on the purpose of the group: **treatment groups** and **task groups.** She also quotes Toseland and Rivas (1995, 14) as they differentiate between the two types:

> The term treatment group is used to signify a group whose major purpose is to meet member's socio-emotional needs…. In contrast, the term task group is used to signify any group in which the major purpose is neither intrinsically nor immediately linked to the needs of the members of the group. In task groups, the overriding purpose is to accomplish a mandate and complete the work for which the group was convened.

Treatment groups gather for the purpose of meeting the therapeutic objectives of the group members. Individuals work as a group to address problems that they experience personally. The three types of treatment groups are family or household groups, therapy groups and self-help or peer groups.

- **Family or household groups** consist of family or household members. They may be members of the opposite or same sex, with or without children. Family group work or counselling is most effective when the issues that need to be addressed require interaction between family members.

- **Therapy groups** consist of individuals who do not share a household together or have any kind of relationship with one another outside the group setting. They are people seeking individual assistance. Interaction in a group environment is merely part of the therapy for the individual members. The group has no purpose outside of its therapeutic objectives.

- **Self-help or peer groups** consist of people who have similar problems or interests and believe that working and interacting together will provide opportunities for all the group members to grow and change. A social worker may or may not guide the group.

- Group Work Intervention: Tasks and Group Phases

Successful group work intervention involves an understanding of group intervention tasks and the stages of group development. Group workers need to be aware of the group intervention tasks necessary to help maintain and guide a group. In a group, the tasks take place in a group context and therefore generally pass through identifiable stages of development. Often the specific social work interventions or tasks are most effective at particular group development stages.

For successful group work intervention, it is also important to know how to identify the **stages of group development**. The intervention tasks for group work will be quite different depending on the type of group (e.g., self-help or treatment), but the stages of group development will often be the same for each type of group. By identifying the group's stage of development, workers can better help the group meet its needs and goals.

SELF-HELP GROUPS

The number and significance of self-help groups in Canada is increasing. Self-help groups are voluntary groupings of people who come together for mutual assistance in addressing a common need or problem, or to bring about personal or social change. Self-help groups are voluntary mutual aid groups, which may or may not involve a social worker.

Self-help groups are also emerging on the World Wide Web at a rapid rate. Go to your favourite web search engine and type in self-help groups—you will find many sites available. Besides providing emotional support, these sites offer practical, valuable insights gained through first-hand experience of the same situation. Many self-help groups advocate to bring about policy changes for the benefit of all who share the group's concern. National self-help organizations offer support through newsletters, hotlines, and assistance in starting groups.

TALKING STICK

The "talking stick" is often used by First Nations to ensure that everyone's message and opinion is heard by the group, but it can be used in a variety of social work groups.

One stick or feather (or almost any object) is required, and the group usually positions itself in a circle without obstructions in the middle. Each group member can speak only when he or she has the stick. The speaker passes the stick to the next person who wants to speak.

The method ensures that everyone can contribute without interruption, and encourages shy members to participate.

The stages of group development are:

1. *Orientation stage.* Group members commit to the group and task roles begin to emerge.

2. *Authority stage.* Members challenge each other and there is often conflict over power and control issues. Although conflicts are usually resolved through the sharing of feelings, members frequently drop out at this stage.

3. *Negotiation stage.* Group norms and task roles are designated and accepted and group cohesion and sharing increases.

4. *Functional stage.* Integration enables the group to implement plans and accomplish tasks. Few groups reach the end of this stage.

5. *Disintegration stage.* Groups may fall apart during any of the stages, but once the group feels that its goals have been accomplished, groups often disband. Social workers may also bring a treatment group to an end to enable the members to move on.

Throughout these stages, social workers will undertake specific tasks. Depending on the type of group, social workers will take on any or all of the following tasks:

- *Facilitation.* This is the most frequent role for social workers in non-treatment groups. The goal is to enable the group to function smoothly by asking questions, helping the group stay on topic, summarizing decisions and being supportive of members.

- *Co-ordination.* This more administrative task involves monitoring the task completion by group members, and helping the group plan future activities.

- *Therapy.* This is a broad task category and can include any of the skills discussed previously in the discussion of intervention with individuals. Often, social workers are working with "the multi-person client," such as a family. The focus is often on issues around group interaction and communication.

- *Conflict resolution.* While not always identified as a group work task, conflict resolution is increasingly a task of social workers (especially in child welfare, family therapy and international human rights work). The core elements include defining it as a group (rather than an individual) problem, listening to the different points of view and seeking to draw out common ground. The aim is to create a "win-win" situation and encourage co-operation.

• Group Work Intervention Steps

The steps for social work with groups are similar to those for work with individuals except that they involve groups of people.

- *Intake.* During intake, the social worker acknowledges the client's need, collects information from the client (for example, self-referral or referral by someone in the community), assesses the client's situation and his or her capacity and motivation to change, and determines the agency's capacity to help the client by using any type of group that it has available.

During group work, the social worker will be involved in facilitation, co-ordination, therapy or conflict resolution. Frequently he or she will be involved in all these activities.

- *Assessment and planning.* The worker completes a preliminary assessment of the client's situation or problem, provides a potential group process intervention plan and proposes a potential group to the client or adds the client's name to a waiting list.

- *Group intervention.* In working with groups, the social worker may do any of the following:

  - help the group to find common ground in terms of the issues they wish to deal with;
  - anticipate obstacles to the group work experience and bring them to the group's attention;
  - educate the group, providing information and support thought to be useful to the group;
  - contribute thoughts, feelings, ideas and concerns regarding the group work experience (drawing upon insights derived from similar group work experience);
  - define the needs and limitations of the group-social worker relationship; and
  - monitor the group's progress and provide ongoing evaluation of the group experience.

- *Evaluation and termination.* The final stage deals with issues that arise from terminating the group experience, such as evaluating the group process with the group and the social work supervisor. The worker may terminate the relationship with the group or mutually agree with the group members to end the group process.

TEN RULES OF COMMUNITY ORGANIZING

1. Nobody's going to come to the meeting unless they've got a reason to come to the meeting.

2. Nobody's going to come to a meeting unless they know about it.

3. If an organization doesn't grow, it will die.

4. Anyone can be a leader.

5. The most important victory is the group itself.

6. Sometimes winning is losing.

7. Sometimes winning is winning.

8. If you're not fighting for what you want, you don't want enough.

9. Celebrate!

10. Have fun!

SOCIAL WORK WITH COMMUNITIES

Social work with a community (or community work, as it is usually called) is often either not addressed in social work texts or is limited to a few pages at the back. Students are left with little knowledge of what community work is and often feel that it is too complex or too abstract for them to learn. They end up deciding that they would rather work directly with people or that community work is for social activists only. In this book, community work is given equal treatment.

Community work can be thought of in different ways. It may be a **geographic community** as defined by a specific neighbourhood, city district or local ward, with specific geographical boundaries. It might also be a **membership community** as defined by a sense of belonging to a specific group; for example, the gay and lesbian community, the black community, the Native community and so on. Or, it may be a **self-help community** consisting of persons with similar problems or difficulties; for example, those living with addiction, disability or unemployment, or coping with illness or the death of a loved one. Community work is frequently a central part of international social work or social work in developing countries. (This type of community work is discussed in more detail in Chapter 13, which deals with international social work.)

• Four Models of Community Work

The nature of community work differs depending on the perspective informing one's practice. A useful approach is Rothman's **model of community development**, which allows one to see the differences between the various forms of community development discussed and debated in Canada today. Rothman's typology regards community work as a continuous process and one that includes the staff who sustain and plan the process (Rothman 1970, 474). To this model, we would add a fourth component, "participatory action research" (PAR).

Community social work can therefore be seen as consisting of the following four types:

- *Locality development.* Community action for change involves the participation of a broad range of people in the community who focus on goal determination and action. This model emphasizes community building to enable people to solve their own problems. It is closely associated with adult education and self-help. Within this model, the primary problems are identified as anomie (disorganization), lack of communication and lack of problem-solving capacities. The basic strategy is to involve a broad cross-section of people in determining and solving their own problems, with the aim of achieving consensus and increasing communication among the various groups. Members of the local power structure are encouraged to become involved as well and are seen as potential collaborators in a mutual venture. The definition of community in locality development is geographic; that is, the community is composed of people in a specific geographic area who share common interests or reconcilable differences. Organizations involved in locality development may include overseas development programs, neighbourhood workers and consultants to community development teams. Historically, settlement houses were of this type.

- *Social planning.* When individuals plan and gather data about problems in order to choose the most rational course of action, they are engaged in social planning. The focus is on rational, deliberately planned and controlled change. Social planning involves people in the community to varying degrees, depending on the nature of the problem. The approach focuses on gathering information about problems and making rational decisions for change. The change strategy may seek consensus or may acknowledge conflict. Social planning focuses more heavily on gathering information than on changing the system. This model's definition of community is functional and may include a segment of a community in which the people are clients of a particular service or face a particular problem. The client population are considered to be consumers or recipients. Typical organizations may include social planning councils, welfare groups or government-sponsored organizations.

- *Social action.* Social action organizes disadvantaged groups in the community to re-distribute power, resources or decision making. It involves the disadvantaged segments of a community, those in need of more resources or improved facilities, in accord with social justice or democracy. The change strategy is to work with a community to investigate and identify issues and to organize people to take action against groups who are exploiting or oppressing the disadvantaged groups. It can involve conflict, confrontation, direct action or negotiation. Social action is concerned with the shifting of power relationships and resources and sees issues as revolving around conflicting interests, which may not easily be reconciled. Typical social action initiatives include poverty activists, peace groups, civil rights groups, welfare rights groups, trade unions, partisans and liberation movements.

- *Participatory action research.* Research that is directed towards changing the structures that promote inequality is called participatory research. Participatory research is similar to the social action model, but emphasizes the direct participation of the disadvantaged segment of the community in the entire research and action process. This emphasis is based on the belief that people must produce their own body of knowledge, representing their own history and lived experience, in order to redress social inequality. The basic change strategy for social workers is to help identify local social problems, to design action research in collaboration with local people, to collect information and to use that information to confront power structures with the need for structural change. Participatory researchers are critical of the standard social planning model. They argue that, when doing "social planning," researchers more often than not work for the existing power structure—outsiders design the studies, and the results of their studies primarily benefit people in

SUGGESTIONS FOR GROUP FACILITATION

- Ensure that there is an agenda and a note-taker.
- Encourage the expression of all facts, feelings and opinions.
- Handle strong disagreement immediately.
- Help everyone to participate.
- Break into small groups and present back to the large group to build consensus.
- Keep discussion relevant to the topic at hand.
- Keep track of time.
- Encourage people to pursue action items.

VIRTUAL COMMUNITIES

Several websites provide community workers, individuals and groups with a place on the Internet to learn, meet and organize.

They offer on-line access to a variety of groups including PeaceNet, EcoNet, WomensNet, and AntiracismNet as well as daily headlines, advocacy tips, calendars of events and work opportunities.

power. The plan, therefore, ignores the capability of local residents to form their own questions, design their own studies, collect their own information and, most importantly, use the knowledge gained for their own benefit. The results are then subject to market forces and tend to benefit the powerful over the powerless. (PAR is discussed further in Chapter 13, page 246.)

Every practising social worker will at some point become involved in community work of some kind or other. This is particularly true for those who emphasize changing social structures or changing the client's immediate social environment. Like individual work and group work, social work with communities is a challenging area. It involves working with individuals and groups in tandem, and therefore it requires a unique set of skills. Students sometimes see community work as an optional field of knowledge, one in which they are unlikely to be involved. In fact, community work can be immensely satisfying as a main area of work, and a working knowledge of it is essential for anyone who wishes to become a well-rounded and effective social work practitioner.

• Virtual Community Work

Today, the Internet makes it possible for community workers and activists to expand their networks by identifying and contacting people in other communities who have similar interests and concerns. This could be loosely referred to as a kind of **virtual community work**. Its importance should not be minimized.

By joining the appropriate Internet-based discussion lists and news groups, social workers can identify and communicate with people in other communities who are working on similar issues. By sharing information, strategies and advice, the effectiveness of efforts may be enhanced. For example, human rights workers have dramatically improved the effectiveness of Urgent Action work to call attention to human rights violations by spreading the news via the Internet. As well, Jubilee 2000, a global movement for Third World debt relief, was organized primarily using Internet communication. A social worker in the community work field can be certain that there is a group on the Internet with similar interests. And, as globalization increasingly affects our economy and the nature of social issues, there is growing importance in connecting with other groups and individuals.

Social workers worldwide are beginning to use the Internet to organize and mobilize on behalf of disadvantaged groups in society. These individuals are turning to the Internet as a way to connect with each other, learn from each other and challenge what they see as injustices in society. Grassroots activists are finding that they can interact on the Internet without the restrictions normally associated with official social services agencies. Social workers are using the Internet to connect not only with those in distant areas of Canada but with like-minded people in other countries. The new communications technology has opened up possibilities for conducting social work more effectively, and knowledge of this technology will be increasingly important to social workers in the future.

• **Community Work Intervention Steps**

The worker will take the following steps for social work with a community.

• **Entry**

The entry step is comparable to the intake step of the social work relationship with individuals. In this step, the community usually consults a community worker about its particular problem. The social worker acknowledges and responds to the community's need or is hired by someone to help the community. For example, the Canadian International Development Agency (CIDA) might hire a social worker to go to Kenya to assist a community in organizing to meet their health needs.

The worker needs to start slowly by getting to know the local contacts and developing an understanding of the power relations in the community. The community leaders need to be informed about what the worker intends to do. If the community feels that what is being proposed is not valuable, then it is best to know this at the outset—and perhaps leave, rather than wasting the time of the worker and the community.

Bill Lee, an accomplished community organizer in Canada, believes three primary principles must be adhered to at this stage: (1) the organizer must begin where the people are and respect their value system; (2) his or her contacts must be broad (and include not only the elite or powerful); and (3) he or she should attempt to find out who in that particular context has the power and credibility to mobilize and organize others into action (Lee 1996, 60).

• **Data Collection and Analysis**

It is important that the social worker work with key members of the community to determine what information and efforts are required. One of the common goals of community work is to increase self-reliance within the community. This goal will be hampered if the social worker enters the community as an expert and undertakes top-down social action. Development goals can also be negatively affected when only the elite, or people with high social status, are participating. It is critical that power be equally distributed in decision making.

The social worker and members of the community

- collect information from interviews, questionnaires and observation (individuals and groups);

- document and analyze the community in order to determine who the stakeholders are or what the distribution of power is (major/minor stakeholders/powerholders);

- determine how community needs can be met;

- ask how the community will evaluate the intervention; and

- propose a plan and ask how the community will react to the proposed intervention plan.

Rural communities are often in need of social workers.

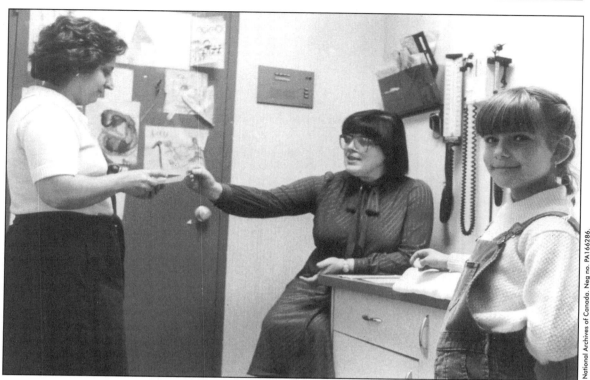

All types of social work and approaches share a body of knowledge, skills and values that are designed to empower people and promote their well-being.

National Archives of Canada. Neg no. PA166286.

In recent years, community social workers have become somewhat concerned with research itself as a social process and have begun to question the role of the "independent" researcher. In this context, some social workers have found the idea of participatory research to be useful (see the discussion on participatory action research above, on page 83). Here, research is conducted not only by the social worker but includes the direct participation of the community members. Certainly this can be an effective way to do research in communities, and it may, in some cases, be the only way.

As with other aspects of community work, the type of research that would work best in any particular situation needs to be evaluated and discussed with the community. In some cases, the best arrangement might be a conventional study; in others, a participatory model; and in still others, some combination of the two.

• Goal Setting

The social worker brainstorms with the community to establish goals, evaluates the goals in terms of their feasibility, sets priorities with the community and provides education to community members. Again, the maximum participation of community members from all social levels is critical.

• Action Planning

The social worker, working with members of the community, creates an action plan. The plan will include action steps, implementation steps, monitoring and evaluation steps, and re-planning steps. Generally the plan should be a participatory process and may include:

- what action or change will occur;
- who will carry it out;
- when it will take place, and for how long;
- what resources (i.e., money, staff) are needed to carry out the change; and
- communication (who should know what).

• Action Taking

In its simplest terms, this step involves the implementation of the action plan on the part of the social worker and the community. However, "action taking" is not a separate activity; the worker and people in the community have been taking action throughout the entire process.

What most clearly distinguishes this stage is that action is being taken more by the members of the community than by the social worker. Seeing a self-reliant community begin to improve its situation is one of the most rewarding aspects of being a community social worker.

• Evaluation and Termination/Re-planning

In the evaluation stage, the social worker and the community evaluate the intervention and re-plan in the light of its effectiveness. Evaluations in community work increasingly involve the direct and active participation of the community's members.

Evaluating the success of the intervention and planned activities is a critical part of any organizing effort, and it is important not to wait until the completion of the organizing effort to evaluate its effectiveness. The following questions provide a basic framework for a more extensive evaluation. Try discussing these questions at an early stage.

1. Are we moving closer to achieving our intended objectives?
2. What other unintended impacts and effects have resulted?
3. What activities in particular are contributing to the achievement of our objectives?
4. Are there better ways to achieve the desired results?
5. Are our actions and work helping us to gain support in the community?

An evaluation of results might reveal that the reason objectives have not been met is that the strategy was correct but not implemented effectively. For example, the actions may have been timed inappropriately or the actions were too infrequent or not carried through thoroughly. Revisions to strategy are frequently necessary. Action-evaluation-action is a cycle that allows the worker and the community to change tactics. The central indicator for evaluating success is, of course, whether your efforts have created the change you desired.

A COMMUNITY TOOL BOX

This website contains 46 chapters of information and tools to help social workers be more effective community organizers.

For instance, there are sections on leadership, strategic planning, community assessment, advocacy, grant writing and evaluation. Each section includes a description of the task, advantages of doing it, step-by-step guidelines, examples, checklists of points to review and training materials.

The website is at:
http://ctb.lsi.ukans.edu

REFERENCES

• Lee, B. 1999. *Pragmatics of Community Organization.* Mississauga: Common Act Press.

• Rothman, J. 1970. Three Models of Community Organization Practice. In F. Cox et al., eds., *Strategies of Community Organization* (pp.22-39). Illinois: Peacock Press.

• Siporin, M. 1975. *Introduction to Social Work Practice.* New York, N.Y.: Macmillan Publishing.

• Toseland, R., and Rivas, R. 1995. *An Introduction to Group Work Practice.* 2d ed. Boston: Allyn and Bacon.

• Turner, F.J. 1999. *Social Work: A Canadian Perspective.* Scarborough: Prentice-Hall, Allyn & Bacon Canada.

CONCLUSION

To be successful in the three fields of social work (social work with individuals, group work and community work), a social worker requires a variety of technical skills as well a commitment to certain basic humanitarian values.

Social work with individuals, or one-on-one practice, moves from intake, assessment and planning to intervention. The intervention is the action stage in which the issues and concerns of the client are addressed. These interventions will not only be directed at the individual client, but will often include actions at the group, community, institutional, policy or political level. The evaluation and termination phase terminates the intervention and determines whether or not it was effective. It also includes a review of clients records. Keeping accurate client records according to agency policy and the *Code of Ethics* is critical to ensuring effective continued care and protecting the client should his or her records be subpoenaed for a court case.

Social work with groups is increasingly being used as a practice technique due to its proven success with particular groups of people, including abused women, homeless people, youth, and people with various mental illnesses, to name a few. For the group worker, it is crucial to understand both effective practice techniques and the stages of group development.

Community work, another growing field, can take many forms including developing the capacity of a locality, planning services for a group or community, or challenging power structures to advocate for rights or access to resources. In community work, the participation of community members in decision making and the actions undertaken is critical. Virtual community organizing or on-line social activism is another rapidly growing social work field as citizens use new communications technology to challenge the globalization of power. In a sense, it is a kind of "globalization from below."

All types of social work and approaches share a body of knowledge, skills and values that involve a commitment to humanitarianism and egalitarianism aimed at empowering people and building on their strengths, whether as individuals, groups or communities.

TWO APPROACHES TO DIRECT PRACTICE

The Generalist Approach

Generalist social work education is widespread in undergraduate and introductory training in Canada. It is particularly common as an approach for beginning students in the United States, as the Council on Social Work Education (CSWE) requires a "generalist orientation" at the undergraduate level.

The generalist approach evolved from attempts by social workers to address issues in a way that goes beyond diagnosing individual problems by looking only at the individual factors. Practitioners recognized that it is also important to examine elements such as the family, community and institutions in society. Whereas those formulating a structural approach looked to power theory and political economy theory, those developing the generalist approach adopted "systems theory." Systems theory focuses on the systems in the person's immediate environment that may be causing the individual's problem.

With the generalist approach, the worker is trained to use the problem-solving process in combination with **systems theory** to assess and intervene to establish the social functioning of individuals, families, groups, communities or organizations. Social systems theory provides a framework for understanding how systems such as the individual, the family, the small group, the school, the church, the social agency, the community and societies interact and relate causing both private problems and public issues. When assessing the situation with the client, the social worker decides which system is the appropriate unit of attention or focus.

The generalist approach integrates knowledge about human behaviour and knowledge about the influence of social environment on behaviour. It is therefore the job of the generalist practitioner to understand both the personal reasons for the client's behaviour and also the environmental factors influencing this behaviour. For example, in being presented with a case of child abuse, the social worker would look at each of the separate factors. First, the parent may have alcohol abuse problems, may have a low income or problems with anger control. The family may be one where the parents are separated and hostile towards one another. The community may include support groups that would be appropriate for the child and the parent. In the institutional area, the child welfare worker may have such a large caseload that individual attention is non-existent and resources for family education are limited.

As with the structuralist approach, there is no unanimous agreement as to the meaning of generalist practice. The above overview highlights the key points where there is some consensus.

The Structuralist Approach

Though the term appears to have originated in the United States, the structural approach to social work is largely a Canadian development.

Social workers taking a more "structural approach" frequently arrive at this approach from a critical analysis of the outcomes of their own interventions. Workers who previously concentrated only on personal factors or interpersonal interactions between individuals find that, by ignoring the broader social structures that shape the individual's problem, they are minimizing the very changes required to alleviate their client's difficulty (as well as those of many others experiencing the problem). They find that it is more effective to focus on the root causes of the problems at hand and deal with the client's personal issues or behaviour at the same time.

The skills involved in structural social work are of course similar to the generalist approach and draw on the same sense of humanism, empathy and reflection. It is the way in which the social worker analyzes problems and the type of actions that result from this analysis that distinguishes the structural approach. The structural social worker is concerned with helping the individual deal with a difficult problem, but he or she is also concerned with changing the overall situation that is causing the problem, whenever that is possible.

Structural social work, then, can be defined as practice that focuses on the impact of wider **social structures** on personal problems. It involves a critical analysis of these structures, whether they are based on class, race, age, gender, ability or sexuality. These include primary structures—such as patriarchy, racism, capitalism, heterosexism, ageism and ableism—as well as secondary structures such as personality, family, community, and bureaucracy.

Advocates of structural social work emphasize the links between a person's feelings and behaviour, and the larger society. Client empowerment and social worker activism are emphasized. The structural approach works simultaneously at liberating people and transforming social structures. Individual and social changes are seen as inextricably related.

Like the generalist approach, the structuralist approach requires that the social worker be skilled in casework, family counselling, group work and community organizing, as well as have a deep knowledge of social policy and social welfare. Structural social work differs in that it goes beyond an analysis of the immediate family and community as external factors and looks to the broader analysis of socioeconomic factors such as class, gender and race.

CHAPTER 5: SOCIAL WORK WITH INDIVIDUALS, GROUPS AND COMMUNITIES

Concepts

- Social work with individuals
- Group work
- Community work
- Social work practice
- Praxis
- Intake
- Assessment and planning
- Intervention
- Evaluation and termination
- Confidentiality
- Treatment groups
- Task groups
- Family or household groups
- Therapy groups
- Self-help or peer groups
- Stages of group development
- Geographic community
- Membership community
- Self-help community
- Model of community development
- Virtual community work
- Systems theory
- Social structures

Discussion Questions

1. What are the three fields of social work practice and how do they differ?

2. What steps does a social worker usually follow in providing help to: (a) an individual; (b) a group; (c) a community?

3. Social work practice involves continually reflecting with the client on past actions. Explain this process.

4. What is a community and what different types of communities exist?

5. What are the main features of community-based social work?

6. What is the key feature of participatory action research and what is the role of the social worker?

7. What is the significance of the new information technology for community organizing?

8. Explain what is meant by the "generalist" and the "structuralist" approaches to social work practice.

Websites

- **A Community Toolbox**
  http://ctb.lsi.ukans.edu

  This website contains information and tools to help social workers be more effective community organizers. The core of the Tool Box is the "how-to tools." These sections explain how to do the different tasks necessary for community development.

- **Charity Village**
  http://www.charityvillage.com

  Defines itself as Canada's supersite for the non-profit sector. It has 3,000 pages of news, jobs, information and resources. The resources section of the site should connect you with a cause or group that interests you. You can even volunteer or donate on-line.

- **Canadian Social Work Discussion Group**
  http://groups.yahoo.com/group/csocwork

  This is a listserv that enables social workers in Canada to discuss general practice issues as they arise.

  Go to the website to subscribe.

6

Social Work with Children and Youth

Child Protection and Family Support

Social workers have always been at the forefront in advocating for improvements in policy and services for children and youth. From their unique vantage point, social workers know that children are not only the most vulnerable citizens of Canada, they are also our hope for the future.

The 1995 federal budget marked a turning point for social services across Canada. The budget determined that social funding would be substantially cut in an all-out effort to reduce the government deficit. More recently, in 1999, the Liberal government announced a new era of government surplus, thus opening up the possibility of a renewed commitment to social welfare. Whether this will come to pass remains to be seen.

In Canada, provincial, territorial, Aboriginal and private non-profit child welfare agencies are mandated to protect children under the age of sixteen. The agencies are legally obligated to look into allegations of child abuse and neglect and are, for the most part, crisis oriented. More recently, child protection services have come under scrutiny as a result of high-profile child deaths during custody. For example, in April 1996, the Office of the Coroner for the Province of Ontario and the Ontario Association of Children's Aid Societies, with support from the Ministry of Community and Social Services, established a task force to undertake a review of the children who had died while receiving child welfare services.

Child welfare is a major area of employment for social workers today. It is also one of the most difficult areas of work for practitioners in terms of the heart-wrenching cases that can arise and the often complex ethical issues involved. This chapter provides an overview of the child welfare system in Canada. It examines:

- the current and historical organization of child welfare in Canada;

- the extent of child neglect and abuse;

- the state of child welfare legislation and the work of the child welfare agencies;

- the process of removing a child from the home when the child is in need of protection; and

- other social services available for children and youth.

Our most vulnerable citizens and our hope for the future.

Public Archives of Canada. Neg no. PA-118220.

THE ORGANIZATION OF CHILD WELFARE

In Canada, child welfare work is largely the domain of social workers, and much of the social worker's daily activity involves complex and sensitive issues surrounding children and their families. Across the country, child welfare is highly regulated and involves a variety of activities:

- *Family support and prevention.* Providing a range of family programs and services in order to maintain healthy families, support families at risk and protect children.
- *Child protection.* Protecting children at risk by removing them from *their families and by finding them substitute care.*
- *Child placement.* Finding temporary substitute care such as foster and group homes for children who cannot continue to live with their parent(s) or guardian(s).
- *Adoption.* Finding permanent homes for children who cannot live with either of their parents.
- *Foster care.* Recruiting foster homes, providing training and support and monitoring of foster homes. When children and parents must be separated due to abuse, neglect, maltreatment or special medical circumstances, substitute care is often provided by foster families.

Canadian social workers also provide a wide variety of important services for children and youth in the form of in-home services and out-of-home services.

In-home services are provided to help a household or family members live together harmoniously in a secure and safe environment. The main categories of in-home services include family counselling services, parenting supports, child protection, in-home child care, homemaker services and family educational services.

Out-of-home services are implemented when the home situation becomes unsuitable for the upbringing of a child. These services include foster care, adoption, day care centres, community supports (e.g., the Community Action Program for Children and Aboriginal Head Start), group homes, institutional care, parenting self-help and empowerment groups, and family housing assistance.

PROVINCIAL LEGISLATION

Each of Canada's ten provinces and three territories has different organizations and legislation governing child welfare. As well, provincial services for children and youth may be provided by a branch of the provincial government or by a private or non-profit agency. In some provinces, such as Nova Scotia, there is a mixture of private and public delivery.

In each jurisdiction, a wide variety of child and family services are provided. For example, in Ontario, the Children's Aid Societies (CAS) provide ongoing counselling for youth and families. They have adoption departments, which also provide adoption disclosure for older adopted children desiring information on their biological family. Children under the age of eleven are adopted through the CAS. The CAS also provide foster care services and group home facilities, and there is an increasing need for this as the CAS take more children into care. In order to keep children in the home, the CAS now provide family services. There is also the Parent Assessment Resource (PAR) program, which is a child-management program that helps parents and children to "get along."

Besides the child protection agencies, there are a variety of youth and children agencies across the country. The Ottawa-based Youth Services Bureau (YSB) is representative of many such child and youth programs. It provides community programs involving work with families in the home as well as individual counselling. It has a residential program for girls under sixteen years of age to help build their self-esteem as well as a six-month transitional residence program for youth sixteen years of age and older who are not quite ready to live on their own and require skills development. The YSB also provides an observation and detention home for young offenders and another residence for youth with drug and alcohol-related problems.

Similarly, in Alberta, Child Focus Services Ltd. operates a child assessment and treatment program in Calgary through three transition houses. The methods used with the children are non-threatening and encourage the children to express themselves through activities such as play and art work. The children are placed in groups of approximately five. Workers create reports to assess the children and recommend various intervention strategies, which may include advocacy and further discussion about family violence. These reports are shared with the parents or guardians to encourage them to actively participate in the therapeutic process.

An overview of a selection of provincial systems is provided below.

- First Nations child welfare services are provided by either the provincial agency on behalf of the federal government or directly by First Nations agencies as negotiated under the federal government's 1995 policy on Aboriginal self-government. Arrangements must be negotiated individually with each First Nation and generally involve federal and provincial representatives.

- In British Columbia, child protection services are provided by the Ministry for Children and Families, a branch of the provincial government, and are legislated by the 1996 *Child, Family and Community Service Act.* The Ministry states that its role is to ensure a child-centered, integrated approach that promotes and protects the healthy development of children and youth while recognizing their lifelong attachment to family and community (British Columbia Ministry for Children and Families 1999).

- Alberta child protection services are provided by Alberta Family and Social Services, which is run by the provincial government of Alberta.

- In Manitoba, child protection services are provided through non-governmental "Child and Family Services Agencies," which

Child welfare can involve teenagers as well as children.

are mandated under the *Child and Family Services Act* of 1986. These are overseen by the provincial Ministry of Family Services.

- In Ontario, child protection services are delivered through fifty separate Children's Aid Societies (CAS). These community organizations are legislated under the *Child and Family Services Act* 1984 to investigate allegations of abuse and neglect, provide services to families for protecting children and to prevent circumstances requiring the protection of children, and provide care or supervision for children and provide adoption services. As of January 1, 1998, the provincial Ministry of Community and Social Services assumed 100 percent funding of Children's Aid Societies.

- The New Brunswick provincial government provides child protection services through its Family and Community Social Services (a department of the Ministry of Health and Community Services).

- The Children's Aid Society of Halifax provides services in Nova Scotia. Under the *Children and Family Services Act* of 1990, child protection workers and designated social workers in child welfare agencies investigate all reports of alleged child abuse and neglect. There are twenty child welfare offices throughout the province. Six are district offices of the government and fourteen are privately run societies and/or family and children's services agencies. The Mi'kmaq Family and Children's Services Agency provides services for Native families living on reserves.

- The Newfoundland Minister of Health and Community Services has proposed a Bill, Respecting Child, Youth and Family Services, to replace the present *Child Welfare Act.* The new Act represents a fundamental shift in the way child welfare services will be provided in the province. The legislation supports a move away from remedial approaches towards prevention and early intervention strategies, with services delivered by community-based agencies.

- In Prince Edward Island, the proposed *Child and Family Services Act* includes major changes in child welfare practice, including a lowering of the age in defining a child from eighteen to sixteen years, the inclusion of progressive and preventive approaches, and a tightening of time frames, particularly for younger children.

- The government of the Northwest Territories provides child protection services through its Department of Health and Social Services. The government recently implemented the new *Child and Family Services Act* and the *Adoptions Act.* The new Act defines "best interests of the child" with the recognition that differing cultural values and practices must be respected. Under the new Act, applicable Aboriginal organizations must be informed whenever someone who is eligible to become a member of the organization has a child protection case proceeding to court. This creates an opportunity for the organization to provide input, particularly on customs and traditions that may be unique to the Aboriginal organization and may be important in the development of a case plan for the child and family.

- Saskatchewan has a *Child and Family Services Act*. Bilateral agreements continue to be negotiated between Saskatchewan Social Services and First Nations Bands for the control and delivery of child and family services on reserves.

HISTORY OF CHILD WELFARE

As is clear from the above, over the years, each of the provinces has accumulated an imposing array of child welfare legislation. Nevertheless, certain patterns can be discerned in the history of child welfare in Canada. Below is a discussion of these trends.

• Pre-Industrial Child Welfare: Pre-1890

The problems of child abuse and neglect did not suddenly appear in the twentieth century. The children of "traditional," rural settler families typically worked at farming along with other family members and household employees. The mother was responsible for family care needs, such as cooking, cleaning and nursing. The father was responsible for the economic survival needs of the family. The wife and children existed as economic dependants of the family patriarch, the husband and father. Patriarchal authority was reinforced by the state through a variety of laws and practices.

By contrast, Aboriginal communities had rather more benevolent ideas concerning the raising of children. First Nations believed that a child belonged to his or her people, and that a child was a gift from the Creator. They believed that this connection of child to community was non-discretionary–he or she simply belonged to the nation and it was the responsibility of all to meet the child's needs.

In 1792, The Province of Upper Canada proclaimed that the Common Law of England would be the law in force for the new province. This body of law was exceedingly harsh towards children. For example, Upper Canada introduced the first Act concerning children in 1799. It was called the *Orphans Act*, and it gave town wardens the power to bind a child under fourteen to an employer as an apprentice. In 1827, this Act was replaced with the *Guardianship Act*, which allowed guardians to be appointed by the court. The guardian then had the right to bind the child as an apprentice.

The period from 1867 to 1890 saw the introduction of new laws that changed the exalted position of husbands and fathers. The legislative right of men to inflict arbitrary and severe punishment on their wife and children was beginning to be challenged. These new laws also affected the treatment and rights of children. The period began with amendments to Ontario's *Apprentices and Minors Act* (1874) and saw the introduction of compulsory education, regulation of work hours, the right of women to hold property and the rise of new and improved social agencies. For the first time, courts would decide whether a child's best interests would be better served with his or her family, one parent or an employer. The role of the family in the early laws in Canada did not

CHILD WELFARE LEGISLATION

The federal government's Human Resources Development Canada (HRDC) department's website keeps up-to-date information on new child welfare legislation across the country. This is located at: http://www.hrdc-drhc.gc.ca/socpol/cfs/cfs.shtml

National Archives of Canada.

The late 1800s saw a marked increase in child welfare laws.

National Archives of Canada. Neg no. PA123686.

The Ontario Association of Children's Aid Societies (OACAS) is a membership organization, representing fifty Children's Aid Societies in Ontario, based in the community and governed by voluntary boards of directors.

extend beyond its value as an economic unit. Therefore, families that were poor were viewed as moral and economic threats, and their children were to be "bound out" to proper self-supporting families who would not taint the children with their parental failure.

It should also be noted that the system of child welfare, as it was emerging, would be used by governments in an attempt to dismantle Native communities and assimilate Native children into mainstream Canadian society. The *Indian Act* of 1876 exemplified the colonizer's views towards First Nations and their children. A primary thrust was to "Christianize" Natives, beginning with the children. Beyond outlawing traditional ceremonies, such as the potlatch, the laws of the day attempted to eradicate Native culture by taking Native children out of First Nations homes and communities and placing them in residential schools administered by the Christian churches. (For more on the residential schools, see Chapter 9, page 165.)

• A New Era in Child Welfare Legislation: 1890-1940

There was a marked increase in government involvement in children's issues in the late nineteenth and early twentieth century. Legislation was enacted that allowed the state to remove children from the care of their parents or guardians. The federal *Juvenile Delinquent Act* of 1908 and the Ontario *Act for the Prevention of Cruelty to Children* of 1893 were both aimed at the protection of children. The legal mandate for promoting the "best interests" of children was given to the state. The state could decide whether or not parents were good or bad and had the authority (through legislation and the courts) to remove children from homes and put them into care.

Until this time, children generally were not seen as needing special care or nurturing; their needs were ignored and severe punishment was meted out to enforce rules. In the 1890s, Canadian provinces began to establish commissions to inspect the working conditions for children in factories. Many children as young as eight and nine years of age were employed, and inspections often revealed a callous disregard for the welfare of the children by factory owners. For example, there were repeated reports of poor ventilation and a lack of sanitary equipment. As well, the children were receiving no education while working in the factories, which contributed to the large number of illiterate adults across the country. As a result, new legislation was passed to regulate working conditions and hours of work. For example, Ontario passed the *Factory Act* and the *Regulation of Shops Act*. Eventually, the age level of those considered to be children was raised to sixteen years.

Several important women's organizations emerged in the late nineteenth century that affected the rights of children. The Women's Missionary Societies, which originally had an evangelical approach, began addressing the needs of women and children. The Women's Christian Temperance Union, founded in 1874, emphasized the prohibition of the sale of alcohol. Their broader social goals were aimed at helping children and included ensuring child protection, establishing reformatories for juveniles and building cottage-style homes to replace institutional care. The Young Women's Christian Association (YWCA) addressed the needs of urban working women, including assisting them with their children. The National Council of Women, formed in 1893, was an alliance of women's organizations aimed at co-ordinating policies at a national level. They considered many women's issues to be "mothering" issues, and their goal was to bring private mothering practices to public and national attention.

In Toronto, John Joseph Kelso, a journalist who had been raised in a single-parent family, began organizing meetings to address the problem of street children and their abuse. He was critical of the care provided by many of the private charities and orphanages, such as Maria Rye's Our Western Home for Girls at Niagara-on-the-Lake. He believed the children suffered from careless policies, lack of supervision and a lack of inspection or visitation. Kelso's work resulted in numerous changes to child welfare services in Ontario and in Canada. The Toronto Children's Aid Society was incorporated in 1891, with Kelso serving as its first

J.J. KELSO

Irish immigrant, journalist and child welfare pioneer, J.J. Kelso helped found the Toronto Humane Society in 1887, which concerned itself with the prevention of cruelty to children and animals. He became superintendent of neglected and dependent children until his retirement in 1934. During this time he was instrumental in helping to establish Children's Aid Societies throughout Ontario-sixty by 1907-and in British Columbia, Manitoba, Prince Edward Island and Nova Scotia during the first two decades of the 1900s.

His influence led to the Ontario *Children's Protection Act*, the first in Canada. He was a skilled organizer and a tireless promoter of children's rights who firmly believed that wide community mobilization is required for social change. His fresh and new ideas on children are exemplified in his presentation to the Social Service Congress in 1914 in which he said, "The child is the central figure in all social reform."

National Archives of Canada.

president. In 1892, the name was changed to the Children's Aid Society of Toronto, and a charter was granted to carry out the administration of the *Act for the Prevention of Cruelty and Better Protection of Children*. He played a pivotal role in the formation in Ontario of a Royal Commission on Prisons and Asylums in 1890, the formation of the Toronto Children's Aid Society in 1891, the creation of an office for the protection of children, and the *Children's Protection Act* of 1888, which is the forerunner of the current *Child and Family Services Act*.

The passing of the 1893 *Children's Protection Act* in Ontario ushered in a new era of modern child welfare legislation protecting children from abuse and neglect. The notion of neglect, which is still controversial today, stated that a child found sleeping in the open air was considered to be neglected. Those found guilty of mistreating a child were sentenced to three months of hard labour. The idea of foster homes, supervised by Children's Aids Societies, also originated with this Act. In 1908, the *Child Welfare Act* repealed some of the more draconian aspects of the previous Act and provided for procedures to rehabilitate mistreated children. Between 1891 and 1912, sixty Children's Aid Societies sprang up in Ontario. In 1912, they joined together as the Associated Children's Aid Societies of Ontario, now known as the Ontario Association of Children's Aid Societies (OACAS).

The obligation on the part of society to protect children began to crystallize during this period. A new notion of "childhood" emerged in the late nineteenth century. Prior to this, children had been regarded in the same way as adults. Children were now beginning to be seen to be qualitatively different from adults, as being in an important stage of development, a stage of life important to the later development of the person. This was a primary shift in thinking.

• Modern Child Welfare Policy: 1940-Present

Since 1940, literally hundreds of provincial laws have been passed that affect child welfare. While each province has distinct and separate legislation, several national trends have emerged:

- a shift from a volunteer to a professional service system;

- the development and implementation of risk assessment models and standardized record keeping;

- provincial governments' acceptance of direct responsibility for the delivery of child welfare services through public financing, agency reporting and provincial supervision;

- a shift from institutional and protection-oriented services to non-institutional and prevention-oriented services;

- a shift towards legislation that emphasizes the "best interests" of the child over a model that stresses keeping children in their families;

- an improvement in the capacity of Aboriginal agencies to provide services under Aboriginal leadership.

During the mid-1950s and 1960s, the near total reliance on foster homes and large-scale institutions such as orphanages and training schools came under scrutiny. Increasingly, child welfare agencies dealt with children who were older than the tiny passive victims of the past. These older children had emotional problems and exhibited more troublesome behaviour. Social workers were spending a lot more time with foster parents, families and the children themselves. By the end of the 1960s, the number of foster care homes was declining.

In response, two alternatives to foster homes and large-scale institutions emerged. First, treatment regimes were emphasized. This involved many different kinds of treatment, ranging from strict discipline to a more permissive approach that concentrated on free expression and creativity. Second, group homes were launched. Reformers noted that children were being shuffled from foster home to foster home. One out of every three permanent wards of the court could expect to be placed five or more times in the care of various foster parents. The children simply were not able to adjust. Both the government and social workers believed that group homes would be less stigmatizing and impersonal than the large institutions of the past and more able to meet the adjustment needs of the children. They hoped that group homes would provide the children with the remedial help they needed.

In the 1970s, there was increased concern about the damaging effects of child welfare agencies on children in their care. Advocates for reform believed that too much attention had been directed towards the family's inability to meet the needs of children and not enough to the impact of child welfare interventions, in particular the effects of substitute care. This new generation of reformers argued that children were coming out of the child welfare system more damaged than when they went into it.

Some of this concern was reflected in a new 1978 *Child Welfare Act* in Ontario, which defined child abuse for the first time. However, it wasn't until Ontario's *Child and Family Services Act* of 1984 that this concern was expressed in legal language. The 1984 Act begins with a statement of principles that includes: "The least restrictive or disruptive course of action should be followed keeping the child in the home, if possible. Social workers can no longer 'apprehend' a child unless imminent risk can be shown." In 1990, new legislation in Ontario shifted to stating that the paramount purpose was "to promote the best interests, protection and well-being of children."

Many similarities can be noted in provincial child welfare legislation across the country. The provincial Acts of the 1970s and early 1980s emphasized the least disruptive course of action in addressing the abuse and neglect of children. The child was to remain in the home if at all possible. The more recent provincial Acts have swung back to the notion of acting in the best interests of the child. Several widely publicized deaths of children who were left in the home caused a reaction on the part of some provincial governments. The Acts now call for the quicker removal of children who may be in danger. As well, the expansion of the notion of neglect has increased the likelihood that social workers will determine that a child needs to be removed and placed in care.

CHILD POVERTY RATES BY PROVINCE

- Newfoundland—25.1%
- Quebec—23.8%
- Manitoba—23.6%
- Nova Scotia—19.1%
- Saskatchewan—18.7%
- New Brunswick—18.0%
- Ontario—17.5%
- Alberta—17.1%
- British Columbia—14.8%
- PEI—12.4%
- Canada—19.0%

Source: Prepared by Canadian Council on Social Development, using Statistics Canada's *Survey of Labour and Income Dynamics* (1998).

CHILD TAX BENEFIT

- In 1998, the Government of Canada increased the Canada Child Tax Benefit (CCTB) for low-income families by adding the new National Child Benefit Supplement. This resulted in an increase in Government of Canada benefits for about 1.4 million Canadian families with 2.5 million children.

- In its 1999 budget, the Government of Canada announced further increases to the National Child Benefit Supplement, taking effect in July 1999 and July 2000. In July 1999, the maximum supplement increased by $180 per child per year.

• Funding Child Care

From 1966 to 1996, the cost of children's services was shared between the federal and provincial governments. Under the Canada Assistance Plan (CAP), the federal government paid 50 percent of the costs of provincially administered child services and was responsible for 100 percent of Aboriginal child services. Since 1996, federal funding of provincial social assistance, post-secondary education, hospital and health care as well as social services has been provided in a lump sum based on a per-person calculation under the Canada Health and Social Transfer (CHST).

The 2000 Budget announced a $2.5 billion increase for CHST to help provinces and territories fund post-secondary education and health care, but nothing was added for child welfare services. Increasingly, local municipalities must help to pay for child welfare services. (For more on this topic of federal funding, see the section entitled "Federal Funding for Provincial Medicare" in Chapter 6, page 125.)

THE DILEMMA OF PROTECTION AND THE "BEST INTERESTS" OF THE CHILD

The primary response to child abuse and neglect in Canada is through its provincial child protection systems. The provincial child welfare laws require that all cases of suspected child abuse and neglect be reported and investigated. Various actions or interventions occur if an investigation indicates a child is in need of protection. Responses range from the provision of counselling and support services to the family, to the temporary or permanent removal of the child from the home, to the removal of the abuser or abusers from the home. In the most serious cases, abusers may be convicted of a crime if the abuse can be proven under the Criminal Code of Canada.

Child protection agencies have long grappled with the dilemma of deciding when children should be brought into the care of the state and when they should be left in the home. The social worker operates with the knowledge that she or he must obtain and assess as much background information as possible and use the information to make judgements regarding the parents and the child's best interests, all the while knowing that the process is not an exact science. As one CAS administrator put it, "The work is not for the faint of heart. It is not a vocation for those who are just 'well-meaning.'" The work requires knowledge, stamina, exceptional versatility and an ability to find common ground with parents in order to secure safety for children.

Throughout the history of modern child protection legislation in Canada, the terms "best interests of the child" and "least restrictive" intervention have been debated, and Acts have been passed that move between the two approaches. The **"best interests" approach** emphasizes the protection and well-being of the child, whereas the **"least restrictive" approach** emphasizes the least disruptive course of action that will leave the child with his or her family, if at all possible.

Deciding what is in the best interests of a child can be difficult. The social worker makes the initial decision to remove a child from the home, but the case must go before a judge for a final decision. When provinces have had "best interest" legislation, the number of children taken from their families has generally increased, in some cases quite dramatically. On the other hand, a few high-profile cases in which children have been harmed as a result of being left in a potentially harmful situation has led several provinces to change their "least restrictive" legislation. There is no easy solution. The state, however, must consider the damage that may be caused by removing many more children from their families and placing them in less than ideal situations in group homes.

In Nova Scotia, for example, the following factors are considered in deciding which criteria are to be used by social workers and the courts when trying to decide on the best interests of the child:

1. what are the child's physical, mental and emotional needs and what is the appropriate care or treatment to meet those needs,

2. the child's cultural background and religious faith,

3. the importance for the child's development of a positive relationship with a parent and a secure place as a member of a family,

4. the child's relationships by blood or through an adoption order,

5. the importance of continuity of care: is it likely that the child will be moved from one agency or home to another?

6. the child's views and wishes must be respected,

7. the risk that the child may suffer harm through being removed from or kept away from the care of a parent, and

8. the degree of risk, if any, that justifies the finding that the child is in need of protection (Nova Scotia Department of Community Services 1990).

For example, section 22 (j) of the *Children and Family Services Act* states that, in the case of neglect, a child is in need of protective services when he or she "has suffered physical harm caused by chronic and serious neglect by a parent or guardian of the child, the parent or guardian does not provide, or refuses, or is unavailable or unable to consent to services or treatment to remedy, or alleviate the harm" (Nova Scotia Department of Community Services 1993, 17). In the same province, a child is considered in need of protective services when "the child has suffered physical harm, inflicted by a parent or guardian of the child or caused by the failure of a parent or guardian to supervise and protect the child adequately." However, the Act does not provide clear and specific directions as to what a social worker must do. Rather, it provides only general guidance on what a social worker or judge must consider when deciding what to do.

More recent Ontario legislation, on the other hand, is directive in declaring what a social worker must do to protect the best interests of the child. In 2000, the Ontario government stiffened its previous legislation with the *Family Services Amendment Act*. The words "least restrictive" were removed to ensure that the "best interests" clauses were clearly paramount. It also expanded the reasons for finding a child in need of

"Being a social worker is probably one of the toughest jobs on the face of the earth because not only do you have to take into consideration how the family operates, and you can go back generations to see how things have developed, but you also have to take into consideration who you are and how you react to things. So, there are a lot of variables going on at all times and so what I try to do is make sure that I ask all the questions that I need to ask."

—Anonymous social worker

CHILDREN IN CARE

The latest evidence suggests that there has been a resurgence in the number of children in care. In all of Canada (excluding Quebec) there was a 20% increase between 1990 and 1997.

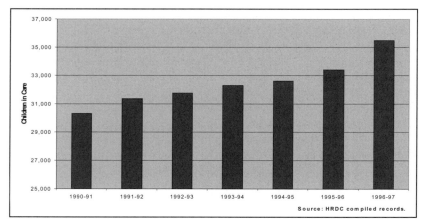

Figure 6.1: Children in Care, 1990-1997.

protection. For instance, the word "neglect" was specifically included, and the threshold for risk of harm and emotional harm to children was lowered.

• Criticism of Policies

There has been much debate about and criticism of current legislation and policies with respect to protecting children. For example, child welfare agencies in Canada are not mandated to protect a child from the abuses of poverty or other social problems—these are not considered to be protection issues. Strong arguments have been made for having children's agencies do more work as child advocates on prevention programs or on raising issues of poverty. In fact, when government finances are strained, as they are now, prevention programs are the first to be cut. Governments talk of using the "least restrictive" measures and keeping children in the home, but at the same time, they are often not willing to fund the prevention programs needed to carry this out. Consequently, programs are increasingly reactive and crisis-oriented.

On the other side, arguments have been made that child welfare agencies should be involved only in straightforward protection issues, such as neglect or abuse. These criticisms rest on a widespread belief that child welfare agencies are sufficiently intrusive and should not be concerned with broader social issues as well.

CHILDREN IN CARE

The numbers of children in care tell part of the story. Consistent with the hopes of the 1978 and 1984 Ontario legislation, there was a decline of children "in care" between 1971 and 1988. In this period, the CAS reported an increase of 160 percent in the number of families served, but the number of children in care decreased by 45 percent (Trocmé 1991, 63). However, the trend has completely changed. The 1994 and 2000 changes in legislation emphasized the best interests of the child, and the number of children in care has again increased. The latest total of 14,219 children in care in Ontario represents an increase of nearly 34 percent from January 1995 (OACAS 2000).

A similar trend exists in other provinces as well, although the increases are not as dramatic. Alberta Children's Services (1999-2000, 38) reports that the number of children under permanent state guardianship increased from 3,862 to 4,318 during 1999-2000. This represents an increase of 12 percent. British Columbia reports (Ministry for Children and Families 1998-99) that 9,813 children were under state care in 1999, an increase of 4.8 percent over the previous year. The British Columbia Ministry emphasizes court order supervision in the home, rather than state custody of children at risk. They report 1,355 children under ordered supervision—an increase of 39 percent over 1998. In all of Canada (other than Quebec), the number of children in care increased by 20% between 1990 and 1997 (CASSW 2001).

The increase in the number of families involved with child welfare agencies can be partly explained by population growth, but the increased economic stress families are experiencing is certainly an important factor. Poverty rates have increased, the number of families living below the poverty line has gone up, as has the number of children living in poverty. There has been an increase in the number of lone-parent families living in poverty, with the attendant stress this entails. In particular, a large and growing proportion of the low-income population consists of lone-parent families headed by women: "While slightly over half (54.3 percent) of all poor children live in two-parent families, the trend is toward more poor children living in lone-parent households; in 1981, 34.3 percent of all poor children lived in lone-parent families; by 1991, this figure had risen to 45.3 percent" (Ross, Shillington, and Lochhead 1994, 61, 122-23).

Social workers are presented with a persistent dilemma in their daily practice; namely, to what extent they and their agency should take into account the broader social context of individuals, families and communities. Before taking a child from a home, for example, should the social worker consider such things as economic stress caused by family poverty (say, in the case of single-parent family)? Should the social worker first seek ways to address and rectify obvious economic problems? These are judgements individual social workers currently make largely on their own, without clear direction from child welfare or other legislation.

NATIONAL YOUTH IN CARE NETWORK

The National Youth in Care Network is a "by youth, for youth" organization. This national charitable organization was started by a small group of young people in care from across Canada in 1985. The group shared a feeling of powerlessness–they felt strongly that the child welfare system had taken away their control over their own lives.

The Network exists to help members find their voice and regain control over their lives through support, skill building and healing opportunities. Young people in and from care can support, educate and advocate for each other.

Check out their website at: http://www.youthincare.ca

THE INCIDENCE OF CHILD ABUSE

Child abuse entails the betrayal of a caregiver's position of trust and authority over a child. It can take many different forms.

- **Child abuse**–the physical, psychological, social, emotional and sexual maltreatment of a child, whereby the survival, safety, self-esteem, growth and development of the person are threatened. Separate categories include physical abuse, sexual abuse and emotional abuse.

CHILD ABUSE

The Investigation and Protection Services branch of the Ontario Association of Children's Aid Societies reports the following statistics:

CAS responded to 65,542 inquiries in the 12 months from April 1, 1999, to March 31, 2000.

CAS received 55,572 referrals, which were assessed as requiring no investigation.

CAS completed 63,712 investigations in 1999-2000.

There were 18,136 open protection cases on April 1, 2000.

There were 6,518 other child welfare cases open on April 1, 2000.

There were 204,487 inquiries, referrals, investigations and assessments, protection and prevention services provided to children and families in 1999-2000.

Source: OACAS 2000.

- **Neglect**–sustained deprivation of food, clothing, hygiene, shelter and other needed care so as to cause, or potentially cause, physical, emotional, developmental or psychological harm.

- **Physical abuse**–physical assaults such as hitting, kicking, biting, throwing, burning or poisoning that cause, or could cause, physical injury as well as behaviours or omissions that cause, or could cause, physical injury to a child.

- **Sexual abuse**–any sexual exploitation of a child whether consented to or not. It includes touching of a sexual nature or any behaviour of a sexual nature towards a child.

- **Emotional abuse**–emotional attacks or omissions that cause, or could cause, serious emotional injury, including the behaviour of parents or guardians who do not take an interest in their child; for example, not talking with or hugging their child, or being emotionally unavailable to their child. This could also include repeated threats, confinement, exposure to violence, ongoing humiliation and ridicule, and attacks on a child's fundamental sense of self.

There are no national statistics on the prevalence or incidence of child abuse. Each province or territory compiles its own figures using its own definitions. A recent national survey, the Canadian Incidence Study of Reported Child Abuse and Neglect (CIS) provides national estimates on the incidence of child abuse and neglect (Trocmé et al. 2001). This information will establish a baseline for future incidence rates of reported child abuse (for the report, see the Child Maltreatment Division at the Health Canada website: http://www.hc-sc.gc.ca).

The CIS collected information about children and their families as they came into contact with child welfare services over a three-month sampling period, from October to December 1998. The report presents data on physical abuse, sexual abuse, neglect and emotional maltreatment based on 7,672 investigations from fifty-one sites in all provinces and territories. The following are some of the main findings:

- Of the 135,573 child maltreatment investigations in three months of 1998, 45 percent were substantiated, 22 percent remained suspected and 33 percent were found to be unsubstantiated. Overall, 2.2 percent of Canadian children were investigated for maltreatment during the three-month period.

- Less than 1 percent of Canadian children were maltreated in the three-month period as measured by substantiated investigations.

- Child maltreatment investigations were divided into four primary categories. Of all investigations, 31 percent were physical abuse, 10 percent were sexual abuse, 40 percent were neglect, and 19 percent were emotional maltreatment.

- Thirty-four percent of the physical abuse investigations were substantiated. This compares with 38 percent for sexual abuse, 43 percent for neglect and 54 percent for emotional maltreatment.

- Substantiated cases of physical abuse consisted of:
  - inappropriate punishment (69 percent of physical abuse cases),
  - Shaken Baby Syndrome (1 percent),
  - other forms of physical abuse (31 percent).
- The most common forms of substantiated sexual abuse included:
  - touching and fondling of the genitals (68 percent of sexual abuse cases),
  - attempted and completed sexual activity (35 percent),
  - adults exposing their genitals (12 percent).
- The most common forms of substantiated neglect included:
  - failure to supervise leading to physical harm (48 percent of neglect cases),
  - physical neglect (19 percent),
  - permitting criminal behaviour (14 percent),
  - abandonment and educational neglect (12 percent and 11 percent respectively).
- Substantiated cases of emotional maltreatment included:
  - exposure to family violence (58 percent of emotional maltreatment cases),
  - emotional abuse (34 percent),
  - emotional neglect (16 percent).
- Seventy-seven percent (77 percent) of substantiated cases were referred to social service agencies:
  - parent support programs (31 percent),
  - parent counselling (39 percent),
  - parent drug/alcohol counselling (17 percent),
  - child psychiatric/psychological services (23 percent), or
  - child counselling (23 percent).

The Ontario Association of Children's Aid Societies also provides the following statistics on child maltreatment and neglect on their website (http://www.oacas.org):

- the incidence of child maltreatment is estimated to be one in five children;

- 33 percent of sex offenders experienced some form of sexual trauma as children;

- 80 percent of female prisoners were victims of child physical or sexual abuse;

- 80 percent of people with eating disorders experienced some form of abuse and/or witnessed violence between their parents as a child;

- children with a history of sexual abuse are seven times more likely to become alcohol and/or drug dependent;

- suicide prevention programs find that children with a history of sexual abuse are ten times more likely to attempt suicide;

REASONABLE DISCIPLINE

Attitudes towards discipline and punishment of children are changing in Canada. Parents have a lot of discretion but some forms of punishment are clearly abusive and against the law. Many Canadians believe that physical force is an unacceptable means of disciplining children.

The law currently allows parents to use "reasonable force" to discipline children. What is reasonable depends on the situation, but judges have indicated that forms of physical punishment that were acceptable in the past may no longer be permitted. Clearly, any injury that requires medial attention is not reasonable discipline. Physical discipline that results in bruising, welts or broken skin would also almost certainly be considered abuse.

- child prostitution prevention programs for ages nine and up find that 99 percent have a history of child abuse;

- 85 percent of runaways served by Covenant House in Toronto have been sexually abused;

- children with a history of child abuse are more likely to have psychiatric and other health problems, commit crimes, drop out of school or be unemployed.

Over the past two decades, there has been a dramatic increase in both reports of suspected abuse and neglect and in the number of children found to be in need of protection. Even with these increased numbers, there are still many cases of child abuse that are not reported. People working with children, including professional social workers, may not report child abuse because they do not recognize its signs and symptoms. They may also resist admitting that it is really happening or convince themselves that it is not serious enough to report. Other factors inhibiting voluntary reporting are the nature of family problems related to child abuse and neglect, the sense of secrecy and shame surrounding child maltreatment, the possible consequences of intervention by child protection authorities or police, and the fact that many of the victims are young and relatively dependent.

Children may want to disclose their abuse, so it can be stopped, but they are often afraid that no one will believe or help them. They may be afraid of what will happen. Abusive parents frequently warn their children not to tell anyone about their actions. They may convince the child that the abuse is the child's fault and that telling someone will only get them into more trouble.

STEPS IN PROVIDING CHILD WELFARE SERVICES

A key component of child protection services is risk assessment. A discussion paper on best practice in child welfare assessments issued by the Children's Aid Society of Metropolitan Toronto (which can be found on-line at http://.casmt.on.ca/best1.html) gives a fairly complete overview of the process of assessment and the principles for service. **Risk assessment** has been defined by the Children's Aid Societies of Ontario as an educated prediction regarding the likelihood that a child will be maltreated based on a careful examination of pertinent data.

Research has identified the risk assessment factors that correlate with the abuse of children. This research is useful, but with some factors there are questions. Risk assessments are not foolproof and must be used in conjunction with worker judgement. The research helps in supporting casework judgement, standardizing decision making, providing a teaching tool, focusing service plans on risk and demonstrating accountability. Workers therefore require a sound knowledge of the risk factors to enable them make judgments that are supported by credible information.

It is important to note that it is not only child protection workers who have a responsibility to report suspected instances of child abuse or neglect. Every member of society has a responsibility to report child abuse or neglect when there are reasonable grounds for believing a child may be in need of protection. People in professions that bring them into contact with children have a particular responsibility to ensure that young people are safe. In the course of their duties, they have a professional **duty to report** if they have reasonable grounds to suspect that a child is or may be suffering abuse. If professionals do not report their suspicion of child abuse or neglect, they can be convicted for such and fined up to $1,000. This professional duty to report affects the following persons:

- health care professionals, including physicians, nurses, dentists, pharmacists, psychologists;
- teachers and school principals;
- social workers and family counsellors;
- priests, rabbis and other members of the clergy;
- operators or employees of day nurseries;
- youth and recreation workers (but not volunteers);
- police officers and coroners;
- solicitors;
- service providers and employees of service providers; and
- any other person who performs professional or official duties with respect to children.

Child welfare service procedures are detailed in provincial standards manuals. Specific criteria for determining whether or not a child is in need of protection are found in provincial child welfare Acts. These Acts outline the conditions under which children are considered to be in need of protection. In general, the steps for providing child welfare services in Canada are as follows:

• 1. Initial Response to Reports of Abuse

The person receiving the report of child abuse must exercise careful judgement. Workers should collect accurate information from various sources, such as from the child, other family members, anonymous neighbours and other callers, and from persons with well-meaning intentions as well as persons intending to make malicious accusations. Even though decision making may be difficult and emotional, workers must make decisions that are in the best interests of the child.

The Response Steps are as follows:
- Receiving the report
- Obtaining complete information from the informant
- Assessing the motivation and credibility of the informant
- Checking records
- Determining if investigation is necessary
- Developing initial investigation plan
- Documenting the reported abuse

CHILD ABUSE

- It is estimated that there were nearly 12,000 investigations of child sexual abuse in Ontario in 1993. Sexual abuse was substantiated in 29% of these cases and suspected in another 27%.

- In British Columbia, more than 500 complaints of sexual abuse were received in March 1992.

Source: The National Clearinghouse on Family Violence, on-line at: http://www.hc-sc.gc.ca/hppb/familyviolence/csaeng.html

PARENTING IN CANADA

The Canadian Resource Centre on Children and Youth (CRCCY) has published a pamphlet called "Parenting in Canada." The pamphlet provides general information and answers questions frequently asked by parents.

It is available on-line at: http://ia1.carleton.ca/52100/m18/pam.html

• 2. Investigation

The social worker should obtain detailed and complete information using interviews, observations, assessment, service reports from professionals, and by checking available records. All decisions must be based on detailed, accurate and documented evidence. Workers must make crucial decisions at this juncture in response to the following questions:

- Has the child been abused?
- What are the immediate safety needs of the child?
- Is there a risk of future harm?
- What is the capacity of the family to protect the child?
- What services are required by the child and family?

All provincial child welfare Acts empower child protection workers to enter premises to remove children whom they deem to be in need of protection. Workers will frequently interview children at school, as this is considered a safe and familiar environment. Interviewing children requires considerable skill.

As mentioned, the assessment of risk to the child is increasingly seen as the key component of child welfare practice (see above, page 106). While each province and, indeed, each local agency has its own policies and procedures, general investigative guidelines are common. An investigation includes the following steps:

1. Conduct a telephone interview with the person who reported the alleged abuse and any others who have information.

2. Search existing Society records for any present or past contact with the family, the alleged abuser or the child.

3. Contact the Child Abuse Register to ascertain if the alleged abuser was registered in the past, and if so, what the details were of that registration. Contact any child welfare authority that previously registered the alleged abuser.

4. See the child who is alleged to have been abused and conduct an interview using methods appropriate to the child's developmental stage and ability to communicate.

5. Ensure that the alleged abuser is interviewed by the police and/or a Society worker pursuant to the protocol established between the Society and the police.

6. Interview the parent or person having charge of the child, if they are not the alleged abuser.

7. Interview other potential victims (for example, siblings, other children in the home, classmates).

8. Gather evidence from other professionals involved in the investigation, (for example, medical, law enforcement, educational).

9. Gather information from other witnesses.

Assessing the urgency of a response is critical. The child who is the subject of a report of abuse must be seen as soon as possible, but generally not later than twelve hours after receipt of the report. To assess urgency, the social worker should consider the child's age, the nature of the alleged abuse, the known injury to the child, the potential for the child to suffer physical harm, the availability of possible evidence (for example, visible marks) and the immediate need for counselling or support. The worker should ensure that a medical examination is performed when there is a need to document the child's condition. A medical examination may also be necessary to ascertain whether the child has been harmed. This can be arranged by obtaining the co-operation of the parent. However, if the parent's co-operation cannot be obtained, the social worker may apprehend the child and authorize the examination without parental consent.

• 3. Verification

Agencies generally have written policies and procedures outlining the process and factors to be considered when a verification decision is made. The verification decision must be made at a formal meeting in consultation with the social worker's supervisor and/or higher authorities. The worker should record the process of verification and the standards of proof for making the decision in the case file.

There are generally four possible investigative outcomes:

* The complaint is not verified, and child abuse does not appear to exist.

* Child abuse is verified, but the child remains in the home. This outcome occurs when the abuse has been perpetrated by a non-family member.

* Child abuse is verified, and the child remains in the home but may be in need of protection. With this option, a plan must be developed to ensure the child's safety, including a schedule of visits and restricted access by some family members. This approach is consistent with the philosophy of taking the "least restrictive" course of action necessary to protect the child.

* Child abuse is verified, and the child is removed from the home. The child welfare agency must decide on and seek from the court a report order that it believes to be the least restrictive or disruptive. **Court order** options include the placement of the child with some other person subject to the agency's provision, child welfare agency wardship, Crown wardship, or consecutive child welfare agency wardship and supervision order.

• 4. Assessment Report and Service Plan

If abuse is verified, the law requires a complete assessment and plan of service for the child and family. The assessment report should address numerous issues, including a description of the nature of the abuse, precipitating factors, the nature of the dispute, family dysfunction, family background, parental capacity, family relationships, family strengths, service needs, child development, and the risk of further abuse to the child. The service plan should include the specific risk factors, service needs, strategies and service providers, ongoing care responsibility and co-ordination, expectations, review dates and client involvement in the development of the service plan.

• 5. Case Management

Careful record keeping is mandatory in all child welfare agencies. If called upon, a worker must be able to substantiate the decisions made. Supervision, consultation, review and decision making occur frequently during the management of all child abuse cases. The approach should be co-ordinated with other service providers. All agencies have strict documentation requirements.

SOCIAL SERVICES FOR CHILDREN AND YOUTH

Many families and individuals experience stress due to problems that are not restricted to the poor, the uneducated or the unmotivated. These difficulties may take a number of forms, such as addiction or substance abuse, wife assault, eating disorders and so forth. Some of these problems involve children and youth. There are a number of programs, agencies and organizations that exist to assist these families and are, in the broad sense of the word, concerned with child "well-fare." These include the youth services agencies bureau, crisis intervention and residential treatment centres, youth addiction centres, shelters for homeless youth and income support programs.

Income support programs can be seen as a form of child welfare, because they provide families with financial support and thereby indirectly help children. There are also services directly concerned with the protection and care of children, which provide supportive services for families and alternative care for children, either temporarily or permanently. When parents or legal guardians are unable or unwilling to look after their children adequately, according to community and legal standards, then communities must resort to such services.

• Services for Young Offenders

An issue that has recently received much media attention in is that of violence and youth. The *Young Offenders Act* (YOA) was enacted in 1982 and has been in force since 1984. The Act is criticized for being too lenient with young offenders and for failing to adequately protect society, despite the 1995 YOA reforms. These reforms provided for harsher measures for dealing with serious, persistent offenders. Such measures include presumptive transfers to adult court for those aged sixteen and seventeen who are accused of violent crimes, increases in the maximum sentences for murder, the obligation to keep youth court records for at least ten years if the youth re-offends, the loosening of restrictions on the admissibility of a young person's admission of guilt to police, and the ordering of medical and psychological evaluations for repeat offenders or serious offences. Another provision is a direction to youth court judges to increase the use of community-based sentences for youth not committing offences involving serious personal injury.

An increase in policing, courts and prisons fails to address the roots of the problem, which often lie far outside the reach of these institutions.

How serious a problem is youth crime? According to 1999 statistics, only 21 percent of all offences with charges laid are by youth (Statistics Canada, Cansim Matrices 2198, 2199). A large portion (43 percent) of youth crimes are property crimes, and most of these involve theft or break-and-enter charges. In fact, overall violent youth crime rates in Canada have been steadily decreasing since 1995 (Savoie, n.d.). Youth violent crime is 21 percent of the youth total (19 percent according to the Cansim data), with the majority of these offences involving minor assaults. In light of this decrease, or at least stability in youth crime, the federal government's controversial and harsher new legislation, the *Youth Criminal Justice Act* (see sidebar on the next page), appears to be a response, not to reality, but to public perceptions.

The *Young Offenders Act* has been criticized for being a corrections-focused and individualized approach, with decreased room for family or community-based rehabilitative measures. As well, many social workers are concerned that cuts to preventative programs will result only in a dramatic increase in both the number and proportion of youth taken into custody or incarcerated. Front-line social workers in correction facilities, child welfare services and youth service have advocated for decades for an approach that recognizes the societal, family and individual factors that are at the root of youth crime. Societal factors include poverty and unemployment, substandard housing, high urban mobility, racism, homophobia and lack of resources in the community. Family factors include abuse of children, the witnessing of violence, usually against the young person's mother, lack of or inadequate supervision by parents,

YOUNG OFFENDERS BEWARE!

While youth crime is declining (charges against 12-17 year-olds fell by 7% in 1998-99), Canada still incarcerates a higher ratio of young people than does even the United States. About one-third of roughly 70,000 youths convicted of an offence in 1988-99 received a jail sentence, though only a fraction involved serious violence.

The planned overhaul of the 1984 *Young Offenders Act* has been approved by the House of Commons and, in principle, by the Senate. The legislation is to receive further review by the Senate in the fall of 2001.

The new legislation, the *Youth Criminal Justice Act*, draws a distinction between violent and non-violent crime and allows judges more discretion in non-custodial sentencing (probation, community work, restitution), thereby keeping young offenders out of prison (which most agree does more harm than good).

The federal legislation has become a political and constitutional issue, however. It seeks to reduce the age at which children charged with a serious crime can be sentenced as adults from 16 years to 14. This is totally unacceptable in the province of Quebec, which has the lowest conviction rate for juvenile offenders, a tradition of leniency and overall success with dealing with youth caught up in the law. Based on their successes, Quebec politicians, unlike those in other provinces, maintain that lowering the age would be a big mistake.

excessively harsh discipline, spousal conflict, the father's absence, parental alcohol or substance abuse, and parental and sibling psychiatric problems. Individual factors include poor school performance and learning disabilities, school attendance problems and drop out, low self-esteem, rejection by peers and/or association with a delinquent peer group, alcohol or substance abuse and psychiatric problems (Child Welfare League of Canada 1995, 8). Social workers point out that a punitive approach using incarceration does not deal with these factors.

Indeed, studies would seem to support the claim by social workers that such measures do not reduce violent youth crime. A European study concluded that an increase in the number of police, courts and prisons fails to combat the crime problem as the roots of crime lie outside the reach of these institutions (Waller 1989). The Honourable Herb Grey, Solicitor General for Canada, summed it up when he said that if the answer to the problem of youth crime were longer sentences, then the United States would be the safest place in the world.

INCOME SECURITY FOR CHILDREN

Income security for children is affected by all the income security programs that relate to the income of families with children, specifically, Social Assistance, the Canada Child Tax Benefit (CCTB), Employment Insurance and the recent National Child Benefit (NCB). The CCTB/NCB, in particular, affects children as it is paid only to families with children.

The CCTB/NCB is a joint initiative of the federal government and provincial and territorial governments. It was the first social program credited to the co-operation between provincial and federal levels of government that underpinned the Social Union Agreement. The goals of the CCTB/NCB are to help prevent and reduce the depth of child poverty, promote attachment to the work force, and reduce overlap and duplication between Canadian and provincial/territorial programs.

The stated rationale for discontinuing the universal and widely accepted Family Allowance and replacing it with a program targeted at the poor is that the CCTB/NCB will begin to remove child benefits from welfare, assist parents with the cost of raising children and make it easier for low-income parents to support their families through employment without resorting to welfare. It remains to be seen whether or not the CCTB/NCB will continue to receive the support of the public when the majority middle class do not benefit from the program.

With the NCB supplement program, the government aims to both reduce child poverty and promote the attachment of parents to the workforce. To accomplish this, provincial governments are allowed to reduce their Social Assistance expenditures to families by the same amount as the increase in NCB. The catch is that the savings must be used for other programs for low-income families with children. In short, the children in families of the working poor receive more, and children in families on welfare receive less.

Has this shift in government policy towards targeting benefits to poor families with children affected the poverty rates of children in Canada? A review of trends over the past twenty-four years shows that income inequality has worsened among families with children. In 1973, the poorest quintile of families (that is, the poorest 20 percent of families) earned only 5.3 percent of all market income (that is, earnings from employment and private investments). By 1996, they received only 2.3 percent of market income. The next poorest quintile of families also lost some of their share of market income—experiencing a drop from 13.5 to 11.1 percent. Meanwhile, the top quintile of families saw their share of market income rise over the same period from 38.4 percent to 43.2 percent. After factoring in the redistributive effects of government taxes and transfers—such as welfare payments, Employment Insurance benefits and child benefits—the distribution of family income is somewhat improved, but it has become even more unequal over time. The two lowest or poorest quintiles continue to receive a vastly smaller share of total family income than does the top quintile. (For the statistics upon which this analysis is based, see http://www.ccsd.ca/facts.html.)

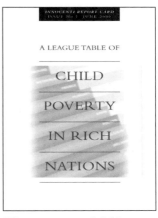

"The persistence of child poverty in rich countries undermines both the equality of opportunity and commonality of values. It therefore confronts the industrialized world with a test both of its ideals and of its capacity to resolve many of its most intractable social problems."

Source: UNICEF, *Child Poverty in Rich Nations*, Innocenti Report Card (June 2000).

According to the United Nations Children's Fund report, *Child Poverty in Rich Nations*, one in six of the rich world's children—47 million —remains poor, despite a rapid increase in national incomes in developed countries (UNICEF 2000, 2). In Canada, according to the report, 15.5 percent of children—one in every six—lives in relative poverty (p.4). The report adds that the lack of adequate economic opportunity, and not the composition of the family, is primarily to blame for placing children in dire economic straits.

Unlike other rich countries, however, the poor children in Canada are more likely than not to live in lone-parent households. The percentage of lone-parent mothers living in poverty in 1981 was 53.5, and this figure had increased to 56 percent by 1997 (Ross et al. 2000). Canada's social expenditures have failed to meet the needs of children, unlike those of other countries. Having a well-developed social safety net has worked well in Sweden, Norway, Denmark and Finland. For example, Sweden has the highest rate of children living in lone-parent families but has the lowest child poverty rate.

EARLY CHILDHOOD DEVELOPMENT SERVICES

Guided by the spirit of provincial and federal co-operation contained in the Social Union Agreement, both levels of government have agreed to the importance of **early childhood development**. This priority was identified and developed under the National Children's Agenda (NCA) document negotiated between provincial and federal governments in 1999-2000. In support of this initiative, the federal government has agreed to contribute $2.2 billion for early childhood development over five years, beginning in 2001-02.

Provincial and territorial governments have agreed to use this increased funding to promote healthy pregnancies, births and infancy; improve parenting and family supports; strengthen early childhood development, learning and care and strengthen community supports. This initiative will provide better access to services such as pre-natal classes and screening, pre-school programs and child care, parent information and family support, and community supports. Each provincial or territorial government will be able to tailor its early childhood development services to its specific circumstances and be in a better position to commit to improving children's services and addressing such requirements as the need for affordable child care spaces throughout Canada.

CHILD PROTECTION WORKER "BURNOUT"

Child social work is a noble occupation, to be sure, but a disconcerting phenomenon has recently received considerable attention—the extent of worker **"burnout"** among dedicated child welfare workers in particular. It is perhaps wise, therefore, to raise a note of concern.

The term *burnout* refers to the anxiety resulting from increased workplace pressure and increased workloads. This type of stress occurs among social workers and others who are faced with increasing responsibility and less and less control over how the work is to be completed. Across Canada, this condition seems increasingly to have become the norm for child welfare workers.

A recent study found that social workers employed by the Children's Aid Society of Toronto showed traumatic stress scores "considerably higher" than those of workers in other emergency services, such as firefighters and ambulance paramedics (Philip 2001). The study, conducted by the Ontario Association of Children's Aids Societies, found that mounting caseloads and a mismatch between the time allotted by provincial regulations for investigation and assessment (12.5 hours) and the actual required time of 19.3 hours are causing undue stress and the departure of many workers.

In response to a number of high-profile inquests into the deaths of children in care, provincial governments are mandating new administrative requirements. It is fast becoming impossible for the workers to comply with the mounting paperwork and computer work within the time allotted. And, of course, a failure to comply with administrative requirements places the onus for any mistakes squarely on the worker. Undoubtedly, such high levels of stress are directly linked to the workers' lack of control over work processes while bearing total responsibility for the outcomes. When combined with larger caseloads and the significant emotional stress of the work, it should not be surprising that worker burnout results.

The ultimate victims of this state of affairs of course are the children themselves. Dedicated individuals enter this area of the profession with the intention of doing good work and helping children and families as best they can. If they are to remain, and if others are to be attracted to this important field of social work practice, working conditions must be improved. The current round of government cutbacks is taking a severe toll on these social workers and, in turn, on the children they are seeking to help.

CONCLUSION

Only recently has child maltreatment received recognition as a significant social problem, although child abuse and neglect has a long history. In 1893 the passing of the *Children's Protection Act* in Ontario ushered in a new era in modern child welfare legislation protecting children from abuse and neglect. The following years saw a range of provincial legislative Acts, as child welfare was, and still is, defined in the Constitution as a provincial jurisdiction. Modern child welfare work has continued to struggle with dilemmas such as protection verses family preservation, or the "best interests" of the child verses the "least restrictive" measures of intervention.

Child welfare work is the most common field of work for graduating social workers today. The field is changing rapidly and workers need continually to update their skills and learn new techniques. For example, research has been done to identify the risk assessment factors that correlate with the abuse of children, and workers are expected to apply this in their practice. The first step in the overall process of child protection is to obtain and record the initial response from a variety of sources to the report of abuse. Next, the worker determines if the child has been abused, any safety concerns, future risk, the capacity of the family to protect the child and any services that will be required. Verification decisions are critical in today's litigation-filled society, so the worker must document both the evidence of abuse and standard of proof. Finally, the social worker needs to complete a plan of service for both the child and family and keep careful records of the implementation of the plan.

Doing social work on behalf, or with, children and youth includes more than child protection work. Social workers work with children and youth in variety of roles. Other social work settings include day care, foster care, adoptions, residential group homes, youth corrections, various income security programs and child care, to name a few. In all these settings, social workers have always been at the forefront in advocating for improvements in policy and services for children and youth.

Social work recognizes that children are not only the most vulnerable citizens of Canada, but they are also our hope for future. That is why social workers continue to enter this field, despite its difficult conditions and high attrition rates. While working with abused children and the people that abuse them may not be pleasant, it is indispensable in a civilized and just society. It will, no doubt, continue to be a key field of activity for social workers.

REFERENCES

- Alberta. 1999-2000. *Annual Report.* Alberta: Children's Services.

- British Columbia Ministry for Children and Families. 1998-99. *Annual Report.*

- Canadian Association of Schools of Social Work. 2001. *In Critical Demand: Social Work in Canada, Final Report.* Ottawa.

- Child Welfare League of Canada. 1995. *The Young Offenders Act, Its Implementation and Related Services: A Child Welfare Perspective.* Ottawa: CWLC.

- Nova Scotia Department of Family Services. 1990. *Children and Family Services Act.*

- Nova Scotia Department of Community Services. 1993. *Advisory Committee Report on Children and Family Services Act.* December 9.

- Philip, Margaret. 2001. Children's Aid Staff Face Burnout. *The Globe and Mail,* February 20.

- Ontario Association of Children's Aid Societies. 2000. *OACAS Facts.* Available at: http://www.oacas.org

- Ontario Ministry of Community and Social Services. 1999. *Annual Report.*

- Ross, David P., E.R. Shillington, and C. Lochhead. 1994. *The Canadian Fact Book on Poverty.* Ottawa: CCSD.

- Ross, David P., Katherine Scott, and Peter Smith. 2000. *The Canadian Fact Book on Poverty.* Ottawa: CCSD.

- Savoie, Josée. n.d. Violent Youth Crime. *Juristat.* Catalogue No. 85-002-XPE, Vol. 19, No. 13. Ottawa: Statistics Canada.

- Statistics Canada, Cansim Matrices 2198 and 2199. Cat. No. 85-205-XIB.

- Trocmé, N. 1991. Child Welfare Services. In Child, Youth and Family Policy Research Centre, *The Sate of the Child in Ontario.* Don Mills: Oxford University Press.

- Trocmé, N., et al. 2001. *Canadian Incidence Study of Reported Child Abuse and Neglect: Final Report.* Ottawa, Ontario: Minister of Public Works and Government Services Canada.

- UNICEF. 2000. *Child Poverty in Rich Nations.* Innocenti Report Card. United Nations Children's Fund.

- Waller, Irvin. 1989. *Current Trends in European Crime Prevention: Implications for Canada.* Ottawa: Supply and Services Canada.

CHAPTER 6: SOCIAL WORK WITH CHILDREN AND YOUTH

Key Concepts

- In-home services
- Out-of-home services
- Best interests approach
- Least restrictive approach
- Child abuse
- Neglect
- Physical abuse
- Sexual abuse
- Emotional abuse
- Risk assessment
- Duty to report
- Court order
- Early childhood development
- Burnout

Discussion Questions

1. Identify and discuss three phases in the history of child welfare.
2. Explain what is meant by the "least restrictive" and the "best interests" approaches to child protection cases.
3. What is the extent of youth in care in Canada and how does this match up with government policy in this area?
4. What is the extent of child abuse today in Canada?
5. What are the steps to be followed in providing child welfare services?
6. What are some of the issues that trouble youth who are in care?
7. How has provincial child welfare legislation changed in the past few years in ways that you see as positive? How has it changed in ways that you see as negative?

Websites

- ### Child & Family Canada
  http://www.cfc-efc.ca

  A unique Canadian public education website. Fifty Canadian non-profit organizations have come together under the banner of Child & Family Canada to provide quality, credible resources on children and families on an easy-to-navigate website. The "library" provides access to over 1,300 documents on child welfare.

- ### Child Welfare League of Canada
  http://www.cwlc.ca

  The CWLC is an organization active in Canadian policy, research and advocacy. The site contains an issue-specific search engine for those doing research in the child welfare area.

- ### The Ontario Association of Children Aids Societies
  http://www.oacas.org

  The voice of child welfare in Ontario, dedicated to providing leadership for the achievement of excellence in the protection of children and in the promotion of their well-being within their families and communities.

- ### Child Welfare Resource Centre
  http://www.childwelfare.ca

  This website offers an excellent list of web links, an on-line CHAT group, and an e-mail discussion list. This would be a good place to start exploring the field of Canadian child welfare.

7
Social Work and Health

Medicare at Risk

Canadians generally see their health care system as exemplifying many deeply held Canadian values, such as equity, fairness, compassion and respect for the fundamental dignity of all. Social workers have been at the forefront of defending this publicly funded system and promoting healthy living and illness prevention. They have an increasingly important role in health care delivery.

Social workers play a key role in the provision of health services in Canada. The range of services they provide includes medical social work (such as social work with individuals, group work, discharge planning, family consultation, patient advocacy, counselling of terminally ill patients, training and policy analysis) as well as community-based and preventative services (such as health promotion and education, self-help group formation, community development and advocacy). In hospital care settings, social workers are often part of a multidisciplinary team that provides a unique holistic perspective to health care. This holistic perspective is not only concerned with the treatment of illness, but also with the promotion of wellness and the consideration of the social, economic, spiritual and cultural needs of the health services client.

This chapter begins by looking at the relationship between economic inequality and health status, or what is known as the "health gap." It then gives an overview of the history of public medical care in Canada, the current *Canada Health Act* and the role of the federal government and the provinces in the provision of health care. Several contemporary issues are discussed, including universality, privatization, extra billing and user fees. It also looks at the recent agreement between the federal government and the provinces to restore federal funding to the health care system. Finally, the chapter examines the role of social workers in medical social work, community health centres and social work with people who have contracted HIV/AIDS.

Public health significantly reduces the "health gap."

HEALTH AND INEQUALITY

Despite the availability of public health care across the country, there is a serious **health gap** between the rich and the poor in Canada. The rich are healthier than the middle class, who are in turn healthier than the poor. The well educated are healthier than the less educated, the employed are healthier than the unemployed and so on.

TOWARDS A HEALTHY FUTURE

The federal, provincial and territorial Ministers of Health released, in September 1999, the public policy report *Toward a Healthy Future: Second Report on the Health of Canadians*. This landmark report examines all the major factors or "determinants" that influence the health of Canadians of all ages. The Report makes a special effort to look at the effects of socioeconomic status and gender on health. A complementary report, *Statistical Report on the Health of Canadians* (1999), was produced through a partnership of Health Canada, Statistics Canada and the Canadian Institute for Health Information.

The key messages from *Toward a Healthy Future* are provided in *Building a Healthy Future*, which is intended for health intermediaries and the general public.

These reports are available on-line at: http://www.hc-sc.gc.ca/hppb/phdd/report/toward/eng/index.html

A 1990 report by the National Council of Welfare focused on the link between health status and income. For this report, the population was divided into five groups according to income (known as a quintile distribution by income). The analysis examined a number of measures of health status in relation to the distribution of income. The report found that the poorer the neighbourhood, the shorter was the average life expectancy of its residents. Fifty percent of men residing in the poorest neighbourhoods will live to age seventy-five, while almost 70 percent of men who live in the richest neighbourhoods will reach this age. Similarly, babies born to parents in the poorest neighbourhoods are twice as likely to die before their first birthday than babies born to parents in the richest neighbourhoods. And, lower-income Canadians experience fewer years of good health throughout their lives (National Council of Welfare 1990a, 99).

In 1990, Wilkins, a representative of the Canadian Centre for Health Information at Statistics Canada, appeared before a parliamentary committee studying child poverty. On the basis of evidence gathered over thirteen years of study, Wilkins concluded that,

> based on the best data currently available for Canada, it appears that the health problems of poor children begin before birth and continue to place these children at greater risk of death, disability and other health problems throughout infancy, childhood and adolescence (Ibid., 103).

A 1990 federal Health and Welfare document, *Achieving Health for All*, noted that "the first challenge we face is to find ways of reducing inequities in the health of low- versus high-income groups in Canada" (National Council of Welfare 1990b, 105).

A more recent 1996 study found that there is a gap between the rich and the poor for most types of illnesses and for almost all causes of death. Moreover, only 47 percent of low-income Canadians rate their health as excellent or very good compared to 73 percent of Canadians in the high-income group (Federal, Provincial, and Territorial Advisory Committee on Population Health 1996, 14). Commenting on the importance of relative poverty in 1999, the same committee stated that "there is strong evidence that the health of a given population depends on the equality of income distribution rather than on average income. The greater the disparities between rich and poor, the greater the health consequences" (Federal, Provincial, and Territorial Advisory Committee on Population Health 1999, 49).

In other words, the "health gap" in Canada is serious–people who are living at a socioeconomic disadvantage are more susceptible to illness and early death.

HEALTH STATUS OF ABORIGINAL PEOPLES

Aboriginal peoples have the poorest levels of overall health, located as they are in the lowest quintile of the Canadian socioeconomic hierarchy. For status Indians living on reserves, the average life expectancy in 1991 was 65.7 years for men and 73.0 for women (compared to 74.1 for men and 81.2 for women in the general population). As well, infant

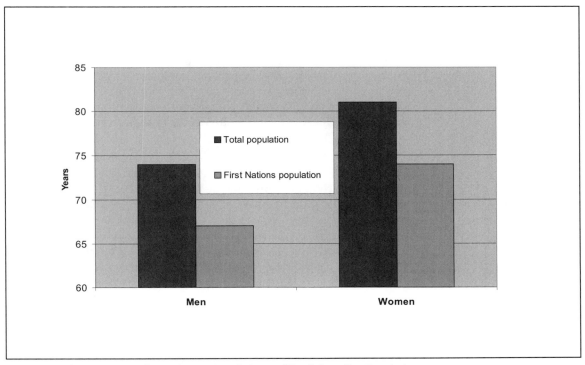

Figure 7.1: Life Expectancy of First Nations Population and Total Canadian Population.
Source: Department of Indian Affairs and Northern Development (Status Indians); Statistics Canada, *Births and Deaths* (1993).

mortality for status Indians was 17.2 deaths per thousand in 1986, twice the Canadian average of 7.9. Diabetes rates among First Nations people are from three to five times the national average (Assembly of First Nations 1999).

The Canadian Institute of Child Health describes the problems faced by Canada's Aboriginal peoples:

> The pattern of disease among Canada's Native people resembles the main killers of the developing world. Infections and parasitic and respiratory diseases, often helped by malnutrition, account for most deaths under one year of age. Accompanying these are "diseases" of economic under-development. Many Native people live in poverty and consequently, when compounded by the implicit and explicit racism of our society, they are doubly oppressed. The state of poverty in which they live makes them particularly vulnerable to health hazards (National Council of Welfare 1990a, 108).

Improving the health of Native Canadians involves addressing the factors associated with poor health, such as poverty, unemployment, inadequate housing and so forth. The health and social problems of Aboriginal peoples do not require only corrective medical procedures; they require fundamental changes in the social conditions in which they live.

HISTORY OF HEALTH POLICY

Canadians have not always had ready access to quality health care. Prior to the late 1940s, access to health care was based solely on one's ability to pay. Access to health care did not become a governmental concern until illness threatened to hamper the supply of workers for industry, and even then, the road to a state-funded health insurance plan was not smooth. **Universal public health care** took over five decades to evolve.

The history of health care in Canada begins with the in-home care provided by women as midwives and caregivers and by healers and shamans in First Nations communities. Health care knowledge was passed on by mothers, grandmothers or other elders. By the late 1700s, male allopathic practitioners sought to overthrow the power of the traditional female practitioners. The first Canadian medical school was established in 1824, and in 1869, government legislation gave the male allopathic practitioners or physicians control over medical education (Clarke 1990). Women were actively excluded from access to medical schools by the male-dominated medical associations.

One of the first pieces of government health care regulation was a directive in 1832 by the Upper Canada Sanitary Commission and Board of Health pertaining to the quarantine and sanitation of immigrants infected with cholera. More extensive public health measures, including the *Food and Drug Act*, the *Narcotics Control Act* and the establishment of hospitals and asylums, were introduced later in the nineteenth century (Clarke 1990).

The British North America Act of 1867 established the jurisdictions of the federal and provincial governments in delivering health services. The management and maintenance of health institutions became the responsibility of the provinces. Nevertheless, the larger tax base of the federal government allowed it to continue to influence Canadian health policy.

From 1880 to the 1950s, there were a variety of **pre-payment health plans** in place across Canada, sponsored by local governments, industries and volunteer agencies (Vayda and Deber 1995). By 1934, there were twenty-seven different hospital-sponsored pre-payment plans in six of the provinces. For example, a payroll-deduction plan existed for miners in Nova Scotia and Ontario, and the Municipal Doctor System, which paid physicians on an annual contract basis, had been established in Saskatchewan in 1914. Medical associations and hospitals also developed health insurance plans in Ontario, Manitoba and Nova Scotia. In 1939, the first Canadian Blue Cross plan was formed in Manitoba, with most provinces following suit in the 1940s. These voluntary insurance plans did not cover all medical services, and they were available only to those who could afford to pay the premiums.

While people struggled to obtain health insurance, provincial governments often backed down from its provision under pressure from the medical profession. For example, in British Columbia, relief workers, the One Big Union and the Co-operative Commonwealth Federation

National Archives of Canada. Neg no. PA128016 (NFB).

Eye examination in a Newfoundland school, 1949.

(CCF) put intense pressure on the Patullo government to institute comprehensive health insurance in the 1930s. In 1933, the Patullo government included health care as a key component of its election platform. The Bill passed third reading, but because of opposition from doctors, Patullo refused to give effect to the legislation. In Alberta, health insurance plans were blocked by the powerful Medical Association.

Debates about health insurance also occurred within the field of social work. The 1942 Heagerty Report and the 1943 Marsh Report both recommended comprehensive state-funded health insurance. The more conservative Social Service Council, led by Charlotte Whitton (see page 46), opposed state-funded health insurance.

FEDERAL INVOLVEMENT

Several factors precipitated more active federal involvement in medical insurance. When the issue of public medical insurance first arose in the 1920s in British Columbia, it was considered to be a provincial matter. But in the 1930s, working Canadians were devastated by economic depression, and political unrest was widespread. Because many people were unable to pay for medical expenses, some doctors found the idea of public medical insurance attractive—at least the bills for medical care would be paid.

In 1942, the Heagerty Report proposed a federally funded, two-stage health insurance scheme. The plan was accepted by labour and the medical profession but foundered because of federal-provincial animosity. In 1945, the Royal Commission on Dominion Provincial Relations (established in 1939) produced the Green Book, which placed on the table a whole series of proposals to the provinces, including proposals regarding health care. The proposals reflected a reasonable ordering of priorities—extending the unemployment insurance system, instituting federal programs of unemployment assistance and health insurance, and improving old age pensions—and called for the federal government to help finance health and social services programs in return for the provinces' renouncement of their claim to income and corporate taxes. The provinces, particularly Ontario and Quebec, turned the federal offer down. There was a "lack of agreement on the tax-sharing formula and federal interference in matters that were considered to be provincial jurisdiction under the B.N.A. Act. Ontario considered health insurance in particular, to be the responsibility of the provincial government" (Cumming 1985, 51).

By the end of World War II, however, children's allowances and unemployment insurance were in place. And in 1947, the first scheme for the public insurance plan for hospital services was instituted in Saskatchewan. The scheme did not provide funding for personal medical care received in a doctor's office, but it did provide financing for emergency services, curative medicine and surgery in hospitals.

In 1957, the *Hospital Insurance and Diagnostic Services Act* was passed. In the Act, the federal government agreed to finance 50 percent of the cost of provincial acute and chronic hospital care (although mental hospitals, tuberculosis sanatoria and custodial care institutions, such as nursing homes, were excluded, and patients still had to pay a daily user fee for hospital services). This legislation encouraged the development of hospital insurance plans, and by 1961, all provinces and territories had signed agreements with the federal government for limited, in-patient hospital care that qualified for federal cost sharing.

Public medical care insurance that included coverage for visits to, and services provided by, physicians outside of hospital began in Saskatchewan. With hospital insurance plans, the possibility of financial ruin due to ill health remained, and the CCF government in that province considered more comprehensive medical coverage to be necessary. The doctors in Saskatchewan eventually won the right to opt out of the plan, but the CCF adamantly opposed them, arguing that this would create a two-tiered system. Even though the plan was limited due to the resistance of the physicians, it provided the foundation for future progress.

The powerful Canadian and American Medical Associations continually blocked plans to replace fee-for-service with salaried physicians. Even today, many physicians resist efforts to replace the current, privately based delivery of medical services with salaried physicians delivering public medical care.

• Medical Care Act, 1968

In 1962, Conservative Prime Minister John Diefenbaker appointed Justice Emmett Hall to chair a Royal Commission on Health Care. In 1964, the Hall Report disclosed that 7.5 million Canadians did not have medical coverage and recommended that a comprehensive, publicly administered universal health service plan be implemented. Hall's proposal received massive grassroots support. Women's organizations and organized labour were particularly positive about national medical care insurance. The federal minority Liberal government that followed Diefenbaker's Conservative government was supported by the newly established New Democratic Party, which supported universal health care. The physicians threatened to strike but were unsuccessful in reversing the tide, and the *Medical Care Act* was passed in 1968.

The 1968 *Medical Care Act* provided for an equal federal-provincial cost sharing of non-hospital medical services. By 1972, all provinces and territories had extended their plans to include physician's services. Funding was made available to provinces if their services met the criteria of comprehensiveness, accessibility, universality, portability and public administration. Under the new legislation, physicians were permitted to opt out of the plan and extra billing was permitted.

In 1979, the Hall Commission reported that public health care in Canada was still under threat. Extra billing on the part of physicians and user fees levied by hospitals were creating a two-tiered system. The federal government responded by imposing a dollar-for-dollar penalty on federal transfer payments to provinces that allowed extra billing or user fees. This penalty remained in the 1984 *Canada Health Act* and is included in both the current Act and the Social Union Agreement.

National Archives of Canada. Neg no. PA130735 (Louis Jaques).

Diefenbaker appointed Royal Commission on Health Care.

CANADA'S MEDICARE SYSTEM

Today, Canada has a health care system that is funded by government insurance, but medical care itself is privately delivered by physicians who are self-employed or employed by physician-owned corporations. The system is an interlocking set of ten provincial and two territorial health insurance plans. Known as **Medicare**, the system provides access to universal, comprehensive coverage for hospital, in-patient and out-patient physician services.

Behind the Canadian health care system is a constitutional agreement between the federal government and the provinces. Under the agreement, the jurisdiction over most aspects of health care is provincial. The system is referred to as a "national" health insurance system because all provincial and/or territorial hospital and medical insurance plans are linked through adherence to national principles set at the federal level.

The *Canada Health Act* (CHA) passed by Parliament in 1984 is the cornerstone of the Canadian health system. It replaced the existing *Hospital Insurance and Diagnostic Services Act* and the *Medical Care Act* of 1968. It reaffirmed the commitment to a universal, accessible, comprehensive, portable and publicly administered health insurance system. The CHA aimed to ensure that all Canadians had access to necessary health care on a pre-paid basis. It established criteria and conditions that the provinces and territories must satisfy to qualify for their full share of the federal transfers for health care services. The purpose was to "establish criteria and conditions in respect of insured health services and extended health care services provided under provincial law that must be met before a full cash contribution may be made."

Each province must meet the following five criteria in order to receive funding from the federal government:

- **Public administration.** Pursuant to section 8, the health care insurance plan must be administered and operated on a non-profit basis by a public authority, responsible to the provincial government and subject to audit of its accounts and financial transactions.

- **Comprehensiveness.** Pursuant to section 9, the plan must insure all insured health services provided by hospitals, medical practitioners or dentists, and, where permitted, services rendered by other health care practitioners.

- **Universality.** Section 10 requires that 100 percent of the insured persons of a province be entitled to the insured health services provided for by the plan on uniform terms and conditions.

- **Portability.** In accordance with section 11, residents moving to another province must continue to be covered for insured health services by the home province during any minimum waiting period imposed by the new province of residence, not to exceed three months. For insured persons, insured health services must be made available while they are temporarily absent from their own provinces on the basis that: (a) insured services received out of a province, but still in Canada, are to be paid for by the home province at

CANADA HEALTH ACT

The primary objective of the health policy is stated in Section 3 of the Act: "It is hereby declared that the primary objective of Canadian health care policy is to protect, promote and restore the physical and mental well-being of residents of Canada and to facilitate reasonable access to health services without financial or other barriers."

That Act goes on to state that health insurance "must provide for insured health services on uniform terms and conditions and on a basis that does not impede or preclude, either directly or indirectly whether by charges made to insured persons or otherwise."

The *Canada Health Act*, as with all of Canada's legislation, is available on-line at: http://laws.justice.gc.ca

host province rates unless another arrangement for the payment of costs exists between the provinces. Prior approval may be required for elective services; (b) out-of-country services are to be paid, as a minimum, on the basis of the amount that would have been paid by the home province for similar services rendered in the province. Prior approval may also be required for elective services.

- **Accessibility.** By virtue of section 12, the health care insurance plan of a province must provide for: (a) insured health services on uniform terms and conditions and reasonable access by insured persons to insured health services unprecluded or unimpeded, either directly or indirectly, by charges or other means; (b) reasonable compensation to physicians and dentists for all insured health services rendered; payments to hospitals in respect of the cost of insured health services.

Commitment to the "five principles" was recently reaffirmed, after intense negotiations, in the Social Union Agreement of 1999 between the federal government and all provinces and territories (except Quebec). The Agreement, entitled *A Framework to Improve the Social Union for Canadians*, attempted to define how power and responsibility would be divided. It also attempted to smooth relations between the federal government and the provinces following the fall-out from the unilateral federal changes to funding in the *Canada Health and Social Transfer Act* (CHST). (For background information on the Social Union Agreement, see Chapter 2, page 34.)

HOW DOES MEDICARE WORK?

The purpose of Medicare is to insure the patient against the costs of personal, private care. The individual physicians retain their private status and continue to operate on a fee-for-service basis; they are not salaried employees. The insurance is paid for through our tax system. In that sense, Medicare is a social insurance system, and since we all pay and we all benefit, it is a type of universal social insurance program. Each patient has a number, and each medical procedure has a definition and a designated number. Using the patient number and the number of the medical procedure, the physician bills the provincial administration for costs. In this system, the physician determines the range and the extent of care necessary, including referral to specialists and hospital, whether for a physical or psychiatric illness.

Each province has legislation that regulates the medical profession and health professions. The province determines which services are covered by its plan and also determines under what conditions health practitioners—whether psychologists, social workers, massage therapists, midwives, physiotherapists, speech pathologists, chiropractors and so forth—are permitted to provide services. Fee schedules for physicians are determined by negotiation between the provincial government and the provincial medical association. Wages and salaries for nurses and hospital staff are determined by negotiation between provincial hospital associations and the staff. The provinces also have a range of labour relations laws that establish the conditions of collective bargaining for health professionals and staff. For example, in some provinces health care workers have prescribed procedures to follow during collective bargaining that lead to a contract establishing wages, salaries and working conditions.

Each provincial government legislates what health services are available in that province. The province contracts with hospitals to provide these services. The hospital and the province sign a contract; the patient is not a direct part of the agreement. Patients, sometimes aided by private insurance, must pay for services not covered by the plan but provided by the hospital (such as semi-private or private rooms).

In short, then, Canada has a predominantly publicly financed, privately delivered health care system that can described as an interlocking set of ten provincial and three territorial health insurance plans. Known to Canadians as "Medicare," the system provides access to universal, comprehensive coverage for medically necessary hospital, in-patient and out-patient physician services. This structure results from the constitutional assignment of jurisdiction over most aspects of health care to the provincial level of government. The system is referred to as a "national" health insurance system in that all provincial/territorial hospital and medical insurance plans are linked through adherence to national principles set at the federal level (Health Canada 2000).

• Federal Funding for Provincial Medicare

Since the late 1940s, the federal government had been providing funds to support post-secondary education across the country. In 1964, they decided to create one piece of legislation through which it would provide funding to the provinces to support both hospitals and post-secondary education. After Medicare was instituted, grants to the provinces were linked to support for hospitals and post-secondary education in the *Established Programs Financing Act* of 1967. The arrangement was to be renegotiated every five years. Negotiations took place in 1972, 1977, 1982, 1987, and 1992. In 1992, the review was postponed until 1994.

In 1977, the nature of the grant program changed from its original base of "conditional funding"–the federal government's 50 percent was conditional on the provinces contributing their 50 percent share. The federal government stated that the program was too costly, and the grant was converted to a "block grant" of a given amount of money. It was no longer a "cost-sharing" program, and the provincial government receiving the money was not obligated to spend it in the areas of education and health. As part of the new 1977 Established Programs Financing (EPF) regime, the federal health transfer took the form of roughly equal portions of cash transfers and tax transfers. To provide the tax transfer, the federal government reduced its personal and corporate income tax rates, which allowed the provinces to raise their tax rates by the same amount. As a result, revenue that would have flowed to the federal government began to flow directly to the provincial governments. (This transfer of taxation rights is frequently missed when examining federal participation in health funding.)

FROM HALL TO ROMANOW

In 1964 Emmett Hall was asked "to look into the existing and future need for health services and to recommend measures to ensure that the best possible health care is available to the people of Canada." The report of the Hall Commission was a landmark in Canadian history. It helped to set the stage for the Medicare that Canadians know and cherish as an essential part of what defines us today.

In 2001, Allan Rock, the federal Minister of Health, announced the Commission on the Future of Health Care in Canada under Mr. Roy Romanow. The Commission is to recommend policies and measures that will give Canadians a sustainable and universally accessible health system over the long term. The Romanow report is due in November 2002.

HEALTH EXPENDITURES

In 1996, hospital expenditures represented the largest category of expenditure at 34.2% of total health expenditures, followed by physicians and drugs at 14.4% each.

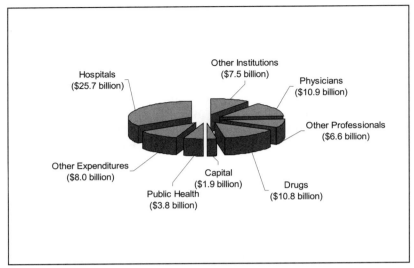

Figure 7.2: Percentage Distribution of Health Expenditures by Category of Expenditure, 1996.
Source: Health Canada and CIHI.

In 1986, increases in block funding were limited to the Consumer Price Index (CPI), less 2 percent. In 1990, Bill C-69 froze block funding at 1989-90 levels for 1990-91 and 1991-92. For 1992-93 and beyond, block funding was to be limited to Gross National Product (GNP) growth, less 3 percent. In short, the federal government limited the funds available to pay for health care in Canada throughout the 1990s, forcing the provinces to pay more in order to maintain services. Poorer provinces found it harder to finance health care and were forced to reduce services.

In 1996, the EPF and the Canada Assistance Plan (CAP), which funded social assistance and other social services, were replaced by the *Canada Health and Social Transfer Act.* The CHST is not subject to regular re-negotiation. Monies granted through CHST can be used for health, post-secondary education and Social Assistance and/or services, and provinces are free to spend as much of this on health care as they wish.

In 1997-99, funding from the federal government dropped significantly. By 2000, however, it was back at 1996 levels. Canada spent an estimated $75.2 billion on health in 1996, or $2,511 per person and 9.5 percent of Gross Domestic Product (GDP). In 1996, hospital expenditures represented the largest expense item at 34.2 percent of health spending (Health Canada 1997, 3). In 2000, the federal government transferred $30.8 billion to the provinces through CHST; $9.5 billion in equalization transfers to less prosperous provinces; and $3.2 billion in direct health spending for First Nations and Inuit, military personnel, health promotion and protection, innovation and research, and health information.

Data on the funding of health care can be found at the Health Canada website at http://www.hc-sc.gc.ca.

Government cutbacks have targeted health and education.

USER FEES AND EXTRA BILLING CONTROVERSY

By the early 1980s, doctors were charging fees beyond the scale of payments established by the provinces in negotiation with the Canadian Medical Association. These **extra-billing** charges threatened the principle of accessibility, one of the five principles of the *Canada Health Act*. Many doctors maintained that extra billing was their right in a free enterprise society—if patients did not want to pay the fees, they could try to find a doctor who did not charge extra fees. For its part, the federal government argued that extra billing made it impossible to ensure the same health services for all citizens at a reasonable cost. For example, if a majority of specialists in a certain field practised extra billing, it would be difficult for patients to locate a specialist who did not charge fees beyond those prescribed by the Medicare system.

At the same time, **user fees**—an extra fee above the scale rate—were being charged by hospitals and other medical institutions for individual use. For example, the Quebec government wanted to introduce user fees to raise revenue and deter what it called the "frivolous" or unnecessary use of medical facilities. It was also argued that user fees would establish a direct relationship between the patient and the service provider and would allow the individual to contribute to his or her own medical health care.

In response, in 1984 the federal government brought in the *Canada Health Act*, reiterating the five principles. The purposes of the *Hospital Insurance and Diagnostic Services Act* of 1957 and the *Medical Care Act* of 1968 were reasserted; extra billing and user fees were effectively eliminated. The provinces were permitted user fees and extra billing, but the federal government reduced the grant to the provinces by a dollar for every dollar raised through either user fees or extra billing. Consequently, the provinces gained no additional funds. Because of the *Canada Health Act*, extra billing and user fees had disappeared by 1987. Under the *Canada Health Act*, the federal government could levy penalties on provinces and territories that did not comply with the Act.

• The Issue of User Fees

User fees are small charges that the patient must assume for hospital and physician services. Their rationale and their existence is a matter of dispute. Those in favour contend that user fees prevent the frivolous use of services, raise revenue, remind the user that the service is not truly free and therefore begin a shift towards the creation of a private market for medical services.

Critics contend that user fees prevent access to services by people who are most vulnerable, for example, those with low incomes. Moreover, they argue that user fees do not prevent the abuse of health services because small fees do not deter the more affluent users of services who therefore tend to benefit more than lower income users. As well, user fees establish a **two-tiered system** of health service, with those who can pay the extra fee or who work for employers who have extended health benefits being more privileged than others. It is also contended that user

HOW THE SYSTEM WORKS

Canada does not have a system of "socialized medicine,"with doctors employed by the government. Most doctors are private practitioners who work in independent or group practices and enjoy a high degree of autonomy. Private practitioners are generally paid on a fee-for-service basis and submit their service claims directly to the provincial health insurance plan for payment.

When Canadians need medical care, in most instances they go to the physician or clinic of their choice and present the health insurance card issued to all eligible residents of a province. Canadians do not pay directly for insured hospital and physicians' services, nor are they required to fill out forms for insured services. There are no deductibles, co-payments or dollar limits on coverage for insured services.

WHAT THE ACT SAYS

EXTRA-BILLING: In order that a province may qualify for a full cash contribution referred to in section 5 for a fiscal year, no payments may be permitted by the province for that fiscal year under the health care insurance plan of the province in respect to insured health services that have been subject to extra-billing by medical practitioners or dentists.

USER CHARGES: In order that a province may qualify for a full cash contribution referred to in section 5 for a fiscal year, user charges must not be permitted by the province for that fiscal year under the health care insurance plan of the province."

Source: Canada Health Act, 1984, c. 6, s. 18. 19.

fees have little effect on controlling the demand for health services, because the suppliers of the services—the physicians and health product suppliers and manufacturers—directly influence that demand.

• The Issue of Extra Billing

Extra billing is an extra charge levied by the physician beyond the negotiated or scheduled rates set by the provinces. Extra billing has been a part of Medicare from its beginning. Until the passage of the *Canada Health Act* in 1984, all provinces except Quebec permitted extra billing.

Those who support extra billing argue that doctors should have the same right as others to charge what the market will bear; doctors' incomes are not keeping pace with inflation and are limited by Medicare. Extra fees ensure that the client determines the service. They also reduce the frivolous use of medical services, promote efficiency and lower health care expenditures. Opponents argue that, with extra billing, health care is not free to each individual. People with low incomes are deterred from obtaining health care, and a two-class system of health care is thereby created. Doctors can charge different prices for the same service, and medical care will become just another commodity.

THREATS TO UNIVERSAL HEALTH CARE

An ageing population and ever-spiraling health care costs are challenging enough, but those who defend universal health care are facing yet another formidable foe: large American health care delivery corporations, ever alert to the opportunity to make a profit from a system under strain. In this context, defenders of universal care will need to be even more alert to the danger signs, such as the following:

- *Comprehensiveness.* Some provinces have attempted to reduce medical costs by reducing comprehensiveness—that is, the range of what are considered to be "medically necessary" services. This is not covered by the *Canada Health Act*, which states that the provinces must determine which services are "medically necessary."

- *Contracting out.* There are also concerns regarding the administration of hospitals. Governments are **contracting out** the management of some hospitals to private companies. If the company generates additional funds for the hospital, it can claim those funds as profit. For example, in Alberta, Bill C-11 of 2000 encourages the establishment of private, for-profit hospitals. Also, some services, such as catering, laundry and cleaning, have been contracted out to private, for-profit organizations. While not contrary to the letter of the *Canada Health Act*, the Alberta legislation threatens universal health care in Canada as it builds into hospital care the concept that patients can be charged privately for non-insured clinical services while they are receiving an insured service. This interferes with the Medicare norm of reasonable access. It may also activate troublesome provisions under the North American Free Trade Agreement (NAFTA) by binding succeeding Alberta governments to deal with for-profit hospitals and by allowing foreign companies to claim to an international arbitration tribunal that they should be allowed into all provinces because the Alberta law has the effect of changing federal legislation.

- *Privatization.* One the biggest threats to our public system of health care is the current movement to privatize care in some provinces, particularly in Alberta and Ontario. Several trends indicate increased **privatization** in our health care system, including:
  - the "de-listing" of services covered by Medicare (e.g., specific medical procedures, support services, drugs);
  - the transferring of care out of areas covered by Medicare (e.g., acute care in hospitals) to areas that are not (e.g., home care);
  - the contracting out of "non-core" medical services (labs, ambulances and rehab services) to private companies;
  - the contracting out of services (laundry, meal preparation, cleaning and maintenance, materials handling, information management, and disposal services) to private companies;
  - the contracting in of management services, leading to the redesign of management practices in accordance with private sector criteria.

- ### The Debate over Privatized Health Care

Canadians are entering a period of agonizing discussion over whether public health care should be privatized along the American model. And the final outcome of this public debate, in terms of continuing universal medical care, is by no means certain.

The Canadian Health Coalition, a coalition of groups favouring the expansion of quality public health care, has argued that the costs of privatization far outweigh the benefits (Canadian Health Coalition 2000). Their research reveals that

- *A private system is more complex to administer, and therefore more costly.* For example, in the U.S., health care administration cost $361 per capita in 1995, compared to $119 in Canada. Health care consumes 14 percent of economic resources in the U.S., compared with 9 percent in Canada.

- *A private system provides less coverage.* Private insurance firms refuse insurance to those with known medical conditions, or set rates so high that the average person cannot afford them. In the U.S., about 44 million citizens are unable to afford health insurance.

- *A private system yields poorer results.* Infant mortality and social inequality are higher with a private system; the U.S. has the highest infant mortality rate among countries belonging to the Organization for Economic Co-operation and Development (OEDC).

- *A private system is more prone to fraud.* A national study produced by Harvard Medical School in 1998 concluded that "large scale fraud has become routine" in the profit-driven health care sector. The study cited U.S. General Accounting Office estimates that "about 25 percent of all home care agencies (most of which are for-profit) defraud Medicare" (Center for Health Program Studies 1998).

THE U.S. EXPERIENCE

"The US experience demonstrates that private sector involvement in health care delivery is neither more efficient nor effective. Because 'customers' (known in Canada as 'Patients') are charged for each and every cost item, the typical US hospital employs 50 billing personnel; a Canadian hospital employs only three or four on average."

"To use the words of University of British Columbia health economist Robert Evans, 'the US health care system scores relatively badly on every dimension and from every perspective: public satisfaction, measured health outcomes, overall cost, efficiency, coverage, equity of access, equity of finance.'"

"The US experience of privatized health care continues to provide Canadians with the best reasons for defending, and strengthening, our own cherished public system."

Source: Canadian Health Coalition, *Health Alert: Newsletter 2000* (Ottawa).

PROVINCIAL HEALTH CARE WEBSITES

Provincial and territorial governments are responsible for the delivery of Canada's health care and hospital services. To find out more about health care in your province or territory go to:

- BC Ministry of Health
  http://http://www.gov.bc.ca/healthplanning
- P.E.I. Health
  http://www.gov.pe.ca/infopei/Health
- Alberta Health
  http://www.health.gov.ab.ca
- Saskatchewan Health
  http://www.gov.sk.ca
- Manitoba Health
  http://www.gov.mb.ca/health
- Ontario
  http://www.gov.on.ca/health
- Ministère de la Santé et des Services sociaux du Québec [French only]
  http://www.msss.gouv.qc.ca
- New Brunswick Department of Health & Community Services
  http://www.gov.nb.ca/hcs
- Nova Scotia
  http://www.gov.ns.ca
- Newfoundland Dept. of Health
  http://www.gov.nf.ca/health
- NWT Dept. of Health & Social Services
  http://www.hlthss.gov.nt.ca
- The Yukon
  http://www.gov.yk.ca

The provincial websites change occasionally. An up-to-date list is available at Health Canada: http://www.hc-sc.gc.ca/english/about.htm

- *A private system removes money from the system.* In the private sector, some money is always used to pay back investors. The average health maintenance organization (HMO) in the U.S., for example, devotes 14 percent of its premiums to overhead and profits (Canada's public system uses a mere 0.9 percent by comparison) (Evans 1998, 45). In Canada, much of this profit would go to U.S. companies.

- *A private system raises costs.* Private firms have a stake in costs going up, because higher costs mean higher profits; there are no internal checks and balances to control costs within the private sector. This, says University of British Columbia health economist Robert Evans, is the real agenda behind corporate pressure to reduce public health spending (Evans 1998). According to Professor Pat Armstrong of York University, "it is mainly [this] increase in private expenditures that makes Canadian spending on health amongst the highest in the world" (Armstrong 1997, 21).

Apart from being more economical, public Medicare has several important advantages over a private health care system. First, public financing spreads the cost of health care across society, rather than only to those who are unfortunate or sick. Second, financing health insurance through the taxation system is efficient, since it does not require the creation of a separate collection process. Third, Medicare encourages Canadians to seek preventive care services and to treat problems before they worsen and treatment is more costly.

Many Canadian businesses also recognize and support Canada's universal Medicare system since it provides a competitive advantage with other countries. For example, lower employee benefit costs and a healthy and mobile workforce are attractive advantages. Also, the portability principle of Medicare ensures that workers can move from province to province and still be covered by health insurance.

• Cost Reductions

Medical care costs in Canada have been rising steadily because of the ageing of the Canadian population, the emphasis on curative and high technology medicine, the increasing demand for hospital services and for expensive equipment, and the increasing fees of medical personnel. **Cost containment** has become an area of major concern and will certainly be a focus of the newly formed Commission on the Future of Health Care in Canada (the Romanow Commission; see page 125), due to report in November 2002.

The issue of spiraling costs is one that advocates of public health care take very seriously. Nevertheless, they also insist that keeping operating costs under control is not a valid justification for greater privatization. In the 1970s and early 1980s, many provincial governments attempted to lower hospital costs by reducing the range of services covered or by approving smaller budgetary increases. They also began to permit hospitals to introduce cost-cutting measures, such as fees for emergency care, fees for use of ward beds, contracts with private management companies to manage hospitals, and the contracting out of services such as food or laundry. Provincial governments also closed institutions and sought methods of increasing revenue, such as extra billing by doctors and an increase in Medicare premiums. Such measures tend to undermine public support for Medicare and open the door to privatization.

On the plus side, provincial governments have also begun to address **preventive medicine** and community-based care and have considered experimentation with community-based health and social service centres, such as the community health centres in Ontario. This important step in the right direction is discussed below.

• Community Health Centres

In the 1970s, the federal government recommended the establishment of **community health centres** (CHCs) with the intention of providing primary care, health promotion and prevention services using salaried primary health care professionals. Studies have found that CHCs provide better primary care, decrease the costs of patient care and decrease hospitalization rates. For example, CHC patient care costs were found to be 17 percent lower than hospital costs in Saskatchewan and 25-30 percent lower for Ontario (Angus and Manga 1990).

CHCs tend to network with other health and social services agencies and are accountable to their communities through community boards. They operate on the premise that communities should work together to "own" health care services. They frequently address a variety of issues affecting health, such as violence, housing, literacy, workplace hazards and poverty through programs and social action.

An important advantage of the CHC model is the focus on prevention, education, community development, social action and health promotion. CHCs tend to address four determinants of health: living and working conditions, social support, individual behaviour and genetic make-up. Social workers are central to the provision of both direct care and community development in CHCs.

CHCs are funded primarily by provincial grants. Additional funding is often obtained from United Way, foundations and federal government programs. Funding is allocated either through a global budgeting process, based on services directed at populations, or through capitalization funding, where fixed sums are established for each registered client based on need as a reflection of age, sex, key demographic factors, and prevalence and severity of chronic illness.

In 1995, there were 300 CHCs providing services to 13 percent of Canadians (Albrecht and Lapointe 1995). The use of CHCs is most widespread in Quebec where there are 161 centres known as CLSCs (centres locaux des services communautaires). Ontario is second highest with 56 centres. They are less widespread in the other provinces, due to a lack of political will and opposition by physicians, many of whom are opposed to being paid a salary. CHCs are also associated with the poor and other marginalized groups rather than as being of potential benefit to all. There is, however, a growing interest in the CHC model across the country, both as a way to cut costs and as a community-based approach.

Creative health initiatives reach out to those in need.

MEDICAL SOCIAL WORK

One of the chief settings for **medical social work practice** is the hospital. Almost every hospital in Canada has social workers in its departments, including emergency services, oncology, pediatrics, surgery, intensive care, rehabilitation, gerontology and orthopaedics. The type of work performed by social workers in hospitals is wide ranging and includes direct casework, group work, discharge planning, family consultation, advocating for patients, counselling terminally ill patients, training other professionals and policy and administration. The role of social workers in health care is of vital importance and is increasing along with the understanding that illness is greatly affected by social and environmental factors, and that preventive and educational approaches are both effective and cost-efficient.

When working in a hospital setting, the social worker is often a member of a team that includes other health professionals. The team approach is increasingly used to help ensure that each patient's physical, psychological, social, and cultural needs are being met. The role of social workers is becoming more central in this holistic approach to health care. The **holistic approach to health care** involves taking into account not only the physical aspects of health, which have commonly been addressed by physicians, but also the social, cultural, mental and spiritual aspects of the patient.

In addition to hospital work, social workers are also involved in other health care settings, such as local medical clinics, community health centres and specialized care agencies (such as HIV/AIDS clinics, addiction treatment centres, family planning, pre-natal care, long-term care, home care, hospice care, nursing homes and services for people with disabilities). Social workers are also active as health promoters, community developers and policy advocates in the health field. For example, a social worker may work with a community health centre to promote an aspect of healthy living in the community. Through this work, social workers are at the forefront in addressing primary health care-prevention, health promotion and self-care.

Three health areas where the role of social work is growing are in mental health, HIV/AIDS and addictions treatment. Within all three areas social workers are developing innovative treatment and health promotion methods.

• Mental Health and Social Work

It is estimated that one in five Canadians will be affected by a mental illness at some time in their lives. Social workers are playing an increasingly important role in promoting the mental health of Canadians. The World Health Organization (WHO) considers mental well-being as an integral part of the general definition of health. In the Preamble to the WHO Constitution, for example, health is defined as "a state of complete physical, mental and social well-being and not merely the absence of disease or infirmity."

National Archives of Canada. Neg no. PA113286.

Many retirement homes now employ health care workers.

© Dick Hemingway

Homelessness is all too common in Canadian urban centres. Countless numbers are sleeping on the street each night across the country, seemingly with no let up in sight.

Mental illness is the term used to refer to a variety of diagnosable mental disorders. Mental disorders are health conditions that are characterized by alterations in thinking, mood or behaviour (or some combination thereof) associated with distress and/or impaired functioning. Mental illness implies significant clinical patterns of behaviour or emotions associated with some level of distress, suffering or impairment in one or more areas of functioning (school, work, social and family interactions). At the root of this impairment is biological, psychological or behavioral dysfunction, or a combination of these (Canadian Psychiatric Association 1996).

The Canadian Mental Health Association (CMHA) exists to promote the mental health of Canadians, and employs an increasing number of social workers. Each year, CMHA provides direct service to more than 100,000 Canadians through the combined efforts of more than 10,000 volunteers and staff in locally run organizations in all provinces and territories, with branches in more than 135 communities. Each region, city or province has a CMHA that has social workers providing services to the local community. All CMHA mental health projects are based on principles of empowerment, peer and family support, participation in decision making, citizenship and inclusion in community life.

AIDS IN CANADA

Since the beginning of the HIV epidemic in Canada, there has been a steady decline in the proportion of gay men among new infections, from over 80% during 1981-83 to 29.5% in 1996. Recently, there has been a sharp increase in the proportion of injection drug users (IDU) among new infections, from less than 10% before 1986 to 24% in 1987-90 and to 46.9% in 1996.

There were an estimated 4,600 women living with HIV infection at the end of 1996 and women were estimated to comprise 22.6% of new HIV infections in Canada in 1996, an increase from less than 10% before 1986 and 14% in 1987-90.

Source: Health Canada, *HIV/AIDS epi Update* (2000) Available on-line at: http://www.hc-sc.gc.ca/hpb/lcdc/bah/epi

Social workers in CMHA-run programs assist with employment, housing, early intervention for youth, peer support and recreation services for people with mental illness, stress reduction workshops and public education campaigns for the community. In addition, social workers act as advocates to encourage public action and commitment towards strengthening community mental health services and legislation and policies affecting services.

• Social Work and HIV/AIDS

The human immunodeficiency virus (HIV) is a sexually transmitted and blood-borne retrovirus that undermines a person's immune system. AIDS is the final stage of HIV in which the immune system is destroyed. Health Canada reports that at the end of 1996, an estimated 40,100 Canadians were living with HIV infection (including those living with AIDS). During 1996, there were an estimated 4,200 new HIV infections in Canada.

HIV/AIDS has been identified as the leading contemporary global health concern. Estimates by the Joint United Nations Programme on HIV/AIDS (UNAIDS) and the World Health Organization (WHO) indicate that, by the beginning of 1998, over 30 million people had been infected with HIV and 11.7 million people around the world had already lost their lives to the disease. The virus is reported to be spreading, with nearly 16,000 new infections a day. In 2000, one in every 100 adults in the most sexually active age bracket (ages fifteen to forty-nine) was living with HIV. However, only a tiny fraction are aware that they have been infected. As people can live for many years before showing any sign of illness, the HIV virus can spread undetected (UNAIDS/WHO 1998).

People diagnosed with HIV/AIDS face a great many difficult issues. Upon detection of HIV or AIDS, an individual must first deal with the illness itself and his or her own possibly impending death. He or she must also confront social and economic problems, such as dealing with social stigma, rejection by friends and relatives, maintaining a work life, health insurance and medication costs, and maintaining interpersonal relationships. Women face special challenges as often services do not exist for them and they frequently must deal with child care concerns.

The services that social workers deliver for people with HIV/AIDS include public education and prevention initiatives, primary care, hospital care, home care, hospice care, support groups, family support and advocacy. Social workers provide information and education, form support groups, make referrals to community resources and prepare discharge plans.

In a hospital setting, social workers play a pivotal role as part of the health care team. In many cases, the social worker is the only person in the hospital who deals with non-medical or non-physical needs. Generally, a social worker will meet with a person with HIV/AIDS, dealing with his or her social, emotional, spiritual and economic needs. They also work with family members and friends to provide both information and support.

TEP Photo Archives, Toronto.

Most public hospitals employ social workers full time to work with other health care practitioners in alleviating the demands on a seriously underfunded medical care system across the country.

• Addictions and Social Work

The treatment of addictions is a growing concern of governments. **Addiction** can be defined as a compulsive need for, or persistent use of, a substance known to be harmful. For example, nearly one in ten adult Canadians (9.2 percent) have problems with excessive alcohol consumption. Others experience problems with narcotics, tranquilizers, sleeping pills, cocaine, LSD and cannabis. A review of addictions in Canada is provided in *Canadian Profile*, published jointly in 1999 by the Canadian Centre on Substance Abuse and the Centre for Addiction and Mental Health (see http://www.ccsa.ca). There are hundreds of treatment programs across Canada, with twenty-four in the Ottawa area alone.

Social workers are at the forefront in developing innovative ways to help people with addictions. Increasingly social workers in addictions treatment programs are taking a **harm-reduction approach** instead of an abstinence approach to treatment. Just over one-half of the Ottawa area programs, for example, list abstinence as their treatment goal, while the other agencies list reduced consumption as the treatment goal. The

REFERENCES

- Albrecht, Dennise, and Patrick Lapointe. 1995. Community Health Centres in Canada: In a Land of Opportunities and Threats. Paper presented to the International Conference on Community Health Centres, Dec. 3-6.

- Angus, Douglas E., and Pran Manga. 1990. Co-op/Consumer Sponsored Health Care Delivery Effectiveness. Ottawa: Canadian Co-operative Association.

- Armstrong, Pat. 1997. Privatized Care. In Pat Armstrong et al., eds., Medical Alert. Toronto: Garamond Press.

- Assembly of First Nations. 1999. First Nations Health Priorities 2001-2002. Ottawa: AFN.

- Assembly of First Nations. 2000. First Nations Health Priorities 2001-2002. Ottawa: AFN.

- Canadian Centre on Substance Abuse. 1999. Canadian Profile: Alcohol, Tobacco and Other Drugs. Ottawa: Canadian Centre on Substance Abuse and the Centre for Addiction and Mental Health.

- Canadian Health Coalition. 2000. Health Alert: Newsletter 2000. Ottawa. Available at: http://www.healthcoalition.ca

- Canadian Psychiatric Association. 1996. Mental Illness and Work. Ottawa.

- Center for Health Program Studies. 1998. For Our Patients, Not for Profits: A Call to Action, Chartbook and Slideshow. The Center for Health Program Studies, Harvard Medical School/The Cambridge Hospital.

- Clarke, Juanne. 1990. Health, Illness and Medicine in Canada. Toronto: McClelland and Stewart Inc.

- Cumming, M.M. 1985. An Historical Review of Medical Insurance Legislation in Canada and the Effects of Dominant Ideology. Unpublished Master's Thesis, Carleton University School of Social Work, Ottawa.

- Evans, Robert G. 1998. Health Care Reform: Who's Selling the Market, and Why? Journal of Public Health Medicine 19, no.1: 45-49.

- Federal, Provincial, and Territorial Advisory Committee on Population Health. 1996. Report on the Health of Canadians. Ottawa.

latter is consistent with a harm-reduction approach, which seeks to minimize or reduce the adverse consequences of drug use.

Social workers using a harm-reduction approach believe that people can overcome an addiction in incremental steps and be successful. The focus may be on safer use patterns rather than on immediate deterrence of use. This approach overcomes the assumption that those who unwilling to abstain are not worthy of help, and those who do not abstain are failures. The harm-reduction approach is concerned with being non-judgmental and increasing the individual's health and well-being.

FIRST NATIONS HEALTH

As noted earlier, the federal government through Health Canada has a special responsibility for the delivery of health care services to First Nations and Inuit communities. They are obligated through treaties to fund 100 percent of the cost of First Nations health care.

The Aboriginal population in Canada is quite varied, with numerous distinct cultural and political organizational structures, each with unique concerns and needs. In general, poverty and a lack of economic and educational opportunity have severely affected the health of the Aboriginal population. The health status of Aboriginal people is much worse than that of the average Canadian, and the Assembly of First Nations (AFN) states that the health gap between First Nations people and the general population is widening.

While health care services have eased this situation somewhat, they have also contributed to the gradual erosion of traditional Aboriginal holistic approaches to health and healing. The Assembly of First Nations Health Secretariat, AFN National First Nations Health Technicians Network (NFNHTN) and the AFN Chiefs Committee on Health (CCOH) have identified seven health priorities: sustainability, health research, jurisdictional issues, mental health, children's health/gender health, smoking, and environmental health and infrastructure (Assembly of First Nations 2000).

Generally, First Nations leaders wish to see an integrated, holistic, interdepartmental and interorganizational strategy to address the inequities in health and social service delivery. They also believe that jurisdictional issues between the federal and provincial governments with respect to responsibility for First Nations health care need to be removed, particularly in light of provincial health care reform. They also support the Canadian public's demands to save Medicare and eliminate the widening health status gap between First Nations and the general population (Assembly of First Nations 2000).

An example of a new program that is meeting the health care needs of First Nations is Aboriginal Head Start (AHS). AHS projects typically provide half-day pre-school experiences that prepare Aboriginal children for their school years by meeting their spiritual, emotional, intellectual and physical needs. Aboriginal Head Start projects are run by locally managed Aboriginal non-profit organizations that see the parent and/or caregiver as the natural advocate of the child.

CONCLUSION

The *Canada Health Act* (CHA) of 1984 is the foundation of the Canadian health system. The CHA establishes the federal government's commitment to transfer money to each province and territory in Canada to enable them to deliver universal, accessible, comprehensive, portable and publicly administered health insurance. Public concern was recently heightened, however, when in 1996 the federal government substantially reduced the funding transferred to the provinces, and some provincial governments began to look favourably on private hospital administration and user fees.

Recent provincial trends indicate that equal access to the same health care services is diminishing and that the gap between the rich and poor is increasing. Several provinces are trying to move towards user fees, extra billing and the privatization of some services. This movement has the potential to lead to a two-tier health care system in Canada. The experience in the U.S. shows us that this type of system increases the disparity between the rich and poor and leads to a more costly, wasteful and inefficient system of delivery.

On a positive note, our current socialized system is enabling all provinces to shift away from an emphasis on health treatment towards a more comprehensive and integrated view of health. All levels of government are looking at ways to adapt our current system. The emphasis within the health care system on institutionally based delivery models (i.e., physicians and hospital-based care) is moving increasingly towards community-based models that focus on health promotion and prevention. Social workers are often at the forefront in advocating for, and providing, primary, community-based and preventive health care.

In the health field, social workers work in a variety of capacities. While the primary setting for medical social work is the hospital, social workers also provide direct services in community centres, specialized facilities and alternative care settings. While social workers in hospitals frequently feel that their role is not respected, it is fast becoming more central as health care becomes more holistic in its approach. A holistic approach to care includes not only the physical aspects of health that are commonly addressed by physicians, but also the social, cultural, mental and spiritual aspects of the patient. The wide skill set of social workers ensures that they will be invaluable as part of multidisciplinary and holistic health care teams in Canadian health care settings.

- Federal, Provincial, and Territorial Advisory Committee on Population Health. 1999. *Toward a Healthy Future: Second Report on the Health of Canadians.* Ottawa. Available at: http://hc-sc.gc.ca

- Health Canada. 1997. *National Health Expenditures in Canada, 1975-1996: Fact Sheets.* Ottawa.

- Health Canada. 2000. *Canada's Health Care System.* Available at: http://www.hc-sc.gc.ca

- National Council of Welfare. 1990a. *Health Care Report.* Ottawa.

- National Council of Welfare. 1990b. *Achieving Health for All.* Ottawa.

- UNAIS/WHO. 1998. *Report on the Global HIV/AIDS Epidemic* (June).

- Vayda, Eugene, and Raisa B. Deber. 1995. The Canadian Health Care System: A Developmental Overview. In R.B. Blake and J. Keshen, eds., *Social Welfare Policy in Canada: Historical Readings* (pp.311-325). Toronto: Copp Clark Ltd.

CHAPTER 7: SOCIAL WORK AND HEALTH

Key Concepts

- Health gap
- Universal public health care
- Pre-payment health plans
- Medicare
- Public administration
- Comprehensiveness
- Universality
- Portability
- Accessibility
- Extra-billing
- User fees
- Two-tier health system
- Contracting out
- Privatization
- Cost containment
- Preventive medicine
- Community health centres
- Medical social work practice
- Holistic approach to health care
- Mental Illness
- Addiction
- Harm-reduction approach

Discussion Questions

1. What is the "health gap" in Canada and why should we be concerned about it?
2. Canada's health care system is publicly financed but largely privately delivered. Explain.
3. What are the five fundamental principles of Canada's health care system?
4. What do you think about user fees and extra billing?
5. What are some signs that the universal public health care is being eroded in Canada?
6. What are some of the arguments against a private health care system based on the model in the United States?
6. How can governments continue to finance universal medical care in an "era of constraint"? What alternatives are there to cutbacks and privatization in health care?
7. What are some the key challenges facing medical social workers today?

Websites

- **Health Canada on-line**
  http://www.hc-sc.gc.ca
  Health Canada is the federal department responsible for helping the people of Canada maintain and improve their health.

- **Canadian Health Network**
  http://www.canadian-health-network.ca
  The Canadian Health Network (CHN) is a national, bilingual Internet-based health information service. Through CHN, the Canadian public and health intermediaries alike can find excellent resources provided by health information providers across Canada.

- **Canadian Health Coalition**
  http://www.healthcoalition.ca
  The Canadian Health Coalition is dedicated to preserving and enhancing Canada's public health system for the benefit of all Canadians. Founded in 1979, the coalition includes groups representing unions, seniors, women, students, consumers and health care professionals from across Canada.

- **World Health Organization (WHO)**
  http://www.who.int
  World Health Organization (WHO) is an agency of the United Nations and is based in Geneva. WHO was established in 1948 and is "the directing and coordinating authority on international health work." WHO is responsible for helping all peoples to attain "the highest possible levels of health." In 1987 the organization had 166 member countries. Dr. Gro Harlem Brundtland took office as Director-General of the World Health Organization on 21 July 1998. Her term of office is five years.

Social Work with Women

A Feminist Approach

As with other approaches to social work, feminist social work practice seeks to understand a client's situation by acquiring knowledge of the client's history, family and social relations, and cultural context. However, in analyzing individual problems and working out effective interventions, the feminist approach gives greater emphasis to the harmful role of patriarchal relations within the family and within the wider society.

One of the defining social characteristics of the second half of the twentieth century was the increased labour force participation of women. Indeed, the participation rate for Canadian women more than doubled over the thirty-year period from 1961 (29 percent) to 1991 (60 percent). The social implications of this economic fact were phenomenal (Gunderson 1998). Among other things, it gave rise to the dominance of the two-earner family. It precipitated a marked increase in the demand for child care, part-time work and flexible work arrangements, and in pressure for legislation that would foster and ensure equality between men and women. What feminist author Betty Friedan referred to in the 1950s as "the problem with no name" very soon received a name and a solution—women's inequality and women's liberation.

This chapter begins by looking briefly at the important role women have played in the history of Canadian social work. It reviews the current economic context and the serious individual and social problems inherent in a society organized along patriarchal lines. Finally, it outlines the main principles of the "feminist approach" to social work practice and the role of social workers in dealing with key problems faced by women in Canadian society today.

SOCIAL WORK BEGINNINGS

In Canada, the movement for greater participation of women in public life arose at the end of the nineteenth century. It had a number of major strands, including the temperance movement, women's missionary and charitable activities, and the suffragette movement. The temperance movement focused on the abolition of alcohol (because of its devastating effects on male breadwinners and therefore on women and children); missionary and charitable activities were an opportunity for women to become involved in public life beyond their role as caregivers in the family; and the suffragette movement sought to establish the

Social problems are inevitable in patriarchal societies.

voting rights of women. Women became involved in the Women's Christian Temperance Union, the National Council of Women (founded by Lady Aberdeen), the Young Women's Christian Association (YWCA) and church missionary societies and charities, such as the Protestant Orphans Homes, homes for unmarried mothers, homes for the aged and settlement houses.

Women were also involved in campaigns to improve the conditions for nursing mothers through the provision of pure milk, in organizations that provided care for victims of tuberculosis and other illnesses, and in providing assistance to families of veterans during and after World War I. When the federal government agreed to pay an allowance to support the families of men who died in the war, a group of Manitoba women (including suffragette leader Nellie McClung) campaigned for a similar benefit for the widows and children of men who died in peacetime. The Mothers' Allowance established by the Manitoba government in 1916 was the first legislated welfare program, and it soon became available in all Canadian provinces.

These early women's organizations were the forerunners to the profession of social work. Participation in these organizations as well as in employment during the war in jobs vacated by men at the front led to an increased role for women in public life, and to the acquisition of the vote. Together these political and social changes opened the door for women who wanted to participate in public affairs.

Women in early social work were typically **maternal feminists**. They felt that women's nurturing and caring qualities and understanding of children were important in the reformation of society. The Child Welfare Council, for example, was composed of maternal feminists who entered social work because of their concern for families and mothers and poor children in particular. Although they brought women into public life and social work, these early maternal feminists now tend to be viewed as quite conservative, insofar as they supported more traditional conceptions of the family in which women were expected to stay in the home.

Given the expectations on women to maintain family life, it is not surprising that it was largely single women who sought employment in the social work field and in other professions. Moreover, at this time salaries were typically low in comparison to those of men with similar qualifications: "excluded in large part from the male-dominated fields of business, government, and the professions, a new generation of college-educated middle class women after the turn of the century, provided a large pool of available labour for the emerging fields of nursing, teaching, library science and social work (Struthers 1991, 128). Delegates to a 1929 conference on equal pay pointed out that "the same salary which will attract superior women will interest only mediocre men" (Ibid.).

The ensuing Depression of the 1930s, followed by World War II, did little to change this situation. It was only later, in the 1960s, that this began to change dramatically with the wholesale expansion of employment in the social services sector.

National Archives of Canada. Neg no. PA165610.

Many women perform double duty, at home and at work.

EQUAL PAY AND EMPLOYMENT EQUITY LEGISLATION

Although more and more Canadian women entered the labour force from the 1950s onward, they seldom did so on equal terms with men. The industries and occupations initially open to women were generally the less prestigious ones. Their incomes were far inferior to those of men in the same occupations, and justifications for this fundamental inequality seemed to be readily available. In addition to economic inequality, patriarchal family and social relations were still in force. In many households, women were expected to tend to their children, husband and household affairs as well as earn an income outside the home.

Nevertheless, there were many legislative changes and important policy initiatives in the post-war period that were aimed at fostering greater equality for women at work. These included: (1) equal pay policies (including pay equity or equal pay for work of equal value) designed to improve women's pay; (2) equal employment policies (including employment equity) designed to help women's employment and promotion opportunities; and (3) other facilitating policies (such as child care and parental leave) designed to put women on an equal footing with men in the labour market. (For a discussion of the women and the Canadian labour market, from which much of this information is derived, see Gunderson 1998.)

Equal-pay policies. During the 1950s and 1960s, every Canadian province enacted legislation requiring equal pay for similar or substantially similar work. During the 1970s, both Quebec and the federal government introduced pay equity legislation that required equal pay for work of equal value (allowing comparisons between occupations). In the 1980s, most other jurisdictions followed suit, at least with respect to public sector employment. In Ontario, most establishments are required to have a pay equity plan in place regardless of whether there has been a complaint, and this applies to both the private and public sector.

Equal employment and employment equity. All Canadian provinces now have equal employment opportunity legislation in place, usually as part of their human rights codes. This legislation prohibits discrimination on the basis of race, age, religion, nationality and sex. The prohibition of discrimination on the basis of sex was generally added during the 1960s and 1970s. Employment equity legislation, however, was not introduced in Canada until the 1980s. The first legislation took effect in 1986 and applied only to Crown corporations and federally regulated employers with 100 or more employees. In 1996, it was expanded to include the federal public service. Employment equity is also required of federal contractors. In Ontario, employment equity was legislated in 1994 but was repealed in 1995. Employment equity may also be required by cities and municipalities. Canadian research evidence as to the effect of employment equity legislation is thin, although what does exist suggests small improvements in occupational advancement and wages for women and visible minorities. One study, reported by Gunderson, found that only slightly more than one-third of firms where employment equity was required had effective procedures in place to administer the policy (Gunderson 1998).

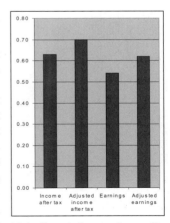

Male-Female income inequality index (Statistics Canada, 1997).

Facilitating programs. Many other changes have been introduced to help put Canadian women on an equal footing with men in the labour market. These include changes in divorce laws, policies against sexual harassment at work, expanded maternity leave provisions, policies to protect part-time and temporary workers and policies designed to ensure women have equal access to higher education. Such policies have undoubtedly helped to equalize the situation for women, though there is still the overriding concern that women leave their places of work only to find that they have still to assume the main burden of work at home and in the family.

PERSISTENT PROBLEMS

While the new legislation and strategic policy initiatives have undoubtedly helped to improve the position of women in Canadian society, there is a growing realization that employment legislation in itself has not resolved many of the underlying problems. In many areas of economic and social life, women are still vulnerable. Gunderson lists some of these areas:

- *Poverty.* Women today constitute a substantial share of the working poor. This is in large part due to the high poverty rates of unattached women under sixty-five (38.5 percent, compared to 33.4 percent for men); unattached women sixty-five and older (42 percent, compared with 27.2 percent for men); and single mothers with children under eighteen (57.1 percent) (National Council of Welfare 1999, 98).

- *Part-time work.* Women still constitute a large proportion of part-time workers in Canada and as such are usually underpaid and particularly vulnerable in periods of economic downturn. There needs to be more protection put in place for part-time workers.

- *Minimum-wage legislation.* Since women are still most often found in minimum-wage jobs, they are obviously most in need of minimum-wage legislation. Minimum-wage laws are inconsistent across the country and minimum-wage levels are inadequate.

- *Public sector wage controls.* Because women are overrepresented in the public sector, wage controls for public sector workers have a disproportionate effect on women.

- *Day care.* Expansion of quality day care is obviously of enormous importance to working mothers. A national program of quality day care, along the lines of the plan in Quebec, is needed.

- *Free trade and globalization.* The era of globalization poses new threats to women, since competition from low-wage countries affects those concentrated in lower-wage jobs. These are legitimate concerns that have not yet become a major part of the "free trade" debate in this country.

- *Government pension programs.* As women often do not have private pension plans, and since their working careers are often interrupted, initiatives are needed to protect women in retirement.

Gender equality report
(Statistics Canada, 2000).

Table 8.1: Full-year Work as a Share of All Work in Selected Occupations

Occupation	Total	Male	Female
Total all occupations (economy-wide)	51.6%	57.6%	44.7%
Social service managers	71.8%	78.2%	68.1%
Social workers	63.5%	73.2%	60.4%
Family, marriage and related counsellors	52.8%	62.6%	48.8%
Probation officers and related	74.7%	77.8%	71.6%
Community and social service workers	51.0%	56.6%	49.0%
Head nurses	60.9%	68.6%	60.4%
Registered nurses	45.7%	62.7%	44.7%
Psychologists	50.0%	62.3%	42.7%
Secondary school teachers	67.2%	75.5%	59.1%
School and guidance counsellors	48.9%	58.5%	43.4%

Source: CASSW, *In Critical Demand: Social Work in Canada, Final Report* (Ottawa, 2001).

- *Occupational health and safety.* Legislation in this area is particularly important since a disproportionate number of women are employed by smaller, non-unionized establishments.
- *Recessions.* Economic downturns, seemingly inevitable under our economic system, disproportionately affect women since they tend to be typically "the last hired and first fired."
- *Unemployment insurance programs.* These programs can work against women in that longer eligibility periods make it difficult for them to collect unemployment insurance.

Despite all the changes in the area of pay equity and employment equity, there is a continuing need for social policy makers and social work practitioners to be aware of the economic problems women still face *as women.* These problems are widespread, persistent and undoubtedly factor into many problems social workers are likely to encounter in their practice.

SEXISM AND GENDER EQUALITY

Before going on, it may be useful to distinguish a number of key terms.

The two terms gender and sex are frequently used interchangeably. **Sex**, of course, identifies the biological differences between women and men. **Gender**, on the other hand, has come to refer to the characteristics that identify the social relations between men and women or the way that this relationship is socially constructed. Gender is a relational term similar to the concepts of class and race, and it is an analytical tool for understanding social relations and processes. *Gender equity* refers to the process or measures taken to compensate women for historical and social disadvantages they have suffered, which leads to gender equality.

In considering Canada's adherence to Articles 16 and 17 of the covenant, the United Nations concluded:

"The Committee notes with grave concern that with the repeal of CAP and cuts to social assistance rates, social services and programmes have had a particularly harsh impact on women, in particular single mothers."

Source: Report of the Committee on Economic, Social and Cultural Rights, United Nations, Concluding observations, Section 22 (1998).

Gender equality means that women and men live in an environment that affords them equal opportunity to realize full human rights, to contribute to national, political, economic, social and cultural development, and to benefit from the results. Gender equity and gender equality form the basis upon which the principles of a feminist social work practice are based.

Sexism refers to prejudice or discrimination based on a person's sex. It is a system of discriminatory interrelated physical and social controls, derogatory beliefs and institutional- and societal-level policies. Sexism can be both blatant and subtle; it can take the form of derogatory language and put-downs or result in the denial of job or career opportunities based on a person's sex. Sexism can be so extensive, commonplace and internalized that it is not initially visible. Acknowledging that sexism can and does have a significant impact on the daily lives of women in Canada can be a difficult process for many individuals. It is sometimes easier to accept traditional roles and norms, which are comfortably familiar. Sexism is rooted in the patriarchal family system.

Patriarchy literally means the "rule by the father" but, in a broader sense, it has come to mean the domination of society by men. Men are still the major stakeholders in Canadian society, men continue to be represented in higher numbers in positions of authority and male interests continue to take precedence over those of females. Given the deep-rootedness of the patriarchal family system—and with it sexism and gender inequality—the prospect of eradicating widespread sex discrimination in Canadian society may seem a little daunting. While one should not minimize the difficulties, it is important to note that great strides have already been made by the women's movement, particularly in the last period. The future looks brighter than ever and social workers and others have every reason to be optimistic as they join this struggle.

PRINCIPLES OF FEMINIST PRACTICE

Social work, like many other things, was greatly influenced by the women's movement of the 1960s. Many Canadian social work schools began looking at different ways to practice social work that addressed the concerns of the movement. Students began to voice concerns about clinical approaches to social work that were not seen as relevant to women issues, and did not fit in with what was happening in society. Students were demanding that social work schools look more critically at social problems and develop programs that would be more responsive to women's issues.

The early feminist movement dramatically changed social work education and practice. Feminist theories offered different ways of seeing (or asking questions) and of understanding women's lives and experiences, the nature of inequality between the sexes and gender relations in society. Feminist therapy, for example, has its origins in the women's liberation movement of the 1960s and 1970s – women's **consciousness-raising groups** began to question gender-based roles and power relations in Canadian society. By sharing their experiences, they began to understand how each woman's experience was not unique but shared a common ground with those of other women. In a manner often similar to structural social work, feminist therapy holds that theories of human behaviour must be understood within the broader social context.

There are different definitions of feminism and numerous formulations and debates in **feminist theory**. There is, however a common core theory asserting that sex-role stereotypes and social structures perpetuate women's subordination. Feminist principles and concepts are similar to those of social work practice, such as the empowerment of the individual and examining society through a critical lens. Several of the principles are common to social work in general; egalitarian client-therapist relations and working at both the individual and social levels are key elements, although to varying degrees.

In the book *Feminist Practice in the 21st Century*, Helen Land, a University of Southern California professor and accomplished feminist clinical practitioner, discusses the following thirteen components of **feminist social work practice**:

- *Validating the social context.* Feminist therapists emphasize the effects of social context or structures on the difficulties of the client as the client and the worker jointly assess them.

- *Re-valuing positions enacted by women.* Social workers see the activities and stances assumed by women, such as nurturing, co-operating and caregiving, as vitally important and valuable. Society and mainstream psychotherapies, on the other hand, are viewed as placing more value on the activities of men, such as competition and upward mobility.

- *Recognizing difference in male and female experience.* Feminist social workers suggest that, to understand the emotional worlds of women, therapists must understand how the oppressive structures in society affect women. They maintain that mainstream theories are gender-blind and ignore the different experiences of women and men.

- *Re-balancing perceptions of normality and deviance.* The need for re-balancing perceptions of normality refers to the belief "that behaviour which is conceived as being dysfunctional or deviant by our society often reflects behaviour of less-privileged groups, such as women, people of colour, poor people, older people, and gay men and lesbians" (p.6).

- *Inclusive stance.* This stance enables feminist counsellors to challenge narrow assumptions, and to include the experiences and values of all people regardless of ethnicity, class, sexual orientation, age or ability.

- *Attention to power dynamics in the therapeutic relationship.* This aspect ensures that the therapist works towards an egalitarian relationship between client and worker. This is seen to empower or increase the client's strength for self-advocacy.

- *Recognizing how the personal is political.* This important component acknowledges that personal difficulties faced by clients (and workers) may reflect an historical and political context, which is gener-

PART-TIME WORKERS

An increasing number of young men and women are working part time, usually because they cannot find full-time employment. Nearly 43% of young workers had part-time jobs in 1994, up from 30% a decade earlier. Among young women, the rate rose from 34% to 48%; for young men, the rate increased from 27% to 38%.

In the social work field, full-year, full-time work as a percentage of all work is as follows:

- Social Workers, 63.5% (Males, 73.2%; Females, 60.4%)
- Community & Social Service Worker, 51.0% (Males, 56.6%; Females, 49.0%)

Source: CASSW, *In Critical Demand*, p.40.

ally called patriarchy. Patriarchy can be defined as social relations in society whereby men maintain control and authority over women's lives.

- *Deconstructive stance.* The deconstructive stance attempts to uncover and examine how social relations of patriarchy maintain the male-dominated world. The therapist continually questions dominate notions of what is right and wrong, normal and abnormal.

- *Partnering stance.* This stance asserts that disclosure about personal experiences by a therapist is helpful to a client, especially if common experience is apparent. This aspect is contrary to traditional psychotherapy, which holds that professional distance is preferred.

- *Inclusive scholarship.* In challenging the traditional notions of objective science, feminist scholarship frequently emphasizes both qualitative (such as interviews or case studies) and quantitative (numerical frequencies and statistics) research methods. As well, it stresses beginning with women's experience and what actually happens in the world, rather than with abstract theoretical models that claim to represent reality.

- *Challenging reductionist models.* "Reductionist" refers to the practice of reducing gender-based behaviours to simple cause-and-effect models, which stereotype and limit our understanding. For example, there is the stereotype of women as being naturally more emotional, and men, more objective. The feminist social worker would challenge these reductionist models.

- *Empowerment practice.* Empowerment practice means that the worker and client develop goals together, with the focus on empowering the client to change structures and environments rather than on helping the client adapt to, and cope with, oppressive structures.

- *Myth of value-free psychotherapy.* Feminist therapists reject the idea that a person can be value-free in their practice and believe that the therapist must be explicit about her own biases and values. As well, they would assist the client in discovering and taking ownership of their own values.

Regardless of the approach to social work one chooses, these components of feminist social work practice offer a way of seeing and understanding women's lives that will aid both in helping individual clients and in changing structures and policies in Canadian society that shape inequality and oppression.

FEMINIST PRINCIPLES IN PRACTICE

Incorporating feminist principles into one's social work practice is not an easy task. To begin, it is important to value women's experience and identity, and recognize that women have been socially subjected to unfounded negative stereotypes. Myths, such as "women are the weaker

National Archives of Canada. Neg no. PA112749.

Women have been relegated to less-skilled, part-time jobs.

sex" and "a woman is nothing without a man," must be rejected, and the strength of women and the positive aspects of women's traits must be stressed. Social workers who incorporate these principles value the diverse experience of all their clients, women and men.

In addition, social work informed by feminist principles identifies power differences and examines how this affects both the therapeutic relationship and the client's life, thereby linking the personal and political. A worker may use "how" questions to assist clients in relating lived experience, facts and context. For example, while a client is recounting a bad experience, the worker may ask, "How does this experience relate to the fact that you are black or a woman?" or "How is your situation similar to that of other women?" This type of question may help a client analyze their situation or experience.

Identifying and critically analyzing behaviours, rather than interpreting and labeling them, enables women to replace powerlessness and helplessness with strength and determination. This feedback allows women to check the validity of their observations and challenge those they see as inaccurate. This in turn fosters self-esteem and an egalitarian client-therapist relationship. Another process that encourages self-esteem and egalitarianism is worker self-disclosure. The sharing of relevant personal information with a client on the part of the social worker allows the client to see that they have a common experience of oppression and face many of the same problems. This helps women to differentiate between individual and social problems and thereby eliminates some of their self-blame. Listening and validating the experiences of women is one of the most important aspects of applying feminist principles. No one except the woman who has experienced the events of her life can really know what it was like. This voicing of her experiences begins the process of healing.

A short illustration may demonstrate how feminist principles can be incorporated into social work practice. A feminist understanding of violence against women has dramatic implications for practice. Social workers who work with abused women generally consider not only individual or inner factors but also the community and environment in which the client lives. Any worker would consider the safety of the woman and ensure that they met in a safe place. The feminist social worker, however, would add the principles discussed above to inform a practice that recognizes the social context of the violence. It is understood that an abused woman may feel alone—she may feel that she is the only one in the world who is abused. She may not have a telephone because the batterer has ripped it from the wall. She may be prohibited from having friends or leaving the house or seeing relatives. All these factors can be seen as part of the power that a man within our society can exert over a woman. The feminist social worker would also emphasize that institutional and social change are required. Not only service deficiencies would be addressed, but also the assumptions and views held by society that perpetuate the dominance of women by men. This may involve linking together women with common experience or supporting the efforts of a women's advocacy group.

Feminist social workers often work with women who have been abused, partly because of the extent of the problem and partly because their training often equips them to help. Social workers drawing from feminist principles will avoid blaming the woman or looking for weaknesses or pathologies within the woman to explain the violence. They will avoid minimizing or ignoring the responsibility of the violent partner for his actions, or overlooking the social values and institutions that condone violence against women and children. This approach is perhaps best illustrated by social work practice as it is implemented at **transition houses** for battered women and their children. Transition houses are responsive to the needs of the abused woman and her children, are sensitive to the power relations within traditional family structures and emphasize social change. Because of their success, the number of transition houses or shelters is growing. A total of 90,792 women and children were admitted to 413 shelters for battered women across Canada in 1997-98 (Trainor 1999, 1). While they are becoming a primary resource for women and their children, they face serious funding problems.

Social workers who work with women and who are influenced by feminist principles often include community work in their practice. In their work with women with disabilities, social workers realized that, in order to counter barriers faced by women, they needed to link with other organizations. Women with disabilities had formed their own organization, the Disabled Women's Network (DAWN), and social workers soon learned that an important component of their work was to support the efforts of such groups. Rather than advocating for each individual woman, feminist social workers discovered that they could be more effective by linking and supporting groups that advocate for themselves.

Male social workers can also incorporate feminist principles into their practice. Male practitioners working with the New Directions program in Ottawa, for example, use feminist principles to help men who have abused women in relationships. The program attempts to help the men take responsibility for their abusive behaviour and to view it within the context of a male-dominated society. This involves helping the men to see their behaviour within its political context. The history of abuse that many of the men have experienced is also addressed and common experience between the men is explored.

There are obviously many occasions when it is more appropriate that a female worker, rather than a male, works with women in need. For example, when working with women who have been sexually abused or raped, the presence of a male social worker is clearly not appropriate. It is generally recognized that women should counsel such victims. This work normally takes place in settings such as rape crisis centers and women's shelters.

One of the first items of attention for the social worker on these occasions is to determine the current danger to the woman. Following this, social workers provide a rage of services, including twenty-four-hour crisis lines, accompaniment to the hospital, police station or court, individual counselling, group counselling, social and political action to raise awareness of conditions that perpetuate violence against women,

National Archives of Canada. Neg no. PA149410.

Federated Women's Institutes of Canada delegates, 1957.

advocacy, information and referrals, and self-defence training. Female social workers who do this type of work not only need knowledge of feminist principles but also specialized knowledge regarding women's issues and the facilities that are available in the community.

Social workers must keep case records or written documents that detail the client's situation, the intervention and the outcomes. However, practitioners who follow feminist principles and who work with abused women increasingly find the requirements of case records to be troublesome; they find it difficult to keep accurate records that might be used against a woman if a defence lawyer subpoenaed them. Bill C-46, the Rape Shield Law, is intended to protect women from character attacks by defence lawyers and restricts the questioning of women regarding their sexual histories. To compensate for this restriction, lawyers are subpoenaing women's counselling and medical records. Social workers need to be mindful of this when writing case notes. One worker stated that, when she is writing case notes, she assumes that a judge is looking over one of her shoulders and the client is looking over the other. Social workers must be careful not to write items that might be misinterpreted. Subjective comments and judgements should be avoided.

Social work practitioners who work with women need to understand the full range of factors that shape a woman's life, such as her economic, social and legal circumstances. For example, issues such as poverty, abuse, pregnancy and child care are often raised within women's addiction treatment services. Specialized programs may be offered for lesbians, such as those offered at the Centre for Addiction and Mental Health in Toronto. The Amethyst Women's Addiction Centre in Ottawa provides a four-phase program for women addicted to alcohol or other drugs. It provides assessment, pre-treatment involving individual counselling and weekly groups, an intensive ten-day treatment including group therapy and/or education and a two-year follow-up service. Individual and group support for problem gambling is also available. In these programs, social workers focus on creating a supportive environment and address the difficulties, other than addiction, faced by the woman.

It is important for social workers to help empower the women with whom they work. This may involve sharing relevant personal information with the client or may involve all-women group work that helps women share and understand the experiences that have influenced them as women. Empowerment takes place in many social service agencies. Child protection agencies throughout Canada generally provide support services for single mothers and seek to empower them. Such services are frequently offered only when the agency believes that a child may be at risk of abuse, but several agencies are providing early support services for specific groups, such as teen mothers. Generally, family support workers develop interventions that will help the parents make the changes necessary for the safety and well-being of their children. These interventions may include providing parents with knowledge of and support with home management, family life routines, bonding and attachment, parenting skills, constructive discipline techniques, family communication and access to community resources. Feminist social

PROMOTING GENDER EQUALITY

In 1995, the federal government adopted a policy requiring federal departments and agencies to conduct a gender-based analysis of future policies and legislation, where appropriate. *Gender-based Analysis: A Guide for Policy Makers* is a "hands-on" working document developed by Status of Women Canada to assist in the implementation of this government-wide policy.

The guide details how government policies and social programs can be analyzed to ensure that they promote gender equality. It is available on-line at: http://www.swc-cfc.gc.ca/pube.html

workers may use self-disclosure and all-women groups to develop a sense of solidarity and empowerment, and emphasize treating mothers with respect.

Social work with homeless women may use both the micro and macro practice skills of feminist social work. Shelters for homeless women exist in most Canadian urban centres. Social workers provide food, shelter and supportive counselling on an emergency basis. Women are provided with a safe, supportive place in which to identify their needs and develop a plan to achieve their goals. Social workers in these settings offer crisis, short-term, individual and group counselling; assessment and referrals; programming services; food and health services; and housing support. A needle exchange, computers and telephones are also available. Feminist social workers would use their macro skills to lobby government for housing and employment, or to help women's groups to organize and gain power over their own lives.

VIOLENCE AGAINST WOMEN

In 1867, the year of Canada's confederation, wife abuse was written into the English Common Law. According to the law, it was acceptable for a man to beat his wife with a whip or stick as long as it was no bigger than the circumference of his thumb (hence, some say, the phrase "rule of thumb"). Upon marriage, a woman became the property of her husband, and her husband then owned all of her assets. There was little or no recourse under the law for assaults against her person. The *Married Woman's Property Act* was enacted in England in 1870, which emancipated the wife and gave her control over her own property. Ontario granted this right to women in 1872.

It was not until the early twentieth century that women were recognized as having legal rights and were able to vote. The **suffragette movement** campaigned for the right for all women to have the right to vote. Most Canadian women were given the right to vote between 1916 and 1922. Those who resided in Quebec did not receive the right to vote until 1940. The status quo prevailed regarding domestic violence; what happened behind closed doors was considered to be nobody else's business. Police were reluctant to respond to calls of domestic dispute, and the courts did not take the matter seriously. As a result, many domestic disputes were not reported to the authorities. It was not until the 1980s that mandatory charging policies took effect across Canada. Formal training was established in Canadian police forces to assist officers in determining a proper course of action when responding to domestic disputes, as well as to help them recognize chargeable assaults.

• Statistics on the Abuse of Women

Many feminist social workers take exception to the phrase "family violence"; they believe it glosses over the fact that it is usually men who are violent against women, and not a family who is violent. Statistics Canada reports that the rate of violence experienced in a marriage or common-law relationship is 8 percent for women and 7 percent for men

(Statistics Canada 2000, 5), though social workers in the field generally believe this to be a dramatic underestimation. Women and men also report very different forms of violence. Women in violent relationships are more likely to report more severe forms of violence—for example, women are more than twice as likely as men to report being beaten (25 percent verses 10 percent) and five times more likely to report being choked (20 percent verses 4 percent). Men, on the other hand, are more likely to report being slapped or having something thrown at them. Unfortunately, Statistics Canada combines these very different "forms of violence" into one statistic. Between 1978 and 1997, 1,485 women and 442 males in Canada were killed by their spouses (National Clearinghouse on Family Violence 2001).

Other figures indicate that about 29 percent of women married or living in a common-law relationship are likely to be abused (Rodgers 1994). The National Clearinghouse on Family Violence reports that nearly 22 percent of the women who experienced violence never told anyone about the abuse. Evidence also shows that the period immediately following her departure is the most dangerous for a woman who is leaving an abusive relationship and that women are more at risk of being murdered or experiencing severe violence at this point than at any other. Several attempts at violence might be made before a final separation results. From 1974 to 1992, a married woman was nine times more likely to be murdered by her partner than by a complete stranger.

• Explaining Violence against Women

Violence against a woman by a man is a social act, a behaviour for which the perpetrator is accountable to the community. A variety of theories have been advanced to explain why this phenomenon occurs in Canadian society. Each of these attempts to conceptualize violence against women contains a great deal of truth, and any social work assessment of a situation of violence by a man against a woman needs to consider the following major theories: power theory, learning theory, anger-control theory and cycle-of-violence theory.

Power theory. This theory argues that wife abuse is a societal problem that occurs because of the power imbalance between men and women, specifically, because of the dominance of men and men's roles. Wife abuse continues because there has been historical acceptance of abuse and of men's right to control women, even by force. This theory maintains that society must change its attitudes, values and responses with respect to women if wife abuse is to be prevented. This theory is consistent with a structural or feminist approach to social work.

Learning theory. The main idea behind this theory is that violence is a behaviour learned in childhood. Boys learn that it is okay to be violent, and girls learn that it is okay to be on the receiving end of violence—this is what relationships are about. This theory holds that all children in our society are socialized to accept violence and that this, coupled with the different roles into which boys and girls are socialized, supports and perpetuates abuse. Children who witness violence in the home are much

MYTHS AND FACTS ABOUT FAMILY VIOLENCE

MYTH. Family violence occurs most often in lower-income families.

FACT: Family violence is not related to economic status or to ethnic, racial, social or particular age groups. Family violence cuts across all age and social boundaries.

MYTH. Family violence is only about physical abuse.

FACT: Family violence includes physical and sexual assault, emotional and psychological abuse, intimidation, neglect and financial and personal exploitation. Abuse may result in injury or significant emotional or psychological harm.

MYTH. People who are abusive are "mentally ill."

FACT: People try to explain or excuse family violence by saying abusers are "mentally ill." This implies that abusers are not responsible for their actions. People who work with family violence problems say that most abusers are not mentally ill. They take advantage of a power imbalance to hurt and control others.

———

Source: Adapted from the National Clearinghouse on Family Violence, *Family Violence Awareness Information for People in the Workplace* (Ottawa: Health Canada, 2001).

THE GENERATIONAL CYCLE OF VIOLENCE

Some research has suggested that witnessing violence against one's mother by one's father will increase the likelihood that a son may be violent towards his own spouse later in life (Rodgers 1994). The 1993 Violence Against Women Survey showed evidence to support the theory of the generational cycle of violence.

According to the survey, men who witnessed violence by their fathers were three times more likely than men without these childhood experiences to be violent towards their wives. The VAWS also found that in 39% of violent relationships, children witnessed the violence.

more likely to become abusers or be abused. The emphasis here is on changing the behaviour of the perpetrator.

Anger-control theory. This theory focuses on the idea that men must be held accountable for their violent behaviour. They must learn to deal with and control their anger and express it in more appropriate ways. This theory does not attempt to explain the root cause of wife abuse, and in that, it is different from the other two theories. Instead, it focuses on poor anger control—if men could control their anger, violence would stop. It is a changed-behaviour model. Within this theory, a criminalization and a punishment-based social work approach would be the most successful.

Cycle-of-violence theory. This theory does not explain why violence occurs; rather, it explains what happens in individual relationships in terms of a three-step process. First is the tension-building phase. In this phase, the woman sees that tension is building in the relationship and that there is going to be an explosion. The man is expressing more anger every day. He may be kicking the dog or yelling at the children. The second phase in the process involves an acute battering incident. The tension has reached a point where the violence erupts against the woman. She is abused, hit, bruised and battered. This is usually a shorter phase than the first, lasting from between two and twenty-four hours. The third phase is called the honeymoon period. In this phase, the man says he is sorry; he should not have done it; I love you; don't leave me; it will never happen again. The man will call relatives to ask them to convince the woman to return to him. If the woman has left during the second phase, she might return to him during this phase. Statistics show that a woman is usually abused and leaves many times before she leaves for the final time. The honeymoon period is a very powerful phase. Women want to believe that their partner has changed; they may also feel that it will be their fault if the marriage breaks down as they perhaps didn't work hard enough at the relationship. Some women stay for the sake of the children or believe that a bad marriage is better than no marriage at all. Statistics show that single mothers are among the poorest in our society, and this is where income security programs come into play.

These theories are useful in that they look at different aspects of the problem of violence against women. In one's daily practice, a concrete assessment that takes account of the specifics of the situation will always be needed so as to ensure that any intervention addresses the full range of possible solutions.

• What Is the Role of a Social Worker?

The role of social workers in helping abused women may include crisis intervention, support and empowerment, support group facilitation and the provision of information.

A social worker in a shelter will frequently be the first person a woman meets when she flees a violent situation. At this critical time, it may be necessary to discuss the cycle of violence and point out that the violence is likely to occur again. The social work process will be assisted by conveying the message that the violence is not her fault and that she is not the only woman to experience this kind of violence.

The social worker should ultimately support the woman in whatever decision she makes and provide her with the kind of support and education she needs to make a good decision. While it is very frustrating for a social worker to see a woman go back to an abusive relationship, sometimes several times, the worker must be sure not to take the power of decision away from the woman, as that has been her experience throughout her relationship. The social worker should empower the woman to make this important decision about her life.

Within this context, the social worker may partake in one or several of the following activities:

- Intervene in a crisis, which may involve the identification and assessment of danger to the women and her children;

- Facilitate an empowerment approach with the woman;

- Listen to what the woman has to say and empathetically respond, sharing one's personal experience if appropriate;

- Connect the woman to a support group of women who have had a common experience;

- Teach the woman how to assess the assault/homicide potential in domestic and other situations;

- Make an appropriate referral, for example, if the woman has immediate financial needs;

- Teach the woman how to recognize abuse, name the problem and its source and avoid self-blame;

- Advise the abused woman of her legal rights and link her to legal resources, thereby avoiding the traditional practice of "revictimization";

- Mobilize safety, legal and community resources effectively (e.g., linkage to a children's protective service, arranging admission to a shelter for abused women, finding a translator for an immigrant woman, linking a rape victim with an advocate, providing support for caregivers as a means of preventing abuse of home-bound older persons);

- Implement agency policy regarding mandated reporting and keep accurate records, including dental and other X-rays, as these can possibly aid later legal action;

- Use the consultative process (know whom to call under what circumstances, and do it) and review one's referrals and interventions with other health care providers;

- Complete the crisis management and follow-up referral or treatment steps while withholding judgement and the imposition of values on the woman and her significant others;

- Provide follow-up counselling to the woman and her assailant.

WHITE RIBBON CAMPAIGN

On December 6, 1989, a man walked into a classroom at Montreal's Ecole Polytechnique, ordered the men to leave, and proceeded to shoot and kill 14 women in what is now referred to as the Montreal Massacre.

In 1991, sparked by this horrifying event, a handful of men in Canada decided they had a responsibility to urge men to speak out against violence against women. They decided that wearing a white ribbon would symbolize this opposition.

The White Ribbon Campaign is the largest effort in the world of men working to end men's violence against women. In addition to wearing a white ribbon—the symbol of commitment to end violence against women—the campaign provides educational programs in high schools, community centres and workplaces, along with local shelters, help lines and other women's anti-violence programs.

POVERTY AMONG OLDER WOMEN

Poverty rates among older Canadian women in 1997:

- All women, 24%
- Women in families, 5.4%
- Unattached women, 49.1%

Source: Statistics Canada, *Income Distribution by Size in Canada, 1997*, Catalogue No. 13-207-XPB (Ottawa, 1999).

Support groups are frequently a key component of social work with abused women. Support groups can empower women in a number of ways: they help to reduce isolation and allow women to meet other women who share their experience; they can help women to develop an understanding of the power and control that are at the root of battering and learn what actions they can take to change the situation; they can be a forum for women to exchange information, practical help and emotional support; and they can allow women to explore their self-image and appreciate their own strengths and accomplishments.

OTHER AREAS OF SOCIAL WORK INTERVENTION

Violence against women is one of the main areas where social workers intervene directly on behalf of women in need. Three other areas are discussed briefly below: women in poverty, social work with older women, and women battling with HIV/AIDS.

• Women and Poverty

Mounting numbers of low-income women, and especially lone-parent mothers, are receiving social services across Canada. Indeed, the **feminization of poverty** has become a household term. Currently, almost 19 percent of adult women live below the Statistics Canada Low Income Cut-Off (Townson 2000, 1). Moreover, women appear to be falling further and further into poverty. There were a total of 93,000 lone-parent mothers with incomes of less than 50 percent of the poverty line in 1997. This was roughly double that of 47,000 in 1989, a year before the 1990-91 recession (National Council of Welfare 1999, 54).

In 1993, 81 percent of Canadian families with children under the age of seven living in poverty were headed by lone parent mothers; in other words, 60 percent of lone-parent mothers lived in low-income situations. Twenty-eight percent of visible minority women and 33 percent of Aboriginal women also lived in low-income situations (Hay 1997, 116).

In working with low-income women, social workers need to be aware that women's poverty is caused by different factors than men's poverty. Canadian studies have found that men's poverty is usually more directly related to low-wage employment, whereas women's poverty arises from additional factors such as divorce and separation, and their responsibilities as mothers, homemakers, caregivers and nurturers. Even though more and more women have paid employment, many are still dependent on the income of a spouse. This has led many women to conclude that they are "only one man away from welfare" (Townson 2000, 6).

Issues pertaining to gender inequality need to be addressed in order to tackle women's poverty in Canada. Beyond understanding the unique issues affecting low-income women, social workers should challenge governments at all levels to develop specific strategies to deal with women's employment, child care, old age security, family law, social assistance rates and general income security.

Because they tend to live longer and have lower income levels, Canadian women rely more heavily on home care services than men.

• Social Work with Older Women

Since a large proportion of the elderly population are women, social work with older adults is often considered a woman's issue. Such work is sometimes called **gerontological social work**. As the Canadian population ages, this field of practice is rapidly expanding. Twelve percent of Canada's current total population are seniors; by 2041, this will have risen to 23 percent. Practitioners in this field need specialized knowledge of health care issues, poverty, housing and mental health, including knowledge of the ageing process and the issues surrounding Alzheimer's disease.

Numerous social workers work with the elderly in home care, as a significant proportion of home care clients are seniors. **Home care** involves the provision of health-related care by one person to another in the client's home. Home care services generally include the provision of health services by two tiers of workers: *professionals,* such as social workers, physicians, nurses, physiotherapists, occupational therapists, speech therapists and dieticians, and *unregulated workers,* such as homemakers, personal support workers and personal care attendants.

Due to the ageing of the Canadian population and health reforms that emphasize keeping the elderly in their homes rather than in hospitals and other institutional settings, home care is becoming increasingly important as part of both the acute care system and the provision of care to those with long-term needs. However, home care has been unevenly developed across Canada and is not always accessible. In some provinces, such as Ontario, home care is increasingly being provided by large American health care corporations.

CARE BY DEFAULT, NOT BY DESIGN

A report card issued in August 2001 by Canada's Association for Retired Persons (CARP), entitled *Home Care by Default, Not by Design,* states that the responsibility for home care is being dumped by governments onto families, not-for-profit groups, volunteers and the private sector. Moreover, no improvement has been made since a similar CARP study in 1999.

Other key problem areas include the need for the development of a country-wide home care strategy, the lack of national standards, and difficulty attracting and retaining qualified staff.

CARP notes that the problems with home care will approach crisis proportion as Canada's population ages.

The home care report is available online at: http://www.50plus.com/carp

A progress report on home care in Canada.

Home care delivery falls within provincial jurisdiction. In Canada there are at least 663 agencies providing home care services, with 93 percent of delivery agencies receiving some government funding and just over 50 percent receiving all of their funding from government sources. The home care workforce is largely unregulated and largely composed of women. Many work part time and must hold multiple part-time jobs to make an adequate income. They receive few fringe benefits and career options within the field are few.

Many Canadian social workers are convinced that nothing short of a universal and comprehensive national home care system is necessary, since home care is not currently regulated by any provincial or federal legislation, nor is it included in the *Canada Health Act.* In 1997-98 Canada spent only 4 percent of total public health care dollars on home care. The piecemeal development of these services has left many women without programs that properly meet their physical, emotional and social needs.

In May 2001, the Canadian Health Coalition (CHC) released a research report exposing the federal government's role in shifting home care policy from health care to private industry. The report, entitled *Home Care: What We Have and What We Need,* is available on the CHC website at: http://www.healthcoalition.ca. In August 2001, a major report by Canada's Association for Retired Persons (CARP), the largest seniors' group, pointed out that home care is poorly funded and doesn't come close to meeting the needs of Canadians, despite government promises (see sidebar).

• Women and HIV/AIDS

More and more Canadian women are becoming infected with HIV, especially those who use injection drugs and whose sexual partners are at increased risk for HIV. Pregnant women are at risk of transmitting HIV to their unborn children. Detecting HIV infection before or during early pregnancy can reduce the likelihood of vertical transmission of HIV (from mother to infant) by up to two-thirds if the woman and her child are offered timely antiretroviral treatment.

The HIV/AIDS epidemic in Canada was initially concentrated among gay men. Since the mid-1980s, HIV/AIDS has increasingly affected other groups, such as injection drug users (IDUs), male heterosexuals and women. The total number of AIDS cases among adult women (delay adjusted) increased from an average of less than 10 cases per year in the early 1980s to an average of 143 cases in 1995-97. In addition, the proportion of AIDS cases in adult women has increased over time, particularly recently, from 5.2 percent of all AIDS cases before 1990 to 6.7 percent during 1990-1995, and 13.6 percent in 1996-97. The proportion of female AIDS cases attributed to injection drug use has increased sharply, from 6.4 percent before 1990 to 20 percent during 1990-95, and 23 percent in 1996-97 (Health Canada 1998).

All women, and especially women of childbearing age, should have access to HIV testing, counselling and care. Social work practitioners often provide counselling and are increasingly engaged in efforts to secure specific services for women affected by AIDS. The spread of AIDS to women is affecting the number of women who live in poverty, are homeless or are in violent relationships. Because social workers are at the front lines helping women in need, they are in an ideal position to address the AIDS problem.

CONCLUSION

The women's movement dramatically changed the status of women in Canadian society. Legislation and policies on employment equity, pay equity, abortion rights, discrimination in employment and education, and specialized health programs have been pursued—yet equality for women is still far from being achieved. Increasingly, women who are not attached to a man are poor. Women of colour and Aboriginal women are even poorer, and employed women are sex-segregated in low-wage jobs.

Social workers need to help women at both the personal and political level. In helping women deal with personal problems, social workers need to analyze the social and economic context of women's problems. The feminist approach emphasizes the harmful role of patriarchal relations within the family and within the wider society. The recognition that sex-role stereotypes and social structures perpetuate women's subordination also necessitates a response that addresses the institutions, structures and policies in Canadian society. Social workers should not minimize the importance of helping women deal with personal changes in their attitudes, behaviours and relationships, but workers also need to challenge the ways in which sexism supports oppression and inequality.

Since the early 1970s, social workers have been concerned with eliminating sexism from social work education and thereby enabling graduating social workers to work more effectively with women. Facts about the historical roots of patriarchy and gender inequality are generally woven into the curriculum, and feminist social work practice skills are increasingly taught in both core and specialized courses. Social workers need to continue to be aware of how sexism pervades practice, and understand the social, economic and cultural context of women's problems.

REFERENCES

- Canadian Health Coalition. 2001. *Home Care: What We Have and What We Need.* Prepared by Coleen Fuller. Ottawa. Available at: http://www.healthcoalition.ca

- Gunderson, Morley. 1998. *Women and the Canadian Labour Market: Transitions Towards the Future.* Ottawa/Toronto: Statistics Canada/ITP Nelson.

- Hay, D. 1997. Campaign 2000: Child and Family Poverty in Canada. In J. Pulkingham and G. Ternowetsky, eds., *Child and Family Policies: Struggles, Strategies and Options.* Halifax: Fernwood Publishing.

- Health Canada. 1998. *HIV and AIDS in Canada: Surveillance Report to December 31, 1997.* Ottawa: Health Canada, Division of HIV/AIDS Surveillance.

- Land, Helen. 1995. Feminist Clinical Social Work in the Twenty-first Century. In Nan Van Den Bergh, ed., *Feminist Practice in the 21st Century.* New York: NASW Press.

- National Clearinghouse on Family Violence. 2001. *Family Violence in Canada: Facts.* Ottawa: Health Canada. Available at: http://www.hc-sc.gc.ca/hppb/familyviolence/family.htm

- National Council of Welfare. 1999. *Poverty Profile 1997.* Ottawa: National Council of Welfare.

- Rodgers, K. 1994. Wife Assault: The Findings of a National Survey. *Juristat* 14, no.9. Ottawa: Statistics Canada, Canadian Centre for Justice Statistics.

- Statistics Canada. 2000. *Family Violence in Canada: A Statistical Profile.* Ottawa: Statistics Canada.

- Struthers, James 1991. How Much is Enough? Creating a Social Minimum in Ontario, 1930-44. *The Canadian Historical Review,* 72: 1, 39.

- Townson, M. 2000. *A Report Card on Women and Poverty.* Ottawa: Canadian Centre for Policy Alternatives.

- Trainor, C. 1999. Canada's Shelters for Abused Women. *Juristat* 19, no. 6. Ottawa: Statistics Canada, Canadian Centre for Justice Statistics.

CHAPTER 8: SOCIAL WORK WITH WOMEN

Key Concepts

- Maternal feminism
- Equal-pay policies
- Employment equity
- Facilitating programs
- Sex
- Gender
- Sexism
- Patriarchy
- Consciousness-raising groups
- Feminist theory
- Feminist social work practice
- Transition houses
- Suffragette movement
- Power theory
- Learning theory
- Anger-control theory
- Cycle-of-violence theory
- Feminization of poverty
- Gerontological social work
- Home care

Discussion Questions

1. What was the general approach of the early women who were involved in social work?
2. List and define five persistent problems that women in Canadian society confront.
3. What is meant by *the feminization of poverty*?
4. Define and compare the terms *gender equity* and *gender equality*.
5. List and define five components of feminist social work practice.
6. Describe two ways in which social workers put feminist principles into practice.
7. What is the generational cycle of violence?
8. What are two theories that explain violence against women?
9. What is the role of social workers when working with women who have been abused?

Websites

- **Status of Women of Canada**
  http://www.swc-cfc.gc.ca
  Status of Women Canada (SWC) is the federal government agency that promotes gender equality and the full participation of women in the economic, social, cultural and political life of the country. SWC focuses its work in three areas: improving women's economic autonomy and well-bring, eliminating systemic violence against women and children and advancing women's human rights.

- **Gender-based Analysis: A Guide for Policy-making**
  http://www.swc-cfc.gc.ca/publish/gbagid-e.html
  This "hands-on" working document developed by Status of Women Canada is a must read for social workers interested in analyzing social policy to assess the differential impact of proposed or existing policies, programs and legislation on women and men. The guide is divided into three sections: Section 1 defines key concepts and provides the rationale for gender-based analysis; Section 2, Policy Development and Analysis Process, outlines a commonly accepted policy analysis process and highlights how sensitivity to gender can be integrated into this process; and Section 3, Gender-Based Analysis Methodology, offers a step-by-step process for gender-based analysis.

- **National Clearinghouse on Family Violence**
  http://www.hc-sc.gc.ca/hppb/familyviolence
  National Clearinghouse on Family Violence is a national resource centre for those seeking information about violence within the family and new resources being used to address it.

9
Social Work and Aboriginal Peoples

The Canadian Legacy

"Government policies have been singularly aimed, for over a century, at reducing the differences that exist between Aboriginal life and the mainstream of Canadian society in the hope that Aboriginal peoples would disappear as distinct societies. The extent to which Aboriginal peoples have retained their distinctiveness is a testimonial to their strength and endurance as peoples"—*Justice Murray Sinclair,* Aboriginal Justice Inquiry of Manitoba (Manitoba 1991, 97).

This chapter examines social work with Aboriginal peoples. To understand this aspect of contemporary social work and social welfare, however, it is necessary to begin with the history of relations between Aboriginal peoples and the European settlers who made Canada a colony, first of France and then of Britain.

With the founding of Canada, the social relations between the original inhabitants and the colonizer were expressed in the *Indian Act* and the reserve system. These continue to shape contemporary relations between Aboriginal peoples and mainstream Canadian society. The chapter begins by briefly describing the Aboriginal peoples of Canada. It continues with a brief review of the history of colonialism in Canada and its contemporary legacy. It then goes on to examine the residential schools and early child welfare systems, which were attempts by the government to wipe out Aboriginal societies altogether. The chapter examines the issues pertaining to providing welfare and social work services to Aboriginal peoples, and outlines the basic principles that underlie an Aboriginal approach to a social work practice. The factors that make a variety of social work interventions successful are discussed, as well as the question of who will provide services to Aboriginal peoples.

WHO ARE ABORIGINAL PEOPLES?

Aboriginal peoples are the original inhabitants of this portion of landmass known as Canada. It is generally agreed that Aboriginal peoples have lived upon this land for thousands of years. The term *Indian* is widely understood to have originated with explorers who thought they had reached India in their search for a passage to the east. Today the term is used to define a group of indigenous people registered as such according to the *Indian Act*. Menno Boldt states that the term *Indian*

Land claims focus on need for Aboriginal self-government.

"My heart is a stone. heavy with sadness for my people; cold with the knowledge that no treaty will keep the whites out of our land; hard with determination to resist as long as I live and breathe. Now we are weak and many of our people are afraid. But Hear Me: a single twig breaks, but the bundle of twigs is strong. Someday I will embrace our brother tribes and draw them into a bundle and together we will win our country back from the whites."

—Tecumseh, Shawnee Chief, circa 1795.

"serves the Canadian government as a convenient political, legal, and administrative categorization of the culturally diverse first peoples of Canada" (1993, 192).

The term *Indian* is a generic one. It is used in much the same way as *Native,* as a means of "outside-naming" those "who are descendants of the first inhabitants of what is now Canada." The term *Aboriginal,* another all-encompassing term, "appears to be associated with a general, emerging emancipation of Aboriginal peoples from domination of all sorts by the settler society" (Chartrand 1991, 3-4). Of course, the Aboriginal peoples have their own names for themselves in their respective languages: Anishnaabe, Inuit, Innu, Nuu-chah-nulth, and Métis. The Inuit are Aboriginal peoples of Canada "that have traditionally used and occupied, and currently use and occupy, the lands and waters" ranging from the Yukon and Northwest Territories to northern Quebec and Labrador (Indian and Northern Affairs Canada and Tungavik 1993, 4). A large portion of their traditional territory has been recognized as the Nunavut Settlement Area. The agreement between the Inuit of Nunavut and the federal government recognizes that the Inuit are best able to define who is an Inuk according to their own understanding of themselves. Like other Aboriginal peoples, the Inuit have a richness of diverse cultures and ways of living.

The Métis have often been neglected in the consideration of the Aboriginal peoples of Canada, an injustice that obscures their role in the westward expansion of this country. Unlike other Aboriginal peoples, the Métis cannot assert that they have inhabited this continent *as a distinct people* for many thousands of years. According to Purich,

> most often, the term Métis is used to refer to the descendants of the historic Métis–that is, those whose origin can be traced back to the Red River in the early 1800s. These are the people, now located mainly in the prairies and the north, who formed a language and culture, which was a unique blend of Indian, and European cultures (Purich 1988).

When Europeans began to arrive on this continent, Aboriginal peoples numbered between 500,000 and 2 million. They lived a wide variety of lifestyles, depending on the natural resources available to them. The oral traditions of some Aboriginal cultures assert that the pre-contact population was even greater than the estimates of anthropologists and historians. Across Canada, there were approximately fifty Aboriginal languages spoken, which made up eleven main language groups. Within each Aboriginal language there are also several dialects. For example, the Algonkian language group includes Ojibway, which in turn includes Saulteaux, Odawa, Potowatomi and others. Aboriginal nations were also characterized by a rich diversity of social organization, including systems of governance, health care practices, and cultural and spiritual rituals. These social aspects were not separated into functionally specialized institutions, but were organized holistically. Such social organization usually included some formal means by which different nations agreed to co-exist. Some, such as the Haudenousaunee or the Mi'kmaq, formed confederacies.

POVERTY AND CANADA'S FIRST NATIONS

The policy best described as **colonialism** amounted to nothing less that an attempt to completely subjugate the Aboriginal peoples. As a direct result, among other things, to this day income levels for the Métis and Inuit communities and those living on and off reserves continue to be lower than for the rest of Canada. Aboriginal people are more reliant on various forms of social assistance as a major source of income than the rest of the Canadian population (Royal Commission on Aboriginal Peoples 1996, 168). A primary factor contributing to the high rates of poverty among Aboriginal people is unemployment. In 1995, only 25.3 percent of Aboriginal people had full-time, year-round employment, and 38.4 percent of working-age Aboriginal people were unemployed (Lee 1999, 11).

A lack of economic development, unemployment and reliance upon social assistance, as well as a host of other social problems including alcohol and drug addictions and family violence, are related to the loss of language and traditional cultural practices. Aboriginal peoples are incarcerated in correctional centres and penitentiaries more than other groups. Aboriginal people are twice as likely to be imprisoned and are more likely to receive a full prison sentence than non-Aboriginal people. The rate of suicide and suicide attempts is at least three to four times higher among Aboriginal peoples, especially among those fifteen to twenty years old, than the rest of Canadians (Royal Commission on Aboriginal Peoples 1995).

These poor social conditions have caused many Aboriginal peoples to leave their own communities for urban centres, particularly within the last thirty years. However, poverty doesn't disappear when Aboriginal people reside in cities. In 1996, 44.5 percent of Aboriginal people lived in metropolitan areas of Canada. Half of these live in the prairie provinces. Winnipeg has by far the largest Aboriginal population at 43,200 or almost 20 percent of the total urban Aboriginal population (Lee 1999, 9). Of the total Aboriginal urban population, 50.4 percent live below Statistics Canada's Low-Income Cut-off (LICO), sometimes referred to as the poverty line, as compared to 21.2 percent of the non-Aboriginal population. Perhaps the most shocking statistic is that 77 percent of Aboriginal lone-parent families live below this line. The poorest urban Aboriginal people live in Saskatoon (63.7 percent), Regina (62.2 percent) and Winnipeg (60.5 percent) (Lee 1999, 10).

Interestingly, while the mainstream Canadian population ages and its birth rate declines, the Aboriginal population continues to grow. Moreover, Aboriginal populations are on average younger than the general Canadian population. Currently, the median age of Status Indians recognized as Indians under the *Indian Act* is ten years younger than the Canadian median age, and for Inuit it is twelve years. While the Canadian population, as a whole, is ageing into retirement, Aboriginal populations are moving from youth into working age (Canadian Medical Association 1993, 7). Unless action is taken soon, social problems in Aboriginal communities are likely to become even more acute.

ON THE WEB

- A good place to search for web links on Canadian Aboriginal peoples is http://www.ayn.ca
- The "5000 year heritage" of the Inuit is on the Inuit Tapirisat of Canada website at: http://www.tapirisat.ca
- A good internationally focused site is at http://www.nativeweb.org

Aboriginal children at Red Cross Centre, circa 1940.

Table 9.1: A Comparison of Selected Characteristics of Aboriginal Ancestry Population with the General Population of Canada

	Aboriginal Ancestry	General Population	Aboriginal Condition
Total population	1,101,960	28,528,125	4% of Canada
% off-reserve	79%	–	227,285 on reserve
% under 15 years	34%	20%	Much younger
% over 65 years	3%	12%	Four times fewer
Unemployed rate	20%	10%	Twice as high
Average income for those 15+	$17,823	$25,435	One-third less
Average income for those 65+	$15,866	$21,028	One-quarter less
65 years+ with private pensions	8%	19%	One-half as many
65 years+ with investment income	9%	28%	One-third as many
Incidence of low-income families	35%	16%	Twice as many
Children under 15 living in lone-parent families	30%	16%	Almost twice as many
Lone-parent unemployed rate	26%	16%	One-third higher
Own home	44%	70%	One-third fewer

Source: Statistics Canada, 1996 Census.

HISTORY OF ABORIGINAL PEOPLES

The relationship between Aboriginal peoples and Europeans was initially harmonious and mutually advantageous. During the sixteenth and seventeenth centuries, Aboriginal peoples served as partners in exploration and trading. Later, as the English and the French became locked in an imperialistic struggle for control over the North American continent, the relationship with the Aboriginal peoples evolved into a military alliance. As European peoples and their governments exerted military dominance over the territories that had been inhabited by the indigenous peoples, and as those territories bore the weight of the incursion of settlers, the role of Aboriginal peoples changed from one of military allies to one of irrelevance (Miller 1989, 84).

The movement westward by Europeans in the later eighteenth and nineteenth centuries caused increasing displacement and conflict for the Aboriginal peoples who lived on the land that the newcomers wanted for agriculture and homesteads. The presence of Aboriginal peoples on these lands demanded a response from the European governments. With the colonization of what would become known as Canada, the land's original inhabitants became **"the Indian problem,"** and impediments to "civilization." Colonial representatives and, later, government officials devised various schemes to address the Indian problem, including land-cession treaties and assimilation policies. Such schemes came at an exorbitant cost, not only financially, but more importantly in terms of the loss of Aboriginal lives and ways of living.

With the signing of **land-cession treaties** and the adoption of a succession of *Indian Acts*, the government of Canada changed its relationship with the continent's first inhabitants in the later nineteenth century. "The intention of the civil government, now that Indians no longer were militarily useful, was to concentrate Indians in settled areas, or reserves; to subject them to as much proselytization, schooling, and instruction in agriculture as 'circumstances' made necessary" (Miller 1989, 100).

The **Indian Act** sought to define strictly who would be considered an Indian so as to exert government authority over Aboriginal peoples. The Act fragmented the Aboriginal population into legally distinct groups with different rights, restrictions and obligations. Canada is one of the few countries to have legislated separate laws for a specific group based on race or ethnicity.

The *Indian Act* was, and still is, a piece of social legislation of very broad scope, which regulates and controls virtually every aspect of Native life. The so-called **Indian Agent** administered the Act in Aboriginal communities. These agents were to displace traditional Aboriginal leaders so as to institute a new way of living consistent with the intentions of the government. The Indian agents had extraordinary administrative and discretionary powers. In order to ensure this, Clause 25 of the Act established the government's guardianship over Indian lands.

The social control aspects of the *Indian Act* placed Indians in the position of a colonized people. The Act spelled out a process of enfranchisement whereby Indians could acquire full Canadian citizenship only by relinquishing their ties to their community; that is, by giving up their culture and traditions and any rights to land. Consequently, the cost of Canadian citizenship demanded of an Aboriginal person far surpassed that for an immigrant to Canada. The Canadian government saw the *Indian Act* as a temporary measure to control Aboriginal peoples until they had been fully assimilated through enfranchisement. It was not until 1960, however, that the government changed the policy and granted Indians the right to vote in federal elections. For the first time, citizenship for Aboriginal peoples was not conditional upon their assimilation into mainstream Canadian society.

The situation among the Métis in the same time period, the late nineteenth and early twentieth centuries, was unique. The Métis in western Canada could seek to become status Indians by aligning themselves to certain treaty areas or they could "take scrip." The **scrip system** entitled the bearer of a scrip certificate to either land or money; in exchange, the person who took scrip gave up all further claims to land. Although the scrip system offered to the Métis was different from the treaty-making process for Indians, the result was the same. Neither Métis nor Indian felt that they had been treated fairly (Purich 1988, 125).

The *Indian Act* also governed the Inuit. No land was formally set aside for their exclusive use nor were any treaties signed between the Canadian government and the Inuit peoples. Because of the extensive mineral and oil exploration on their lands, Inuit communities have been relocated, forcing a change in their lifestyle. One gross example of the nature of state intervention in Inuit lives is the **disk list system**. As

BILL C-31

Provisions of the *Indian Act* had been criticized for discriminating against Indian women. Bill C-31, passed in 1985, amended status and band membership provisions, reinstating status to women who had married a non-Native. The concept of enfranchisement, voluntary or otherwise, was totally abolished, and those who lost status through enfranchisement had their status restored. First-generation children of restored persons were granted first-time status.

As of 1995, Bill C-31 had added 95,429 persons to the status Indian population in Canada, more than half of them (57.2 percent, 54,589) women.

Source: Royal Commission on Aboriginal Peoples, *Perspectives and Realities*, vol. 4 (1996), Sec. 3.2.

Assimilationist policies reject rights to self-government.

Table 9.2: Aboriginal Population by Poverty Status, Age Group and Poverty Rate, 1996 (Census Metropolitan Areas)

	Total	Poor	Poverty Rate (%)
Aged 14 and younger	69,800	42,900	61.5
Aged 15 to 24	39,600	20,800	52.5
Aged 25 to 34	42,600	20,300	47.7
Aged 35 to 44	32,800	13,300	40.5
Aged 45 to 54	19,700	7,000	35.5
Aged 55 to 64	9,600	4,200	43.8
Aged 65 to 74	4,300	1,700	39.5
Aged 75 and older	1,800	700	38.9
Total	220,200	111,000	50.4
Women	117,000	61,700	52.7
Men	103,200	49,300	47.8
Total	220,200	111,000	50.4

Source: Prepared by the Canadian Council on Social Development using 1996 Census data, custom tabulations.

bureaucrats could not or would not formally acknowledge the Inuktitut names for individuals, the disk list system assigned a numbered disk to each Inuk in order to identify them. Although not universally employed, the disk list system "ultimately came to define the quasi-legal Eskimo status which had an impact on virtually all aspects of Eskimo social life as an intensely administered population within Canadian society" (Smith 1993, 64).

Once land was ceded and Canadian settlements had been established, Aboriginal peoples were shunted aside onto small parcels of land largely devoid of any economic potential. This land could not be used as collateral to develop business ventures, given that Indian land was held in trust. It has been argued that by confining Aboriginal peoples to reserves, Inuit communities and Métis settlements that

> the welfare of Aboriginal societies was systematically neglected. Famines and tuberculosis were allowed to virtually decimate Aboriginal communities, unaided except for relocation of survivors to state institutions. Housing provided was of the poorest quality, and health care and education were until quite recently, left to the Church (Scott 1994, 7).

The federal government established the Department of Indian Affairs as the main vehicle to regulate and control Aboriginal movement and ways of living.

The *Indian Act* certainly seems to be out of step with the bulk of Canadian law. It singles out a segment of society– largely on the basis of race– removes much of their land and property from the commercial mainstream, and gives the Minister of Indian & Northern Affairs and other government official a degree of discretion that is not only intrusive but frequently offensive. The Act has been roundly criticized. Many want it abolished because it violates normative standards of equality, and these critics tend to be non-Aboriginal; others want First Nations to be able to make their own decisions as self-governing polities and see the Act as inhibiting that freedom. Even within its provisions, others see unfair treatment between, for example, Indians who live on reserves and those who reside elsewhere. In short, this is a statute of which few speak well. (Bill Henderson has annotated the *Indian Act*, and placed it on-line at http://www.bloorstreet.com/200block/sindact.htm.)

RESIDENTIAL SCHOOL SYSTEM

The now infamous **residential school system** was established in the mid-1900s by Indian Affairs in conjunction with the Christian churches. Residential schools were

> a place where a large number of people lived and worked together cut off from both the wider First Nation and mainstream societies. In contrast to "day schools" where children came and went on a daily basis, residential schools separated children from their families and communities for extended periods of time, in some instances for years (Assembly of First Nations 1994, 3).

Native children were removed from their Native communities and placed in residential schools. By restricting Native culture and language, the schools sought to fulfill the **assimilationist policies** of the federal government. The curriculum used in the schools emphasized work and religious instruction rather than academic learning. The children were denied their language, spiritual rituals and, more importantly, access to their families. Aboriginal children were subject to emotional, physical and sexual abuse in these schools.

As a result of their having resided within an institution that regulated every aspect of their lives, the Aboriginals' decision-making skills were impaired: "residential schools were no preparation for life in any type of community" (Armitage 1993, 142). Some struggled with drug and alcohol addiction and problems with mental health that arose from the psychological trauma they had endured. Many found themselves with a limited ability to parent their own children as parenting models had been unavailable to them.

While many individuals who emerged from these institutions retained a positive outlook and an intact psyche, a true testament to their adaptability and resilience, it must be stressed that the residential school experience systematically crippled many Aboriginal children and families. This legacy will take many generations to heal.

• Child Welfare and "The Scoop"

In 1951, the *Indian Act* was amended such that provincial laws of application (and therefore child welfare legislation) applied to reserves (Timpson 1990, 54). With this legislative change, the government's approach to Aboriginal assimilation veered from residential schools towards the apprehension and placement of Native children in non-Native foster homes.

THE *INDIAN ACT* REVISITED

In the spring of 2001, the federal government initiated a controversial process of "grassroots consultations" with Native peoples on changes to the *Indian Act*. For its part, the Assembly of First Nations (AFN), Canada's largest Aboriginal group, boycotted the consultations.

The more than 630 chiefs of the AFN promised an "aggressive, strategic plan of action" if the consultations, limited to improving Native governance and accountability on reserves and reforming the voting system, did not include the AFN and if the proposed changes were not broadened to include wider Aboriginal concerns such as treaty implementation and other topics.

Aboriginal children at a residential school, 1894.

National Archives of Canada. Neg no. C26448.

National Archives of Canada. Neg no. PA42122 (Dept. of Interior).

Residential school. The intent of the disastrous residential schools policy was to erase Aboriginal identity by separating generations of children from their families and socializing them in mainstream culture. Above: Aboriginal pupils at the Roman Catholic Mission in Fort Resolution, N.W.T.

Child welfare agencies assumed responsibility for services to Aboriginal communities. The agencies received many reports of alleged neglect and abuse from teachers, police, clergy, government bureaucrats and social workers. These reports often reflected value judgements involving the dismissal of parenting styles that were effective within the context of Aboriginal communities, stereotypes and outright racism.

One result is what is known as **"the Scoop**." In the 1960s, massive numbers of children were removed from their communities and placed in non-Aboriginal foster and adoptive homes. Throughout the 1960s and 1970s, Aboriginal children were increasingly placed in care facilities, which effectively removed them from their families, sometimes permanently. By the later 1970s and early 1980s, at any given time one in seven status Indian children was not in the care of his or her parents, and as many as one in four status Indian children was spending at least some time away from the parental home (Armitage 1993, 147). Between 1959 and 1970, the percentage of Native children made legal wards of the state increased from 1 percent of all children in care to 30-40 percent (Fournier and Crey 1998, 83).

Canadian child welfare authorities now recognize the damage caused by this approach, and the federal government has made efforts to fund Aboriginal child welfare agencies. In 1990-91, the federal government funded 36 Aboriginal child and family agencies, covering 212 bands; in this same period, a total of $1.5 million over a period of two years was allocated to First Nations for the development of Aboriginal child and family service standards.

Most Aboriginal child care agencies have adopted placement protocols that specify the following placement preferences: first, with the extended family; second, with Aboriginal members of the community with the same cultural and linguistic identification; and third, other alternative Aboriginal caregivers. As a last resort, placement is considered with non-Aboriginal caregivers. Some work has been done to develop culturally appropriate standards for selecting Aboriginal foster caregivers.

In many provinces, developing Aboriginal family and child welfare services is difficult. In 1981, the federal government entered into agreements with the provinces, insisting that child and family services established under the agreements and operating under delegated authority from the province must adhere to provincial regulations. For example, Tikinagan Child and Family Services in northwestern Ontario was mandated in 1987 under the *Child and Family Services Act* to provide services in child welfare. Forced by legislative mandates, they became indistinguishable from white-operated children's aid societies. Although the communities recognize that they must implement a child welfare approach consistent with an Aboriginal approach to social work, the system prohibits this.

GOVERNMENT POLICY OBJECTIVES

In *Arduous Journey: Canadian Indians and Decolonization*, Roger Gibbins and Rick Pointing outline the major goals or policy motifs of national government public policy towards Aboriginal peoples (Gibbins and Ponting 1986). These were as follows:

Protection. Some officials developing Indian policy were very aware of the problems of alcoholism, greed and prostitution that flourished on the frontier of Canada. Some had humanitarian goals and sought to protect Indians until they could be assimilated into white society. This led to laws prohibiting the sale of Indian land, the use of alcohol by Indians and the prostitution of Indian women. These officials saw the reservation system as a way to isolate and protect Indians. It can also be argued that these goals of protection were mostly illusory, glossing over the underlying goal of exploitation. For example, by isolating Indians on reserves the government was free to exploit other vast Indian lands.

Assimilation. The central pillar or thrust of federal government Indian policy was the goal of assimilation. Unquestionably the goal was to prepare Aboriginal peoples for absorption into Canadian society. It was desired and expected that eventually all Indians would give up their Native customs, culture and beliefs and become like those of the dominant society. The failure of this assimilation process can largely the attributed to barriers posed by systemic and societal discrimination. As Gibbins and Pointing state, "government policy tried to induce Indians into a mainstream that was unwilling to receive them." Another aspect of this failure is the extent and success of Indian activism.

ABORIGINAL CHILDREN IN CARE TODAY

"The Scoop" of the 1960s appears to be occurring again today, and recent data shows that it may, in fact, be worse.

For example, Saskatchewan, Alberta and British Columbia report disturbingly high rates of Aboriginal children in care and receiving child welfare services.

Saskatchewan reports that 57% of children in care were Aboriginal and another 10% were Métis (Saskatchewan Social Services Annual Report, 1999-2000, p.47). In B.C., 30.2% of children in care in 1999 were of Aboriginal background. And Alberta reports that 37.7% of children receiving child welfare services were Aboriginal, although they comprise only 7.5 of the total population.

Sources: Saskatchewan Social Services, *Annual Report, 1999-2000*, p.47; British Columbia Ministry for Children and Families, *Sharing the Challenge: 1988/1999 Annual Report*, p.23 (http://www.mcf.gov.bc.ca/pubs/title.htm); Alberta Ministry of Children's Services, *Children's Services Annual Report (2000)*, p.35 (http://www.acs.gov.ab.ca).

THE INNU OF LABRADOR

The terms of union under which Newfoundland joined Confederation in 1949 make no mention of Aboriginal peoples. Arrangements for service delivery to the Innu and others were made later, under a series of federal-provincial agreements. Until recently, the government of Newfoundland provided all health, education, welfare and related services, and the federal government contributed 90 percent of the cost of programs the province chose to deliver. The federal government has now begun to provide direct funding to the Innu for some—but not all—health and social programs.

The Innu have long held that federal refusal to treat them in the same way they treat First Nations registered under the *Indian Act* for purposes of program and service delivery constitutes discrimination, an infringement of their rights as Aboriginal people, and an abrogation of fundamental federal responsibilities.

Source: The Final Report of the Royal Commission on Aboriginal Peoples (1996). The Institute of Indigenous Government makes this material available: http://www.indigenous.bc.ca/rcap.htm

Christanization. A central component of assimilation was the process of Christanization. To the colonial government, the civilizing of the Indians was synonymous with their Christanization. Aboriginal ceremonies and cultural practices were officially discouraged or outlawed. Education through church residential schools was seen as a way to destroy the social, spiritual and cultural systems and relations of the Indians and replace them with the beliefs of mainstream Canadian society. Because the residential schools isolated Indians from the mainstream, they worked at cross purposes to the goal of assimilation. They were the source of great antagonism in Native communities and continue to be so to this day.

Enfranchisement. As discussed above (p.163), this was the method envisioned for Indians to obtain citizenship and thus be fully recognized as Canadians until the 1960s.

Land surrender. The desire by the government to obtain land held by Aboriginal peoples for the settlement of non-Aboriginal people was a primary goal. Reserves were seen as a way to move Indians into agriculturally based communities, both to assimilate them and to free vast tracks of land for non-Aboriginal settlement. As immigration increased, the government moved to make more and more "excess Indian land available for non-Indian settlement." Further to this end, numerous treaties were signed between Indians and colonial officials between 1670 and 1923. While the treaties were quite different in their terms and complexity, they generally served to establish peaceful relations, institute payments and gain the surrender of land. The major treaties were signed in the west, starting with treaty #1 in 1871 and ending with treaty #10 in 1906. This allowed the vast territories of the west to be settled and the construction of the CP railway. It is important to note that no treaties were signed between the First Peoples of Quebec, the Maritimes and most of British Columbia. In fact, almost half of the population of registered Indians did not sign land treaties. These land treaties (in many cases, the lack of them) are currently in dispute across the country.

Government authority. As discussed above, a major goal of the *Indian Act* was to give sweeping power and authority to the colonial administrators. This external political control is a fundamental aspect of colonization. In the case of Canada, it was explicitly embodied in the *Indian Act.* The assistant deputy minister of Indian Affairs branch described the *Indian Act* as follows: "The Indian Act is a lands act. It is a municipal act, an educational act, and a societies act. It is primarily social legislation, but it has a very broad scope: there are provisions about liquor, agricultural and mining as well as Indian lands, band membership and so forth. It has elements that are embodied in perhaps 2 dozen different acts of any of the provinces and overrides some federal legislation in some respects.... If has the force of the criminal Code and the impact of a constitution on those people and communities that come within its purview" (Gibbins and Ponting 1986, 19).

• Health Care

Until the mid-1900s, the federal government directly delivered virtually all programs and services to First Nations. In the 1950s, the responsibility for health care was transferred to the medical services branch of the Department of Health and Welfare. This led to the development of a system of primary care clinics, public health programs and regional hospitals for Aboriginal peoples.

Unfortunately, this change did not mean an end to the denigration of Aboriginal cultures or the isolation of Aboriginal peoples from their own societies. Health care was still provided by non-Aboriginal practitioners who had little or no sensitivity to the differing cultural and social systems among Aboriginal peoples. Well into the twentieth century, for example, the *Indian Act* outlawed the spiritual ceremonies of Aboriginal peoples, reflecting the assumption that indigenous healing methods were non-existent or ineffective. As a result, "encounters were often clouded by suspicion, misunderstanding, resentment, and racism" (Scott 1994, 8). These feelings were exacerbated when Aboriginal peoples were removed from their communities to outside medical facilities for treatment.

For decades the Innu of Labrador have been dealing with the problems of serious substance abuse and suicide among their children, yet appropriate services within the community are still lacking. In November 2000, Peter Penashue, president of the Innu Nation, reported that there were at least 30 children sniffing gas in a community of only 1,200 residents. The chief of Labrador's largest Innu community requested that the Newfoundland provincial government take gasoline-sniffing children out of the community to ensure they received treatment. The chief had long complained that neither social workers on the reserve nor the local police had the authority to pick up these children and place them in treatment.

This tragic situation sparked debate about the role of non-Aboriginal social workers in relieving the Innu situation. The historical legacy of government policy characterized by colonization and assimilation had left the community without opportunities or prospects. Child welfare workers historically assisted in the assimilation policy by apprehending Aboriginal children and placing them in non-Native foster homes. Many were rightly sceptical of the help that outsiders could provide.

On the other hand, the Band Council and chief of the community, faced with a desperate situation in relation to Aboriginal youth, were asking for help. Government child welfare authorities were presented with an ethical dilemma in choosing how to respond to the request for assistance. Would they, as they had done so often, take the children out of the community and risk perpetuating the history of assimilation or would they develop the capacity of the local community to deal with these problems? In the end, the children were taken to Aboriginal care centres elsewhere.

This case highlights the importance of addressing the social and economic concerns of Aboriginal communities before such tragic circumstances develop.

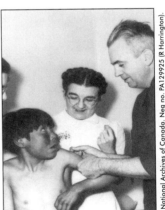

Inuit child is vaccinated, Port Harrison, Quebec, 1947.

• Income Security Programs

Although income security in Canada is supposedly available to every citizen who meets the conditions of a particular program, a double standard has existed for Aboriginal peoples. Until the early 1900s, any kind of monetary relief, taken from the trust accounts of Indian bands, was granted at the discretion of the local Indian agent. The decision to grant relief was based on the old practice of distinguishing between the "deserving" and the "undeserving" poor–and Indians were generally considered undeserving. "Non-registered Indians, Métis and Inuit were on the periphery of the Indian relief system although their economic circumstances were similar to, or worse than, those of the 'Indians'" (Moscovitch and Webster 1995, 212).

Early in Canada's history, government officials issued rations to Aboriginal peoples. These were grossly inadequate and were used just as much as a means to sanction behaviour as for relief (Moscovitch and Webster 1995, 211). When "the first universal and statutory old age pension was enacted in 1927 it excluded Indians and Inuit, but was available to the Métis" (Scott 1994, 18). The first *Unemployment Insurance Act*, passed in 1940, also excluded most Aboriginal people from eligibility (Ibid., 20).

Between 1951 and 1966 the Indian relief system collapsed and was replaced by access to the mainstream welfare state (Moscovitch and Webster 1995). This occurred after the development of several federal acts related to income security, amendments to the *Indian Act* in 1951 and the establishment of the Canada Assistance Plan. Through the development of an administrative structure with huge discretionary powers that minimized community control, the government of Canada effectively came to control the day-to-day lives of Aboriginal peoples.

In short, in the words of Manitoba Justice Murray Sinclair, "it is crucial to recognize that the social condition of Aboriginal people is a direct result of the discriminatory and repressive policies that successive European and Canadian governments have directed towards Aboriginal people" (Manitoba 1991, 92). Yet, despite their best efforts, the Canadian government failed to either assimilate or eradicate the Métis, Inuit and other First Nations.

ABORIGINAL SOCIAL WORK PRACTICE—FOUR PRINCIPLES

Two factors make it difficult to formulate a comprehensive **Aboriginal approach to social work** practice. First, a single Aboriginal culture or worldview upon which to base a uniform approach to social work does not exist. The First Nations of Canada are exceedingly diverse, with many languages, cultures and traditions, and for this reason Aboriginal peoples have a variety of healing and helping philosophies and techniques. Second, a legacy of mistrust and animosity exists towards those in the helping professions, including social work. The process of colonialism featured gross violations of fundamental human rights, leaving untold scars and social problems in many Native communities; a process

TEP Photo Archives, Toronto.

The age profile of the Native population is relatively young.

in which social workers participated. An Aboriginal approach to social work needs to be flexible enough to incorporate a variety of healing methods and must avoid repeating the historical processes of colonialism. It is therefore crucial that the approach be based on the wants of Aboriginal peoples and give power to Aboriginal communities and Nations.

An Aboriginal approach to social work does not mean that mainstream methods are of no value; an Aboriginal approach can be integrated with Western social work practices and standards. The Nechi Institute (http://www.nechi.com), founded in 1974 by a group of elders located in Edmonton, is a good example of a training organization that incorporates both traditional Aboriginal and Western standards. Their holistic approach is based on the belief that true physical, mental, emotional and spiritual healing occurs when an individual is in harmony with his or her environment. They also contend that problems must be understood within the context of history, community setting, personal experience, culture and the social institutions that have had influence on the individual.

The development of an Aboriginal approach to social work practice should be consistent with four key principles. These principles are: (1) the recognition of a distinct Aboriginal worldview; (2) the development of Aboriginal consciousness regarding the impact of colonialism; (3) an emphasis on the importance of cultural knowledge and traditions; (4) utilizing the concept of Aboriginal empowerment (Morrissette, McKenzie, and Morrissette 1993, 91). These principles need to be practiced simultaneously along with adherence to a holistic approach, a belief in equity, Aboriginal self-control and a respect for diversity.

• Distinct Aboriginal Worldview

The first principle acknowledges and appreciates that there is a distinct **Aboriginal worldview**. The First Nations of Canada are diverse and culturally distinct, and therefore each may have a different approach to healing and helping. While Aboriginal peoples do not have one single philosophy or worldview, one can draw upon the fundamental differences between Western Euro-Canadian and Aboriginal worldviews. For example, the concept of the circle captured in the Medicine Wheel illustrates the notion of balance prevalent in Aboriginal societies, in contrast to the typically linear models of cause and effect common in Western society.

• Impact of Colonialism

The second principle involves an analysis of the impact of colonization, which has greatly contributed to the current situation in Aboriginal communities. Colonizers attempted to subordinate Aboriginal peoples and displace traditional spirituality, governance systems, leadership and knowledge by using missionaries, residential schools, child welfare and artificial legal distinctions in the *Indian Act*. Using the reserve system and treaties, the colonizers also sought to subordinate Aboriginal economic systems in order to facilitate the extraction of benefits for themselves. A

INUIT CHILDREN'S HEALTH

Research published in the *Canadian Medical Association Journal* (June 2001) provides the latest in a growing body of scientific and anecdotal evidence that there are serious medical health problems among Aboriginal children.

A case study of Baffin Regional Hospital in Iqaluit involving infants under six months of age suggests that Inuit babies have among the world's highest rate of lung infections. "There is a real problem," said Anna Banerji, the study's lead author. The hospital admission rate is "comparable to a rate that you would expect in the developing world, not in Canada." Older children are also plagued by chronic lung disease, according to Banerji, who said some pre-school children have lungs that resemble those of long-time smokers in their 70s.

Medical officers believe that tackling issues like nutrition, housing, overcrowding, air quality and smoking are the best way to cut the rates of respiratory illness.

recognition and analysis of colonialism will assist the social worker in framing problems, in recognizing solutions that emphasize self-determination and in seeing the importance of the reclamation of Aboriginal culture and identity in the social work process.

Residential schools and child welfare work in First Nations communities are illustrative of the damage done by colonialism. Even today, social work with Native families is premised on the Western perception that individuals are members of nuclear families that provide economic support and affection, and that individuals can turn to specialized institutions for problem-specific help. This is not consistent with the Aboriginal view. Aboriginal peoples often perceive themselves to be members of a family network in which everyone is obliged to contribute their resources and support all community members. These dissimilar conceptions of family, community and social obligation lead to different ideas about how to carry out social work, as described by an Anishnabe social worker and his colleagues:

> Members of the Aboriginal community potentially (and normally do) play multiple roles in relation to one another–friend, neighbour, relative, and community service volunteer, as well as job-related service giver and receiver roles. All of these roles are reciprocal, each (at least potentially) being played by each person in relation to all others in the community.
>
> The individual or family who is the focus of concern assumes the role of "client" [in the] system–a more dependent and generally stigmatized role. In like manner, the community member functioning in the job of human service worker is cast in the role of "worker"–a more powerful and generally more expert role. The worker is not seen by formal human service agencies as an individual simply fulfilling an expected role in the mutual aid system of the Aboriginal community. In the formal system, the worker-client role relationship becomes single faceted rather than multiple, and uni-directional (helper-helped) rather than reciprocal. Both worker and client become removed and isolated from the interpersonal network that gives their needs and behaviour meaning and that will ultimately provide the support and resources, or obstacles, to satisfaction of those needs.

The discrepancy between Aboriginal ways of helping and conventional social work services are even more pronounced when the worker is an outsider to the community. The conventional methods of social work, in which community members are required to turn to outside agencies for help, weakens internal bonds of mutual aid. People in Aboriginal communities begin to question their ability to help one another as they are unable to contribute to the external social work process that becomes the community's source of help. This situation fosters dependent relationships and weakens the traditional community bonds of mutual aid.

• Cultural Knowledge and Traditions

The third principle of **reclaiming Aboriginal culture** emphasizes an awareness of and reflection on common aspects of culture and identity.

National Archives of Canada. Neg no. PA141513.

Frobisher Bay General Hospital, 1959.

By examining Aboriginal history, culture and traditions and dispelling the conventional views of Aboriginal reality flowing from colonialism, Aboriginal people can begin to see the underlying causes of their individual problems. Of course, there may be differences in how much individuals identify with traditional Aboriginal culture and therefore in how much the reclamation of Aboriginal culture will assist in social work intervention. Some will adhere to the teaching of elders and follow traditional ways, while others may not.

In many cases, traditional healing techniques and teachings will be combined with non-traditional methods. This combining of traditional healing and mainstream techniques is evident at the Strong Earth Woman Lodge in Manitoba, where the power of Aboriginal spirituality and traditional teachings is combined with crisis intervention techniques. Working with the Sagkeeng First Nation they have a holistic healing centre based on Native spirituality and traditional teachings. They see holistic healing as the healing of the mind, body, emotions and spirit. Traditionally, this is done through sweat lodges, fasting, vision quests, herbal medicines, ceremonial healing with the eagle fan and rattles, in which sacred songs and the drum are key components; traditional teachings at the sacred fire; sharing circles; individualized counselling; and guidance and direction through traditional teachings.

The Strong Earth Woman Lodge incorporates any or all of these into an individualized program based on the needs of each client. All clients are instructed in the seven sacred teachings and are encouraged to seek understanding of the four elements—fire, earth, water and air—and the four directions. The seven sacred teachings are respect, love, courage, humility, honesty, wisdom and truth. These teachings are carried by the spirits of the Buffalo, Eagle, Bear, Wolf, and Sabe, which is the Giant Beaver and Turtle respectively.

The Strong Earth Woman Lodge offers 24-hour care service towards holistic healing for grieving, loss of identity and suicide crisis intervention. Native spirituality fills the spiritual vacuum in the lives of people traumatized by residential schools and allows clients to find healing for sexual, emotional, mental and physical abuses. Strong Earth Woman Lodge is also a place for Native people just wanting to learn their culture. Although the lodge is based on Native spirituality, it welcomes people from all faiths and from all nations.

The lodge is located on traditionally sacred grounds seventy miles northeast of Winnipeg and is run by Native women and men under the direction of the Creator (Eyolfson 1992).

• Empowerment

In the context of social work, **Aboriginal empowerment** emphasizes the participation of community members in promoting self-determination and social change. The tragedy of the Innu Nation of Labrador illustrates how important empowerment is to community healing. As noted above, Chief Tshakapesh stressed the need to involve Innu members in finding the necessary long-term solutions to the problems of substance abuse and suicide among their children. He criticized the

National Archives of Canada. Neg no. PA161452 (NFB).

Health concerns are serious in Aboriginal communities today.

federal and Newfoundland governments for imposing unsuccessful programs on his community in the past: "We are here today because the solutions didn't work. We will never allow others to control our future."

At the Royal Commission on Aboriginal Peoples hearings, Aboriginal representatives made a distinction between a healing centre that adopts a holistic approach and a health centre dedicated to reacting to specific problems. At its most basic level, the principle of empowerment implies that services must be defined by the needs and situation of the person seeking help. In the Innu case, social welfare agencies continued to react with problem-specific solutions rather than taking the lead from the Innu community.

THE MEDICINE WHEEL AND SOCIAL WORK

Traditionally, many Aboriginal people have used some form of **Medicine Wheel** to underpin their approach to healing. Medicine Wheels are generally rock structures, the majority of which are found in Alberta. The basic teaching of the Medicine Wheel common to most First Nations is the four sacred directions of North, South, East and West. Each represents part of the way we live. For social work practice, these sacred directions represent aspects of life that must be considered when looking at a social problem.

The circle shape of the Wheel is representative of the fact that we are all one and that the entire universe is connected. In the original Medicine Wheels, each corner represented a different animal. Each animal had its own personality trait (that is, introspection, wisdom and so on). An individual who desired to be a complete human being would figure out which animal he or she most related to. The individual's life task would then be to explore other characteristics of the Wheel and thereby find balance.

The Medicine Wheel can potentially teach social workers to balance or consider all aspects of a presenting problem. In many Aboriginal societies, the Medicine Wheel is the symbol of holistic healing, embodying the four elements of whole health:

- spiritual health, which can mean many things depending on the individual's approach to spirituality, and may include participating in ceremonies, gaining traditional knowledge and exploring his or her spiritual heritage;

- mental health, which includes education, knowledge of Aboriginal history and cultural contributions, and activities that promote self-confidence;

- physical health, including nutrition, sports and recreation, and cultural activities; and

- emotional health, gained through access to sharing circles, counsellors and elders.

The Medicine Wheel defines what is commonly referred to as a **holistic approach to healing** (looking at the physical, emotional, spiritual and mental aspects of a problem or situation). It emphasizes that an

National Archives of Canada. neg no. PA92366 (W.A. Steel).

Recognizing and incorporating Aboriginal traditions is key.

Aboriginal approach to social work is one that avoids deep involvement with only one aspect of the problem. The four directions can help the social worker see all aspects of the problem being presented. For example, an approach that stresses the mental or psychological aspects of a problem is not consistent with Medicine Wheel teachings. Social workers using the Medicine Wheel to inform their practice would begin with the physical aspect, and then move to the mental, the emotional, and the spiritual. After going around the wheel completely, the social worker would begin again, looking at the problem at a deeper level.

The tragedy of the Innu of Davis Inlet in Labrador illustrates the importance of the four directions to healing in Aboriginal communities. The community captured national attention in January 1993 when television stations across the country reported numerous youth suicide attempts. Seventeen youths were sent to the Poundmaker Lodge in Alberta for substance abuse treatment, yet when the youth returned to the community, many resumed abusing substances. Their bodies had been healed, but there was nothing to nourish their mind, emotion or spirit. In order to have a lasting effect, healing must address not only individuals, but also the community; not only the physical, but also the spiritual, emotional and mental aspects of life. The initiative to heal must holistic and must come from, and be rooted in, the community.

The holistic approach to healing at Matootoo Lake successfully benefits young women and men. Traditional teachings are offered at Matootoo Lake, near the Peguis First Nation in Manitoba. *Matootoo* is the Ojibwa word for sweat lodge and is a place where traditional elders used to come for specific medicines. The teachings presented at Matootoo Lake prepare young women for their emotional, physical and spiritual transition to womanhood. A major goal of the program is to reduce the number of unplanned pregnancies by helping young women acquire confidence in their ability to deal with sexuality. A parallel program for boys is designed to enhance their self-esteem, develop respect for girls and women, and raise awareness of issues such as violence against women. The program has a great deal of local credibility, and the demand for services outstrips availability. The program exemplifies how a properly structured social work approach, rooted in the community, can successfully heal.

• Aboriginal Social Work Interventions

The Medicine Wheel illustrates the difference between Aboriginal approaches and mainstream approaches. Recognition of this distinction, and a willingness to learn new ways of thinking about problems, are the first steps in developing an Aboriginal approach to social work.

The use of the Medicine Wheel and a holistic concept of healing by social workers is increasing in Aboriginal communities across Canada. If an individual commits an offence against their family or community, everyone involved is brought together to resolve the situation in a way that meets everyone's needs. Under the rubric of social work intervention, new names, such as alternative measures, restorative justice,

"[T]he expertise of Inuit women in dealing with social issues is being recognized, but how can social issues be separated from economic issues? Where is unemployment, poverty and dependence separate from physical and emotional well-being or from the problems of youth suicide, alcohol and drug abuse, and ill-nourished children? Economic development cannot be isolated in a category of its own; all policies and programs must be designed, or redesigned, to include a more holistic perspective."

– Simona Barnes, Pauktuutit, Ottawa, Ontario, November 2 1993.

Source: The Final Report of the Royal Commission on Aboriginal Peoples. Perspectives and Realities (Ottawa, 1996).

sentencing circles, community justice forums and circle of healers, are being given to the traditional healing process.

Community healing centres that incorporate an Aboriginal approach to social work are opening across Canada. These centres provide a forum for exploring how Aboriginal and Western approaches can be brought together to meet Aboriginal community needs. Traditional healers, elders, community health representatives, medical interpreters, nurses, addiction counsellors, midwives, therapists, social workers, doctors, psychologists and rehabilitation specialists may all come together, depending on the situation in the community. Having a range of healers from both Aboriginal and Western professions and traditions enables a holistic healing to occur.

There has also been a marked increase in the number of **healing lodges** that provide residential treatment for people who are overwhelmed by social, emotional and spiritual problems. There are currently approximately fifty treatment facilities that provide Aboriginal residential healing. The Nechi Institute and Poundmaker's Lodge in Alberta, for example, provide healing and lodging for people dealing with addictions. First Nations and Inuit have identified the need for an increased number of similar lodges, since most Aboriginal people suffering from addictions and substance abuse continue to receive treatment in urban medical facilities, isolated from their community and culture.

The integration of an Aboriginal approach to healing with mainstream social work services is not always straightforward. Federal and provincial governments often legislate the work of social workers in state agencies. To secure funding for these needed services, First Nations are obliged to follow these rules and procedures. However, First Nations are developing intervention processes that slot Aboriginal healing practices into the legislated practices. For example, a child welfare worker may apprehend a child who has been abused as stipulated by legislation and the court system. The next step, however, may be a holistic conflict-resolution sentencing circle based on an Aboriginal approach to healing.

In their *Atikamekw Social Policy* regulations, the Atikamekw Nation stipulates an intervention process that is responsive to the social needs of Atikamekw communities and is a part of a self-government process but also complies with provincial government legislation. They outline fairly typical mainstream "temporary measures for protection of a child or youth," and then proceed to detail Aboriginal processes of healing. These processes include Family Council, the Circle of the Wise Counsel, and a Circle of Helpers. The Family Council process involves numerous family members and community participants. In a case where the family, friends and community cannot resolve the problem adequately, a Circle of the Wise Counsel replaces the Family Council. The Circle of Helpers, which includes social workers, is responsible for implementing the intervention plan. The social worker is called a Community Protection Delegate, signifying that the worker represents the protection interests of the community.

The community healing centres and the child welfare policy of the Atikamekw demonstrate how the incorporation of mainstream social work techniques into an Aboriginal approach to healing can work as effective social work practice models. Once again, at the root of this success is the recognition of a distinct Aboriginal worldview, the development of Aboriginal consciousness regarding the impact of colonialism, an emphasis on cultural knowledge and traditions, and the empowering of communities to control their own future.

URBAN SOCIAL SERVICES FOR ABORIGINAL PEOPLES

Many Canadians think of Aboriginal people as living on reserves or in rural areas. This is a misperception, since almost half of Aboriginal people in Canada live in cities and towns. As many Aboriginal people live in Winnipeg as in the whole of the Northwest Territories. Aboriginal people who live off the reserve are often left with no alternative to mainstream conventional social work services, as few urban centres offer distinct Aboriginal social services..

Many Aboriginal people migrating to urban centres are women moving to the city to escape abuse, seek healing or find employment. This naturally distances Aboriginal women from their community support networks and makes it very difficult for them to maintain a connection to their culture. Access to their teachers, grandmothers, clan mothers and healers is limited. Off-reserve Aboriginal women have also found mainstream social work services to be less than welcoming.

Aboriginal women have voiced their desire for their own organizations in urban centres to meet their distinct needs. At the Royal Commission on Aboriginal Peoples hearings, women stated that the existing services were not culturally sensitive nor designed with an Aboriginal approach to social work in mind.

> Our women face racism and systemic stereotyping at every turn. For Aboriginal women, this racism and stereotyping is rampant right through the system, from the police to the courts, child welfare agencies to income security. Although the law is supposed to treat everyone equally, we all know this is not an Aboriginal reality (Hall 1992).

They have developed a fear and distrust of social work agencies and believe that they are not treated equally by mainstream services.

> When a non-native woman goes in they don't even bother to take her children away. They are there to comfort her and give her counseling. When people like me or someone else goes in, right away they take their children. You really have to fight to hang on to them. You really have to prove yourself as a mother, and the other non-native women do not have to do so (Ellison 1992).

Aboriginal people have found that mainstream social work services rarely offer traditional spiritual practices, access to elders, healing medicines or women's teachings that reflect Aboriginal values. They have also found that the social workers in mainstream agencies are neither trained to be culturally aware and sensitive nor know how to deal with

From H. Kesketh Pritchard, *Trough Trackless Labrador* (New York: Sturgis and Walton, 1911).

An Inuit woman with her children in Labrador.

issues critical to Aboriginal women, such as cultural expectations with regard to family roles and the impact of colonization.

Social work for Aboriginal people living in non-Aboriginal communities requires a combination of specific services geared to the distinct needs of Aboriginal women and men and the development of culturally competent social workers in mainstream services that do not re-victimize and isolate. Aboriginal men and women have voiced a strong desire for culturally appropriate services, and have worked to develop Aboriginal urban institutions and networks. Non-Native social workers can play a role in providing social work services to Aboriginal people, both in Aboriginal communities and in urban settings. To do so, however, requires a commitment on their part to develop and apply knowledge and skills that are attuned to the culture and traditions of Aboriginal peoples.

WHO WILL PROVIDE SERVICES TO ABORIGINAL PEOPLES?

The social service and health problems that have long plagued Aboriginal peoples are well documented, and much more remains to be changed before their state of health and well-being is comparable to that of the general population. Individuals, private organizations and governments have had much to say about what is needed to address these issues. However, these recommendations still tend to be embedded in attempts by Euro-Canadians to define the role of Aboriginal peoples in Canadian society and to impose that role upon them, attempts that have to this point abjectly failed.

It is time to acknowledge that non-Aboriginals can no longer presume to institute their will upon the Métis, Inuit and other Aboriginal peoples. Aboriginal peoples across Canada are finding their own voice and, with that, the hope of establishing political, financial and moral control over their lives. Eventually there will be a dialogue and partnership with the rest of Canada in addressing the issues facing their communities, whether those communities are on traditional lands or within the urban centres of Canada.

The demographic information presented at the beginning of this chapter is not the whole story. An important part of the picture is the persistent and tenacious resistance on the part of Aboriginal people to efforts to eradicate both them and their distinct ways of living. Also part of the picture is Aboriginal economic development, the resurgence of Aboriginal languages, the assertion of Aboriginal education with a culturally based curriculum, the development of working models for Aboriginal justice systems, and Aboriginal control of the development and delivery of health care systems, no longer exclusively based upon the Western Euro-Canadian medical model but increasingly integrating Aboriginal medicines and healing ceremonies.

Aboriginal people are healing from the ravages of the residential schools and child welfare system and from the results of the systemic racism and discrimination within Canadian society—including drug addiction, suicides and family violence. They are in the process of

Provincial Archives of Newfoundland and Labrador (PANL B10-148).

An Innu couple in Labrador, circa 1910.

Part of a support rally during the Oka crisis in 1990. Banner reads: "In Support of Mohawk/Native Sovereignty."

redefining themselves in light of their traditional cultural practices. Perhaps most important, or in concert with all of these seemingly discrete efforts, is the reaffirmation of Aboriginal rights to land, rights that are inextricably linked to the development of the principle of **Aboriginal self-government**. Where the federal government might think that it would be *granting* self-government, Aboriginal peoples assert that they are seeking the formal recognition of rights that already exist: the rights to self-government that existed prior to European incursions.

A surge of **Aboriginal political activism** that began in the 1970s has led to the development of several national organizations representing and uniting distinct constituent groups. Among these organizations are: (1) the Assembly of First Nations, which represents status Indians who reside on Indian reserves across Canada; (2) the Inuit Tapirisat of Canada, representing Canada's Inuit population; (3) the Métis National Council; (4) the Congress of Aboriginal Peoples, representing off-reserve Aboriginal peoples; and (5) the Native Women's Association of Canada. These national organizations are generally affiliated with provincial and/or territorial and local groups that lobby the Canadian government to develop inclusive policies to protect the rights and interests of Aboriginal peoples, rights guaranteed in section 35 of the *Canadian Charter of Rights and Freedoms*. They also seek to educate governments and Canadians about the issues facing Aboriginal peoples.

In addition to these national organizations, there are grassroots organizations that provide direct services in Aboriginal communities. Indian and Inuit communities in particular are seeking responsibility for the administration of social programs devolved to them from the federal government. The Métis have historically advocated for inclusion within mainstream services, but have recently made strides in developing their own services related to education, economic development and social support, among others. The Nunavut Land Claims Agreement provides for mechanisms to assist the majority of Inuit living in Canada in developing cultural and social services in the new territory of Nunavut. Tripartite agreements between an individual Aboriginal organization and the federal and provincial governments are another means of enabling Aboriginal peoples to deliver services. These include agreements that provide for child welfare services, elementary and secondary education and policing, as well as social assistance and community health prevention and treatment programs.

In some cases, provincially funded organizations are the main service providers, especially in the case of elementary and secondary education or child welfare services. However, since the late 1970s, there has been an overall shift towards community control. For example, in 1969 the YWCA opened a second-stage supportive housing facility (first stage is an emergency shelter) for status Indian women in downtown Toronto. When it opened, it was called simply "Y Place." Aboriginal women gradually became more involved in the operation of the facility and, in 1973, renamed it *Anduhyaun*, Ojibwa for "our home." Anduhyaun still provides Aboriginal women and their children with a culturally based supportive environment and the resources to work on a variety of problems, including abusive relationships, family and marital breakdown, legal and financial difficulties, and alcohol and drug abuse. Other services help the women find housing, medical services, further education, skills development and employment. It also operates a food bank.

Within grassroots organizations such as Anduhyaun, it is still a challenge to balance the dictates of provincial or federal legislation and administrative criteria with the determination to provide culturally based and culturally appropriate services. This balance is not easily struck because often there are philosophical differences between Aboriginal and Canadian models of service delivery. This means that it has been difficult for Aboriginal peoples to secure stable funding for programs and services that supersede the limitations of the funding criteria for mainstream programs and services. For example, Indian Child and Welfare Services for reserves are funded by Indian Affairs, who may not necessarily provide funding for prevention programs such as courses in traditional parenting styles; instead, funding may be based simply upon the number of children taken into care.

In the past, service providers (including social workers) have usually been non-Aboriginal people who lived outside the community they served or only lived in the community for a short period of time. This is beginning to change. Communities are increasingly looking within their own ranks to find the human resources to build an infrastructure to heal and foster well-being. This option is becoming more and more viable as more Aboriginal people complete a mainstream professional education and as the communities themselves begin to create training programs that prepare community members to deliver specific kinds of programs and services. Self-government will create a situation where Aboriginal peoples take control of their own destinies in this area as well.

National Archives of Canada. Neg no. C102583 (Henry Metzger).

Self-government of Aboriginal communities is critical.

The KeKiNan Centre was started by the Manitoba Indian Nurses Association and the Indian and Métis Senior Citizens Group of Winnipeg in 1991 to provide culturally appropriate services. It was the first urban senior citizens home for Aboriginal people. It is an example of how holistic approaches can improve the quality of life for Aboriginal people. The Centre provides geriatric care for Aboriginal elders in Winnipeg, thirty enriched (or supportive) housing units and a number of personal care (geriatric) units. The philosophy of KeKiNan is consistent with an Aboriginal approach to social work, as it seeks to ensure that the people at the Centre play a major role in making decisions that affect their lives. The Centre provides cultural understanding and respect and empowers the seniors by assisting them in becoming active in the healing of the larger community. The seniors become role models for the Aboriginal youth by teaching about culture and traditions.

THE ROYAL COMMISSION ON ABORIGINAL PEOPLES

Many of the above conclusions were also reached in the recent **Royal Commission on Aboriginal Peoples**. The Final Report in 1996 brings together six years of research and public consultation on First Nations issues. This is the most extensive research to date and provides the basis for significant strides forward. Among the many issues discussed, the Report examines the need for Aboriginal people to heal from the consequences of domination, displacement and assimilation. The foundation for a renewed relationship, according to the Report, involves recognition of Aboriginal nations as political entities.

At the core of the 440 recommendations contained in the Report is a rebalancing of political and economic power between Aboriginal nations and other Canadian governments. The Report points to five key themes:

1. Aboriginal nations have to be reconstituted.

2. A process must be established for the assumption of powers by Aboriginal nations.

3. There must be a fundamental reallocation of lands and resources.

4. Aboriginal people need education and crucial skills for governance and economic self-reliance.

5. Economic development must be addressed if the poverty and despondency of lives defined by unemployment and welfare are to change.

As part of this, there also has to be a sincere acknowledgment by non-Aboriginal people of the injustices of the past.

• Social Services

With respect to social services, the Royal Commission recommends incorporating traditional knowledge and training in the development of Aboriginal health and social work. The Report also recommends that mainstream social work and social service systems be adapted to complement Aboriginal institutions. An additional recommendation is to

ROYAL COMMISSION ON ABORIGINAL PEOPLES

The *Final Report of the Royal Commission on Aboriginal Peoples* (RCAP) represents the most concise and comprehensive distillation of material on First Nations issues ever published. The Institute of Indigenous Government website makes the entire 3,200-page Report accessible through on-line search features and download capabilities.

The Report can be found at: http://www.indigenous.bc.ca/rcap.htm

REFERENCES

• Armitage, Andrew. 1993. Family and Child Welfare in First Nation Communities. In Brian Wharf, ed., *Rethinking Child Welfare in Canada*. Toronto: McClelland and Stewart Limited.

• Assembly of First Nations. 1994. *Breaking the Silence: An Interpretive Study of Residential School Impact and Healing as Illustrated by the Stories of First Nations Individuals*. Ottawa: Assembly of First Nations.

• Boldt, Menno. 1993. *Surviving as Indians: The Challenge of Self-Government*. Toronto: University of Toronto Press.

• Canadian Medical Association. 1993. *Submission to the Royal Commission on Aboriginal Peoples*. Ottawa: Canadian Medical Association.

• Chartrand, Paul. 1991. Terms of Division: The Problems of Outside-Naming for Aboriginal People in Canada. *Journal of Indigenous Studies* 2, no.2: 1-22.

• Ellison, K. 1992. Aboriginal Women's Council of Saskatchewan. Saskatoon, Saskatchewan. Presentation to RCAP (28 October).

• Eyolfson, C. 1992. Strong Earth Woman Lodge, Fort Alexander, Manitoba. Presentation to RCAP (30 October).

• Gibbins R., and J. Rick Ponting. 1986. Historical Overview and Background. In J. Rick Ponting, ed., *Arduous Journey: Canadian Indians and Decolonialization*. Toronto: McClelland and Stewart.

• Fournier, S., and E. Crey. 1998. *Stolen from Our Embrace*. Vancouver: Douglas & McIntyre Ltd.

• Hall, D. 1992. Ikwe Widdjiitiwin. Winnipeg, Manitoba. Presentation to RCAP (23 April).

• Indian and Northern Affairs Canada and Tungavik. 1993. *Agreement Between the Inuit of the Nunavut Settlement Area and Her Majesty the Queen in Right of Canada*. Ottawa: Indian and Northern Affairs Canada.

• Lee, K. 1999. Measuring Poverty among Canada's Aboriginal People. *Insight* 23, no.2. Ottawa: Canadian Council on Social Development.

• Manitoba. 1991. *Report of the Aboriginal Justice Inquiry of Manitoba, Volume I: The Justice System and Aboriginal People*. Winnipeg: Province of Manitoba.

bring housing and community infrastructure up to prevailing Canadian standards. Finally, the Report emphasizes the importance of political and economic restructuring for Aboriginal communities to achieve whole health.

The Report notes that Aboriginal peoples want to develop and control health and social services for both urban and on-reserve communities. The control of social services by external agencies and bureaucracies continues to frustrate attempts to organize holistic responses to need, and variations in available services reflect systematic inequities rather than adaptations to community diversity. The fact that health and social services are under the authority of provincial legislation while funding obligations are a federal responsibility often creates barriers. First Nations are asking that federal, provincial and territorial governments, in consultation with Aboriginal nations and urban communities of interest, co-operate to establish funding and programming mechanisms.

Beyond the development of services controlled by Aboriginal people, the Report outlines how the transformation of mainstream social services could make a more positive contribution to the well-being of Aboriginal people. Owing to the small population and remoteness of many Aboriginal communities, some health and social services, particularly specialized services, may be available only from mainstream providers. Initiatives to improve the effectiveness of mainstream health and social service programs have taken many forms, including:

• affirmative action and employment equity hiring policies;
• specialized Aboriginal units staffed by Aboriginal employees within larger mainstream programs;
• cross-cultural education programs for non-Aboriginal staff;
• Aboriginal input into mainstream programs and decisions; and
• Aboriginal customary practices included in the services offered by mainstream agencies.

• Healing

A prominent theme throughout the Report is the restoration of Aboriginal health from the wounds of culture loss, paternalistic and racist treatment, and official policies of assimilation. The Report details how healing is already under way in many communities and how this needs to increase by building on Aboriginal traditions, culture and worldviews. According to the Report, restoring communities and nations to unity and harmony is an extension of healing at the personal level. Such healing must be accompanied by self-government.

The Royal Commission on Aboriginal Peoples acknowledges that the convergence between Aboriginal perspectives and Western science provides a powerful basis for this work. The Report advocates the adoption of a strategy based on equitable access to services and equitable outcomes, on holistic approaches to treatment and preventive services, on Aboriginal control of services, and on a diversity of approaches that respond to cultural priorities and community needs. The core of the strategy is to develop a system of healing centres in urban, rural and reserve settings for front-line services, and healing lodges for residential treatment. The centres would operate under Aboriginal control and deliver integrated health and social services. Sagamok Anisshnabek First Nation, a reserve of just over 1,000 people, developed such a centre.

The Report acknowledges that Aboriginal people have also developed alternative correction programs that work. Although they are still few and far between, they bear little resemblance to conventional correctional services. The Aboriginal approach typically involves a healing lodge, bush camps and wilderness programs. They also work with traditional skills and spiritual practices. In taking a "justice as healing" approach, they look at the whole of the person's life.

CONCLUSION

Aboriginal peoples in Canada comprise 4 to 5 percent of Canada's total population. They include the Métis, the Inuit and a wide variety of other First Nations. They endure conditions found only in the poorest countries of the world. Poverty (35 percent below LICO) and unemployment (38.4 percent) are widespread. The situation is not only unjust, it is a national disgrace.

The *Indian Act*, residential schools and other government policies are the immediate roots of today's problems, which began with attempts by the European settlers to subjugate Aboriginal peoples and take away their rights to the land. Gradually, much of this is being acknowledged, as evidenced by the 1996 Royal Commission on Aboriginal Peoples and its 440 recommendations.

Social justice and self-determination for the First Nations of Canada are principles upon which to build effective social work with Aboriginal peoples. The traditional Medicine Wheel provides a useful starting point. It encourages service providers to consider all aspects of problems that arise. Social workers with an understanding of such an approach are already breaking new ground by initiating community healing centres, implementing restorative justice, setting up healing lodges, developing innovative child welfare policies, creating culturally appropriate urban social services and establishing holistic health care programs.

There is much that remains to be done to reverse the damage done to Aboriginal communities across Canada, and social workers, Aboriginal and non-Aboriginal, will play an important part in this process.

- Miller, J.R. 1989. *Skyscrapers Hide the Heavens: A History of Indian-White Relations in Canada.* Revised Edition. Toronto: University of Toronto Press.

- Morrissette V., B. McKenzie, and L. Morrissette. 1993. Towards an Aboriginal Model of Social Work Practice: Cultural Knowledge and Traditional Practices, *Canadian Social Work Review* 10, no.1 (winter): 91-108.

- Moscovitch, Allan, and Andrew Webster. 1995. Aboriginal Social Assistance Expenditures. In Susan Philips, ed., *How Ottawa Spends 1995-96: Mid-Life Crisis.* Ottawa: Carleton University Press.

- Purich, Donald. 1988. *The Métis.* Toronto: James Lorimer and Company, Publishers.

- Royal Commission on Aboriginal Peoples. 1995. *Aboriginal Self-Government: Legal and Constitutional Issues.* Ottawa: Canada Communications Group Publishing.

- Royal Commission on Aboriginal Peoples. 1996. *Perspectives and Realities.* Volume 4. Ottawa: Canada Communications Group Publishing.

- Scott, Kimberly A. 1994. Aboriginal Health and Social History: A Brief Canadian History. Unpublished manuscript.

- Smith, Derek G. 1993. The Emergence of Eskimo Status: An Examination of the Eskimo Disk List System and the Social Consequences, 1925-1970. In Noel Dyck and James B. Waldram, eds., *Anthropology, Public Policy and Native Peoples in Canada.* Montreal. McGill-Queen's University Press.

- Timpson, Joyce B. 1990. Indian and Native Special Status in Ontario's Child Welfare Legislation: An Overview of the Social, Legal and Political Context. *Canadian Social Work Review* 7, no.1: 49-68.

CHAPTER 9: SOCIAL WORK AND ABORIGINAL PEOPLES

Key Terms

- Aboriginal peoples
- Colonialism
- The Indian problem
- Land-cession treaties
- Indian Act
- Indian Agent
- Scrip system
- Disk list system
- Residential school system
- Assimilationist policies
- The Scoop
- Aboriginal approach to social work
- Aboriginal worldview
- Reclamation of Aboriginal culture
- Aboriginal empowerment
- Medicine Wheel
- Holistic approach to healing
- Healing lodges
- Aboriginal self-government
- Aboriginal political activism
- Royal Commission on Aboriginal Peoples

Discussion Questions

1. What bearing does the history of the relationship between Aboriginal peoples and the people of Canada have on the social welfare of Aboriginal peoples?

2. What was the reasoning behind the residential schools?

3. What were the six major goals of public policy in relation to Aboriginal peoples as identified by Gibbins and Ponting?

3. What are the four principles of an Aboriginal approach to social work?

4. Why does one need to be careful in describing a uniform Aboriginal approach?

5. What is the relevance of the Medicine Wheel for social work? How can it inform our approach to social work practice?

6. Is there a way for non-Aboriginal people to work productively with Aboriginal peoples and under what circumstances might this take place?

Websites

- **Aboriginal Canada Portal**
  http://www.aboriginalcanada.gc.ca
  This is a window to Canadian Aboriginal on-line resources, contacts, information, and government programs and services. The portal offers ease of access and navigation to listings of Aboriginal associations, businesses, organizations, bands, communities, groups, news and so forth.

- **Report of the Royal Commission on Aboriginal Peoples (RCAP)**
  http://www.indigenous.bc.ca/rcap.htm
  The Final Report of the Royal Commission on Aboriginal Peoples brings together six years of research and public consultation on Indigenous issues. This website makes the entire report accessible through on-line search features and download capabilities.

- **Assembly of First Nations (AFN)**
  http://afn.ca
  The AFN is the national representative/lobby organization of the First Nations in Canada. Their website has up-to-date news and information about First Nations people.

- **Congress of Aboriginal Peoples (CAP)**
  http://www.abo-peoples.org
  The Congress of Aboriginal Peoples was founded in 1971 as the Native Council of Canada (NCC). It was established to represent the interests nationally of Métis and non-status Indians, a population that out-numbered all other Native people combined. This is an excellent website with statistics, history and news.

10
Anti-Racist Social Work Today

Resisting Resistance to Change

Racism is the subordination of one group by another using arbitrary physical features such as skin colour. It can occur at individual, institutional or societal levels in the form of attitudes, beliefs, policies or procedures. Anti-racist social work is an approach to practice that aggressively combats racism on all three levels.

_____

R acism is not simply a series of random discriminatory acts against "visible minorities"—it is much more than that. There is a deep-seated ideology underlying racism and this ideology needs to be understood and combated. Is there racial equality in Canada? Do visible minorities still face barriers to success in the workplace and in accessing health and social services? What is the role of the social worker in combating discrimination based on race or ethnicity? These are a few of the questions this chapter will address.

In order to practice anti-racist social work, one must understand the history of racism in Canada, its extent today (for example, the prevalence of hate crimes), and be aware of one's own preconceptions in this area. This chapter introduces students to basic concepts, themes, strategies and practices associated with anti-racism and the role of social work and social workers in combating racism within themselves, their organizations and the wider society. The chapter touches on the following points: the history of racism in Canada in relation to various minority groups (Aboriginal, Chinese, Japanese and Blacks), Canadian immigration policy and the impact of the recent shift in immigration away from Europe to Third World countries, the history and impact of Canada's multicultural policy, the nature and scope of provincial and federal human rights legislation, and the prevalence of hate crimes in Canada today. The key concepts in this area are defined and, finally, the chapter outlines the basis of the new "anti-racism" approach and its application in the field of social work today.

HISTORY OF "RACE RELATIONS" IN CANADA

Canadians take great pride in the ethnic and racial diversity of their country. By comparison with many other countries, there is much to feel good about. However, one need not dig too deeply into Canadian history to see that ethnic conflict and racism are not at all foreign to the

Anti-racist rally highlights the persistence of racism.

185

THE JAPANESE IN CANADA

The evacuation of the Japanese Canadians, or Nikkei, from the Pacific Coast in the early months of 1942 is said by some to have been the greatest mass movement in the history of Canada.

It was not until 1949, four years after Japan had surrendered, that the majority of displaced Japanese Canadians were allowed to return to British Columbia. By then, most had begun a new life elsewhere in Canada. Their property had long before been confiscated and sold at a fraction of its worth.

In 1988, Prime Minister Brian Mulroney formally apologized to Japanese Canadians and authorized the provision of $21,000 to each of the survivors of war-time detention.

Canadian experience and that problems in this area continue to the present day. Racism persists and even thrives in Canada, according to Lincoln Alexander, chair of the Canadian Race Relations Foundation:

> Today I stand before you to say: As Canadians, we are not doing a very good job. We're not making the grade. We get a failing grade when police officers in Saskatoon drive Aboriginal men to the outskirts of town and leave them in sub-zero temperatures without winter coats. We get a failing grade when 600 Chinese arrive by ships off the coast of British Columbia looking for sanctuary in Canada only to be met with fear and even hatred. They were handcuffed like criminals, and today, the future for some of these refugee claimants is uncertain and 35 of them remain in provincial jails. We get a failing grade when our schoolyards become a war zone for some visible minority youth because they're bullied on a regular basis, sometimes with fatal results. We get a failing grade when new immigrants, especially non-white immigrants, subsidize Canada's economy to the tune of 55 billion dollars each year, according to a study done by the University of Toronto, because skills acquired in their homelands are not recognized in this country (Alexander 2001).

We will briefly review some of the history that contributes to this current state of affairs.

Native Canadians and the residential school system. The history of injustice wreaked upon Canada's founding peoples since the Europeans first arrived in North America is widely documented and quite widely known. Perhaps its worst expression is found in the infamous residential school system, which was, for all intents and purposes, designed to obliterate Native society and culture altogether.

The church-government partnership for Aboriginal education lasted from the 1840s to 1969 (the last residential school, Christie Roman Catholic School in Tofino, B.C., didn't close until 1983). It is estimated that from 100,000 to 150,000 Aboriginal children attended residential schools. A 1920 amendment to the *Indian Act* made it mandatory for every Indian to attend. Children stayed at the residence for most of the year, and family visits were limited. The use of the English language became mandatory. The intent of the residential school policy was to erase Aboriginal identity by separating generations of children from their families and socializing them, not in the culture of their ancestors, but in the culture of the Canadian mainstream. This process was often done by force, which resulted in psychological damage to the students. This was social welfare at its worst, and its effects (poverty, family disintegration, poor health, high rates of suicide, high incarceration rates) remain with us today.

One of the main arenas of conflict today between governments in Canada and First Nations is Native land claims. All Aboriginal groups (Inuit, Indian, Métis) have placed claims before provincial and federal governments. More often than not, the desire to expand mineral and resource exploration on Native lands has brought the federal and provincial governments into conflict with the First Nations. These clashes escalated in the 1990s, with the Oka Crisis outside Montreal over incursions into Native land areas, and the celebrated struggle over Clayoquot Sound on Vancouver Island, where Native groups and environmentalists resisted the clear-cutting of ancient forests.

Courtesy of Vancouver City Archives.

Japanese-Canadian fishing boats confiscated during WWII.

Chinese Canadians. Between 1881 and 1884, 15,700 Chinese were brought over from China as contract labourers to work on the Canadian Pacific Railway (Isajiw 1999). Thereafter a series of laws were put in place to exclude or limit the number of Chinese and South Asian immigrants to Canada: the *Chinese Immigration Act* of 1885; the Head Tax of $50 on Chinese immigrants set in 1885 (raised to $100 in 1901 and to $500 in 1904, an average two-year wage for a Chinese person in Canada); the *Immigration Act* of 1910 (which established "undesirable" classes of immigrants); and the *Chinese Exclusion Act* of 1923 (which admitted to Canada only certain specified classes of Chinese and almost stopped Chinese immigration completely). As William Lyon Mackenzie King, then Deputy Minister of Labour, put it in 1907, it is "natural that Canada should remain a White man's country." The tax was eliminated in 1923, but other laws, which made it nearly impossible for Chinese men to bring their families to Canada and forced many to be separated from their wives and children for years at a time, remained in place until 1947 (Ibid.). Recently, the Canadian government was faced with a lawsuit by Chinese Canadians who were demanding compensation for the Head Tax and other racially motivated measures aimed at limiting immigration from China in the first half of the twentieth century. In July 2001, however, a court ruled that the claim could not proceed.

Japanese Canadians. In World Wars I and II, the Canadian government instituted a policy of internment of members of ethnic minority groups whom it defined as "enemy aliens." Immigrants from the Austro-Hungarian Empire, with whom the Allies were at war, were interned, as well as the Japanese in Canada. In both cases the basic human rights of the respective minorities were violated. The homes, businesses and property of Japanese Canadians were confiscated and their lives were turned on end (Isajiw 1999). It was not until four decades later, in 1988, that the government announced a comprehensive settlement with surviving members of the Japanese war-time community.

Jews. In addition to racial categories, racist ideologies may be focused on policies directed towards specific ethnic groups. During and immediately after World War II, the Canadian government was reluctant to admit Jews as refugees to Canada. It undertook informal measures to restrict their immigration. When asked how many Jews would be allowed into Canada after the war, a senior immigration official issued his famous reply: "None is too many." The Canadian government refused entry to a ship called the *St. Louis*, which carried a shipload of Jews desperate to be admitted to Canada. Instead, they were compelled to sail back to Europe on a voyage of the damned. Anti-Semite beliefs and practices are still widespread today.

Blacks in Canada. The first account of the presence of Blacks in Canada was in 1605. Mattheu de Costa was one of the team members with the French explorers who landed in Nova Scotia (formerly Port Royal) in the early seventeenth century. Later, Blacks were brought to Canada by the French as slaves. Slavery was officially introduced in Canada by the French in 1628 and continued by the British until 1833-1834 when slavery was abolished in the British Empire.

THE CHINESE IN CANADA

In 1885, federal legislation was passed to restrict the immigration of Chinese into Canada. A $50 Head Tax was imposed on every Chinese immigrant entering Canada. In January 1901, the tax was increased to $100 per head and raised again in January 1904 to $500.

An excellent website summarizing facts and accounts of the lives of Chinese Canadians since 1858, using text articles and an extensive photo gallery, is located at: http://www.ccnc.ca/toronto/history/index.html

Certificate of Head Tax paid by Quan Lum, 1912.

REMEMBER AFRICVILLE

Canada is a country that prides itself on its multiculturalism and ethnic diversity. But, in the 1960s, a different approach was evidenced in a small village on the edge of Halifax, named Africville.

In the name of urban renewal, this poor Afro-American community, pictured below, was erased. Civil servants insisted that this action was above board and legal and that it was not a example of racism, but few people now see it this way.

Africville was plowed under to make way for a park and a new bridge over the narrows to Dartmouth, between 1964 and 1969. Former residents were moved to nearby public housing in the depressed north end of Halifax.

Africville in the 1960s; now a largely abandoned park.

The next significant early migration into Canada was that of the Black Loyalists, brought by the British in 1784 following the American War of Independence. Hundreds, who had fought for their freedom on the side of the British against the Americans, were brought to Nova Scotia. They were emancipated and promised education, employment and citizenship, but were instead left to fend for themselves. Many were forced back into slavery through abject poverty. The situation forced them to ask the British government in England to send them to Africa. Their request was granted, and in the late 1790s, many were shipped to West Africa to the British colony of Sierra Leon. In response to the need for cheap labour, the British also deceived and brought Maroons (runaway slaves) from Jamaica to work on the fortifications at Citadel Hill in Halifax. These Maroons were militant and refused to be controlled as slaves by white Nova Scotians who used them as forced labourers. Many Maroons were also shipped to Sierra Leone.

Another group of Blacks were taken to Nova Scotia as refugees from the War of 1812 between Britain and the U.S. Most black indigenous Nova Scotians are the offspring of these refugees. It must be understood that on no occasion did Britain free the Blacks from slavery as a humanitarian gesture. They were freed as a war strategy against the Americans who owned them. Finally, Blacks used what is known as the Underground Railroad to escape slavery in the United States between 1820 and 1860. These American Blacks, as fugitives, slaves and as freedmen, formed sizable settlements, particularly in southwestern Ontario and the Maritimes. More recently, however, immigration from the Caribbean accounts for the majority of Canadian Blacks.

While the context is quite different from that in the U.S., there has been a great deal of research documenting anti-black prejudice, racism, discrimination and harassment in Canada. Newspapers in Toronto, Halifax, Ottawa and Montreal have reported numerous incidents involving black youth and the police. In her study of Caribbean people in Toronto, Frances Henry concluded that police-Black community relations are "fraught with tensions" and that "the increased policing to the Black community, stop-and-search procedures and other forms of harassment have exacerbated tensions and contributed to the 'criminalization' of young Black males" (Henry 1994). Similar conclusions were reached by the Ontario Commission on Systemic Racism in the Ontario Criminal Justice System, which reported that discriminatory practices by police against black men were widespread (Ontario 1995).

Canada actively practised slavery until early in the nineteenth century (Sheppard 1997), and even the Black Loyalists who entered Canada as free persons were subject to racist policies. Black Canadians were subject to legislation that enforced segregated schools and communities, and limitations on property rights. In 1939, Canada's highest court concluded that racial discrimination was legally enforceable (Walker 1997). It was not until 1953-54 that Canada deleted from its statutes discriminatory laws that denied Blacks the right to freely pursue formal education, respectable jobs, welfare assistance, and civil and humanitarian rights. For over four hundred years, white Canadians have discriminated against Blacks.

TEP Photo Archives, Toronto.

THE NEW IMMIGRATION

As might be expected in a country comprised largely of immigrants and their descendants, ethnic and race relations in Canada have been heavily influenced by **immigration policy**. Prior to 1967, when important new immigration legislation came into force, "Nationality" was one of the criteria used to qualify for admission to Canada. Canadian immigration policy was undoubtedly Eurocentric; immigration was encouraged from (white) Europe and discouraged from the rest of the world. In 1967, new legislation introduced a point system, whereby prospective immigrants had to qualify based on such criteria as education, work experience, language fluency and age. "Country-of-origin" was no longer an explicit criterion in the selection process. The inevitable consequence of the new legislation was a new wave of skilled immigrants from Asia, Africa and South and Central America.

The shift was quite dramatic. Prior to 1961, over 90 percent of all immigrants were from Europe, and over half of these were from Northern and Western Europe and the United Kingdom. Immigrants from Asia constituted only a small percentage (3.1 percent) of all immigrants arriving in the country. By the 1990s the picture had changed significantly. Europeans made up only about one-fifth of all the immigrants, and the largest number, close to 60 percent, came from Asia. The remaining proportion—almost one-fifth (16.6 percent)—came from Central and South America, the Caribbean and Bermuda, and from the United States. The largest proportion of European immigrants came, not from the United Kingdom or Northern and Western continental Europe, but from Eastern Europe.

With this shift came a substantial increase in the "visible minority" population in Canada. No longer were new immigrants predominantly white Europeans. According to Statistics Canada projections, the number of Canadians in "visible minority" groups is expected to increase to 7.1 million by 2026, up from 2.7 million in 1991 (Kelly 1995; Isajiw 1999). As a proportion of the overall population, this represents a doubling to 20 percent in 2016 from 10 percent in 1991. The largest visible minority group in 1991 (as of 1996) were the Chinese (about 666,000 people), and this group will continue to be the largest over the projection period (nearly 2 million by 2016). The proportion of Canadians who are of Chinese ancestry will grow to 5 percent by 2016. Blacks were the third-largest visible minority group in 1991 (540,000) but are expected to become the second-largest group by 2016 (almost 1.3 million). South Asians will drop from the second-largest to the third-largest group, moving from 543,000 in 1991 to a projected 1.2 million in 2016. West Asians and Arabs will continue to rank as the fourth-largest visible minority over this period (Kelly 1995).

Largely because of the selective process of modern immigration policy, visible minority adults are much more likely to have a university degree and less likely not to have completed high school than are other adults. In 1991, 18 percent of the visible minority population aged fifteen and over had a university degree, compared with 11 percent of other adults (Kelly 1995).

MARY ANN SHADD CARY

Teacher, abolitionist, civil rights advocate, feminist and newspaper editor, Mary Ann Shadd (1823-1893) was an influential voice in the Underground Railroad community in Upper Canada. She was active in Sandwich, Toronto and Chatham, teaching and editing the *Provincial Freeman*, an important newspaper of the Canadian Underground Railroad community.

Shadd broke new ground for women, being not only an early woman newspaper editor, but also the first black woman editor in Canada. She claimed equal rights under the law regardless of colour or gender, while exhorting her community to realize the benefits of self-sufficiency.

There has been a major shift in Canadian immigration trends.

Table 10.1: Immigrant Population by Place of Birth, Showing Period of Immigration before 1961 and between 1991 and 1996

Place of Birth	Period of Immigration*			
	Before 1961	%	1991-1996**	%
United States	45,050	4.3	29,025	2.8
Central and South America	6,370	0.6	76,335	7.3
Caribbean and Bermuda	8,390	0.8	57,315	5.5
Europe	953,360	90.4	197,480	19.0
United Kingdom	265,580	25.2	25,420	2.4
North & West Europe without UK	284,285	26.9	31,705	3.1
Eastern Europe	175,430	16.6	87,900	8.5
Southern Europe	228,145	21.6	52,455	5.0
Africa	4,945	0.5	76,260	7.3
Asia	32,580	3.1	592,710	57.1
West Central Asia & Middle East	4,975	0.5	82,050	7.9
Eastern Asia	20,555	1.9	252,340	24.3
South-east Asia	2,485	0.2	118,265	11.4
Southern Asia	4,565	0.4	140,055	13.5
Oceania & Other	4,250	0.4	9,875	1.0
Total Place of Birth	1,054,930	100.0	1,038,992	100.0

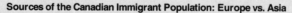

Sources of the Canadian Immigrant Population: Europe vs. Asia

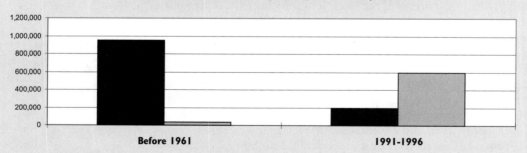

*Non-permanent residents are not included.
**Includes only the first four months of 1996.
Source: Statistics Canada, *Census 1996*, "Population by Selected Age Groups and Sex for Canada, Provinces and Territories," Internet Catalogue No. 93F0023XDB96005, the Nation Series, 1998.

The substantial increase in the visible minority population in recent years has already dramatically affected public policy (e.g., multiculturalism and anti-racism policy), and it seems likely to continue to do so in the future. The new period of ethnic and racial diversity has undoubtedly enriched Canada and the lives of each of its citizens. Certainly, there is no reason why the demographic changes need to result in serious ethnic and racial conflict. Other factors, such as a serious downturn in the economy, and policies and institutional procedures that intervene and foster ethnic and racial divisions, however, will likely affect the social impact of this underlying demographic change.

As a result of the new immigration, there is a new set of issues for social workers and others working in the social services to consider. Social workers are now required to have a greater sensitivity to religious beliefs, cultural events and holidays, and the effects of prejudice and discrimination. Social workers must not only deal with the effects of racism, but also find ways to combat it.

MULTICULTURALISM POLICY

In 1971, Canada became the first country to adopt **multiculturalism** as an official policy. The policy was aimed at a greater integration of Canadian society by providing the diverse ethnic minority groups with a sense of belonging to Canada. Its original aim was to give ethnic minority groups a public recognition of their identity. The policy gave them a chance to reinforce their identity, but within the Canadian context, and with the recognition that ethnic diversity is part of Canadian identity (Isajiw 1999). The basic principles of the policy were expressed by Prime Minister Pierre Elliott Trudeau in his introduction of the policy in the Canadian Parliament on October 8, 1971:

> A policy of multiculturalism within a bilingual framework commends itself to the government as the most suitable means of assuring the cultural freedom of Canadians. Such a policy should help to break down discriminatory attitudes and cultural jealousies. National unity if it is to mean anything in the deeply personal sense must be founded on confidence in one's own individual identity; out of this can grow respect for that of others and a willingness to share ideas, attitudes and assumptions. A vigorous policy of multiculturalism will help to create this initial confidence. It can form the base of a society which is based on fair play for all.

In order to implement the policy, the Canadian government created the Multicultural Directorate, which in turn developed a range of programs designed to help it fulfil the policy's objectives. Wsevolod Isajiw, professor of sociology at the University of Toronto, categorizes these programs under four headings: (1) programs aimed at assisting the cultural preservation, cultural education and growth of various ethnic groups, including their languages; (2) programs aimed at exhibiting cultural differences to the general public; (3) programs aimed directly at the mainstream community in order to develop a greater tolerance or acceptance of ethnic differences, and thus to reduce prejudices and ethnic and racial discrimination; (4) programs aimed at involving ethnic groups and selected ethnic institutions in the mainstream institutions of society (Isajiw 1999).

ANTI-RACIST TRAINING AND MATERIALS PROJECT

Social work professional associations are taking up the challenge of implementing an anti-racist model that respects difference and acknowledges oppression. The Anti-Racist Training and Materials Project, a project of the Canadian Association of Schools of Social Work (CASSW), was designed to build a national infrastructure of regionally strong collegial educational support and scholarship in the areas of anti-racism and anti-oppression.

The project participants concluded that, because racism and diversity are so multi-layered, social work educators need to address them across the curriculum.

For more information, go to: http://www.cassw-acess.ca

In 1988, the *Multiculturalism Act* was passed, restating and reinforcing the 1971 policy and mandating federal departments to ensure equal opportunities in employment for all ethnic and racial groups. The federal multicultural program stimulated the development of other programs and the establishment of other agencies and institutions. Isajiw notes, for example, that a Multicultural Television (MTV) channel went on air in Toronto, and many ethnic programs began to appear on the Public Access Network across the country. In addition, the publication of books and the production of ethnic films has been supported by the multicultural program. In many Canadian provinces, particularly Alberta, Saskatchewan and Manitoba, the idea of multiculturalism has been instrumental in the inclusion of a number of "heritage" languages into regular secondary school programs. In 1996, by a special Act of the federal Parliament, the Canadian Race Relations Foundation was established to deal more directly with issues of race.

Canada's multiculturalism policy has set a positive framework within which all issues relating to ethnic and racial equality are now discussed. Nevertheless, while the policy's impact on Canadian society has been significant, and ethnic and racial groups have experienced some improvement in their conditions, they are still relatively disadvantaged. In a recent report, for example, the Canadian Race Relations Foundation notes that members of visible minority groups continue to have poorer outcomes with respect to employment and income and still face barriers to socioeconomic equality (Canadian Race Relations Foundation 2000).

HUMAN RIGHTS LEGISLATION

All federal and provincial jurisdictions have legislated rights protection laws and have created rights commissions to implement such policy. National **human rights legislation** in Canada began with the passage of the Canadian Bill of Rights in 1960. Later in that decade other provinces enacted similar legislation, and by 1975, all provinces in Canada had human rights codes. Whether a rights violation complaint is heard at the federal or provincial levels is determined by the constitutional division of powers: complaints involving banking, national airlines, railways or federal government employees are in the federal jurisdiction, whereas complaints involving school boards, city government or restaurants are in the provincial jurisdiction. In general, both federal and provincial human rights law prohibits discrimination in all aspects of employment; the leasing and sale of property; public accommodation, services and facilities; membership in labour unions and professional associations; and the dissemination of hate propaganda. Grounds of discrimination vary slightly depending on the jurisdiction.

In 1982, the Canadian Bill of Rights was superceded by the **Charter of Rights and Freedoms.** The *Charter* guaranteed the fundamental freedoms of conscience and religion, thought, belief, opinion and expression (including freedom of the press and other media of communication), peaceful assembly and association. It guaranteed democratic rights, geographical mobility rights, legal rights (including the right to life, liberty

© Dick Hemingway

Part of the multicultural Caribana celebration.

and security of persons), and equality rights that protect against "discrimination based on race, national or ethnic origin, colour, religion, sex, age or mental or physical disability." The *Charter* reinforced the official bilingualism in Canada by affirming the equality of the English and French languages and by affirming the rights of children to be educated in either language. It also affirmed the multicultural character of Canada and recognized the rights of Canada's Aboriginal peoples. Finally, it emphasized that all the rights and freedoms referred to within it are guaranteed equally to male and female persons (Isajiw 1999).

In 1986, the Canadian *Human Rights Act* and the *Employment Equity Act* were passed with the purpose of redressing some of the past injustices against designated groups in Canada. The designated groups are women, persons with disabilities, Aboriginal peoples and visible minorities. The purpose of the **Employment Equity Act** is to ensure equity in the workplace so that no one is denied access to employment for reasons unrelated to merit and skills.

In relation to its own minority groups, Canada is also bound by the international covenants on human rights to which it is a signatory. These include the United Nations Charter of 1945, the Universal Declaration of Human Rights adopted by the United Nations in 1948, the International Convention on the Prevention and Punishment of the Crime of Genocide of 1948, the International Convention Concerning Discrimination in Respect of Employment and Occupation of 1958, the International Convention on All Forms of Racial Discrimination of 1965 (ratified in 1969), the International Covenant on Economic, Social and Cultural Rights of 1966 (ratified in 1976), the International Covenant on Civil and Political Rights (ratified in 1976) and various other resolutions of United Nations assemblies and international conferences (Isajiw 1999).

Passing laws is one thing; implementing them is another. Each province and territory, and the federal government, has a **human rights commission** charged with dealing with abuses. While these commissions have had some success, they have unfortunately often been hampered by limited resources and case backlogs. Furthermore, since such commissions are by their nature complaints-driven, it is generally felt that many victims of discrimination, perhaps themselves new to the country, do not have the financial resources or even the time to report discrimination and initiate the lengthy complaints process.

HATE CRIMES

When people are the targets of violence solely because of who they are, or who they are thought to be, they are the victims of **hate crimes**. The most common targets of hate-motivated crime are Blacks, Jews and gays. It is estimated that there are approximately 60,000 hate crimes committed annually in Canada's nine major urban centres; 61 percent of hate crimes are directed against racial minorities (particularly Blacks), 23 percent against religious minorities (particularly Jews), 11 percent against groups of different sexual orientation, and 5 percent against

---

CONSTITUTION ACT

"Every individual is equal before and under the law and has the right to the equal protection and equal benefit of the law without discrimination based on race, national or ethnic origin, colour, religion, sex, age, or mental or physical disability."

Source: Constitution Act, 1982, s.15, pt.1.

HATE ON THE INTERNET

The electronic transmission of hate propaganda has fundamentally changed the face of racism in Canada. Canada's hate propaganda laws prohibit the dissemination of hate books, and Holocaust denial tracts are not allowed to enter the country. However, the Internet does not recognize international borders, and material prohibited by Canadian law can pass freely and unexamined on the information highway.

Source: Canadian Association of Chiefs of Police, *Hate Crimes in Canada: In Your Back Yard* (1996).

Racist garden ornaments are demeaning and offensive.

ethnic minorities (Roberts 1995). Such crimes create a climate of fear within the entire targeted group.

The promotion of hate based on race, religion, ethnic origin or sexual orientation is widespread. Hate sites on the Internet increased from 50 to more than 800 in the period from 1998 to 2001. The Toronto Police Hate Crimes Unit reports that 19 percent more hate crimes, or 110 incidences, were reported in the first six months of 1999 compared with the previous six-month period. There were 280 reported incidents of anti-Semitic harassment and vandalism in Canada in the year 2000, according to the League for Human Rights of B'nai Brith. This represents a 5 percent increase over the 267 incidents reported across the country in 1999 (League for Human Rights of B'nai Brith 2000).

Individuals who act out conscious feelings of hate, bias or prejudice commit most hate crimes in Canada. A survey in 1994 by Canada's Department of Justice to assess the tone of race relations found that people involved in racially motivated hate crimes tend to be young—in their teens or early twenties—and that the perpetrators of such crimes are not, as some have suggested, experiencing bouts of teenage angst and rebellion (Roberts 1995). To the contrary, the study concluded that young people are acting out on long-held views shared by their families and friends about those unlike themselves. Organized hate groups are responsible for about 5 percent of hate-motivated activities in Canada.

There is a growing consensus on the need for consistent policy and service delivery responses from the criminal justice system at all levels. The federal government demonstrated strong leadership in this area by amending the Criminal Code in 1996 to strengthen sentencing for any Criminal Code offence that is motivated by hate (Bill C-41). The move prompted community discussion, raised overall awareness of the issues and helped to mobilize communities. It also highlighted the need for stronger responses in the communities where hate-motivated incidents occur and may go unreported. In some centres, police services are creating hate crime units in response to demands from marginalized communities who are the targets of hate-motivated crime.

For their part, front-line social workers are using innovative anti-racist approaches that emphasize community empowerment to combat hate crimes. Since hate crimes do not occur in a vacuum, education and effective community work can prevent hate crimes and act as an important complement to hate crime laws. Social workers are involved in outreach and consultation, education and awareness activities, and fostering the creation of advocacy and support groups. In struggling against overt racism of this kind, social workers also work with community organizations to promote an anti-racist perspective through education. This may involve producing brochures on anti-racism, going into schools and engaging students in the issues or speaking out about community conditions and government inaction. With their roots firmly in the locality, community workers can also provide feedback on what works. This kind of collaborative, community-based approach to combating overt racism can help to minimize the extent of hate crime activity and strengthen the resolve and solidarity of its victims.

CONCEPTS AND TERMS

The terms used to describe and understand complex social issues such as race and racism evolve over time. In the 1970s, for example, racism tended to be seen as the result of individual prejudice. Negative and stereotypical attitudes were deemed to be "the cause" of racist discrimination; if individual attitudes were corrected through education and the sharing of cultures, racism would no longer exist. Much of federal multicultural policy is premised on this understanding. More recently, we have seen the emergence of a comprehensive "anti-racist" approach. In general, this has involved a shift from seeing the causes of racism as lying within personal prejudice and individual behaviour to seeing racism as interlinked with the larger structures and social systems in Canadian society. Some of the key concepts in this area are reviewed below.

- **Stereotype.** When applied to people, stereotyping refers to the forming of a fixed picture of a group of people, usually based on false or incomplete information.

- **Prejudice.** Prejudice literally means to "prejudge" others based on preconceived ideas. No law can prevent prejudiced attitudes. However, the law can prohibit discriminatory practices and behaviours that flow from prejudice.

- **Ethnicity/ethnic group.** The term ethnicity refers to the characteristics of a group of people who share a common heritage, identity or origin or are descendants of those who have shared a distinct culture and who identify with their ancestors, their culture or their group. Most commonly, the term *ethnic group* is used to mean "minority" ethnic groups, for example, Blacks, Chinese or Sikhs in Canada (as against the majority ethnic group, white Anglo-Saxons). Interestingly, in today's multicultural Canadian society, the term "ethnic" is used both in a derogatory sense (i.e., as a racist slur) and in a positive sense as describing a group and its food, customs and so forth as being different and interesting.

- **Culture.** The concept of culture generally refers to behaviours, beliefs and practices that are meaningful in terms of some shared, even if implicit, cognitive and value assumptions derived from a unique historical community experience (Isajiw 1999).

- **Ethnocentrism.** Ethnocentrism is an attitude by which members of a group tend to consider their group to be in some or all ways better or superior to other groups. Such an attitude is especially significant in relation to the majority groups because it is conditioned by the positions of power that members of a group hold.

- **Race.** Race is an arbitrary classification of human beings based on skin colour and other superficial physical characteristics. This classification, conceived in Europe in the colonial period, placed the populations of the world in a hierarchical order with white Europeans superior to all others. Modern biologists do not recognize "race" as a meaningful scientific category and recent human genome research is conclusive on this point.

RACISM DEFINED

Racism, as defined in Article 1(1) of the International Convention on the Elimination of Racial Discrimination (1966), includes all three levels of racism:

"Any distinction, exclusion, restriction or preference based on race, colour, descent, or national or ethnic origin which has the purpose or effect of nullifying or impairing the recognition, enjoyment or exercise, on an equal footing, of human rights and fundamental freedoms; in the political, economic, social, cultural or any other field of public life."

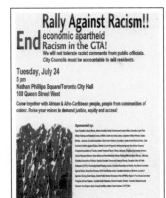

Rallies across Canada unite forces opposed to racism.

EDUCATING AGAINST RACISM

A key component of anti-racism work is education. Researchers have sifted through hundreds of resources to present useful and practical tools for anti-racism training and education. Available in the publication section of the Canadian Race Relations Foundation website at: http://www.crr.ca

"Schools shall be expected to provide evidence of effective progress in attaining multicultural/multiracial diversity given the school's context and mission. Such progress should be evident in curriculum, administration, the selection of faculty and professional staff and in initiatives directed toward their self-awareness and education, in student admissions, and in external relations."

Source: CASSW Accreditation Standards, Sec. 1.11.

- **Visible minorities.** Canadian legislation, such as the *Employment Equity Act*, even today refers to "visible minorities"–defined as "persons, other than Aboriginal peoples, who are non-Caucasian in race or non-white in colour." However the term *visible minority* begs the question: visible by whom? It is probably time to abandon this term.

- **Racism.** Racism is a relationship or attitude based on the subordination of one group by another using arbitrary physical features such as skin colour. One can identify three types of racism: personal racism, cultural racism and institutional racism. Personal racism refers to attitudes and behaviours on the part of individuals that ascribe inferior status to visible minorities. Cultural racism entails beliefs that the cultural or ethnic differences of "others" are inferior. Institutional racism includes discriminatory policies, institutional practices and structures (such as the residential school system or racially based immigration policies). Racism is manifested in overt (obvious and unconcealed) and covert (subtle and hidden) forms.

- **Discrimination.** Discrimination refers to actions, situations or policies that have the effect, whether intentional or not, of putting some people at an unnecessary disadvantage on grounds such as race, sex or religion. Discrimination is usually based on prejudice and stereotypes. Canadian courts have recognized two types of illegal discrimination: (1) direct discrimination; and (2) adverse effects discrimination (also called indirect discrimination or systemic discrimination).

- **Systemic discrimination (or institutionalized racism).** Systemic racism refers to the existence of policies and structures built into our social institutions that serve to subjugate, oppress and force the dependence of individuals or groups. The recent finding by a commission of inquiry of systemic racial discrimination within the Ontario criminal justice system is an example. The forced-assimilationist policies underlying the residential schools were of this kind, as were the pre-1968 Canadian immigration laws that explicitly excluded persons based on their country of origin.

- **Anti-racist social work.** In the past, racism tended to be presented as if it took place only at the individual level (i.e., that there were individuals with racist opinions), and there was a belief that it could be eliminated at this level by education alone. The new anti-racist approach goes beyond this and recognizes that racism is also deeply rooted in the wider institutions of our society—most notably, in employment, education, justice, media, policing, immigration and government policies. Certainly, there is now ample evidence that deep-rooted racism exists. Since social service practitioners carry out their work within these institutions, it is incumbent upon them in the course of their daily work to be aware of this wider problem and to combat racism fully and comprehensively wherever and however it manifests itself.

TOWARDS AN "ANTI-RACIST" SOCIAL WORK: THE PERSONAL, INSTITUTIONAL AND SOCIETAL

What does it mean to practice anti-racist social work? The Canadian Association of Social Workers' code of ethics states that "a social worker shall identify, document, and advocate the elimination of discrimination." As part of this, there is an obligation to not only challenge and eradicate racism in others, and in policies and organizations, but also to examine one's own beliefs and behaviours.

Lena Dominelli, one of the pioneers in developing anti-racist social work, summarized anti-racist social work: "Social work, redefined according to anti-racist criteria, is about realizing significant improvement in the life chances and well-being of individuals regardless of their gender, race, class, age, physical or intellectual abilities, sexual orientation, religious affiliation or linguistic capabilities. Anti-racist social work, therefore, is a bridge between social work in a racist society and social work in a non-racist one" (Dominelli 1988, 164). At the same time, practitioners have emphasized an anti-oppressive framework that recognizes the need to continue the fight against racial oppression but alongside class, gender and other forms of oppression.

Effective anti-racist social work practice addresses these issues at the personal, institutional and societal levels. At the personal level, social workers must ensure that their own practice is free of racism and challenge what are considered to be individual racist practices by others. In other words, workers should be "culturally competent" and aware that cultural practices will vary among the different groups of people with whom they work. The issue of cultural competency also arises within the context of international social work practice (see Chapter 13). At the institutional and societal levels, social service agencies must pursue policies and practices that are non-discriminatory, and legislation and government policies must be changed to remove barriers to racial groups. This includes working to eliminate unintentional racism in policy and procedures.

There are many examples of social workers and social service agencies that integrate an anti-racist approach to practice. Take, for example, the work done by the Nanaimo Youth Services Association in Vancouver, which serves youth and integrates an anti-racism approach within its social services. Social workers at the agency focus on youth with difficulties that affect their physical and/or emotional well-being and development. Services offered include job-readiness training, employment counselling, wage subsidies, community development, internships, housing, supportive living, student summer programs, youth drop-in centre, youth newspaper, work experience, meal program, recycling building materials centre, and a teen talkline. The Supportive Living Program within the association helps facilitate the process of the youths' transition from residential care to successful independent living. The program objective is to obtain input from the caseworker, youth, and when appropriate the caregiver, to develop an individual program plan for the youth. The work done by social workers at the association does not stop with the individual youth. First Nation youth often face racism

ERASING THE HYDRA OF HATE

Try the interactive Internet game "Erasing the Hydra of Hate," developed by the Canadian Human Rights Commission. It may help you examine your knowledge and beliefs in an historical context—the beginning step to applying anti-racist concepts in social work practice.

It can be found at: http://www.crr.ca/eraceit/default.htm

Canada is largely made up of earlier waves of immigrants.

There are a variety of national and provincial organizations fighting racism. Social workers need to link and form relations with such groups.

in finding employment and training opportunities. In this case, social workers relate directly with the community and employers in undertaking awareness training and organizational development activities directed at systemic changes. The workers understand that the youths' difficulties in finding employment cannot be addressed only through education and training of the youth. Barriers and systemic discrimination must also be tackled.

Anti-racist social workers often use an empowerment approach or elicit the direct participation of those affected by racism in developing solutions. The Urban Native Youth Association (UNYA) in Vancouver, for example, was formed to address Aboriginal youth issues when it became apparent that growing numbers of young people were continuing to leave reserves for the city of Vancouver. A disproportionate number of First Nations youth end up on the streets with little or no knowledge of where to go for help. UNYA's goal is to serve as a safe place for Native youth to come and find out about other services in the community and to develop their own solutions. Their involvement in the development of youth services has enabled the youth to raise difficult questions around racism in the community, suggest solutions and work towards implementing the changes. The youth have taken it upon themselves to work with social workers to challenge the racism they confront in their daily lives.

When faced with mainstream services that are not fully meeting their needs, minority communities have sometimes needed to create separate social service agencies to act on their behalf. The Black Community Resource Centre in Montreal helps black English-speaking youth and advocates for systemic change. The centre promotes the social, health, education and economic needs of the youth by collaborating and partnering with black community organizations, public agencies and community-wide agencies. Ethnic-specific centres organize services not only to help people from their specific group, but also to collaborate with other groups to address systemic or structural racism. The Black Community Centre works with community organizations to monitor and review public policy that affects black youth. The centre attempts to improve the cultural and racial appropriateness of other public and para-public agencies by organizing cultural and racial sensitization workshops and works with other black organizations in providing operational support and training. The Centre's approach is two-pronged: it has created a separate agency to address unmet needs, while also working to improve the cultural appropriateness and anti-racist perspective of mainstream agencies.

While working in communities to find alternatives to poverty and unemployment, social assistance workers are also actively challenging the federal government at the level of legislation and policy. In helping First Nations communities, for example, social workers can point to the 1997 Delgamuukw decision, where the court clarified that Aboriginal title to traditional lands and resources cannot be revoked by the Crown, and the now-famous Marshall decision of 1999, where the Court affirmed the right of the Mi'kmaq and Maliseet in Atlantic Canada to earn a "moderate" living from fishing, hunting and gathering.

ANTI-RACISM ANALYSIS TOOL

An anti-racist approach to social work practice emphasizes placing personal difficulties within a larger social context. Not doing so leads to viewing problems as personal pathologies or problems of interpersonal relations and can result in "blaming the victim," thereby diverting attention away from social structures and thus inhibiting social change. The anti-racism analysis tool (see diagram) provides a useful way to apply this approach.

Take, for example, racism in relation to First Nations youth caught up in the criminal justice system, which continues to be one of the most readily apparent examples of institutional racism. Studies show that, provincially, First Nations peoples are incarcerated at rates that are six to seven times higher than the overall provincial rate. In Manitoba, for example, 60 percent of prisoners in provincial jails are First Nations people, while 70 percent of women in provincial jails and 75 percent of juveniles in Winnipeg's detention centres are First Nations people (York 1990). Taken alone, these statistics tend to perpetuate stereotypes and misconceptions about First Nations peoples.

The analysis tool can be used to examine issues arising in the context of the overrepresentation of First Nations people in the criminal justice

E-RACE-IT

Learn about racism and what to do about it on this youth and racism website. Youths talk about their personal experiences of racism throughout the website, located at: http://www.crr.ca

PERSONAL PROBLEMS

Anti-racist analysis: putting personal difficulties in context.

TRANSFORMING OUR ORGANIZATIONS

Social workers sometimes find themselves employed by agencies that do not operate with what they would consider to be an appropriate anti-racism perspective. Doing something about this (hopefully, without losing one's job) is part of anti-racist social work.

How does one approach this difficult task of organizational change? Social workers can promote anti-racist organizational change by using "Transforming Our Organizations," a tool kit for planning and monitoring anti-racism and/or multicultural change in organizations.

For more information on this anti-racism tool, go to: http://www.multiculturalism.org

system. Personal racism can be found in policing practices, since First Nations people are three times more likely to be charged after arrest than non-Aboriginal people. Instances of overt racism by police officers have also been widely reported. At the institutional level, social workers find that few police officers are Aboriginal, almost all judges are white and less than 1 percent of lawyers are First Nations people. This combination often results in lawyers advising First Nations people to plead guilty (75 percent do so) to charges even when they are innocent.

At the ideological level, First Nations people are alienated from the mainstream justice system, which emphasizes an adversarial approach rather than a healing and community approach. Cultural differences and language barriers also compound the problem—for example, almost one-third did not understand the sentencing process (Satzewich 1998). This cultural racism continues in prison where ceremonial and spiritual practices are often forbidden. And, later, only 18 percent of First Nations inmates are released on parole as compared to 42 percent of the general inmate population (Ibid.).

The interplay of all of these factors produces an overall system of racism. Social workers addressing the problem of the overrepresentation of First Nations people in prisons need to work on all levels to achieve a complete and effective solution.

• Example using the Anti-racist Tool

Tom is an eighteen-year-old living in a large hostel run by a family as a profit-making business. The hostel mainly houses young single people with mild disabilities. Tom is Aboriginal and has mild brain damage incurred in a car accident four years ago. He currently works in a day program for people with mild disabilities.

The manager at the hostel referred Tom to a social worker in a local community heath centre because Tom is creating problems at the hostel. He is refusing to clean his room, arguing with the other residents and often causing damage to the common living areas. It is rumoured that he is an alcoholic (these are rumours, without definite evidence). For the first four months Tom lived at the hostel, there were no problems; it has only been in the last month that problems have been reported. Tom will not discuss the reasons for his recent behaviour, and has not responded to requests to follow hostel rules.

The hostel owner arranges an interview between Tom and the social worker. Tom does not want to see the worker, but the owner threatens to evict him if he does not. He admits to the worker that he has caused some damage, but claims that the other hostel residents are ganging up on him and spreading rumours about him because he is Native. He has no friends at the hostel, and no family with whom he could live. His mother has thrown him out of her house because he argued with her new boyfriend. He does not know what he will do if he has to leave the hostel, and would continue to stay there if the other residents would only get off his back. However, he would consider going somewhere else if something became available. He agrees that his behaviour has not been without fault, but blames the manager and residents for setting him off.

National Archives of Canada. Neg no. PA130852 (John Flanders).

Poverty still underlies problems in Aboriginal communities.

There are numerous ways to approach this case, but the social worker who is taking an anti-racist approach avoids jumping to conclusions about Tom's rumoured alcohol abuse. The worker explores the issue with Tom and discovers that Tom does not drink at all. He produces a letter from an elder stating that Tom once had an alcohol problem, but that he has been dry for years. In exploring what "sets Tom off" or makes him angry, the worker discovers that several of the hostel residents taunt him and call him names, such as "drunken Indian."

After the interview with Tom the anti-racist social worker further investigates the hostel, paying particular attention to past reports of problems. The worker finds that there have been reports of racial slurs by a few residents. Working at the personal, institutional and societal levels, the worker undertakes sensitivity training with the hostel residents and the owner, emphasizing the importance of managing an environment that is non-racist. The worker also investigates the reasons for the lack of other hostel opportunities closer to Tom's community, and connects with Native Friendship Centres or other organizations in advocating for such facilities in First Nations communities. The worker explores the possibility of starting a province-wide hostel management diversity training program, and connects Tom with culturally appropriate resources and people. There are a wide variety of options, but the anti-racist social worker addresses the multi-level aspects of the problem and avoids racist stereotyping.

CONCLUSION

Anti-racist social work has an important role to play in creating a non-racist society. It demands that social work practitioners work to change their own awareness and practices, the practice of those around them, institutional policies and procedures, and social relations and systems that operate, both overtly and covertly, to perpetuate racism. The implementation of anti-racist approach requires the employment of workers who have an ability to work across racial divides, and who have an empathy based on knowledge of the differences between people. It also means asserting the fundamental values of being human, of respect and dignity to all.

The anti-racist approach to social work is gaining acceptance in the profession, but challenges remain. Within social work there is a lack of a firm knowledge upon which to form a comprehensive anti-racist practice. Anti-racist social work writers and researchers are few in number, and as a result, it is often necessary to go beyond social work literature. Additionally, social workers who confront racism sometimes face opposition because they are often challenging deeply held beliefs and values. Responding to this will often involve joining with other advocacy and social action groups.

Anti-racist social work practice is a framework for analysis as well as a form of practice pertinent to all aspects of social work, including individual and group counselling, community work, social policy development and advocacy. It is multifaceted and equally relevant for both white and non-white practitioners.

REFERENCES

- Alexander, Lincoln. 2001. Speech to the Canadian Race Relations Foundation's Award of Excellence Symposium, Vancouver. March 2. Available at: http://www.crr.ca

- Canadian Association of Chiefs of Police. 1996. *Hate Crimes in Canada: In Your Back Yard.* Ottawa: Canadian Association of Chiefs of Police.

- Canadian Race Relations Foundation. 2000. *Unequal Access: A Canadian Profile of Racial Differences in Education, Employment and Income.* Available on-line at: http://www.crr.ca

- Dominelli, L. 1988. *Anti-Racist Social Work–A Challenge for White Practitioners and Educators.* London: MacMillan Education Ltd.

- Henry, Frances. 1994. *The Caribbean Diaspora in Toronto: Learning to Live with Racism.* Toronto: University of Toronto Press.

- Isajiw, Wsevolod W. 1999. *Understanding Diversity: Ethnicity and Race in the Canadian Context.* Toronto: Thompson Educational Publishing.

- Kelly, Karen. 1995. Projection of Visible Minority Groups, 1991-2016. *Canadian Social Trends* (summer).

- League for Human Rights of B'nai Brith. 2000. *Annual Audit of Antisemitic Incidents.* Downsview, Ont.: B'nai Brith Canada. Available at: http://www.bnaibrith.ca

- Ontario. 1995. *Final Report of the Commission on Systemic Racism in the Ontario Criminal Justice System.* Toronto: Queen's Printer for Ontario.

- Roberts, J.V. 1995. *Disproportionate Harm: Hate Crime in Canada.* Ottawa: Department of Justice Canada.

- Satzewich, V., ed. 1998. *Racism and Social Inequality in Canada: Concepts, Controversies and Strategies of Resistance.* Toronto: Thompson Educational Publishing.

- Sheppard, Bruce. 1997. *Deemed Unsuitable.* Toronto: Umbrella Press.

- Walker, J. 1997. *Race, Rights and the Law in the Supreme Court of Canada.* Kitchener: The Osgoode Society for Canadian Legal History and Wilfred Laurier University Press.

- York, G. 1990. *The Dispossessed: Life and Death in Native Canada.* Toronto: Little, Brown & Company.

CHAPTER 10: ANTI-RACIST SOCIAL WORK TODAY

Key Terms

- Immigration policy
- Multiculturalism
- Human rights legislation
- Charter of Rights and Freedoms
- Employment Equity Act
- Human rights commissions
- Hate crimes
- Stereotype
- Prejudice
- Ethnicity/Ethnic group
- Culture
- Ethnocentrism
- Race
- Visible minorities
- Racism
- Discrimination
- Systemic discrimination
- Anti-racist social work

Questions

1. Describe three major events in Canadian history that illustrate racial injustice.

2. How has immigration changed in the past twenty years?

3. Describe the origins and basic principles of Canada's multiculturalism policy.

4. What is meant by a "hate crime"? What is the extent of hate crime in Canada? What is the best way to combat such crimes?

5. Explain what is meant by systemic racism and give some examples of systemic racism in Canada.

5. What is anti-racist social work? How has the approach to racism changed in the last decade?

Websites

- **Canadian Race Relations Foundation**
  http://www.crr.ca

  The Canadian Race Relations Foundation is committed to building a national framework for the fight against racism in Canadian society. They have an excellent on-line media centre, publications and an E-Race-It website for youth.

- **Canadian Association of Schools of Social Work-Anti-Racist Training and Materials Project**
  http://www.cassw-acess.ca

  This is a site with an extensive list of resources and materials. These include print journals, organizations, publishers, videos and films, websites, virtual libraries and teaching tools. There are course outlines and papers available for downloading as well. This site also includes numerous bibliographic citations organized by theme. Five themes have been selected as entry points. There are definitions to help you access the right category for your needs. Full-text searches are also available.

- **The World Conference Against Racism, Racial Discrimination, Xenophobia and Related Intolerance (WCAR)**
  http://www.unhchr.ch/html/racism

  The World Conference Against Racism, Racial Discrimination, Xenophobia and Related Intolerance was held in South Africa in 2001. The conference focused on developing practical, action-oriented measures and strategies to combat contemporary forms of racism and intolerance.

11

Social Work and Sexual Diversity

Bisexual, Lesbian & Gay Identities

George F. Bielmeier

Same-sex attraction, love and personal relationships have been given a variety of meanings throughout human history. In the past, however, heterosexism and an emphasis on patriarchy and male power ensured that mainly heterosexual relationships would be publicly sanctioned. This is gradually beginning to change.

———

Concepts of sex, gender and relationship are formulated in our minds early in the socialization process. A four-year-old can identify culturally "appropriate" behaviour, without the sophistication of any critical analysis, but with a moral sense of "right" or "wrong." Within the socialization context is the assumption that the child will form intimate relationships with opposite-sex partners, marry at least one, and reproduce. The universal assumption maintains that female and male were created for each other with a primary function of reproduction, ensuring the survival of the family, community and culture.

Historically, particularly in Western societies, religious organizations assumed a major role in sanctifying these relationships, condemning all others and viewing same-sex relationships as a moral wrong and an abomination to nature and the "divine plan." This view continues to inform and shape personal, social and professional understandings of sex, love, intimacy and relationships. In concert with economic and political arrangements, **heterosexism** has become firmly embedded in social understandings and expectations, marginalizing and oppressing those who express difference.

This chapter examines the major theoretical approaches to sex, gender and sexuality. It then briefly reviews some of the historical background and more recent experience of sexual diversity, and goes on to examine the implications for social work practice today.

THEORETICAL PERSPECTIVES

Critical to an understanding of sex, gender and sexuality are the theoretical perspectives that have been developed and underpin social knowledge and social organization. Since the nineteenth century three major schools of thought have emerged: biological essentialism, social constructionism and, most recently, postmodernism.

Part of a World Pride March in Italy, 2000.

Issues of people who define themselves as transgender or transsexual are not addressed here. These subjects may involve some sex-attraction, but require specific attention and development beyond the scope of this chapter.

• Biological Essentialism

The most established perspective, and the one adopted and promoted by the medical community and other helping professions, is **biological essentialism**. This perspective assumes the origin of all sexual attraction and behaviour is innate and predetermined, a component of the person's biological endowments. Within this school of thought are two major trends. First, it is argued that the "homosexual" is born and should be accepted as such. Second, there is the view of pathology and abnormality, which promotes the need for professional treatment regardless of success, but with the aim of ensuring that the person will not act upon "deviant" sexual drives and desires.

During the late 1860s, with the introduction of the concept of "homosexual" within the German language, the early homosexual movement in Europe adopted and promoted the view of biological essentialism. The term *homosexual* was used by a physician, Karl Marie Kertbeny (known also as Karoly Benkert), who wrote in defence of men criminally charged with sodomy (a term that is not clearly defined and which could include a variety of behaviours). He viewed the act of sodomy as the expression of a particular type of person and, as such, not punishable. What had previously been considered a behaviour became a "sexual orientation" that would define the identity of the person.

More recently, biological essentialism has once again found favour in research that involves attempts to locate the "gay gene" (and, some argue, ensure the social rights of a sexual minority group). Critics of this perspective, however, argue that the reduction of sexual orientation to genetics might also provide society with the knowledge to abort an "unwanted" fetus.

• Social Constructionism

A second perspective, **social constructionism**, gained favour after World War II with a focus on nurture and social learning theories. At the extreme of this theoretical perspective rests the view that the homosexual is not born but is the product of post-natal life experience; in particular, the outcome of the social creation of meaning that is assigned to behaviour.

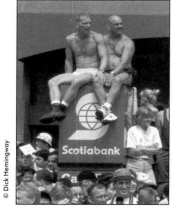

Annual gay pride events help break down social barriers.

While social constructionists acknowledge that biology or genetics has some role and function in same-sex attraction, little attention is given to it. Rather, the historical sociocultural experience is given primacy in the construction of a "homosexual identity and role." Within this view, identity and role are shaped and given specific meaning by social experience (Weeks 1986; 1991). The meaning changes over time and historical periods, and the changing meaning influences the expression of self, both sexually and as an identity. Social constructionism gave rise to perspectives of "choice" and "lifestyles," challenging the innate deterministic understanding of sexual orientation (as advanced by the advocates of biological essentialism). This perspective of choice and lifestyle would be used by religious fundamentalists to condemn the "immorality" of same-sex relationships.

The nature (biological essentialism) and nurture (social constructionism) perspectives characterize most twentieth-century thinking about sex and created the modern discipline of sexology. Each perspective claimed to have the answer to questions about sex, sexuality and sexual identity. Each subscribed to the use of labels and categories to make sense out of sexual expression, particularly same-sex involvement. The inquiries produced a dichotomous view of sexual behaviour as either homosexual or heterosexual, often without comprehensively critiquing the social milieu or the assumptions, mores and values in which these labels and categories were developed.

Within this configuration rests the birth of the homosexual as a distinct personality type, the counter-opposite of the heterosexual. Such a conception allowed those in the medical profession to claim "scientific" knowledge. It also allowed sociological and political thinkers to advance a strategy to secure social and political rights and freedoms for those involved in same-sex behaviour. The conceptualization promoted the view of "other" and "otherness," as distinct from the heterosexual majority group, and thus created social and objectified images of same-sex involvement that religious leaders and organizations would characterize as unnatural, an abomination, a moral wrong and against the "divine plan." (Paradoxically, however, the creation of the separate identity also provided the foundation for the organization of gay male and lesbian liberation that would emerge in the 1960s and 1970s.)

• Postmodernism

Since the early 1990s, a challenge to the perspectives of biological essentialism and social constructionism has emerged through the **postmodernism** critique. While not an internally consistent school of thought, postmodernism challenges the older theories that attempt to discover the origin of human sexual expression from a single cause and an emphasis on one truth, reality or explanation.

The postmodern approach rejects the labels and categories created since the mid-nineteenth century and offers an alternative perspective. This alternative perspective acknowledges "difference" that is personally mediated by life experience and asserts that sex and sexuality are only one of many contested domains of living. Such factors as historical period, ethnicity, financial resources and opportunities all play a significant role in self-definition. Concepts of "homosexual identity," "gay identity," "lesbian identity," "gay community" are rejected, with a recognition that there are differences and diversity among those who experience same-sex attraction and physical involvement.

In the postmodernist critique, each person has a unique definition and means of personal expression, and this may change over one's life span. Some may never use the term *homosexual, gay, lesbian* or *bisexual* but instead may have a fluid and variable way of describing self and experience. Each person will have a unique definition or interpretation based upon his or her position within the world.

FOUR THINGS A SOCIAL WORKER SHOULD KNOW

- **UNDERSTAND HOMOPHOBIA:** Identify homophobia and not homosexuality as the problem.
- **UNDERSTAND ISSUES:** Understand issues confronting gays, lesbians and bisexuals.
- **KNOWLEDGE OF HISTORY:** Have knowledge of the history of discrimination against gays, lesbians and bisexuals.
- **KNOWLEDGE OF SERVICES:** Have knowledge of support services for gays, lesbians and bisexuals that are available in the community.

SYMBOLIC TRIANGLES?

Why is the pink triangle used as the symbol for the gay movement and the black triangle for the lesbian movement?

The pink triangle is a symbol that was used by the Nazi party to identify prisoners in their camps. The Nazis forced certain groups to wear identification badges. The Jews were forced to wear yellow stars of David. Gay men were forced to wear the pink triangle (pointing up).

Women who were considered "anti-social" were forced to wear a black triangle. Some of these women were lesbians, so that is why some lesbians have reclaimed the black triangle.

Postmodernism challenges the "grand theories" and narratives. Attention is given to the use of language and the creation of social knowledge. There is a recognition that many voices have been silenced in the recording of history and that this has ensured that only the most powerful are heard. In the postmodernist view, the homosexual-heterosexual dichotomy is the result of "scientific" explanations of sexual expression that attempt to bring organization to an area of human experience viewed as threatening to a defined social order. This social order is based on a patriarchal system that espouses heterosexism, promotes hierarchical structures and ensures a vision of society that is determined by select but powerful groups.

Within the postmodern view, there is the idea that sexuality is understood, shaped and expressed within particular personal and/or social contexts, and that the experience of pleasure, passion and desire are fluid and potential within each person.

HISTORICAL PHASES IN PERSPECTIVE ON SEXUAL DIVERSITY

Within Canada, as well as other parts of the world, the urban environment provided many opportunities for political and social organizing and this fostered the development of identifiable **gay and lesbian communities**. The urban communities, often referred to as the "village" or "ghetto," all developed after World War II and throughout the 1950s and 1960s. They are an example of the social networks people develop in response to societal dynamics of oppression, prejudice and stigmatization. They have become the "safe space" for those who have not found acceptance or validation in their communities of birth or origin and for those who have not found a place within the predominant heterosexual groupings and institutions that characterize life beyond the family. For some, these communities and institutions are temporary resources and play a minimal role in their life; for others, they have become the centres of social living, a social and recreational space; and for still others, these communities are the milieu for political and social action.

Each decade in the post-war period, including the 1950s, may be roughly characterized by its own theme. Each decade redefined the "gay male" and "lesbian," increasingly challenging earlier definitions and more recently recognizing the diversity of identities that comprise contemporary understandings. The phases and themes are:

  1950s – Oppression;
  1960s – Organization;
  1970s – Liberation;
  1980s – Community Building;
  1990s – Diversity.

• 1950s — Oppression

The 1950s continued the tradition of homosexual oppression, already well established, particularly from the state and the medical and psychiatric community. Views of the homosexual as a social security threat, as a predator upon the young, as mentally ill and as emotionally unstable were well entrenched. Those with same-sex attraction learned to hide and live in secrecy, meeting in places identified as "safe."

Some formal organizing was occurring within cities in the United States, such as Los Angeles, Washington and New York. The Mattachine Society was established, which led to the development of the Homophile Associations that would later characterize Canadian organizing. These early organizations largely accepted the notion of "difference," with some accepting the illness metaphor. However, these organizations attempted to change the negative definitions through education and political reform, promoting the view of the homosexual as a distinct minority group. These strategies were similar to those that took place in Germany from the 1860s through to the early 1930s. The overall approach was to become acceptable to the dominant heterosexual institutions, including the use of social and political change tactics that would not bring a negative response and reinforce the existing social stereotypes.

Secrecy often characterized the membership of these early organizations. Loss of employment, criminal charges and family and community harassment ensured the ongoing oppression of the homosexual, condemning the person to silence and invisibility. Given the conservative social context in Canada, same-sex organizing tended to be restricted to smaller encounters that were generally centred in bars in urban environments, leading to the development of social and support networks (Kinsmen 1996, 224-35).

• 1960s — Organization

The 1960s would witness growing attempts at organizing, particularly in urban environments. Public debates were beginning to emerge about homosexuality. The first Canadian homophile organization, the Association for Social Knowledge (ASK), was formed in April 1964 in Vancouver. ASK would open the first gay and lesbian community centre in 1966 (McLeod 1996, 7, 26).

The late 1960s saw the birth of the liberation movements that would develop in the 1970s. No longer content to allow the slow process of reform to unfold through the beneficence of heterosexual institutions, a more vocal and visible platform was beginning to take shape. The Stonewall Riots in New York City (June 28-29, 1969) became the marker event for a change in political philosophy, objectives and strategies, inspiring and promoting critical thinking within the Canadian context.

The same summer, the **Criminal Code of Canada** was amended, removing "gross indecency" and "buggery" as grounds for criminal charges providing the acts took place in private between two consenting adults of at least twenty-one years of age. While the Amendment to the Criminal Code did not specifically identify gay men or lesbians, it was assumed to indicate a change of social attitude without recognition of the need to examine the broader social and political demands emerging within gay and lesbian movements, demands that involved public and visible recognition.

The AIDS epidemic calls for a major educational effort.

SVEND ROBINSON

First elected to the House of commons in May 1979, Svend Robinson represents the federal constituency of Burnaby-Douglas. He was the first openly gay MP, having come out publicly in the spring of 1988. In addition to his many other achievements, he has received honours for his work for equality for lesbian, gay, bisexual and transgender people.

• 1970s — Liberation

Within Canada, the 1970s would witness the growth of organizations promoting liberation politics and a redefinition of the homosexual. The Gay Liberation Front was formed in Vancouver in 1970 and preceded the development of the Canadian Gay Activist Alliance and the Gay Alliance Toward Equality (McLeod 1996, 54). In Montreal, the Front de Liberation Homosexuelle was organized in 1971 (Kinsmen 1996, 291). Also in 1971, the Community Homophile Association of Toronto (CHAT), which grew out of earlier developments at the University of Toronto, was formed (McLeod 1996, 46). CHAT maintained an educational and counselling function, but Toronto Gay Action developed from within its membership, a group committed to political action for social change. Along with other organizations it would participate in the Canadian Gay Rally on Parliament Hill in 1971. While political change strategies continued to include education, attention was now focused on the oppressive practices within social arrangements. As a result of political organizing in the United States, the American Psychiatric Association removed its classification of homosexuality as a mental disorder in 1973.

Across Canada, groups were forming in major cities to advance gay and lesbian rights. Within the universities, groups were formed to advocate for political change. Within larger urban sites, such as Montreal, Vancouver and Toronto, periodicals and newspapers emerged, providing a voice for gay and lesbian liberation and a forum for critical discussion about sex, identity, community and culture. In 1977, Quebec would become the first province in Canada to ban discrimination on the basis of sexual orientation.

• 1980s — Community Building

The 1980s brought major changes for lesbian and gay communities. Not only did community building continue to grow and flourish, but during the later part of the decade major legal changes were also gained. "Sexual orientation" was included in provincial **human rights codes.** (Rulings by the Supreme Court of Canada have ensured this inclusion in all provinces and territories.)

The 1980s also saw the impact of HIV/AIDS on gay male communities. The lack of response on the part of government agencies and hospitals mobilized the men and women of the communities to organize to meet the needs of those directly affected by HIV. The impact of HIV/AIDS was devastating for many, and some individuals lost their entire network of friends to the disease.

This devastation and loss was intensified by the broader social response that this was the "gay plague" and "divine punishment." The recognition that the virus was not selective, and that in other parts of the world whole communities had died due to the disease, appeared to have no impact. The disease fuelled the response of the moral right in its campaign against lesbian and gay populations and further stigmatized bisexual identities. Opposition did not prevent the Canada-wide development of AIDS Service Organizations, many organized and staffed by lesbians and gay men. And when the government's response

Courtesy of George F. Bielmeier.

Part of a Gay Pride demonstration.

neglected the needs of those affected and infected with HIV, AIDS
Action Now emerged to bring social awareness and political action to
the issues (Kinsmen 1996, 351).

In Toronto, 1981 saw a major initiative following the bath house raids.
On a February night, police raided four bathhouses within the city and
arrested 289 men. The assault raised a consciousness within gay and lesbian communities of the need to protest the police action, and hundreds
of gay and lesbian activists, along with their supporters, took to the
streets and demonstrated within the city core (Kinsmen 1996, 342).

The decade of the 1980s was a paradox. It was a period that saw the
emergence of organized gay and lesbian visibility within social and work
life, but also one that, through continued and renewed social responses
of fear and hatred, combined with the impact of HIV/AIDS, witnessed
threats and violence to this visibility. The 1980s reinforced the ongoing
struggle to challenge oppressive structures and practices with the recognition that legal changes cannot be equated with personal attitudinal
changes.

• 1990s and Today — Diversity

The 1990s continued to be a decade of struggle within gay and lesbian
organizations and activities as well as in the challenging of heterosexist
practices within broader societal arrangements. Virtually every institution has now been confronted about its response to gay and lesbian identities. Some have re-evaluated their assumptions and political stance,
while others have rejected the calls for change and stand firm on their
rejection. The example of The United Church of Canada demonstrates

HISTORICAL OVERVIEW OF DISCRIMINATION

Early immigration laws prohibited the entry of lesbians and gays into this country and immigrants who were found to be lesbian or gay were deported (1952-1977). Criminal law made certain forms of gay male sexual expression illegal and gay men were incarcerated as "dangerous sexual offenders" (1892-1969).

For an historical overview, go to this website: http://ia1.carleton.ca/52100/m21/history.htm

the possibilities for change. Parishioner response has ranged from an acceptance of gay and lesbian ministers to outright rejection, in which whole congregations have left the church.

The 1990s did witness major legislative changes on the national level. These include the passing of Bill C-41 (hate crimes) in 1995, Bill C-33 (amendments to the *Canadian Human Rights Act*) in 1996 and **Bill C-23,** which extends benefits to same-sex couples. Some Members of Parliament did not support the inclusion of sexual orientation, which gave rise to protests in some federal ridings, such as in Nova Scotia. Progress was slower on the provincial level with resistance to recognizing the relationships of lesbians and gay men as "family." This was witnessed in Ontario with the defeat of Bill 167 in 1994, although British Columbia made legislative changes during the summer of 1997.

Within lesbian and gay organizing, as witnessed in the short-lived activist group Queer Nation, issues of difference and diversity are being confronted. This is a task that is both divisive and challenging, one that raises fear yet inspires hope for more inclusive and accepting definitions of human sexuality as people take ownership of their own identity. The voices of bisexual and transgender people are now being acknowledged, confronting the rigid categorization of sexual and gender social practice. The experiences of those confronting multiple oppressions—based on ethnicity, ability, gender and social class, for example—add a further dimension to liberation movements.

SOCIAL WORK PERSPECTIVES ON SEXUAL DIVERSITY

Social work activity promoting the early rights (nineteenth century) of the homosexual appear to have been non-existent. The profession embraced the notion of the heterosexual family structure along with the associated moral and social responsibilities for its members. It joined the medical profession in treating homosexuality as a social and/or sexual disorder and/or deviant. Members of the profession who were involved in same-sex relationships remained silent about them, although they may have been active in other more "respectable" social reform activities that enhanced and expanded the knowledge and practice base of the emerging profession. Whatever voices may have emerged to challenge these perspectives were silenced. Many gay men and lesbians soon learned not to approach the helping professions or discuss their social and/or sexual lives for fear of being viewed as sick or deviant.

Although the American Psychiatric Association dropped the classification of homosexuality as a sexual disorder in 1973, some social workers continued to pathologize same-sex attraction. Clinical social work adopted the traditional psychoanalytic descriptions of the homosexual as regressed, immature and fixated (Strean 1978). No critique was undertaken on how these descriptions were based on social stereotypes and continued to oppress gay men, lesbians and bisexuals.

The 1980s, however, brought a change within the professional understanding of sexual diversity. The change had its roots in the late 1970s, when some gay and lesbian social workers, reinforced by the broader

© Dick Hemingway

Gay rights campaign aligned with other social movements.

gay and lesbian movements, started to "come out" and name their oppression. This influence, and their employment within repressive service delivery structures and practices, promoted their involvement in the development of new professional and self-help services within the community for lesbians and gay men.

Curriculum changes were also occurring within schools of social work. Gender and human sexuality courses emerged, which included views of homosexuality beyond the medical and disease models and spoke to the social construction of sexuality and the impact of heterosexism. By 1986, specific credit courses on "Gay & Lesbian Identities" were being taught within one Canadian school of social work (Ryerson Polytechnic), which challenged the moral and disease metaphors embedded within social work theory. The structural approach to social work practice as formulated by Maurice Moreau (1979) identified within its framework the oppression of lesbians and gay men, challenging the profession to re-think its position and response to issues of sexuality and sexual identity.

Social workers were thus increasingly challenged to consider the social arrangements and ideologies that oppressed people, limiting their life chances and opportunities, and (through internalizing these views) giving rise to self-damaging behaviours such as alcohol and drug addiction and even suicide.

SOCIAL WORK ORGANIZATIONS

Today, to be effective social workers require a critical self- and social awareness about issues of sex, sexuality and sexual identity. Workers need to recognize their comfort level and feel accepting of their own sexual bodies, emotions and feelings. **Internalized homophobia** and attitudes that devalue same-sex relationships need to be acknowledged and challenged. Social workers need to recognize their limitations, both personal and professional, and be able to discuss them with clients. Social workers who self-identify as gay or lesbian need to recognize and acknowledge their own struggles and accomplishments without losing their focus on the unique process experienced by clients.

Both explicit and implicit policies, practices and arrangements within the social agency setting require critical review to identify embedded heterosexism and ensure the inclusion of gay men, lesbians and bisexuals. As part of the examination, staff development activities are necessary to ensure that everyone in the agency has an opportunity to explore their perception of and responses to sexual minority groups. As part of an affirmative-action position, posters, resources and mission and policy statements that demonstrate the inclusion of gay men, lesbians and bisexuals should be visible in reception areas and offices. Social workers need to ensure that their own office libraries include resources that encompass more than the heterosexual experience.

Social workers also have the opportunity to be involved in social change through joining with other groups and organizations. Building solidarity among different identity groups (recognizing that members

HOMOPHOBIA

Homophobia is a pervasive irrational fear of homosexuality. It includes the fear that heterosexuals have of many homosexual feelings within themselves, any overt mannerisms or actions that would suggest homosexuality, and the resulting desire to suppress or stamp out homosexuality.

Gay Pride parade and celebration.

belong to multiple groups based on sex, geography, religion and so on)
involves creating a safe space for critical discussion and learning to facilitate a political and social transformation that seeks social justice for all.
Organizations can become innovative in the development of support
systems. The Children's Aid Society of Toronto, for example, recognizes
the needs and rights of bisexual, lesbian, gay and transgender youth
within its care.

Social workers require more information about the gay and lesbian
community in order to plan social services. It is important to note that,
for the first time, the **Canadian census** for 2001 will ask Canadians if
they live in same-sex relationships. This will assist governments and
agencies in planning to meet the income, security and social service
needs of the gay and lesbian communities.

COMMUNITY AND GROUPS

The scope of social work often encompasses work with community-
based groups and organizations. Being aware and challenging **homophobia** within these settings is crucial if these organizations are to be
accepting and responsive to gay men, lesbians and bisexuals. Working
with issues of difference demands sensitivity, clarity and focus in combination with listening and conflict resolution skills. It has taken thousands
of years to entrench homophobia within social arrangements—it will not
disappear quickly.

In areas where no community-based group or organization exists for
gay men, lesbians and bisexuals, social workers can begin to link people

together, working with them to develop support systems predicated on models of mutual aid and self-help. Such support systems foster positive self-esteem and identity, help to overcome social isolation and allow individuals to begin the process of personal and social change.

In community planning and service-based program development, social workers can play an active role in ensuring the inclusion of all people. By developing educational programs that critically examine heterosexism and homophobia and include strategies for change, social workers can provide the opportunity for silenced voices to be heard, respected and affirmed.

Fostering the development of specific groups that speak to the needs and experiences of gay men, lesbians and bisexuals is essential to any social and community effort at bringing about change. The isolated individual will never come to realize the power of collective action unless he or she is given the opportunity to join with others who experience the same struggle.

Groups need not focus on therapeutic and treatment approaches; too often these encourage the pathologizing of same-sex attraction and homophobia. Groups that affirm the power of people working together and supporting each other, promote understanding and learning, and provide the opportunity to act upon insights in unity and solidarity with others enhance self-identity and community building. As a method of social work practice, social group work promotes the collective capacity of people to respond creatively to the obstacles of social living and, at the same time, find support from and with others.

INDIVIDUAL AND FAMILY

The social worker's initial response to an individual who raises questions about sexual identity is critical. He or she must be cautious not to dismiss the individual's questions and concerns as "a passing phase." Of course, the worker may have no particular expertise within the area, in which case he or she will need to ensure that the person is supported and referred to an experienced worker. Where that social worker has personal awareness and understanding, and a degree of professional knowledge and skill, there will be an opportunity for effective individual and family social work to take place.

"**Coming out**," the political act and strategy of the gay and lesbian liberation movement of the 1970s, is now regarded as an important psycho-social developmental process. It has become the unique challenge for every gay man and lesbian, a task deemed necessary for self-acceptance and relationship development. Research in the area has highlighted various stages of the process, ranging from confusion and denial to pride (Eliason 1996).

Social workers need to be prepared for a variety of individual responses and be prepared to respond to the process of "coming out" at a pace that is supportive of the client. This may involve dealing with the client's feelings of confusion, anxiety, anger, guilt, remorse and self-hate. It may involve time frames that will be viewed as "regressive," with the

BILL C-23, MODERNIZING BENEFITS AND OBLIGATIONS ACT.

Bill C-23 amends 68 federal statutes to provide same-sex couples with the same rights and responsibilities as heterosexual married couples. At the last minute the government introduced a change that excluded same-sex couples from the definition of "marriage."

client renegotiating earlier understandings and perceptions, or it may appear as a "flight" into total self-acceptance. Each response requires discussion, including a critical evaluation with the client in recognizing the strengths and challenges of the response.

Social workers may also, upon request, intervene with the family as they respond to a member's self-disclosure. Some families will never accept a gay or lesbian member, others will only accept the member if same-sex relationships do not become a topic, and still others will eventually embrace the member without conditions. Families, much like the person who is "coming out," need time to integrate and assimilate new information, understanding and awareness. They may also move through feelings of denial, blame and confusion before they can accept a gay or lesbian member. It is critical for the social worker to respond to these feelings and responses without pre-judging the situation. Linking the family to Parents and Families of Lesbians and Gays, for example, or helping them to form their own chapter, could be a critical step in personal and social change.

Social workers may also work with issues of addiction, abuse, relationship breakdown and child custody as they pertain to bisexuals, gay men and lesbians. In such situations, the role that stigma plays in coping behaviours is critical to the assessment and intervention. Social workers also need to be aware of community resources, both professional and self-help, that are responsive to these needs.

Gay and Lesbian Health Service in Saskatoon, for example, works to address the health and social issues faced by the gay and lesbian community. Its workers have found that there is a need for a specialized health centre as lesbians and gay men experience numerous social and personal problems resulting from homophobia in the community and society, but often find it difficult to obtain services. In their experience, social work professionals frequently lack information and knowledge about the gay and lesbian community, particularly with respect to its diversity. The centre is involved in providing direct care, educating the community and building partnerships with professional, support and discussion groups.

LESBIAN AND GAY SUICIDE

The **suicide risk** level of gay men, lesbians and bisexuals is now an area of grave concern. Although governments have been reluctant to act, research suggests that gay men, lesbians and bisexuals (and especially youth) are at higher risk of suicide than their heterosexual counterparts. Studies in the United States, for example, have shown that gay males may be six times more likely to attempt suicide than heterosexual males, and that lesbians may be two times more likely to attempt suicide than heterosexual females (Bell and Weinberg 1978).

A 1994 Canadian study, *Suicide in Canada*, addresses the issue in a limited sense. Gay men are reported to be more likely to attempt suicide in their adolescent years, due to stresses associated with "coming out." Lesbians are more likely to attempt suicide at a later age due to the break-up

Courtesy of George F. Bielmeier.

Students show support for gay and lesbian rights.

of a relationship. The Canadian study reviews studies from the United States that suggest that gay and lesbian youth account for as much as 30 percent of completed suicides each year (Gibson 1989). The suicides are attributed to a society that discriminates against and stigmatizes homosexuals and that fails to recognize that a substantial number of young people have a gay or lesbian orientation (Health Canada 1994).

Social workers are a key part of crisis-intervention teams working in community centres, mental health facilities, self-help services and peer support programs. To work effectively, workers must recognize and address sexual orientation as a key aspect of the person's situation. In suicide prevention and intervention work, social workers must be aware of these dangers and recognize that any suicide prevention intervention needs to focus on ameliorating the societal conditions that contribute to suicide. Efforts should focus on public education to address discrimination and non-acceptance. Suicide intervention includes early recognition of risk, immediate response, resource referrals and ongoing support systems.

CONCLUSION

This chapter provides an introduction to an understanding of same-sex attraction and identity for students of social work. It examined the different theoretical approaches to these issues (biological essentialism, social constructionism and postmodernism). It traced the history of oppression experienced by gays, lesbians, bisexuals and transgender persons and went on to highlight more recent gains in the form of community organizing and improvements in human rights legislation.

Through community work, group work and work with individuals, social workers attempt to provide for the specific needs of lesbians, gay men, bisexuals and transgender persons. Individual-level work may focus, for example, on supporting a person who is "coming out" or on providing specialized services to individuals, couples and their families. HIV/AIDS has taken a particularly severe toll in the gay male community, and the battle against the disease has taken up much energy and time for activists, social workers and medical personnel. Recent evidence suggests that suicide, particularly youth suicide, is also becoming a concern for activists and service workers.

At the policy and program level, social workers continue to advocate for legislative changes such as the recent Bill C-41 (hate crimes) and Bill C-23 (extending social benefits to same-sex couples). They also play a vital role in helping to educate the public about homophobia and the urgency of developing new services that can meet the needs of this community. In these and other areas, social work practitioners work closely with community activists and other service professionals.

REFERENCES

- Bell, A., and M. Weinberg. 1978. *Homosexualities: A Study of Diversity Among Men and Women.* New York: Simon and Schuster.

- Eliason, M. 1996. Identity Formation for Lesbian, Bisexual, and Gay Persons: Beyond a "Minoritizing" View. *Journal of Homosexuality* 30, no. 3:31-58.

- Gibson, P. 1989. Gay Males and Lesbian Youth Suicide. In M.R. Feinleib, ed., *Report of the Secretary's Task Force on Youth Suicide: Vol. 3 Prevention and Interventions in Youth Suicide* (pp. 110-142). Washington, D.C.: US Government Printing Office.

- Health Canada. 1994. *Suicide in Canada.* Ottawa: Health Canada.

- Kinsmen, G. 1996. *The Regulation of Desire: Home and Heterosexualities:* 2d ed., revised. Montreal: Black Rose.

- McLeod, D.W. 1996. *Lesbian and Gay Liberation in Canada: A Selected Annotated Chronology, 1964-1975.* Toronto: ECW Press/Homewood.

- Moreau, M. 1979. Empowerment through Advocacy and Consciousness-Raising: Implications of a Structural Approach to Social Work. *Journal of Sociology and Social Welfare* 17, no. 2: 53-67.

- Strean, H.S. 1978. *Clinical Social Work: Theory and Practice.* New York: The Free Press.

- Strean, H.S. 1983. *The Sexual Dimension: A Guide for the Helping Professional.* New York: The Free Press.

- Weeks, J. 1986. *Sexuality.* London: Ellis Harwood.

- Weeks, J. 1991. *Against Nature: Essays on History, Sexuality and Identity.* London: Rivers Oram Press.

GEORGE F. BIELMEIER is a professor in the School of Social Work at Ryerson University. He is involved in community activism and in initiatives that provide services to sexually diverse populations, and has developed and taught courses on sexual diversity and Queer Issues within the School of Social Work.

CHAPTER 11: SOCIAL WORK AND SEXUAL DIVERSITY

Key Terms

- Heterosexism
- Biological essentialism
- Social constructionism
- Postmodernism
- Gay and lesbian communities
- Criminal Code of Canada
- Human rights codes
- Bill C-23
- Internalized homophobia
- Canadian census
- Homophobia
- Coming out
- Suicide risk

Discussion Questions

1. What are the three theories that are helpful in understanding sexuality? Briefly explain each theory.

2. What are the main characteristics of each decade in the history of the gay and lesbian movement since the 1950s?

3. What changes were made to the Criminal Code in 1969? What is Bill C-23 and why is it important to the social welfare of same-sex couples?

4. What is "internalized homophobia" and why is it important for social workers (and others) to understand it?

5. What is the social work profession's perspective on sexual diversity, and how has it changed in the last two decades?

6. What is "coming out," and what are some of the factors of which social workers should be aware?

7. How serious is the problem of suicide among gay, lesbian and bisexual persons and what are its underlying causes?

Websites

- **Equality for Gays and Lesbians Everywhere (EGALE)**
  http://www.egale.ca
  This national organization is committed to advancing, at the federal level, equality and justice for lesbians, gays and bisexuals. The website has a vast collection of news, articles and resources. Included is a summary of lesbian and gay rights in each jurisdiction in Canada.

- **Gay Canada Website**
  http://www.gaycanada.com
  This is a large website covering most issues. GayCanada, which was started in 1994, focused directly on serving as a resource centre on the Internet. The section on support groups and counselling is most relevant to the work of social workers.

- **Parents, Families and Friends of Lesbians and Gays**
  http://www.pflag.ca
  Information and resources for gay men, lesbians and bisexuals and their families and friends. Most chapters have scheduled meetings that provide support and information.

- **International Gay and Lesbian Human Rights Commission**
  http://www.iglhrc.org
  IGLHRC's mission is to protect and advance the human rights of all people and communities subject to discrimination or abuse on the basis of sexual orientation, gender identity, or HIV status. Their website contains excellent resources, news and urgent action items.

Social Work with Persons with Disabilities

The World of One in Six

Roy Hanes

Person with disabilities is a contemporary term, used, appropriately, to indicate that a disability is only one of many characteristics of the individual. Over the years, such terms as *impotent, defective, crippled, lame, and handicapped* have been used to denote persons with disabilities. The new term reflects a healthy change in social attitudes towards more inclusiveness and less stereotyping of people who have disabilities.

Statistics Canada estimates that there are approximately 4.2 million Canadians who are disabled–that is, about 16 percent of the population. Worldwide, there are approximately 600 million disabled people. Disabling conditions can include sensory disabilities, such as blindness or deafness, mental impairments, psychiatric disabilities, developmental disabilities, intellectual disabilities resulting from trauma and head injury, and learning disabilities. Many disabled persons have more than one impairment.

A number of methods for providing care and services to disabled people have been utilized over the years. These include programs based on the principles of out-of-door relief, indoor relief and scientific charity, the common methods for the provision of relief during the nineteenth and early twentieth centuries. Throughout most of the last century, there was a transition from these charity-aid models to a greater reliance on programs provided by municipal, provincial and federal levels of government. During the latter part of the twentieth century, people with disabilities became involved in civil rights activities. This led, among other things, to the creation of the Independent Living Movement, which advocates for the control of services by disabled people themselves.

This chapter provides background information and guidelines for prospective social workers who may find themselves working with persons with disabilities. After providing some basic statistical information, the chapter surveys the history of social services in this area. It goes on to examine the various theories of disability and the different approaches to serving the needs of those with disabilities, and highlights the importance of the disability rights movement. The second half of the chapter traces the history and philosophy of the Independent Living Movement. Finally, the chapter examines the important role social workers play in helping persons with disabilities.

About one in six Canadians has a disabling condition.

IN UNISON

The *In Unison 2000* report marked the first time that Canada's federal, provincial and territorial governments came together to express a common vision on disability issues. This report provides Canadians with a broad view of how adults with disabilities have been faring in comparison with those without disabilities, using both statistical indicators and examples of personal experiences.

Examples of effective practices that have been implemented across Canada are also woven into the report. The situation of Aboriginal persons with disabilities is specifically highlighted. This report is available at:
http://socialunion.gc.ca/
In_Unison2000

In Unison report provides an overview of disability issues.

THE WORLD OF ONE IN SIX

Statistical information shows that people with disabilities form a large minority of the total population of Canada. They comprise approximately 4.2 million people, of which approximately 275,000 are fourteen years of age and younger. Most people who are disabled become so as a consequence of illness and disease. For example, almost 30 percent become disabled as a result of "current disease or illness" and just over 15 percent become disabled as a result of "past disease or illness." In only 6 percent of the disabled population has disability existed since birth. Being disabled does not mean that the individual will end up in an institution. The degree of disability can be defined as mild, moderate or severe, and most disabled people (92 percent) live in the community while only 8 percent live in group homes, nursing homes or chronic care facilities.

While many causes of disability are linked to the onset of illness or disease, this does not mean that Canadians are unhealthy. It must be stated that most people with disabilities are older Canadians who are susceptible to illness and disease and become disabled as a result. For example, incidences of disability related to hearing loss, vision loss and mobility impairment increase dramatically with age. Whereas the disabled population between the ages of fifteen and twenty-four is only 4 percent of the population of this age group, almost 40 percent of the population of people between the ages of forty-four to sixty-five report a disability, and 72.9 percent of the population of people over the age of eighty-five report a disability. These statistics represent Canada as a whole. They do not show the high levels of disability among specific populations. In Canada, for example, the incidence of disabling conditions such as diabetes and heart disease is much higher in First Nations communities than in mainstream society. Many disabling conditions among First Nations peoples can be attributed to poverty, poor nutrition, poor sanitation, inadequate access to proper health care and so on.

Disabled people have a much higher level of unemployment and a much lower level of education than the general population. The 1991 Health and Activity Limitation Survey carried out by the federal government shows that 26 percent of adults with disabilities of working age (fifteen to sixty-four) have only elementary level education and only 5 percent have university education (Statistics Canada 1991). Levels of poverty are often related to levels of education. Since disabled people have lower levels of education and training, this often leads to higher levels of unemployment and poverty. The 1991 Health and Activity Limitation Survey found high levels of poverty and unemployment among people with disabilities. Almost 60 percent of men and women with disabilities of working age are unemployed (ages fifteen to sixty-four). When examining unemployment rates of men and women with disabilities, there are marked differences between the two populations. Women with disabilities have a much higher level of unemployment than men with disabilities. Almost 50 percent of disabled men of working age are employed, but only 30.7 percent of disabled women of working age are employed.

Since education, training and employment are closely linked to financial status, it should be expected that disabled people make up a large portion of the poor and have lower-paying jobs. The Health and Activity Limitation Survey found that 56 percent of Canadians with disabilities have an annual income of less than $10,000. People with disabilities in the middle- and upper-income brackets are a small percentage: 13 percent have an income higher than $35,000 (Statistics Canada 1991).

HISTORY OF SERVICES FOR PEOPLE WITH DISABILITIES

Prior to the development of scientific medicine, in Western English-speaking societies disability was a social and legal category based on statutes stemming from the English Poor Laws. The Poor Laws, in turn, were based on earlier statutes pertaining to the control of vagrants and paupers (Stone 1984, 29). Restrictive parameters were used to distinguish between the deserving poor and the undeserving poor. The deserving poor included lepers, those who were bedridden, the impotent (or those unable to work) and people above the age of sixty. These were the categories of people with disabilities, and the Poor Laws, as well as other social-legal criteria from the early seventeenth until the late nineteenth century, determined who was considered to be disabled. Persons deemed unable to work were considered deserving of charity and were legally permitted to beg, and would later be supported by the parish. All other groups were required to have a job.

The notion of **disability** originated as a social and/or legal category wherein magistrates were given the responsibility of determining disability and distinguishing between the deserving poor and the undeserving poor. Criteria for determining disability, as well as measures established for the care and relief of disabled people, were brought from Britain to North America. These methods, including out-of-door relief, indoor relief and scientific charity, were utilized throughout Canada from the late eighteenth to the early twentieth century.

Out-of-door relief was a common form of assistance provided to people with disabilities when their families could not take care of them. An early form of out-of-door relief was granted by legally allowing begging, but as time passed, other forms of out-of-door relief supplemented this. These persons were housed in private homes, and funds to cover expenses for food, clothing, shelter and medical care were often provided through municipal taxes, charitable organizations and religious organizations. In essence, out-of-door relief basically meant that disabled people were cared for through non-institutional methods of relief and were more or less part of the community.

Out-of-door relief came to be seen as creating dependency, and institutions such as asylums, poor houses and houses of industry replaced the former methods of out-of-door relief. This marked a significant shift in the philosophy. People with disabilities, who had once been considered part of the social order, came to be seen as nuisance populations. They were to be removed from society and placed in segregated institutions. Families often hid members with disabilities who had not been placed in institutions, as they were deemed to be a source of shame.

DISABILITY STATISTICS

- Over four million (4.2 million) people, or about 16% of the population, reported some level of disability in 1991. 31% of Aboriginal adults report a disability.

- Disability increases with age: in 1991, 7% of children under 15 experienced some level of disability, compared to 14% of adults aged 35 to 54 and 46% of those aged 65 and over.

- Severity of disability also increases with age: in 1991, 2.9% of children with disability had a severe disability, compared to 32.4% for those aged 65 and over.

- Among those with disabilities in 1991 aged 15 to 64 and living in households, mobility disabilities (limited ability to walk, move or stand) were most prevalent, at 52.5%, followed by agility disabilities (limited ability either to bend or dress or to handle small objects) at 50.2%.

- Over two million (2.3 million) people between 15 and 64 years of age, or 13% of the working-age population, reported some level of disability in 1991, up from 10% (1.8 million people) in 1986.

- In 1991, 48% of working-age Canadians with disabilities were employed (1.1 million), up from 40% in 1986; among persons without disabilities, the percentage employed increased to 73% in 1991, up from 70% in 1986.

- Among individuals with a university degree in 1991, the percentage employed was lower for persons with disabilities (67%) than for persons without disabilities (87%).

HEALTH AND ACTIVITY LIMITATION SURVEY (HALS)

The Health and Activity Limitation Survey (HALS), together with the 1983-84 Canadian Health and Disability Survey, is part of Statistics Canada's National Disability Database Program. HALS collects data on persons with disabilities living in Canada. It is a post-census survey of 35,000 individuals living in households and 10,000 who reside in institutions.

In the mid-nineteenth century, the segregation, **institutionalization** and isolation of persons with disabilities became common. The social rejection of "defective" populations was so severe that many disabled people were treated as common criminals and were banned from the streets of towns and cities. Many were charged under vagrancy laws and sent to jail; many of those who were not sent to jail were sent to a local poor house, a house of industry or a lunatic asylum. Provincial governments were reluctant to fund support programs for dependent populations, including disabled people, and coercive means were used to provide for their relief.

By World War II, persons with disabilities had been so totally removed from society that the common belief was that segregation was the natural order of things, that disabled people had always been segregated from their communities.

• Scientific Charity and People with Disabilities

There was a growing movement towards social reform at this time, however, which did bring some changes for the disabled. For example, some provinces introduced special schools for blind and deaf children. Homes for disabled children and adults were built, followed by the establishment of special hospitals and convalescent facilities. Interestingly, many of these developments occurred during a time when provincial governments maintained a laissez-faire attitude towards supporting dependent and disabled populations.

To provide for these populations, various charitable organizations emerged, based on what were considered to be scientific principles. Charity aid workers argued for the improvement of all relief operations. Charity work, they argued, needed to be organized along scientific lines, giving rise to the so-called charity organization movement, or scientific charity. The various Charity Organization Societies (COS) did not usually provide assistance directly. Rather, they investigated claims for assistance, kept records on those receiving assistance and acted as a clearing house for information on recipients. Basically, the COS was a social "watch dog," separating the deserving poor from the undeserving poor. The COS utilized the services of "friendly visitors" whose job it was to investigate claims in a scientific manner.

The social reform movements were a mixed blessing for people with disabilities. Educational and training programs were developed and, to an extent, hospital care was provided. But scientific charity also led to the establishment of coercive laws. In Canada, for example, sterilization laws were introduced by most provincial governments by the late 1920s and early 1930s. Many remained in effect until the late 1970s. Over the years, thousands of disabled people (most often with intellectual disabilities) were sterilized. This policy was in line with the now widely discredited **eugenics movement**, advocated by the fascists in Nazi Germany, among others, and was based on the notion that careful planning through proper breeding is the key to bettering society. For disabled women and teenaged girls, this usually meant a hysterectomy; for teenaged boys and men, sterilization was often achieved through castration.

- **From a Social Category of Disability to a Medical Category of Disability**

The enormous tragedy of World War I brought about changes in the public attitude towards disabilities. "When Johnny came marching home without an arm, without a leg, without an eye, people started looking around for other solutions to the disability problem" (Varela 1983, 31). As a part of this change in attitude following the war, disability changed from a social-legal to a medical category. Medical professionals, primarily from the field of rehabilitation medicine, became the new gatekeepers of the welfare state. Many of the programs and services initially provided only to veterans were extended to the public. For example, many provinces introduced worker's compensation, which led to the payment of disability benefits, including disability pensions, funding for equipment such as wheelchairs, prosthetic and orthotic devices, and vocational training.

The period following World War II also saw significant changes for disabled people, especially in the provision of care and treatment. This era saw the onset of the multidisciplinary rehabilitation team, which included the physiatrist, rehabilitation physician, nurse, occupational therapist, physiotherapist and, later, the social worker, psychologist, vocational counsellor and recreologist. Rehabilitation services for veterans laid the foundation for modern services to people with disabilities.

After the late 1940s, medical and social services were expanded to include disabled people. Special schools, training programs, sheltered work shops, summer camps and recreational programs were established, as well as special trades and industries, special hospitals and after-care facilities.

THE DISABILITY RIGHTS MOVEMENT

While the medical paradigm has provided most of the current categories pertaining to disability, there has been a growing shift towards a social-political paradigm of disability. Since the mid-1970s, many disabled people have become involved in various disability rights organizations and have attempted to challenge the existing medical model of disability.

The rise of **disability rights organizations** in Canada is rooted in the rise of the consumer movement, the civil rights movement, the peace movement, the gay rights movement and the women's movement of the late 1960s and early 1970s. As did the activists in these other movements, disability rights activists attempted to redefine their social status. Rather than be labeled "defective or handicapped," they fought to be considered as members of a minority group. Rex Freiden, writing in *Handicaps Monthly*, suggests that "many disabled people considered themselves members of a minority group related not by colour or nationality but by functional limitation and similar need" (1983, 55).

In the United States, disability rights advocates lobbied for new legislation that would benefit people with disabilities. In 1973, the *American Vocational Rehabilitation Act* was passed, prohibiting discrimination

---

CAUSES OF DISABILITY

- Existed at birth, 115,000 (5.9%)
- Current disease or illness, 574,000 (29.4%)
- Past disease or illness, 297,000 (15.2%)
- Aging, 160,000 (8.2%)
- Accident at work, 150,000 (7.7%)
- Motor vehicle accident, 98,000 (5.0%)
- Other accident, 129,000 (6.6%)
- Work environment, 82,000 (4.2%)
- Stroke, 58,000 (2.9%)
- Violent Act, 18,000 (0.9%)

Source: Statistics Canada, *Health and Activity Limitations Survey* (Ottawa, 1991).

against people with disabilities: "No otherwise qualified handicapped individual in the United States as defined by Section 7 shall, solely by reason of his handicap, be excluded from participation in, be denied the benefits of, or be subject to discrimination under any program or activity receiving federal financial assistance" (Zola 1986, 1).

Similar legislation followed in Canada at both the provincial and federal levels, and in 1982 the rights of disabled people were enshrined in the *Canadian Charter of Rights and Freedoms.* Canada is currently the only country in the world that has guaranteed the rights of disabled people within a constitutional framework. At both the federal and provincial levels, the rights of people with disabilities are protected under human rights legislation. There is also an ongoing attempt to develop legislation at various provincial levels that specifically addresses disabled people. For example, in Ontario there has been a move to introduce an "*Ontarians with Disabilities Act.*"

While there is a common belief that disabled people in Western industrialized societies are accepted as equal citizens, this is not the reality. The degree of acceptance of people with disabilities has not substantially increased, and disability is still highly stigmatized. Disabled people often have difficulty accessing jobs, education, housing and support services. "**Ableism,**" the belief in the superiority of able-bodied people over disabled people, is very evident in Canadian society.

DISABILITY THEORIES

Two points of view dominate a discussion of theories of disability. One is the medical model of disability, and the other is the political rights model. The **medical model of disability** has its roots in rehabilitation medicine, in which the focus of intervention is on the individual. The **political rights model of disability** is concerned with broader social and political change. In one form or another, the differences between these two views have established the parameters of the disability debate in Canada for the past fifteen years.

• Personal Tragedy Theory of Disability

Within the **personal tragedy theory of disability**, disability is viewed as an unfortunate life event in which the individual requires some form of professional and medical assistance (Oliver 1991). This theory holds that disability is primarily a medical problem, and therefore the focus of intervention should be on the disabled individual. Disabled individuals are often seen as having only physical or psychological problems, and interventions should be introduced as a means of "curing" the individual.

According to this theory of disability, persons who become disabled, as well as their loved ones, must go through various stages of psychological and emotional adjustment before they can accept themselves or a loved one as being disabled. Most of the literature regarding the impact of disability on the individual or the family focuses primarily on stages of adjustment. Stages such as shock, denial, grief, loss, reconciliation and

TEP Photo Archives, Toronto.

Disabled persons are not treated as equal citizens.

acceptance have often been applied to describe the emotional functioning of families and individuals who are coping with the sudden onset of disability. Such stage theories are based on a sequential interpretation of coping that involves the following characteristics:

- An individual or family must move sequentially through all of these stages to become fully adjusted.

- There is but one path through the sequence.

- An individual can be placed clearly in one stage or another by analyzing their behaviour.

- There is an optimal length of time for staying in each stage (Oliver 1991).

• Social Oppression Theory of Disability

In contrast to the personal tragedy theory of disability, the **social oppression theory of disability** argues that the problems faced by people with disabilities are not the result of physical impairments alone, but are the result of the social and political inequality that exists between disabled people and able-bodied people (Oliver 1991). Disability issues must be addressed in the context of human rights, and this means dealing with issues of high unemployment, lack of affordable housing, greater accessibility to education, lack of transportation and information and so on. The social oppression theory maintains that disability has been socially constructed as an individual medical problem, laying the framework for the continuous treatment of people with disabilities as second-class citizens. In short, a social oppression theory of disability suggests that disabled people are an oppressed minority group and have needs similar to minority groups.

The social oppression theory offers people with disabilities and their advocates not only a different way of examining disability issues but also a framework for action and change. In varying degrees, a social oppression model of disability has been adopted by disabled persons' movements in Canada, Britain and the United States and has resulted in the politicization of disabled persons. This concept of disability challenges the dominant ideology– that disability is an individual problem requiring individual treatment. Instead, disability issues have been redefined as problems associated with social, political and economic inequality.

During the United Nations International Year of Disabled Persons (1981) and Decade of Disabled Persons (1983-1992), the concept of a human rights approach to disability was expanded. The right of persons with disabilities to the same opportunities as other citizens and to an equal share in the improvements in living conditions resulting from economic and social development was emphasized. For the first time, *handicap* was defined as a function of the relationship between persons with disabilities and their environment. This resulted in the development of the Standard Rules on the Equalization of Opportunities for Persons with Disabilities in 1994. The purpose of the Rules is to ensure that girls, boys, women and men with disabilities, as members of their societies,

UNITED NATIONS

In considering Canada's adherence to Articles 16 and 17 of the covenant, the United Nations concluded:

"The Committee is concerned about significant cuts to services on which people with disabilities rely, such as cuts to home care, attendant care, special needs transportation systems and tightened eligibility rules for people with disabilities. Although the government failed to provide to the Committee any information regarding homelessness among discharged psychiatric patients, the Committee was told that a large number of those patients end up on the street, while other suffer from inadequate housing and insufficient support services."

Source: Report of the Committee on Economic, Social and Cultural Rights, United Nations, Concluding observations, Section 36 (1998).

A Schematic Contrast of the Two Approaches

	Medical Model of Disability	Political Rights Model of Disability
Definition of problem	Physical impairment/lack of employment skills	Dependent on professionals, relatives, etc.
Locus of problem	In the individual	In the environment and rehabilitation process
Solution to problem	Professional intervention by physician, therapist, occupational therapist, vocational rehabilitation counsellor, etc.	Peer counselling, advocacy, self-help, consumer control, removal of barriers
Social role	Patient/client	Consumer
Who controls	Professional	Consumer
Desired outcome	Maximize activities, living skills and gainful employment	Independent Living

Source: Gerben Dejong, Independent Living: From Social Movement to Analytical Paradigm, *Archives of Physical Medicine and Rehabilitation* 60 (1979): 435-446.

may exercise the same rights and obligations as others, and obstacles preventing this are removed. It takes the view that it is the responsibility of each state to take appropriate action to remove such obstacles. The Rules emphasize that persons with disabilities and their organizations should play an active role as partners in this process. Despite the UN ruling, disabled people remain largely disenfranchised—in industrial and developing societies, disabled people remain at the bottom of the socio-economic order.

INCOME SECURITY PROGRAMS

Canada's disability income support system is based on a loosely knit set of programs. These programs have different eligibility criteria, guidelines and procedures. The social and income security programs for disabled people are derived from private and public sources in the form of contributory or non-contributory benefits.

Publicly funded disability programs are programs covered by federal, provincial and municipal legislation. These programs include the Canada Pension Plan–Disability Pension (a federal program), the Family Benefits plan (a provincial program), and the General Welfare Assistance plan (a municipal program). These types of programs are funded through government taxation, and except for the Canada Pension Plan, do not require the financial contribution of recipients.

Privately funded disability programs include programs that are provided through private insurance plans or through long-term disability plans as part of job benefits. These private income security programs are based on the amount of funding that the recipient has contributed directly to the plan, or funding that has been contributed to a plan on behalf of the recipient.

In its analysis of disability benefits provided through Canada's income security programs, the G. Allen Roeher Institute, a research group associated with the Canadian Association for Community Living, wrote about the "insecurity" of these income security programs (G. Allen Roeher Institute 1988). These observations were directed at the Canada Assistance Plan, which had existed since the mid-1960s. Since that time, income security has been radically altered with the introduction of the Canada Health and Social Transfer (CHST). CHST (see p.33) is based on a per-capita grant to the provinces without regard to provincial circumstances or needs. The Canadian Association of Independent Living Centres holds that this has jeopardized the income of disabled people, making their lives more insecure than in the mid-1980s.

While Canadians have a universal health care system, there is no similar system for people with disabilities who require government-funded supports and services. The primary similarity across the provinces is the range and types of supports and services provided. For example, provincial programs, whether in Newfoundland or British Columbia, will cover the cost of wheelchairs, canes, eyeglasses, walkers, attendant care services, home care, transportation and so forth. The differences among the provinces are found in two areas. One is eligibility requirements, which may be different from one province to the next; the other is the amount of funding for supports and services, which may vary from one province to the next. Each province has its own legislation and mechanisms for providing services to disabled people. As a consequence of this lack of universality, the care and treatment of persons with disabilities varies across the country. For example, some provinces, such as Newfoundland, Prince Edward Island, Saskatchewan and New Brunswick, have a single-tier program wherein supports and services are directly funded by the province to the individual in need. Other provinces, such as Nova Scotia and Manitoba, have a two-tier system of support for disabled people—basically, the programs are funded though a system of general welfare assistance at the municipal and/or county level. The province provides the funding, and the money for supports and services is then transferred to the local government, which, in turn, funds the individual.

The types of programs indicated above (one-tier and two-tier systems) are directly related to provincial social welfare spending, but there are also provincial programs based on specific legislation aimed at people with disabilities. In Ontario, disabled people are covered under the *Ontario Disability Supports Program Act*; in British Columbia, they are covered under the *Disability Benefits Program Act*; and in Alberta, disabled people receive benefits through the Assured Income for the Severely Handicapped program. These provincial programs are based on distinct legislation covering people with disabilities and are not directly connected to any provincial welfare legislation.

GAINING ACCESS TO SERVICES

For people with a disability, the first step in gaining access to municipal or provincial programs, such as General Welfare Assistance or Family Benefits, is an eligibility determination carried out by a

EQUALIZING OPPORTUNITIES

Standard rules on the equalization of opportunities for persons with disabilities:

1. Awareness raising
2. Medical care
3. Rehabilitation
4. Support services
5. Accessibility
6. Education
7. Employment
8. Income maintenance and social security
9. Family life and personal integrity
10. Culture
11. Recreation and sports
12. Religion
13. Information and research
14. Policy making and planning
15. Legislation
16. Economic policies
17. Co-ordination of work
18. Organizations of persons with disabilities
19. Personnel training
20. National monitoring and evaluation of disability programs
21. Technical and economic cooperation
22. International co-operation

Available at website: http://www.un.org/esa/socdev/enable/dissre00.htm

Adopted by the United Nations General Assembly, forty-eighth session, resolution 48/96, annex, of 20 December 1993.

CITIZENSHIP

"The concept of citizenship is central to disability issues. Citizenship is the inclusion of persons with disabilities in all aspects of Canadian society — the ability of a person to be actively involved with their community. Full citizenship depends on equality, inclusion, rights and responsibilities, and empowerment and participation....

"A person is able to exercise full citizenship when they do not face barriers that significantly reduce their ability to participate fully in their community. Persons with disabilities and their advocates have argued that ensuring full citizenship is not just the right thing to do, but is also a matter of fundamental rights under Canada's Charter of Rights and Freedoms.

"First Nations, Inuit, and Métis people have a somewhat different vision of citizenship due to their unique position in Canada, as Aboriginal people seek full citizenship both within their own Nations and in Canada."

Source: Federal, Provincial and Territorial Ministers Responsible for Social Services, *In Unison 2000: Persons with Disabilities in Canada* (Ottawa: Human Resources Development Canada).

physician. The physician determines whether or not the applicant has a disability that seriously impedes his or her potential for employment.

Once a medical evaluation has been carried out and the person is deemed to be disabled, a Social Assistance review takes place. First, there is an investigation of assets, which means that a person with a disability cannot have assets beyond a specific limit. For example, disabled people living in Ontario who receive Family Benefits are not allowed to accumulate savings beyond the amount of $3,500. Only in special circumstances, such as the existence of a trust fund, can asset exemption be waived.

Each province has its own types and levels of exemption. Exemptions can include automobiles, farm equipment, tools and so forth. For example, in Quebec, benefits are reduced if the value of the applicant's house exceeds $50,000, and automobiles are exempt only up to a certain amount.

The next step in a Social Assistance review is a needs test. A needs test consists of three basic steps:

1. The applicant's basic requirements for living are identified (food, clothing, shelter, utilities, other household and personal allowances). Each requirement is designated with a maximum dollar allotment, and the requirements are then totaled to determine the funds needed to meet basic needs.

2. The applicant's available financial resources to meet basic needs are determined, that is, income from resources such as other pensions, including public or private funds, savings, money received through paid employment or training programs.

3. The difference between total resources and total basic needs is calculated. A negative remainder indicates a "budget defect" upon which eligibility for assistance is determined.

The amount of assistance will then be assessed according to a variety of factors, including size of family, degree of employability of the head of the family, size and type of accommodation and so on.

In addition to basic financial assistance, disabled people who receive either General Welfare Assistance, Family Benefits or who are covered by the Canada Pension Plan are also entitled to other forms of assistance. These may include dental services, prescription medication, eyeglasses, technical aids and devices, prosthetic and orthotic equipment, wheelchairs, child care subsidies and so forth. These forms of assistance are referred to as "in kind." Recipients who work must notify authorities and are allowed to keep only a percentage of the income, with the remainder being deducted from benefits.

With work-related or contributory income security programs, contributions are made through an individual's employment, and the amount of financial benefits received is based on the amount paid into the plan. The higher the wages and the higher the amount of money paid into the plan, the higher the financial benefits the individual will receive should he or she become disabled.

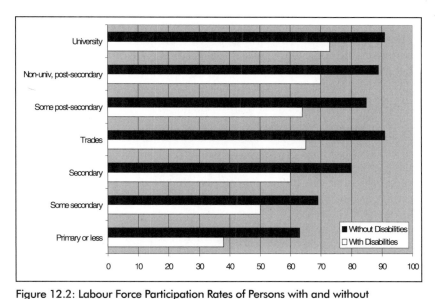

These statistics refer to disabled persons who are actively pursuing employment.

Figure 12.2: Labour Force Participation Rates of Persons with and without Disabilities by Level of Education, 1991.

• Canada Pension Plan

The Canada Pension Plan (CPP) is an example of an income security program based on contributory payments. The federal government operates the CPP in all parts of Canada except Quebec, where there is a similar Quebec Pension Plan (QPP). Workers between the ages of eighteen and sixty-five make contributions based on funds received. Employees and employers pay equal amounts into the plan. Persons over sixty-five have the option of paying into the plan until they are seventy years of age. Persons receiving disability pensions or other pensions do not have to pay into the plan.

Eligibility for CPP benefits is based on the following:

1. A physician must first determine eligibility for benefits.

2. Benefits are granted only to individuals who have either contributed to the plan during two of the last three years or during five of the last ten years.

3. Pension benefits consist of a flat rate plus earnings equal to 75 percent of the retirement pension to which the person would be entitled.

The Canada Pension Plan does not consider the day-to-day financial needs of the disabled individual and his or her family. Low-income workers therefore receive lower benefits and may require additional assistance through other programs such as Family Benefits (GAINS-D) or General Welfare Assistance (Special Needs).

The Canadian Association of Independent Living Centers (CAILC) has a list of all ILCs in Canada at:
http://www.cailc.ca

• **The Poor with Disabilities**

Poverty rates can vary significantly among persons with disabilities. Two-thirds of those who survive on welfare or Social Assistance live in poverty. Many are not eligible for C/QPP or Workers' Compensation benefits due to a lack of past employment. Those who are eligible for C/QPP Disability Benefits are better off, yet more than one-quarter live below the poverty line.

People with disabilities naturally prefer employment as the solution to poverty. Frequently, however, an unaccommodating work environment makes this difficult. The labour force participation rate for all working-age persons with disabilities is lower than that of the general population. As well, the participation rates are lowest for persons with moderate and severe disabilities and are highest for those who have higher levels of education. This data indicates that workplaces need to be more accommodating of people with more severe disabilities, and that increased educational opportunities will contribute to self-reliance.

THE INDEPENDENT LIVING MOVEMENT

The **Independent Living Movement** (ILM) has been a key player in the struggle to achieve human rights legislation for people with disabilities. Originating in the United States during the early 1970s and introduced to Canada in 1979, the Independent Living Movement has become a dominant force in disability rights activity in Canada. In addition to promoting disability rights, ILM promotes the social oppression theory of disability.

The origins of the Independent Living Movement can be traced to the Cowell Residence Program at the University of California, Berkeley. In 1962, Ed Roberts, a post-polio respiratory quadriplegic, became one of the first severely disabled persons to be admitted to the university. A group of students with disabilities began to recognize that medical and rehabilitation professionals largely controlled their lives. They came to realize that the concerns raised by the black and student movements regarding self-determination were very relevant to their lives as disabled people. This consciousness-raising process was accelerated in 1969 when the rehabilitation counsellor assigned to the Cowell Program tried to have two students evicted because she "deemed their educational goals unfeasible and their life styles improper." The Cowell students fought the eviction and won. They went on to form the Physically Disabled Students' Program, which was a radical departure from former practice in the medical and rehabilitation fields.

According to the Canadian Association of Independent Living Centres, the Canadian Independent Living Movement grew out of two central developments: (1) the existing infrastructure developed by the Canadian Consumer Movement in the 1970s, in particular the Coalition of Provincial Organizations of the Handicapped (now known as the Council of Canadians with Disabilities); and (2) the introduction of the Independent Living (IL) philosophy by American disability theorist Gerben DeJong to the Canadian disability community in 1980.

Three events of 1981 were central to the development of IL: (1) the United Nations declaration of the International Year of Disabled Persons, (2) the Canadian government's release of its Obstacles report, and (3) the personal commitment of Henry Enns to the IL philosophy. Each of these events provided legitimacy to the social oppression model of examining disability issues and promoted the philosophy of IL to various levels of government, academics and other disability organizations.

By 1985, Independent Living Resource Centres (ILRCs) were operating in Waterloo, Winnipeg, Thunder Bay, Calgary and Toronto. In 1986, at the first IL conference in Ottawa, the Canadian Association of Independent Living Centres (CAILC) was formed to act as a national co-ordinating body for the ILM and the definition of a Canadian ILRC was developed. In 1997, a total of twenty-two ILRCs were operating across Canada.

• Philosophy of Independent Living

The philosophy of the Independent Living Movement promotes self-direction that enables access to community services and resources, and facilitates full participation in the community. The goal is to foster the self-determination of persons with disabilities according to their individual needs and desires. People with disabilities are encouraged to achieve self-direction over the personal and community services needed to attain their own independent living. The Canadian Association for Independent Living Centres describes the philosophy of ILRCs:

> The Independent Living (IL) approach recognizes the rights of citizens with disabilities to take control of their lives by examining choices, making decisions and even taking risks. The logic behind Independent Living is that people with disabilities are the experts in knowing what their needs are and are able to find solutions to problems surrounding disability issues. The Independent Living philosophy recognizes that people with disabilities have the right to run their own lives, make their own decisions, make their own mistakes and be an active participant in their community (http://www.cailc.ca).

The Independent Living philosophy has three aspects:

1. An approach that empowers consumers to make choices necessary to control their community and personal resources;

2. A set of organizational values or principles: consumer control, cross-disability, community based and full participation. Consumer control means that ILRCs are governed and controlled by persons with disabilities. At least 51 percent of the members of each board of directors must have a disability, and must have a balance of people with and without a disability. Cross-disability means that ILRCs are responsive to persons with all types of disabilities, including mobility, sensory, cognitive, emotional, psychiatric and so forth. The concept of being community based implies that ILRCs are non-profit organizations committed to the development of programs and resources that complement rather than duplicate existing community resources. ILRCs promote the full participation and integration of all persons with disabilities. The

Independent Living approach emphasizes empowerment.

TEP Photo Archives, Toronto.

IMPACT OF INDEPENDENT LIVING RESOURCE CENTRES

A study examined the impacts of ILRCs on individuals with disabilities and the impacts on the community, including formal services/agencies, information groups, families and friends.

The results of this study are available on-line at: http://www.cailc.ca/library/impact.htm

IL philosophy believes that persons with disabilities are citizens with the right to participate in the community life and growth; and

3. An alternative model of program delivery. This alternative program model is one that has been created by and for persons with disabilities.

The Canadian Independent Living model consists of four core programs: information and referral, peer support, empowerment skills development, and research and demonstration. Although each community will have different needs and resources, in general all have these core programs.

1. *Information and Referral:* The Information and Referral program responds to requests from consumers. The Centre attempts to locate the information required or may refer the consumer to another community agency or ILRC program.

2. *Peer Support:* Peer support is consumers talking with and supporting other consumers.

3. *Independent Living/Empowerment Skills Development:* Through appropriate seminars, support and advice, the IL/Empowerment Skills Development program helps disabled people develop the skills that will allow them to advocate for themselves.

4 *Research and Demonstration:* The Research and Demonstration program researches the needs within the community and then promotes the development of services to meet those needs.

CAILC undertook a study of the effects of ILRCs and found that ILRCs succeed, in large part, not simply because they provide an opportunity to learn skills, access information, or receive support, but because they do so in a way that is consistent with the Independent Living philosophy. The Association concluded that improvement in the quality of life for disabled people requires skill development as well as the removal of environmental, social and economic barriers. Individual empowerment was found to be a key benefit. It was particularly important in fostering competency in a variety of community living skills, as well as resulting in increased confidence and self-esteem. Finally, the Association found that individuals involved with some of the programs of the ILRC have knowledge of more programs than they are involved with, and highly value the programs with which they are directly involved and/or see as benefiting others (CAILC 1997).

SOCIAL WORK PRACTICE WITH PERSONS WITH DISABILITIES

Although debates between rehabilitationists and the independent living practitioners have been ongoing for many years, social work in general tends to be dominated by the rehabilitative or medical model of practice. Most social workers that work with disabled people are involved with some aspect of rehabilitative services. These may include services directly associated with hospitals, rehabilitation centres, disabled children's treatment centres, group homes, chronic care facilities

© Dick Hemingway

There is a need for a publicly funded disabilities system.

and sheltered workshops, as well as educational facilities such as schools, colleges and universities. In addition, federal, provincial and municipal governments employ social workers to work with disabled people. Their work may include the provision of direct services, social administration or the development of social policy. Social workers also work with charitable organizations that provide such services.

The role of the social worker varies but one common activity is the focus on individual and family adjustment to disability. This includes the provision of counselling and support services, as well as support in attaining funding for equipment, attendant care services and other resources. Social workers also help clients arrange for social welfare benefits, Workers' Compensation benefits, pensions and so on.

Counselling and resource attainment have been the predominant focus of social work, with less emphasis on civil rights and social and political change. This not to suggest that social workers are not involved in advocacy and community organization, but that the overall focus of social work has been the direct needs of the client population. In fact, the social work profession has come under much criticism from disability rights advocates because of the profession's lack of involvement in social action.

What skills should social workers have to work with people with disabilities? Social workers should have generic practice skills, which include an understanding of individual and family counselling, as well as an understanding of group work and community organization. In addition, to be effective social workers should know mediation and advocacy. Social workers should know about resources and be able to connect clients to these resources (mediation). Social workers should take a stand on behalf of disabled people. This may mean petitioning for more or better services, organizing a protest against the lack of accessible housing, or it might mean leading or supporting boycotts against businesses that are not accessible for people with disabilities (advocacy).

To be effective, social work cannot be restricted to individual or familial models of social work alone but must include a broader framework incorporating the rehabilitative and independent living paradigms. In other words, social workers must be able to help individuals with disabilities as well as their family members cope with disability while recognizing that many of the difficulties facing disabled people stem from broader social arrangements. This requires that social workers become advocates for social and political change, which may lead to a more inclusive and humane society for people with disabilities.

The Independent Living service model involves social workers in completely new ways of service delivery. Social workers who practice following the values and principles of ILM find themselves emphasizing the uniqueness of each individual's situation and encouraging people to make informed decisions and take responsibility for their own lives, even if it involves taking risks. Social work practice within this perspective does not attempt to have the person do something to "fit into" their environment; instead, it is aimed at changing the environment to meet the needs of the individual.

ADVOCACY GROUPS

- Council of Canadians with Disabilities (CCD) is a national organization representing disabled people across Canada. This organization was formerly known as the Coalition of Provincial Organizations of the Handicapped. The CCD is primarily a cross-disability advocacy group representing provincial organizations of disabled people as well as groups such as the Disabled Women's Network, the Canadian Association of the Deaf, the Thalidomide Victims Association of Canada, and the National Network for Mental Health. The CCD's objectives include promotion of full partnership of people with disabilities, self-determination, consumer control, equality and rights.

- Canadian Rehabilitation Council for the Disabled (CRCD) represents 60 organizations of service providers, professional associations and rehabilitation centres across Canada. The CRCD is also linked to international organizations such as Rehabilitation International. The primary focus of the CRCD is to develop rehabilitative programs and services that will contribute to the social and economic integration of people with disabilities.

This type of practice has been found to build self-confidence in the individual. When existing options do not provide an acceptable alternative, individuals are encouraged and assisted to seek their own solutions. Rather than being told that their disability is the barrier, people with disabilities are encouraged to focus on the barriers in society.

SERVING THOSE WITH DISABILITIES

Below is a list of a few **disabilities organizations** that provide services to disabled people.

- *Hearing impairments and deafness.* Canadian Hearing Society (CHS). CHS provides a hearing-aid program, sign language interpretation and technical aid assistance for the hearing impaired. CHS also provides sign language classes, information about hearing loss, referral to community resources and advocacy on behalf of hearing-impaired people.

- *Visual impairments.* Canadian National Institute for the Blind (CNIB). CNIB provides counselling and referrals, rehabilitation teaching, orientation and mobility training, sight enhancement, technical aids, career development and employment services, and library services.

- *Mobility impairments.* Canadian Paraplegic Association (CPA). CPA provides personal and family counselling, educational and vocational counselling, employment referrals placement and counselling, services for locating and adapting suitable housing, assessment and procurement of equipment, financial counselling, information on products and services, and individual advocacy.

- *Learning disabilities.* Learning Disability Association of Canada (LDAC). LDAC is a national, non-profit voluntary organization founded in 1963 and incorporated in 1971. It is dedicated to advancing the education, employment, social development, legal rights and general well-being of people with learning disabilities.

- *Neuro-locomotor impairments.* The Multiple Sclerosis Society of Canada (MSSC). MSSC provides supportive counselling, referral, self-help groups, educational workshops, equipment programs, social and recreational activities, information about MS for health care professionals, and a network of specialized MS clinics. Services vary across the country depending upon the kind of provincial government and community programs available.

- *Intellectual impairments.* The Canadian Association of Community Living (CACL). CACL is a national association representing people with developmental disabilities. It represents ten provincial and two territorial associations as well as 400 local associations across Canada. The primary focus of Community Living Associations is the integration of people with developmental disabilities into all aspects of Canadian society. Services provided by Centres for Community Living include advocacy, research, counselling, housing and supportive services, public education and awareness.

- *Mental health impairments.* The Canadian Mental Health Association (CMHA). CMHA is a national network of 135 branches in communities across Canada dedicated to the promotion of mental health and to ensuring the provision of the best possible services for people with mental health problems.

CONCLUSION

Issues pertaining to social work with disabled persons are very complex, and to be effective in this work requires specialized knowledge and training. The proportion of Canadians affected by some form of disability, and the sheer variety of disabling conditions they experiences, will mean that more resources will need to be devoted in the future to training social workers in this field.

The rehabilitation services are the primary area of social work with disabled persons. These services include hospitals, rehabilitation centres, group homes, chronic care facilities as well as educational institutions. Social workers are also employed by provincial and federal governments and by a variety of charitable organizations, both in the provision of direct services and in the development of social policies. For those involved in direct practice, work centres on counselling and helping with support services, including assisting with access to resources.

Since the 1970s, there has been a shift away from a narrow medical approach of disability to more of a social-political model in which disabled persons are accepted as equal citizens. In line with the newer approach to disability, increasingly social workers are involved in campaigning on behalf of persons with disabilities, as advocates for social and political change. The Independent Living Movement has been a key organization in the promotion of human rights for persons with disabilities. Their successful philosophy is one that promotes self-direction, self-determination and full participation in the life of communities. This shift is to be welcomed and points the way towards significant advances in services and programs and a better life for disabled persons across Canada.

REFERENCES

- Canadian Association of Independent Living Centres. 1997. *A Study on the Impacts of Independent Living Resource Centre in Canada.* Ottawa: CAILC. http://www.cailc.ca

- DeJong, Gerben. 1979. Independent Living: From Social Movement to Analytical Paradigm. *Archives of Physical Medicine and Rehabilitation* 60: 435-446.

- Fawcett, G., and R. Shillington. 1996. Income Support and Tax Relief for People with Disabilities. *Insight,* no.4.

- Federal, Provincial and Territorial Ministers Responsible for Social Services. 2000. *In Unison 2000: Persons with Disabilities in Canada.* Ottawa: Human Resources Development Canada. http://socialunion.gc.ca/In_Unison2000

- Freiden, Rex. 1983. Independent Living in the United States and Other Countries. *Handicaps Monthly* (April), 54B61.

- Oliver, Michael. 1991. *The Politics of Disablement.* London, UK: Macmillan Educational Ltd.

- G. Allen Roeher Institute. 1988. *Income Insecurity: The Disability Income System in Canada.* Toronto: York University.

- Statistics Canada. 1991. *Health and Activity Limitations Survey.* Ottawa.

- Stone, Deborah. 1984. *The Disabled State.* Philadelphia, UK: Temple University Press.

- Varela, Rita. 1983. Changing Social Attitudes and Legislation. In Nancy Crewe and Irving K. Zola, eds., *Independent Living for Physically Disabled People.* San Francisco, Calif.: Jossey-Boss.

- Zola, Irving K. 1986. *The Independent Living Movement: Promises and Challenges.* Ottawa: Proceedings from the Sydney Dinsdale Conference on Rehabilitation, Kune.

Roy Hanes teaches social work at Carleton University. He has a long-standing expertise in social work practice and policy with disabled people.

CHAPTER 12: SOCIAL WORK WITH PERSONS WITH DISABILITIES

Key Terms

- People with disabilities
- Disability
- Institutionalization
- Eugenics movement
- Disability rights organizations
- Ableism
- Medical model
- Political rights model
- Personal tragedy theory
- Social oppression theory
- Publicly funded disability programs
- Privately funded disability programs
- Independent Living Movement
- Disability organizations

Discussion Questions

1. Give some of the basic statistics that capture the extent of disability within the Canadian population.

2. Give a brief description of indoor relief, out-of-door relief, scientific charity, and modern social welfare, showing how each of these delivery models has been applied historically to persons with disabilities.

3. There are two dominant theoretical approaches to disability. Identify and compare these approaches.

4. Briefly trace the origins of the Independent Living Movement and describe its main objectives.

5. List some of the major associations involved in serving the needs of persons with disabilities and describe some of the services they provide.

Websites

- **Disability WebLinks**
  http://www.disabilityweblinks.ca

  This site has been specifically developed for persons with disabilities and the site design, layout and technical features reflect the requirements identified by members of the community and internationally accepted guidelines for accessibility. Human Resources Development Canada is managing the site under the direction of the Federal/Provincial/Territorial Ministers responsible for Social Services.

  For the first time, persons with disabilities across Canada have a dedicated Internet site. Disability WebLinks provides quick access to information on government-related disability programs and services. It is a single-window access to over 1500 federal, provincial and territorial government programs and related services for persons with disabilities. Disability WebLinks provides information on a variety of topics; e.g., accessibility, education, employment, financial supports, health, housing and residential supports, personal supports, rights, tax programs and transportation.

- **Canadian Association of Independent Living Centres (CAILC)|**
  http://www.cailc.ca

  The Canadian Association of Independent Living Centres (CAILC) is a national umbrella organization that consists of local autonomous Independent Living Resource Centres (ILRCs). Their website contains a wealth of information about the topic, including a virtual library.

13

International Social Work Practice

Helping People Help Themselves

Practising social work abroad has always been an important part of what Canadian social workers do. In pursuing the ideals of human rights and sustainable development and in defending oppressed groups, social workers practise in a wide range of governmental, religious and community organizations worldwide. Today, of course, this occurs in the context of the rapid "globalization" of social and economic life.

International social work is a vast field of activity, and the term itself has a variety of meanings. It can refer to comparative social welfare or the examination and comparison of the social welfare systems in different countries. It can also denote work in international organizations, such as governmental or voluntary organizations, assisting in the carrying out of social planning, social development and welfare programs sponsored by such organizations. Finally, of course, international social work can simply refer to day-to-day social work in a country other than one's own.

The history of international social work is certainly a distinguished one. Since the early days of Jane Addams, the profession's first Nobel Prize winner, social workers have worked within various national and international forums struggling for human rights, peace, development and social justice. Social workers have been and remain involved with the resettling of refugees and other persons displaced by war, operating emergency relief services for victims of natural and human-made disasters, advocating on behalf of disadvantaged and vulnerable populations, organizing groups of oppressed people into effective political entities, and otherwise extending various programs of assistance to populations in need. They play an indispensable and often unacknowledged role, often working in very difficult conditions.

This chapter focuses on the work of social workers in "Southern," "developing" or "Third World" countries. It examines the core problems of social and economic development in the modern context of economic globalization. Since those involved in social work at the international level tend to be heavily involved in community development and human rights work, much of the chapter explores these areas. It is important to remember that the work that social workers do abroad is at times very dangerous, and this is further testimony of the dedication of those individuals drawn into the profession today.

Children in a refugee camp in Kukes, Albania.

235

THIRD WORLD

4.4. billion people live in developing countries. Of these:

- three-fifths lack basic sanitation
- almost one-third have no access to clean water
- one-quarter do not have adequate housing
- one-fifth have no access to modern health services
- one-fifth of children do not attend to the end of primary school
- one-fifth do not have adequate protein and energy from their food supplies

Source: *CAFOD Fact Sheet on Poverty* (2001).

"Everyone has the right to a standard of living adequate for the health and well-being of him/(her)self and his/(her) family, including food, clothing, housing and medical care and necessary social services... Everyone has the right to education."

Source: Universal Declaration of Human Rights.

THE GLOBAL ECONOMY AND POVERTY

Any discussion of international social work must acknowledge the enormous economic disadvantages faced by countries in the developing world. The *Progress on Nations* report published annually by the United Nations Children's Fund (UNICEF 2000) shows the brutal social and economic disparities between countries. The following are some of the highlights:

- Among the 192 nations of the world, per capita GNP is as low as $80 and as high as $45,360 a year.
- The under-five mortality rate varies from 4 to 320 deaths per 1,000 live births.
- The maternal death rate ranges from 0 to 1,800 deaths per 100,000 live births.
- The primary school enrolment rate varies from 24 percent to 100 percent of young people.

The World Health Organization (WHO) estimates that malnutrition was associated with over half of all child deaths that occurred in developing countries in 1995. Of the nearly 12 million children under five who die each year in developing countries, mainly from preventable causes, the deaths of over 6 million, or 55 percent, are either directly or indirectly attributable to malnutrition. Poverty, of course, is one of the main causes of malnutrition and early death.

• The North-South Divide

The economic world divides, broadly speaking, along North-South lines (the so-called **North-South divide**), with the countries of the First World awash in relative affluence and those of the **Third World** in abject squalor. This is not to minimize the Third-World-like living conditions of many Aboriginal groups and others in the industrialized world or the grotesquely affluent lifestyles of elites in the Third World. Nevertheless, the countries of the South have 75 percent of the world's people, but only

- 15 percent of the world's energy consumption;
- 17 percent of the world's GNP;
- 30 percent of the world's food grains;
- 18 percent of the world's export earnings;
- 11 percent of the world's education spending;
- 9 percent of the world's health expenditure;
- 5 percent of the world's science and technology;
- 8 percent of the world's industry.

About one-third, or 1.3 billion people, live on an income of less than $1 a day (Catholic Agency for Overseas Development 2001).

The most pressing concern in the poorer countries is social and economic development. Economic development is necessary to overcome the crushing poverty that the vast majority of people in these countries face daily, yet many developing nations serve mainly as a source of raw

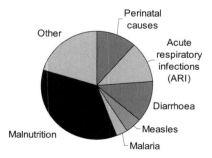

Causes of Child Death Worldwide (Murray and Lopez 1996).

materials and cheap labour for huge international corporations. Indeed, many people would argue that such countries are not so much "developing" as "underdeveloping." The development plans of the International Monetary Fund and World Bank have not led to economic prosperity. What has transpired under the banners of "globalization" and "development" appears to be more a deepening enslavement than economic liberation. (For more on globalization, see Chapter 2, page 36.)

HUMAN RIGHTS AND SUSTAINABLE DEVELOPMENT

In such desperate circumstances, dedicated social workers in these countries quickly realize that opportunities for bringing about effective social change, even on a local scale, are limited. For this reason, international social workers and political activists are increasingly advocating a new approach to development based on adherence to complementary guiding principles.

Two of these principles are: (1) the promotion and protection of human rights, and (2) ensuring sustainable development. A great deal of useful international social work has taken place in pursuit of these key objectives, which are discussed below.

• The Promotion and Protection of Human Rights

Human rights can be defined as those inherent rights without which we cannot truly live as human beings. The idea of human rights is based on an acknowledgment that individuals possess certain inalienable political and civil rights. As well, there are collective cultural, social and economic rights. The notion that there is a duty to protect the rights of all people has become a recognized part of our human heritage.

The recognition of universal human rights was consolidated in the 1948 Universal Declaration of Human Rights by the General Assembly of the United Nations, to which all the major countries of the world are signatories. Its preamble asserts that the "recognition of the inherent dignity and of the equal and inalienable rights of all members of the human family is the foundation of freedom, justice and peace in the world." This declaration is codified and expanded in legislation and regulations around the world.

It is useful to distinguish between three types (or "generations") of human rights. The first type, called *negative rights*, represents civil and political rights as set forth in articles 2 to 21 of the Universal Declaration of Human Rights. These rights ensure protection of basic rights such as freedom from torture, false imprisonment or summary execution. The second type represents *positive rights* or economic, social and cultural rights as detailed in articles 22 to 27 of the Declaration. These rights are aimed at ensuring justice, freedom from want and participation in society. The third type encompasses the *collective rights* contained in article 28, which states that "everyone is entitled to a social and international order in which the rights and freedoms set forth in this Declaration can be fully realized."

IN THE WORLD TODAY...

- 1.3 billion people live in absolute poverty
- 100 million are homeless
- 14 million go hungry every day
- 14 million children under 5 will die this year
- 900 million are without education

Source: CAFOD Fact Sheet on Poverty at: http://www.cafod.org.uk/povertyfs.htm

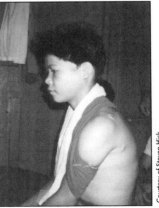

Young boy in the Philippines shot by Marcos military, 1995.

Courtesy of Steven Hick.

Filipino workers protest the displacement of local industries by large global corporations.

The three levels of rights illustrate an evolution is our understanding of human rights and in sociopolitical consciousness. The levels move from a defensive stance (against the violation of basic rights), to an affirmation of the right to meet material needs and participate in society, to an understanding of collective rights and the equitable participation in the production and distribution of resources. The philosophical base of social work loosely corresponds to these three levels. Historically, the profession has tended to focus on meeting needs, rather than affirming rights, but social workers have increasingly moved in the direction of affirming and fostering all three levels of rights.

The International Policy on Human Rights (see Appendix B) adopted by the International Federation of Social Work (IFSW) affirms that all social workers have a special responsibility to advance the cause of human rights throughout the world. In helping individuals, groups and communities to improve their well-being, social workers see the impact of social conditions on the capacity of people to resolve their problems. Because of this, social workers acknowledge that civil and political rights are inseparable from economic, social, cultural and collective rights. The policy asserts that human rights are a common standard and guide for the work of all professional social workers. It points out that social workers not only need to respect human rights, but also to work to oppose and eliminate all violations of human rights.

- **Ensuring Sustainable Development**

Another important concept for international social workers is that of **sustainable development.** The most frequently quoted definition of sustainable development is from the report *Our Common Future* (also known as the Brundtland Report): "Sustainable development is development that meets the needs of the present without compromising the ability of future generations to meet their own needs" (World Commission on Environment and Development 1987, 43).

Sustainable development, then, focuses on improving the quality of life for all peoples of the world without sacrificing the environment. Sustainable development in this sense is not a new idea; Aboriginal cultures have emphasized the need for a holistic approach or harmony between the environment, society and economy. What is new is the articulation of these ideas within the context of global capitalism and an information-based society.

As an important extension to this concept, the International Council on Social Welfare (ICSW; http://www.icsw.org) advocates what it calls "sustainable social progress," which goes beyond ecological and environmental concerns. The members of ICSW believe that, in order to promote sustainable social progress, social workers should support co-operation to strengthen governance and social standards internationally. One area of particular urgency is the implementing of an Anti-Poverty Pact aimed at mobilizing resources to achieve drastic reductions in poverty, especially in developing countries. International sustainable development, in this broader sense, includes all the typical activities that international social workers carry out in enhancing the participation of people in decision making, anti-poverty programs, women's health and promoting peace.

Sustainable development is a central organizing principle for international social workers. Its application involves three basic operating principles:

- *Equity and justice for all:* uphold the rights of the poor and disadvantaged within societies and between nations, and of future generations.

- *Long-term view:* the view that all claims on the earth's resources today have implications for future generations.

- *Structural understanding of the broader society:* it is necessary to fully take into account the many interconnections between individuals, communities, the economy and the environment.

The concept of sustainable development is an important one for international social work practitioners and others. The idea challenges us to think beyond the here-and-now and look to the wider effects of our actions. In essence, the concept is a call to action—a call to do things differently and to realize that our actions have ripple effects throughout our interdependent world.

LEGISLATING HUMAN RIGHTS

The basic legal instruments concerning Human Rights are:

- **Charter of the United Nations (1945)** available on-line at: http://www.un.org

- **Universal Declaration of Human Rights (1948)** available on-line at: http://www.un.org/Overview/rights.html

- **The Covenants on Human Rights (1966)**
  (a) International Covenant on Civil and Political Rights
  (b) International Covenant on Economic, Social and Cultural Rights

- **International Convention on the Elimination of All Forms of Racial Discrimination (1965)**

- **Convention on the Elimination of All Forms of Discrimination Against Women (1979)**

- **Convention Against Torture and other Cruel, Inhuman and Degrading Treatment or Punishment (1984)**

- **Convention on the Rights of the Child (1989)**

- **International Convention on the Protection of the Rights of all Migrant Workers and Members of their Families (1990)**

SOCIAL DEVELOPMENT

Those interested in learning more about the social development approach to international social work can visit the International Council on Social Welfare website at http://www.icsw.org

Explore the social development link and examine the publications and government and organizations links. The publications section contains numerous articles that provide an overview of the situation of children, poverty, employment, health, old age and human development.

Courtesy of Steven Hick.

Filipino children pick through the garbage to survive.

INTERNATIONAL SOCIAL WORK PRACTICE MODELS

Social workers frequently hear the phrase "Think globally, act locally." An international social work career provides the worker with the opportunity to act on major international social issues at home and work abroad to assist people in alleviating the human suffering in their communities.

Within international social work practice, three broad approaches or models can be identified. These are the social welfare model, the new world order model and the social development model. Underlying each model of practice is a particular approach to world poverty, economic development and social work with people in developing countries (Estes 1992).

• Three Approaches to Practice

The more conventional **social welfare model of international social work** is based on the notion that basic social welfare services should be developed in all countries to meet basic human needs. This perspective is largely based on Keynesian economics and American economist W.W. Rostow's "stages of industrialization" theory. Rostow's theory postulates that all societies go through five stages on the road to becoming a developed country: (1) traditional society, (2) long growth preconditions, (3) short period "take-off," (4) a rapid drive to maturity, and (5) the era of mass consumption (Rostow 1960). The goal, then, for social work practice is to help move countries through the necessary stages. An important objective for practitioners is the identification of principles, programmatic approaches and strategies of social welfare development that are suitable for transfer between societies. Social workers following this model of international practice are mainly concerned with the satisfaction of basic social and material needs of people (e.g., minimal standards of living, access to at least basic health, education and other essential social services).

What might be called the **new world order model of international social work** has its origins in the idea that the current world order is not a very democratic one; it is controlled by a relatively small number of wealthy countries that manipulate the international system to their own advantage. Those who practice with this approach in mind are more oriented towards a fundamental rebuilding of the global cultural, social, political and economic structures. Rather than being concerned with incremental change, they are concerned with bringing about widespread change in international institutional arrangements that govern relationships between nations and, within nations, between groups of people. They focus on: (1) the active participation of all relevant sectors in the transformation process, (2) world peace and war prevention, (3) the alleviation of human suffering in the world, (4) the creation of effective systems of social protection and social service provision, (5) increased social and political justice, and (6) the protection and enhancement of the natural environment.

A third approach, which may be referred to as the **social development model of international social work**, falls somewhere between the above two approaches and has its origins in the community development field. Social workers who use this approach to international practice seek primarily to address the immediate causes of human degradation, powerlessness and social inequality, and to guide collective action towards the elimination of all forms of oppression, injustice and violence. They are concerned with the fuller participation of people at all levels of the political and economic systems of their country and with fostering social, political and economic systems that are more humane, inclusive and participatory.

• Respect for Cultural Diversity

Working in another country usually involves being a practitioner in another culture. How does one prepare oneself for such work? How does one ensure that one is culturally sensitive and competent? Is it enough to read about the country, its people and traditions? How does the worker translate this knowledge into a culturally sensitive practice?

There are a variety of definitions of the term **cultural competence** in the social work literature. The notion that predominates is that of cultural literacy. This interpretation emphasizes the need for social workers to gain a deep understanding of the worldview or cultural frame of reference of the client. Thus, for example, the worker must make an effort to understand the history, language and background characteristics of the cultural group with whom they are working. Many social work textbooks take this approach and present general overviews of the various ethno-cultural groups.

However, practitioners working abroad need to be careful to avoid what may amount to stereotypes about other cultures. For example, it would be inappropriate to work in China without considering the cultural differences among the different ethnic groups within the Chinese population. For social workers who are planning to work in another country or region, cultural literacy or learning about the culture of the host country is only the beginning. Social workers need a wider range of cultural competency knowledge and skills. In addition, social workers must take their knowledge of the "other" culture and combine it with an analysis of how their own cultural outlook affects their social work interventions.

WHAT DO INTERNATIONAL SOCIAL WORKERS DO?

Social work, as a helping profession, is especially concerned with the problems and rights of the disadvantaged. In working towards these ends, international social workers can be found undertaking a wide range of activities in a variety of national, international and overseas organizations. These organizations include: (1) international inter-governmental organizations, (2) non-governmental organizations, (3) churches and other humanitarian organizations, and (4) community organizations. These are discussed below.

CULTURAL COMPETENCY

The range of values, knowledge and skills associated with a comprehensive cultural competency approach include:

- Belief in the dignity of all people
- Belief in local and global solidarity
- Knowledge of cultural variations in helping
- Knowledge of historical and systemic racism
- Knowledge of culture as a practice variable
- Knowledge of language and communication styles
- Knowledge of how one's own culture affects practice
- Skills in learning about cultures
- Skills in utilizing the concept of empowerment
- Skills in communication with different cultures
- Skills in openly discussing cultural differences
- Skills in recognizing and combating racism in institutions and structures
- Skills in identifying and using culturally appropriate resources on behalf of clients

• International Inter-Governmental Organizations

Social workers are very active in various **international inter-governmental organizations** (IGOs), of which the United Nations (UN) is best known. Formed at the end of World War II, the UN seeks to develop a framework of international law that will be followed by all nation states around the world. Social workers function in a variety of roles in any of its twelve specialized agencies, including the UN Development Program, UNICEF, World Health Organization, International Labour Office and the UN High Commissioner for Refugees. (For general information and links to its various agencies, go to: http://www.un.org, the UN's main website.)

Within this arena, social workers participate as analysts and as direct practitioners in applying and monitoring the assistance and protection provided by UN declarations and conventions. Social workers also frequently work in a front-line capacity, providing refugee resettlement services, counselling children traumatized by war, distributing humanitarian assistance during disasters or war, or monitoring human rights abuses. In Kosovo, for example, UNICEF provided life-saving assistance for children and women, and social workers were involved in distributing hygiene kits for babies, blankets, water purification tablets and basic medical supplies. They were also a part of trauma teams, along with medical professionals and psychologists, and participated in the long-term relief plans that emphasized support for educational systems and community organizations.

• Non-Governmental Organizations

Social workers are also to be found in the multitude of **non-governmental organizations** (NGOs) around the world. NGOs are international organizations, but they are not directly linked to governments. This allows them more freedom to take up important issues and bring about effective change. NGOs tend to be small dynamic groups that work on a variety of issues related to their particular political or philosophical stances.

Students of social work may find it helpful to do volunteer work for NGOs to build experience and make contacts for future work. Many NGOs have entry-level positions for new social workers without extensive experience. Organizations such as Crossroads International, Canada World Youth and World University Service Canada provide excellent opportunities for social workers to gain international experience.

Social workers working with NGOs frequently find themselves directly participating in peace building and conflict resolution. For example, in the central Caucasus region–Georgia, Armenia and Azerbaijan–social workers are using art therapy to help children heal from the trauma of war and to build peace between the various groups torn by inter-ethnic conflict since the late 1980s. The projects encourage the children to express their thoughts and feelings through coloured pictures and paintings. Both able-bodied and disabled children from all

Courtesy of Steven Hick.

Author at UN food aid supply in Kosovo.

Courtesy of Steven Hick.

Community-based NGOs introduce primary health care using local plants as medicine.

ethnic groups attend the projects, and it is hoped that links will be established between communities by displaying art throughout the region.

• Churches and Other Organizations

Churches and other religious groups and organizations have perhaps the most extensive variety of **overseas humanitarian programs**, and they frequently employ the services of social workers. These groups tend to operate in the poorer countries of Africa, Asia and Latin America.

Few churches still use their programs mainly as a way to recruit into their membership (although some still do). For example, The United Church of Canada has excellent preparation and support programs throughout the world and does not send workers overseas unless they are requested by partner organizations.

As well as church and religious organizations, there are large international grant foundations that employ social workers as consultants, field representatives and as country directors for programs that the foundation supports. The Canadian government also maintains offices in many countries that provide services to visiting Canadians and to local people. These services frequently involve social workers. Other federal government departments, such as the Department of Foreign Affairs (http://www.dfait-maeci.gc.ca), the Canadian International Development Agency (CIDA; http://www.acdi-cida.gc.ca), as well as the International Development Research Centre (IDRC; http://www.idrc.ca), hire social workers to help with their work.

Working directly for the government agencies of other countries is another option for social workers seeking international experience. Such agencies offer a broad spectrum of services to their citizens (e.g., welfare, public health education, development projects and so forth). These agencies are not necessarily international in focus, but they are located abroad and, in this sense, can be considered as part of an international social work career. Generally, however, one must have extensive language skills and direct contacts within the country in order to obtain such a position.

• International Community Work

A common social work activity in developing countries is **international community work**. Social workers work with communities by assisting with problem solving and planning effective social services. They use community work to organize people to bring about major social change between nations, within nations and between groups of people. They work with communities to achieve the fullest participation of community members in transforming various aspects of their lives.

The ultimate goal of community work is the empowerment or fostering of the "sense in people that they have the ability and right to influence their environment" (Lee 1999, 43). Empowering people means that they can create and take action on their own behalf to meet their physical, spiritual and psychological needs and participate directly in the change process. To be able to act on their own behalf, however, people must see themselves as citizens, with the right and ability to express their opinions and acquire resources. Reaching these objectives requires a genuine sense of community: "it is important for the members to have a positive sense of themselves as a distinct group" (Ibid., 31). On the basis of community, new organizations can be built or improved upon and change can be effected.

The Canadian International Development Agency (CIDA), for example, is sponsoring a community-organizing project in Pakistan in which social workers play a key role. The goals of the $4.96-million project are to encourage more of Pakistan's rural poor to become involved in the process of developing their community, as well as to motivate and strengthen community-based organizations and female development organizations, and to encourage other groups to help get their community members involved in addressing development needs. Through this project, about 360 community organizations are being helped to undertake community development.

THE INTERNET AND INTERNATIONAL SOCIAL WORK

Information and communication technology, of which the Internet is a part, is having a significant impact on international social work, as in all other areas of life. The Internet is not only enabling economic globalization, it is also enabling those who wish to connect people and communities for the promotion of social justice and peace. It is currently being used for electronic advocacy, human rights protection and community building.

A CIDA-supported community development initiative.

Courtesy of Steven Hick.

Electronic advocacy might be the best way to conceptualize the importance of informational technology to social work. Electronic advocacy refers to the process of using communication and information technologies to disseminate information and mobilize support from a large constituency to help influence decision-making processes or support efforts at policy change. It may include the use of telephone, fax, television, radio, e-mail, websites, on-line discussion groups, network newsgroups and other modes of communication technologies. These kinds of tools will become increasingly important to social workers in the years to come.

The Internet is also providing new and different ways for people in dispersed communities to connect and advocate for their own rights or the rights of others. These new communities are sometimes called "on-line communities" or "virtual communities" in which people meet, discuss and share information via electronic means. This technology allows social workers to join and connect with people who would have been unreachable in the non-digital era and is becoming part of the skill set of international social workers. Increasingly, the Internet has become a tool for the promotion and protection of human rights. Human rights abuses, by their nature, often necessitate urgent action, and the Internet provides the obvious tool for disseminating immediate information.

It is important to bear in mind that most of the world's peoples do not have access to this technology–a problem sometimes referred to as the **digital divide**. This is an important social justice issue in its own right. Studies show that access to the Internet follows general patterns of social inequality: men have more access than women; higher income more than lower income; young more than old; well educated more than less educated. As information and scientific knowledge becomes increasingly important for economic and social development, addressing the problems associated with unequal access to information technology becomes especially important in the context of international social work.

The Internet, electronic advocacy and virtual communities are already important ingredients of modern social change strategies around the world. As the capabilities and capacity of the Internet increases, new uses and applications for social work will emerge. Intranets will enable organizations to streamline work procedures; virtual office environments will allow international NGOs to work together more effectively; video conferencing will emerge as a key tool for communication. During the Kosovo crisis, for example, the Internet was used to facilitate communication and collaboration within and between social workers in various NGOs.

The recent announcement by the world-renowned Massachusetts Institute of Technology that all of its research material will be available free on-line over the coming years may foreshadow other important developments in this area. The implications of something as simple as this for a poverty-stricken world, where access to scholarly books and research publications is still a major source of educational disadvantage, would be remarkable. If MIT and other institutions hold to their promises, the world could be much richer.

ON THE INTERNET

There are many Internet sites that are useful to the social work student interested in learning more about international social work. Many are mentioned in this chapter. Some places to start are:

- International Federation of Social Workers
  http://www.ifsw.org
- The International Council on Social Welfare
  http://www.icsw.org
- International Development Research Centre
  http://www.idrc.ca

Digital divide: developing world is far behind in technology.

PARTICIPATORY RESEARCH ON-LINE

An excellent collection of on-line articles about participatory research is at: http://www.parnet.org/PARchive

PARTICIPATORY ACTION RESEARCH

Social workers working in overseas communities have widely and successfully employed a technique known as participatory research or **participatory action research** (PAR). Participatory action research has provided social workers with a useful set of techniques with which to effect social change. PAR is a particular approach to knowledge generation, one that views research as the means by which confrontation and action against the causes of injustice, exploitation, violence and environmental degradation can occur.

Social workers using PAR in their overseas community work usually combine three types of activity: investigation, education and action. The objectives are attained through collective processes involving the participation of people who are directly affected by a program or service. People in the community therefore play a large part in all activities on the grounds that those involved on a day-to-day basis, or those who are affected by a particular policy, usually know a great deal about it and should become the centre or beginning point of the social work process.

The notion of power equalization is important to social workers using PAR. Collective inquiry transfers control of knowledge as people move from being mere objects to acting as subjects in their own development process. Empowerment in the context of overseas community work, as developed here, involves giving control over the decision-making process to the members of the community. In CIDA's Southern Africa AIDS Training Program, for example, local organizations are given support in their efforts to serve those most vulnerable to HIV/AIDS. This includes setting up anti-AIDS clubs in schools, visiting orphans, working to keep families together and assisting families with food, counselling and education. To be successful, social workers emphasize that local people have decision-making power in the conception of the program and in its operations.

To take another example, War Child, in conjunction with Street Symphony and The Dandelion Trust in Ethiopia, is working on projects aimed at providing practical aid as well as some fun and greater self-respect to street children. Street Symphony runs drama and dance projects that allow the street children to participate in performances for officials and dignitaries as well as the general public. While being trained as dancers, the children are fed, clothed and provided with a safe home. They learn to express themselves through drama and dance, while also raising awareness of their plight through the performances.

• AH-HAH! Method: A Tool for Working with the Communities

The so-called **AH-HAH! method**, presented in *AH-HAH! A New Approach to Popular Education* (GATT-Fly 1983), was developed in Canada and is frequently used by Canadian social workers in overseas settings. The name refers to the exclamation of "Ah-hah!" emitted by a person at the moment clarity or understanding dawns. The aim of this method is to enable participants to piece together their individual experience in a way that clarifies their understanding of political and

Courtesy of Steven Hick.

Canadian workers apply AH-HAH! method in Kosovo.

socioeconomic systems. It closely follows the principles of Paulo Freire (1970), the Brazilian educator whose work has had a profound impact on education and the struggle for rational development. Freire perfected a method for teaching illiterate people, contributing in an extraordinary way to the inspiration of Latin Americans to participate in the development of their countries.

According to this method, people know the world as they see it, and through this knowledge are able to intervene to transform their situations. The AH-HAH! method involves, in part, the idea of drawing a picture that represents the experiences of the group. In the process, an image of the economic and social system begins to emerge, leading to a discussion of government, legal systems, ownership of businesses, the military and so forth. Problem-posing education of this kind regards dialogue and critical thinking as indispensable to learning. This contrasts with a "banking" perspective towards education, in which participants are treated as empty vessels that must be filled with knowledge and information. The method is highly participatory and transformative, and involves concrete action as its objective.

CONCLUSION

International social work is increasingly being recognized as a crucial area of social work practice. This is due to a number of factors, such as the identification of economic globalization as a factor in world poverty and a recognition that our local concerns are connected to global ones. This internationalization of social problems implies that social workers increasingly need to be knowledgeable and skilled in international social work theory and practice. Social workers accordingly need to acquire new technology skills so as to enhance their ability to work and think locally and globally.

Social workers who do international work do so through an entire network of government and quasi-government agencies. The most prominent of these agencies are those associated with the United Nations and its various bodies, and those agencies associated with voluntary international aid agencies, such as the ones organized by various church and religious organizations. A great deal of useful work is being done through these organizations around the world to alleviate suffering and promote economic growth. However, the scope of the problems facing the poor nations of the world is enormous. Much more support is needed, and much remains to be done.

REFERENCES

• Catholic Agency for Overseas Development. 2001. *Fact Sheet on Poverty.* Available on-line at: http://www.cafod.org.uk

• Estes, R.J. 1992. *Internationalizing Social Work Education: A Guide to Resources For a New Century.* Philadelphia: University of Pennsylvania. Available on-line at: http://caster.ssw.upenn.edu/~restes/iswchart4.html

• Freire, P. 1984. *Pedagogy of the Oppressed.* New York: Herder and Herder.

• GATT-Fly. (1983). *Ah-Hah! A New Approach to Popular Education.* Toronto: Between the Lines.

• Lee, K. 1999. Measuring Poverty among Canada's Aboriginal People. *Insight* 23, no. 2. Ottawa: Canadian Council on Social Development.

• Murray, C.J.L., and A.D. Lopez. 1996. *The Global Burden of Disease.* Cambridge: Harvard University Press.

• Rostow, W.W. 1960. *The Stages of Economic Growth: A Non-Communist Manifesto.* Cambridge: Cambridge University Press.

• UNICEF. 2000. *The Progress of Nations.* Available on-line at: http://www.unicef.org

• World Commission on Environment and Development. 1987. *Our Common Future.* New York: Oxford University Press.

CHAPTER 13: INTERNATIONAL SOCIAL WORK PRACTICE

Concepts

- North-South divide
- Third World
- Human rights
- Sustainable development
- Social welfare model
- Social development model
- New world order model
- Cultural competence
- Inter-governmental organizations (IGOs)
- Non-governmental organizations (NGOs)
- Overseas humanitarian programs
- International community work
- Electronic advocacy
- Digital divide
- Participatory action research
- AH-HAH! method

Discussion Questions

1. What are a few of the indicators of global economic and social inequality?

2. Define the two key concepts that underlie international social work.

3. Define and distinguish the three levels of human rights. Why is it important for social workers to affirm and work towards all three levels?

4. What are the three approaches to international social work practice?

5. Describe the various agencies that employ social workers abroad.

6. How is the Internet changing the way that social workers network and advocate for human rights?

7. What is it about the AH-HAH! method of working in communities that has made it so successful in international social work?

Websites

- **New Internationalist**
  http://www.newint.org

  This monthly print magazine, which first sparked my interest in global issues, is available on-line. It provides a clearly written and concise overview of the important global issues of concern to social workers. An excellent resource to kick-start an essay on international issues.

- **United Nations Development Programme (UNDP)**
  http://www.undp.org

  At the UN Millennium Summit, world leaders pledged to cut poverty in half by 2015. UNDP is charged with helping to make this happen. Their website contains comprehensive related links, publications and various UNDP speeches and reports. Their publications section has numerous complete books on-line including their annual Overcoming Human Poverty Report at http://www.undp.org/povertyreport

- **Heritage Canada, Human Rights Program**
  http://www.pch.gc.ca/ddp-hrd

  This comprehensive website has all the basic information about human rights in Canada and internationally. It contains most of the official UN human rights covenants and an excellent overview of how the international human rights system works.

APPENDIX A

Code of Ethics

Canadian Association of Social Workers
January 1, 1994

[*This Social Work Code of Ethics, adopted by the Board of Directors of the Canadian Association of Social Workers (CASW) is effective on January 1, 1994 and replaces the CASW Code of Ethics (1983). The Code is reprinted here with the permission of CASW. The copyright in the document has been registered with Consumer and Corporate Affairs Canada, registration No. 427837.*]

DEFINITIONS

In this Code,

Best Interest of Client

means

(a) that the wishes, desires, motivations, and plans of the client are taken by the social worker as the primary consideration in any intervention plan developed by the social worker subject to change only when the client's plans are documented to be unrealistic, unreasonable or potentially harmful to self or others or otherwise determined inappropriate when considered in relation to a mandated requirement,

(b) that all actions and interventions of the social worker are taken subject to the reasonable belief that the client will benefit from the action, and

(c) that the social worker will consider the client as an individual, a member of a family unit, a member of a community, a person with a distinct ancestry or culture and will consider those factors in any decision affecting the client.

Client[1]

means

(a) a person, family, group of persons, incorporated body, association or community on whose behalf a social worker provides or agrees to provide a service

    (i) on request or with agreement[2] of the person, family, group of persons, incorporated body, associations or community, or

    (ii) as a result of a legislated responsibility, or

(b) a judge of a court of competent jurisdiction who orders the social worker to provide to the Court an assessment.[3]

Conduct Unbecoming

means behaviour or conduct that does not meet standards of care requirements and is therefore subject to discipline.[4]

249

Malpractice and Negligence

means behaviour that is included as "conduct unbecoming" and relates to social work practice behaviour within the parameters of the professional relationship that falls below the standard of practice and results in or aggravates an injury to a client. Without limiting the generality of the above,[5] it includes behaviour which results in assault, deceit, fraudulent misrepresentations, defamation of character, breach of contract, violation of human rights, malicious prosecution, false imprisonment or criminal conviction.

Practice of Social Work

includes the assessment, remediation and prevention of social problems, and the enhancement of social functioning of individuals, families, groups and communities by means of

(a) the provision of direct counselling services within an established relationship between a social worker and client;

(b) the development, promotion and delivery of human service programs, including that done in collaboration with other professionals;

(c) the development and promotion of social policies aimed at improving social conditions and equality; and[6]

(d) any other activities approved by CASW.[7]

Social Worker

means a person who is duly registered to practice social work in a province or territory or where mandatory registration does not exist, a person practising social work who voluntarily agrees to be subject to this Code.

Standard of Practice

means the standard of care ordinarily expected of a competent social worker. It means that the public is assured that a social worker has the training, the skill and the diligence to provide them with professional social work services.

~ ~ ~

PREAMBLE

Philosophy

The profession of social work is founded on humanitarian and egalitarian ideals. Social workers believe in the intrinsic worth and dignity of every human being and are committed to the values of acceptance, self-determination and respect of individuality. They believe in the obligation of all people, individually and collectively. They believe in the obligation of all people, individually and collectively, to provide resources, services and opportunities for the overall benefit of humanity. The culture of individuals, families, groups, communities and nations has to be respected without prejudice.[8]

Social workers are dedicated to the welfare and self-realization of human beings; to the development and disciplined use of scientific knowledge regarding human and societal behaviours; to the development of resources to meet individual, group, national and international needs and aspirations; and to the achievement of social justice for all.

Professional Practice Conflicts

If a conflict arises in professional practice, the standards declared in this Code take precedence. Conflicts of interest may occur because of demands from the general public, workplace, organizations or clients. In all cases, if the ethical duties and obligations or ethical responsibilities of this Code would be compromised, the social worker must act in a manner consistent with this Code.

Nature of this Code

The first seven statements in this code establish ethical duties and obligations. These statements provide the basis of a social worker's relationship with a client and are based on the values of social work. A breach of any of these statements forms the basis of a disciplinary action. The remaining three statements are characterized as ethical responsibilities and are to be seen as being different from the ethical duties and obligations. These ethical responsibilities are not likely to form the basis of any disciplinary action if breached. However these sections may form the basis of inquiry. These ethical responsibilities may be used in conjunction with breaches of other sections of this code and may form the basis of necessary background information in any action for discipline. Of equal importance, these ethical responsibilities are desirable goals to be achieved by the social work profession which by its nature is driven by an adherence to the values that form the basis of these desirable ethical behaviours.

~ ~ ~

SOCIAL WORK CODE OF ETHICS

Ethical Duties and Obligations

1. A social worker shall maintain the best interest of the client as the primary professional obligation.

2. A social worker shall carry out her or his professional duties and obligations with integrity and objectivity.

3. A social worker shall have and maintain competence in the provision of a social work service to a client.

4. A social worker shall not exploit the relationship with a client for personal benefit, gain or gratification.

5. A social worker shall protect the confidentiality of all information acquired from the client or others regarding the client and the client's family during the professional relationship unless

   (a) the client authorizes in writing the release of specified information,

   (b) the information is released under the authority of a statute or an order of a court of competent jurisdiction, or

   (c) otherwise authorized by this Code.

6. A social worker who engages in another profession, occupation, affiliation or calling shall not allow these outside interests to affect the social work relationship with the client.

7. A social worker in private practice shall not conduct the business of provision of social work services for a fee in a manner that discredits the profession or diminishes the public's trust in the profession.

Ethical Responsibilities

8. A social worker shall advocate for workplace conditions and policies that are consistent with the Code.

9. A social worker shall promote excellence in the social work profession.

10. A social worker shall advocate change

    (a) in the best interest of the client, and

    (b) for the overall benefit of society, the environment and the global community.

Chapter 1. Primary Professional Obligation

1. A social worker shall maintain the best interest of the client as the primary professional obligation.

1.1 The social worker is to be guided primarily by this obligation. Any action which is substantially inconsistent with this obligation is an unethical action.

1.2 A social worker in the practice of social work shall not discriminate against any person on the basis of race, ethnic background, language, religion, marital status, sex, sexual orientation, age, abilities, socio-economic status, political affiliation or national ancestry.[9]

1.3 A social worker shall inform a client of the client's right to consult another professional at any time during the provision of social work services.

1.4 A social worker shall immediately inform the client of any factor, condition[10] or pressure that affects the social worker's ability to perform an acceptable level of service.

1.5 A social worker shall not become involved in a client's personal affairs that are not relevant to the service being provided.

1.6 A social worker shall not state an opinion, judgment or use a clinical diagnosis unless there is a documented assessment, observation or diagnosis to support the opinion, judgment or diagnosis.

1.7 Where possible, a social worker shall provide or secure social work services in the language chosen by the client.

Chapter 2. Integrity and Objectivity

2. A social worker shall carry out his or her professional duties and obligations with integrity and objectivity.[11]

2.1 The social worker shall identify and describe education, training, experience, professional affiliations, competence, and nature of service in an honest and accurate manner.

2.2 The social worker shall explain to the client her or his education, experience, training, competence, nature of service and action at the request of the client.

2.3 A social worker shall cite an educational degree only after it has been received from the institution.

2.4 A social worker shall not claim formal social work education in an area of expertise or training solely by attending a lecture, demonstration, conference, panel discussion, workshop, seminar or other similar teaching presentation.[12]

2.5 The social worker shall not make a false, misleading or exaggerated claim of efficacy regarding past or anticipated achievement with respect to clients.

2.6 The social worker shall distinguish between actions and statements made as a private citizen and actions and statements made as a social worker.[13]

Chapter 3. Competence in the Provision of Social Work Services

3. A social worker shall have and maintain competence in the

provision of a social work service to a client.

3.1 The social worker shall not undertake a social work service unless the social worker has the competence to provide the service or the social worker can reasonably acquire the necessary competence without undue delay, risk or expense to the client.

3.2 Where a social worker cannot reasonably acquire the necessary competence in the provision of a service to a client, the social worker shall decline to provide the service to the client, advising the client of the reason and ensuring that the client is referred to another professional person if the client agrees to the referral.

3.3 The social worker, with the agreement of the client, may obtain advice from other professionals in the provision of service to a client.

3.4 A social worker shall maintain an acceptable level of health and well-being in order to provide a competent level of service to a client.[14]

3.5 Where a social worker has a physical or mental health problem, disability or illness that affects the ability of the social worker to provide competent service or that would threaten the health or well-being of the client, the social worker shall discontinue the provision of social work service to a client

    (a) advising the client of the reason and,[15]

    (b) ensuring that the client is referred to another professional person if the client agrees to the referral.

3.6 The social worker shall have, maintain and endeavor periodically to update an acceptable level of knowledge and skills to meet the standards of practice of the profession.

Chapter 4. Limit on Professional Relationship

4. A social worker shall not exploit the relationship with a client for personal benefit, gain or gratification.

4.1 The social worker shall respect the client and act so that the dignity, individuality and rights of the person are protected.

4.2 The social worker shall assess and consider a client's motivation and physical and mental capacity in arranging for the provision of an appropriate service.

4.3 The social worker shall not have a sexual relationship with a client.

4.4 The social worker shall not have a business relationship with a client, borrow money from a client, or loan money to a client. [16]

4.5 The social worker shall not have a sexual relationship with a social work student assigned to the social worker.

4.6 The social worker shall not sexually harass any person.

Chapter 5. Confidential Information

5. A social worker shall protect the confidentiality[17] of all information acquired from the client or others regarding the client and the client's family during the professional relationship[18] unless

(a) the client authorizes in writing the release of specified information,[19]

(b) the information is released under the authority of a statute or an order of a court of relevant jurisdiction, or

(c) otherwise authorized under this Code.

5.1 The requirement of confidentiality also applies to social workers who work as

(a) supervisors,

(b) managers,

(c) educators, or

(d) administrators.

5.2 A social worker who works as a supervisor, manager or administrator shall establish policies and practices that protect the confidentiality of client information.

5.3 The social worker may disclose confidential information to other persons in the workplace who, by virtue of their responsibilities, have an identified need to know as determined by the social worker.

5.4 Clients shall be the initial or primary source of information about themselves and their problems unless the client is incapable or unwilling to give information or when corroborative reporting is required.

5.5 The social worker has the obligation to ensure that the client understands what is being asked, why and to what purpose the information will be used, and to understand the confidentiality policies and practices of the workplace setting.

5.6 Where information is required by law, the social worker shall explain to the client the consequences of refusing to provide the requested information.

5.7 Where information is required from other sources, the social worker

(a) shall explain the requirement to the client, and

(b) shall attempt to involve the client in selecting the sources to be used.

5.8 The social worker shall take reasonable care to safeguard the client's personal papers or property if the social worker agrees to keep the property at the request of the client.

Recording Information

5.9 The social worker shall maintain only one master file on each client.[20]

5.10 The social worker shall record all relevant information, and keep all relevant documents in the file.

5.11 The social worker shall not record in a client's file any characterization that is not based on clinical assessment or fact.

Accessibility of Records

5.12 The social worker who contracts for the delivery of social work services with a client is responsible to the client for maintaining the client record.

5.13 The social worker who is employed by a social agency that delivers social work services to clients is responsible

(a) to the client for the maintaining of a client record, and

(b) to the agency to maintain the records to facilitate the objectives of the agency.

5.14 A social worker is obligated to follow the provision of a statute that allows access to records by clients.

5.15 The social worker shall respect the client's right of access to a client record subject to the social worker's right to refuse access for just and reasonable cause.

5.16 Where a social worker refuses a client the right to access a file or part of a file, the social worker shall advise the client of the right to request a review of the decision in accordance with the relevant statute, workplace policy or other relevant procedure.

Disclosure

5.17 The social worker shall not disclose the identity of persons who have sought a social work service or disclose sources of information about clients unless compelled legally to do so.[21]

5.18 The obligation to maintain confidentiality continues indefinitely after the social worker has ceased contact with the client.

5.19 The social worker shall avoid unnecessary conversation regarding clients.

5.20 The social worker may divulge confidential information with consent of the client, preferably expressed in writing, where this is essential to a plan of care or treatment.

5.21 The social worker shall transfer information to another agency or individual, only with the informed consent of the client or guardian of the client and then only with the reasonable assurance that the receiving agency provides the same guarantee of confidentiality and respect for the right of privileged communication as provided by the sending agency.

5.22 The social worker shall explain to the client the disclosure of information requirements of the law or of the agency before the commencement of the provision of social work services.

5.23 The social worker in practice with groups and communities shall notify the participants of the likelihood that aspects of their private lives may be revealed in the course of their work together, and therefore require a commitment from each member to respect the privileged and confidential nature of the communication between and among members of the client group.

5.24 Subject to section 5.26, the social worker shall not disclose information acquired from one client to a member of the client's family without the informed consent of the client who provided the information.

5.25 A social worker shall disclose information acquired from one client to a member of the client's family where

(a) the information involves a threat of harm to self or others,[22]

(b) the information was acquired from a child of tender years and the social worker determines that its disclosure is in the best interests of the child.[23]

5.26 A social worker shall disclose information acquired from a client to a person or a police officer where the information involves a threat of harm to that person.

5.27 A social worker may release confidential information as part of a discipline hearing of a social worker as directed by the tribunal or disciplinary body.

5.28 When disclosure is required by order of a court, the social worker shall not divulge more information than is reasonably required and shall where possible notify the client of this requirement.

5.29 The social worker shall not use confidential information for the purpose of teaching, public education or research except with the informed consent of the client.

5.30 The social worker may use non-identifying information for the purpose of teaching, public education or research.

Retention and Disposition of Information

5.31 Where the social worker's documentation is stored in a place or computer maintained and operated by an employer, the social worker shall advocate for the responsible retention and disposition of information contained in the file.

Chapter 6. Outside Interest

6. A social worker who engages in another profession, occupation, affiliation or calling shall not allow these outside interests to affect the social work relationship with the client.

6.1 A social worker shall declare to the client any outside interests that would affect the social work relationship with the client.

6.2 A social worker shall not allow an outside interest:

(a) to affect the social worker's ability to practice social work;

(b) to present to the client or to the community that the social worker's ability to practice social work is affected; or

(c) to bring the profession of social work into disrepute.[24]

Chapter 7. Limit on Private Practice

7. A social worker in private practice shall not conduct the business of provision of social work services for a fee in a manner that discredits the profession or diminishes the public's trust in the profession.

7.1 A social worker shall not use the social work relationship within an agency to obtain clients for his or her private practice.

7.2 Subject to section 7.3, a social worker who enters into a contract for service with a client

(a) shall disclose at the outset of the relationship, the fee schedule for the social work services,

(b) shall not charge a fee that is greater than that agreed to and disclosed to the client, and

(c) shall not charge for hours of service other than the reasonable hours of client services, research, consultation and administrative work directly connected to the case.

7.3 A social worker in private practice may charge differential fees for services except where an increased fee is charged based on race, ethnic background, language, religion, marital status, sex, sexual orientation, age, abilities, socio-economic status, political affiliation or national ancestry.

7.4 A social worker in private practice shall maintain adequate malpractice, defamation and liability insurance.

7.5 A social worker in private practice may charge a rate of interest on delinquent accounts as is allowed by law.[25]

7.6 Notwithstanding section 5.17 a social worker in private practice may pursue civil remedies to ensure payment for services to a client where the social worker has advised the client of this possibility at the outset of the social work service.

Chapter 8. Ethical Responsibilities to the Workplace

8. A social worker shall advocate for workplace conditions and policies that are consistent with the Code.

8.1 Where the responsibilities to an employer are in conflict with the social worker's obligations to the client, the social worker shall document the issue in writing and shall bring the situation to the attention of the employer.

8.2 Where a serious ethical conflict continues to exist after the issue has been brought to the attention of the employer, the social worker shall bring the issue to the attention of the Association or regulatory body.[26]

8.3 A social worker shall follow the principles in the Code when dealing with

   (a) a social worker under the supervision of the social worker,

   (b) an employee under the supervision of the social worker, and

   (c) a social work student under the supervision of the social worker.

Chapter 9. Ethical Responsibilities to the Profession

9. A social worker shall promote excellence in the social work profession.

9.1 A social worker shall report to the appropriate association or regulatory body any breach of this Code by another social worker which adversely affects or harms a client or prevents the effective delivery of a social service.

9.2 A social worker shall report to the association or regulatory body any unqualified or unlicenced person who is practising social work.

9.3 A social worker shall not intervene in the professional relationship of a social worker and client unless requested to do so by the client and unless convinced that the best interests and well-being of the client require such intervention.

9.4 Where a conflict arises between a social worker and other professionals, the social worker shall attempt to resolve the professional differences in ways that uphold the principles of this Code and the honour of the social work profession.

9.5 A social worker engaged in research shall ensure that the involvement of clients in the research is a result of informed consent.

Chapter 10. Ethical Responsibilities for Social Change

10. A social worker shall advocate change

   (a) in the best interest of the client, and

(b) for the overall benefit of society, the environment and the global community.

10.1 A social worker shall identify, document and advocate for the elimination of discrimination.

10.2 A social worker shall advocate for the equal distribution of resources to all persons.

10.3 A social worker shall advocate for the equal access of all persons to resources, services and opportunities.

10.4 A social worker shall advocate for a clean and healthy environment and shall advocate the development of environmental strategies consistent with social work principles.

10.5 A social worker shall provide reasonable professional services in a state of emergency.

10.6 A social worker shall promote social justice.

Notes

[1] A client ceases to be a client 2 years after the termination of a social work service. It is advisable for this termination to be clearly documented on the case file.

[2] This sub-paragraph identifies two situations where a person may be considered a voluntary client. The person who requests a social work service is clearly a voluntary client. A person also may originally be receiving services as a result of the actions of a court or other legally mandated entity. This person may receive a service beyond that originally mandated and therefore be able to terminate voluntarily that aspect of the service. A situation where a person is referred by another professional or family member clearly falls into this "voluntary service" relationship when that person agrees with the service to be provided. This type of social work relationship is clearly distinguishable from the relationship in sub-paragraph (ii) where the social worker does not seek or have agreement for the service to be provided.

[3] In this situation, the social worker is providing an assessment, information or a professional opinion to a judge of competent jurisdiction to assist the judge in making a ruling or determination. In this situation, the relationship is with the judge and the person on whom the information, assessment or opinion is provided is not the client. The social worker still has some professional obligations towards that person, for example: competence and dignity.

[4] In reaching a decision in *Re Matthews and Board of Directors of Physiotherapy* (1986) 54 O.R. (2d) 375, Saunders J. makes three important statements regarding standards of practice and by implication Code of Ethics:

(i) Standards of practice are inherent characteristics of any profession.

(ii) Standards of practice may be written or unwritten.

(iii) Some conduct is clearly regarded as misconduct and need not be written down whereas other conduct may be the subject of dispute within a profession.

[5] The importance of the collective opinion of the profession in establishing and ultimately modifying the Code of Ethics was established in a 1884 case involving the medical profession. Lord Esher, M.R. stated:

"If it is shown that a medical man, in the pursuit of his profession, has done something with regard to it which would be reasonably regarded as disgraceful or dishonourable by his professional brethren of good repute and competency", then it is open to the General Medical Council to say that he has been guilty of "infamous conduct in a professional respect".

[6] This definition except paragraph (d) has been taken from An Act to Incorporate the New Brunswick Association of Social Workers, chapter 78 of the Statutes of New Brunswick, 1988, section 2.

[7] The procedure for adding activities under this paragraph will be established as a bylaw by the CASW Board of Directors.

[8] Taken from: Teaching and Learning about Human Rights; A Manual for Schools of Social Work and the Social Work Profession; U.N. Centre for Human Rights, Co-operation with

International Federation of Social Workers and International Association of Schools of Social Workers, United Nations, New York, 1992.

[9.] This obligation goes beyond grounds of discrimination stated in most Human Rights Legislation and therefore there is a greater professional obligation than that stated in provincial legislation.

[10.] The term condition means a physical, mental or psychological condition. There is an implied obligation that the social worker shall actively seek diagnosis and treatment for any signs or warnings of a condition. A disclosure under this section may be of a general nature. See also 3.4.

[11.] The term objectivity is taken from the Qu6bec Code of Professional Conduct. See Division 2: Integrity and Objectivity (6.0 Qu6bec) November 5, 1979 Vol. 2 No. 30. The term objectivity is stated in the following: 3.02.01. A social worker must discharge his professional duties with integrity and objectivity.

[12.] The provincial associations may regulate the areas of expertise to be stated or advertised by a social worker. This will vary in each province according to its enabling legislation. Where there is not sufficient legislative base for this regulation, the claim of an expertise without sufficient training may form the basis of a determination of unprofessional conduct.

[13.] Even with a distinction made under this section, a social worker's private actions or statements may be of such a nature that the social worker cannot avoid the responsibilities under this Code. See also 6.2 (c).

[14.] This section should be considered in relation to section 1.4 and involves proper maintenance prevention and treatment of any type of risk to the health or well-being of the social worker.

[15.] It is not necessary in all circumstances to explain specifically the nature of the problem.

[16.] Where a social worker does keep money or assets belonging to a client, the social worker should hold this money or asset in a trust account or hold the money or asset in conjunction with an additional professional person.

[17.] Confidentiality means that information received or observed about a client by a social worker will be held in confidence and disclosed only when the social worker is properly authorized or obligated legally or professionally to do so. This also means that professionally acquired information may be treated as privileged communication and ordinarily only the client has the right to waive privilege.

Privileged communication means statements made within a protected relationship (i.e. husband-wife, professional-client) which the law protects against disclosure. The extent of the privilege is governed by law and not by this Code.

Maintaining confidentiality of privileged communication means that information about clients does not have to be transmitted in any oral, written or recorded form. Such information, for example, does not have to be disclosed to a supervisor, written into a workplace record, stored in a computer or microfilm data base, held on an audio or videotape or discussed orally. The right of privileged communication is respected by the social worker in the practice of social work notwithstanding that this right is not ordinarily granted in law.

The disclosure of confidential information in social work practice involves the obligation to share information professionally with others in the workplace of the social worker as part of a reasonable service to the client. Social workers recognize the need to obtain permission from clients before releasing information about them to sources outside their workplace; and to inform clients at the outset of their relationship that some information acquired may be shared with the officers and personnel of the agency who maintain the case record and who have a reasonable need for the information in the performance of their duties.

[18.] The social worker's relationship with a client can be characterized as a fiduciary relationship.

In *Fiduciary Duties in Canada* by Ellis, fiduciary duty is described as follows: ... where one party has placed its "trust and confidence" in another and the latter has accepted — expressly or by operation of law — to act in a manner consistent with the reposing of such "trust and confidence", a fiduciary relationship has been established.

[19.] The "obligation of secrecy" was discussed by the Supreme Court of Canada in *Halls* v. *Mitchell*, (1928) S.C.R. 125, an action brought by a disabled CNR worker against a company doctor who had disclosed the employee's medical history, to the latter's detriment. Mr. justice Duff reviewed the duty of confidentiality:

We are not required, for the purposes of this appeal, to attempt to state with any sort of precision the limits of the obligation of secrecy which rests upon the medical practitioner in relation to the professional secrets acquired by him in the course of his practice. Nobody would dispute that a secret so acquired is the secret of the patient, and, normally, is under his control, and not under that of the doctor. Prima facie, the patient has the right to require that the secret shall not be divulged; and that right is absolute, unless there is some paramount reason which overrides it.

Thus the right of secrecy/confidentiality rests squarely with the patient; the Court carefully provided that there is an "ownership" extant in the confidentiality of the personal information. Duff J. continued by allowing for "paramount" criteria which vitiates from the right:

Some reasons may arise, no doubt, from the existence of facts which bring into play overpowering considerations connected with public justice; and there may be cases in which reasons connected with the safety of individuals or of the public, physical or moral, would be sufficiently cogent to supersede or qualify the obligations prima facie imposed by the confidential relation.

Duff J. continued:

The general duty of medical men to observe secrecy, in relation to information acquired by them confidentially from their patients is subject, no doubt, to some exceptions, which have no operation in the case of solicitors; but the grounds of the legal, social or moral imperatives affecting physicians and surgeons, touching the inviolability of professional confidences, are not, any more than those affecting legal advisers, based exclusively upon the relations between the parties as individuals.

[20.] The master file refers to all relevant documents pertaining to the client consisting of such information as demographics, case recordings, court documents, assessments, correspondence, treatment plans, bills, etc. This information is often collected through various means including electronic and computer-driven sources. However the client master file exists as one unit, inclusive of all information pertaining to the client, despite the various sources of the recording process. The description and ownership of the master file is most often defined by workplace standards or policies. The client's master file should be prepared keeping in mind that it may have to be revealed to the client or disclosed in legal proceedings.

[21.] A social worker may be compelled to reveal information under the section when directly ordered by the court to do so. Before disclosing the information, the social worker shall advise the court of the professional obligations that exist under this section of the Code and where reasonably possible inform the client.

[22.] The case of *Tarasaff* v. *The Regents of the University of California et al.* (1976), 551 p.2d 334 (Cal. Supreme Court) focused on the obligation of a psychiatrist to maintain the confidentiality of his patients' statements in their discussions. In that case the patient told the psychiatrist that the patient had an intention to kill a certain woman. When the patient actually did kill this woman, her parents brought suit alleging that the psychiatrist owed a duty to tell the woman of the danger to her.

It was held that the psychiatrist did have a duty to tell the woman of the threat. The court recognized that the psychiatrist owed a duty to the patient to keep in confidence the statements the patient made in therapy sessions, but held there was also a duty to care to anyone whom the psychiatrist knew might be endangered by the patient. At a certain point the obligation of confidentiality would be overridden by the obligation to this third person. The psychiatrist's knowledge itself gave rise to a duty of care. What conduct would be sufficient to fulfil the duty to this third person would depend on the circumstances, but it might be necessary to give a warning that would reveal what the patient had said about the third party. The court in this case held that the psychiatrist had a duty to warn the woman about the patient's stated intention to kill her, and having failed to warn her the psychiatrist was liable in negligence. Moreover, the court stated that the principle of this duty of care belonged not just to a psychiatrist but also to a psychologist performing therapy. it would follow that the principle would also apply to social workers performing therapy.

[23.] For the purpose of this Code, a child of tender years shall usually be determined to be a child under the age of seven years subject to a determination by a social worker considering the child's social, physical, intellectual, emotional or psychological development.

[24.] This section brings the social worker's outside interest and personal actions in line with the professional duties and obligations as set out in this Code.

[25.] This rate shall be stated on all invoices or bills sent to the client.

[26.] In this situation the professional obligations outweigh any obligations to a workplace.

Ethics of Social Work

Principles and Standards

Adopted by the IFSW General Meeting, Colombo, Sri Lanka, July 6-8, 1994

1. Background

Ethical awareness is a necessary part of the professional practice of any social worker. His or her ability to act ethically is an essential aspect of the quality of the service offered to clients.

The purpose of IFSW's work on ethics is to promote ethical debate and reflection in the member associations and among the providers of social work in member countries.

The basis for the further development of IFSW's work on ethics is to be found in "Ethics of Social Work - Principles and Standards" which consists of two documents, International Declaration of Ethical Principles of Social Work, and International Ethical Standards for Social Workers. These documents present the basic ethical principles of the social work profession, recommend procedure when the work presents ethical dilemmas, and deal with the profession's and the individual social worker's relation to clients, colleagues, and others in the field. The documents are components in a continuing process of use, review and revision.

2. International Declaration of Ethical Principles of Social Work

2.1 Introduction

The IFSW recognises the need for a declaration of ethical principles for guidance in dealing with ethical problems in social work.

The purposes of the International Declaration of Ethical Principles are:

1. to formulate a set of basic principles for social work, which can be adapted to cultural and social settings.

2. to identify ethical problem areas in the practice of social work (below referred to as 'problem areas'), and

3. to provide guidance as to the choice of methods for dealing with ethical issues/problems (below referred to as 'methods for addressing ethical issues/problems').

Compliance

The International Declaration of Ethical Principles assumes that both member associations of the IFSW and their constituent members adhere to the principles formulated therein. The IFSW expects each member association to assist its members in identifying and dealing with ethical issues/problems in the practice of their profession.

Member associations of the IFSW and individual members of these can report any member association to the Executive Committee of the IFSW should it neglect to adhere to these principles. National Associations who experience difficulties adopting these principles should notify the Executive Committee of IFSW. The Executive Committee may impose the stipulations and intentions of the Declaration of Ethical Principles on an association which neglects to comply. Should this not be sufficient the Executive Committee can, as a following measure, suggest suspension or exclusion of the association.

The International Declaration of Ethical Principles should be made publicly known. This would enable clients, employers, professionals from other disciplines, and the general public to have expectations in accordance with the ethical foundations of social work.

We acknowledge that a detailed set of ethical standards for the member associations would be unrealistic due to legal, cultural and governmental differences among the member countries.

2.2 The Principles

Social workers serve the development of human beings through adherence to the following basic principles:

2.2.1. Every human being has a unique value, which justifies moral consideration for that person.

2.2.2. Each individual has the right to self-fulfilment to the extent that it does not encroach upon the same right of others, and has an obligation to contribute to the well-being of society.

2.2.3. Each society, regardless of its form, should function to provide the maximum benefits for all of its members.

2.2.4. Social workers have a commitment to principles of social justice.

2.2.5. Social workers have the responsibility to devote objective and disciplined knowledge and skill to aid individuals, groups, communities, and societies in their development and resolution of personal-societal conflicts and their consequences.

2.2.6. Social workers are expected to provide the best possible assistance to anybody seeking their help and advice, without unfair discrimination on the basis of gender, age, disability, colour, social class, race, religion, language, political beliefs, or sexual orientation.

2.2.7. Social workers respect the basic human rights of individuals and groups as expressed in the United Nations Universal Declaration of Human Rights and other international conventions derived from that Declaration.

2.2.8. Social workers pay regard to the principles of privacy, confidentiality, and responsible use of information in their professional work. Social workers respect justified confidentiality even when their country's legislation is in conflict with this demand.

2.2.9. Social workers are expected to work in full collaboration with their clients, working for the best interests of the clients but paying due regard to the interests of others involved. Clients are encouraged to participate as much as possible, and should be informed of the risks and likely benefits of proposed courses of action.

2.2.10. Social workers generally expect clients to take responsibility, in collaboration with them, for determining courses of action affecting their lives. Compulsion which might be necessary to solve one party's problems at the expense of the interests of others involved should only take place after careful explicit evaluation of the claims of the conflicting parties. Social workers should minimise the use of legal compulsion.

2.2.11. Social work is inconsistent with direct or indirect support of individuals, groups, political forces or power-structures suppressing their fellow human beings by employing terrorism, torture or similar brutal means.

2.2.12. Social workers make ethically justified decisions, and stand by them, paying due regard to the IFSW International Declaration of Ethical Principles, and to the International Ethical Standards for Social Workers adopted by their national professional association.

2.3 Problem Areas

2.3.1. The problem areas raising ethical issues directly are not necessarily universal due to cultural and governmental differences. Each national association is encouraged to promote discussion and clarification of important issues and problems particularly relevant to its country. The following problem areas are, however, widely recognized:

1. when the loyalty of the social worker is in the middle of conflicting interests

   - between those of the social worker's own and the clients
   - between conflicting interests of individual clients and other individuals
   - between the conflicting interests of groups of clients
   - between groups of clients and the rest of the population
   - between systems/institution and groups of clients
   - between system/institution/employer and social workers
   - between different groups of professionals

2. the fact that the social worker functions both as a helper and controller

   The relation between these two opposite aspects of social work demands a clarification based on an explicit choice of values in order to avoid a mixing-up of motives or the lack of clarity in motives, actions and consequences of actions. When social workers are expected to play a role in the state control of citizens they are obliged to clarify the ethical implications of this role and to what extent this role is acceptable in relation to the basic ethical principles of social work.

3. the duty of the social worker to protect the interests of the client will easily come into conflict with demands for efficiency and utility

   This problem is becoming important with the introduction and use of information technology within the fields of social work.

2.3.2. The principles declared in section 2.2 should always be at the base of any consideration given or choice made by social workers in dealing with issues/problems within these areas.

2.4. Methods For The Solution of Issues/Problems

2.4.1. The various national associations of social workers are obliged to treat matters in such a way that ethical issues/problems may be considered and tried to be solved in collective forums within the organization. Such forums should enable the individual social worker to discuss, analyse and consider ethical issues/problems in collaboration with colleagues, other expert groups and/parties affected by the matter under discussion. In addition such forums should give the social worker opportunity to receive advice from colleagues and others. Ethical analysis and discussion should always seek to create possibilities and options.

2.4.2. The member associations are required to produce and/or adapt ethical standards for the different fields of work, especially for those fields where there are complicated ethical issues/problems as well as areas where the ethical principles of social work may come into conflict with the respective country's legal system or the policy of the authorities.

2.4.3. When ethical foundations are laid down as guidelines for actions within the practice of social work, it is the duty of the associations to aid the individual social worker in analysing and considering ethical issues/problems on the basis of:

> 1. The basic principles of the Declaration (section 2.2)

> 2. The ethical/moral and political context of the actions, i.e. an analysis of the values and forces constituting the framing conditions of the action.

> 3. The motives of the action, i.e. to advocate a higher level of consciousness of the aims and intentions the individual social worker might have regarding a course of action.

> 4. The nature of the action, i.e. help in providing an analysis of the moral content of the action, e.g. the use of compulsion as opposed to voluntary co-operation, guardianship vs participation, etc.

> 5. The consequences the action might have for different groups, i.e. an analysis of the consequences of different ways of action for all involved parties in both the short and long term.

2.4.4. The member associations are responsible for promoting debate, education and research regarding ethical questions.

3. International Ethical Standards for Social Workers

(This section is based on the "International Code of Ethics for the Professional Social Worker" adopted by the IFSW in 1976, but does not include ethical principles since these are now contained in the new separate International Declaration of Ethical Principles of Social Work in section 2.2 of the present document.)

3.1 Preamble

Social work originates variously from humanitarian, religious and democratic ideals and philosophies and has universal application to meet human needs arising from personal-societal interactions and to develop human potential. Professional social workers are dedicated to service for the welfare and self-fulfilment of human beings; to the development and disciplined use of validated knowledge regarding human and societal behaviour; to the development of resources to meet individual, group, national and international needs and aspirations; and to the achievement of social justice. On the basis of the International Declaration of Ethical Principles of Social Work, the social worker is obliged to recognise these standards of ethical conduct.

3.2. General Standards of Ethical Conduct

3.2.1. Seek to understand each individual client and the client system, and the elements which affect behaviour and the service required.

3.2.2. Uphold and advance the values, knowledge and methodology of the profession, refraining from any behaviour which damages the functioning of the profession.

3.2.3. Recognise professional and personal limitations.

3.2.4. Encourage the utilisation of all relevant knowledge and skills.

3.2.5. Apply relevant methods in the development and validation of knowledge.

3.2.6. Contribute professional expertise to the development of policies and programs which improve the quality of life in society.

3.2.7. Identify and interpret social needs.

3.2.8. Identify and interpret the basis and nature of individual, group, community, national, and international social problems.

3.2.9. Identify and interpret the work of the social work profession.

3.2.10. Clarify whether public statements are made or actions performed on an individual basis or as representative of a professional association, agency or organisation, or other group.

3.3 Social Work Standards Relative to Clients

3.3.1. Accept primary responsibility to identified clients, but within limitations set by the ethical claims of others.

3.3.2. Maintain the client's right to a relationship of trust, to privacy and confidentiality, and to responsible use of information. The collection and sharing of information or data is related to the professional service function with the client informed as to its necessity and use. No information is released without prior knowledge and informed consent of the client, except where the client cannot be responsible or others may be seriously jeopardized. A client has access to social work records concerning them.

3.3.3. Recognise and respect the individual goals, responsibilities, and differences of clients. Within the scope of the agency and the client's social milieu, the professional service shall assist clients to take responsibility for personal actions and help all clients with equal willingness. Where the professional service cannot be provided under such conditions the clients shall be so informed in such a way as to leave the clients free to act.

3.3.4. Help the client - individual, group, community, or society- to achieve self-fulfilment and maximum potential within the limits of the respective rights of others. The service shall be based upon helping the client to understand and use the professional relationship, in furtherance of the clients legitimate desires and interests.

3.4 Social Work Standards Relative to Agencies and Organizations

3.4.1. Work and/or cooperate with those agencies and organizations whose policies, procedures, and operations are directed toward adequate service delivery and encouragement of professional practice consistent with the ethical principles of the IFSW.

3.4.2. Responsibly execute the stated aims and functions of the agency or organizations, contributing to the development of sound policies, procedures, and practice in order to obtain the best possible standards or practice.

3.4.3. Sustain ultimate responsibility to the client, initiating desirable alterations of policies, procedures, and practice, through appropriate agency and organization channels. If necessary remedies are not achieved after channels have been exhausted, initiate appropriate appeals to higher authorities or the wider community of interest.

3.4.4. Ensure professional accountability to client and community for efficiency and effectiveness through periodic review of the process of service provision.

3.4.5. Use all possible ethical means to bring unethical practice to an end when policies, procedures and practices are in direct conflict with the ethical principles of social work.

3.5 Social Work Standards Relative to Colleagues

3.5.1. Acknowledge the education, training and performance of social work colleagues and professionals from other disciplines, extending all necessary cooperation that will enhance effective services.

3.5.2. Recognise differences of opinion and practice of social work colleagues and other professionals, expressing criticism through channels in a responsible manner.

3.5.3. Promote and share opportunities for knowledge, experience, and ideas with all social work colleagues, professionals from other disciplines and volunteers for the purpose of mutual improvement.

3.5.4. Bring any violations of professionals ethics and standards to the attention of the appropriate bodies inside and outside the profession, and ensure that relevant clients are properly involved.

3.5.5. Defend colleagues against unjust actions.

3.6 Standards Relative to the Profession

3.6.1. Maintain the values, ethical principles, knowledge and methodology of the profession and contribute to their clarification and improvement.

3.6.2. Uphold the professional standards of practice and work for their advancement.

3.6.3. Defend the profession against unjust criticism and work to increase confidence in the necessity for professional practice.

3.6.4. Present constructive criticism of the profession, its theories, methods and practices

3.6.5. Encourage new approaches and methodologies needed to meet new and existing needs.

International Policy on Human Rights

**Approved at the IFSW General Meeting,
Hong Kong, July 21-23, 1996**

Background

History of Human Rights

The history of human rights is that of the struggle against exploitation of one person by another. It is based on the recognition of basic rights founded on the concept of the inherent dignity and worth of every individual.

The recognition was consolidated in the Universal Declaration of Human Rights by the General Assembly of the United Nations. Its preamble asserted "recognition of the inherent dignity and of the equal and inalienable rights of all members of the human family is the foundation of freedom, justice and peace in the world".

The Basic Instruments concerning Human Rights are:

1. Charter of the United Nations (1945)

2. Universal Declaration of Human Rights (1948)

3. The Covenants on Human Rights (1966)

   a) International Covenant on Civil and Political Rights

   b) International Covenant on Economic, Social and Cultural Rights

4. International Convention on the Elimination of All Forms of Racial Discrimination (1965)

5. Convention on the Elimination of All Forms of Discrimination Against Women (1979)

6. Convention Against Torture and other Cruel, Inhuman and Degrading Treatment or Punishment (1984)

7. Convention on the Rights of the Child (1989)

8. International Convention on the Protection of the Rights of all Migrant Workers and Members of their Families (1990)

These global instruments are reinforced by:

1. The European Convention on Human Rights (1950)

2. The American Convention on Human Rights (1969)

3. The African Charter on Human Rights and Peoples Rights (1981)

The Covenants and Conventions are supported by United Nations Declarations:

a) The Rights of Mentally Retarded Persons (1971)

b) The Protection of Women and Children in Armed Conflicts (1974)

c) The Elimination of All forms of Religious Intolerance (1981)

d) The Right to Development (1986)

Violations of Human Rights

Despite these agreements, gross and subtle violations of human rights are perpetrated every day against thousands of people. The phenomenon of the "disappeared", the torture of political prisoners, summary killings and arbitrary arrests, the increasing use of the death penalty, the extortion of confessions by physical and mental abuse, the manipulation of and the intellectual, emotional and moral pressures imposed on individuals in an attempt to condition their personalities, the detention of prisoners without trial, the economic exploitation of adults and children, displacement of populations due to internal conflicts - these and other violations are all too evident throughout the world. The victims of human rights abuses continue to suffer for many years as a result of their experience.

Many factors contribute to the violations of human rights. The collapse of totalitarian regimes in Eastern Europe did not bring an end to the human rights abuses. The resurgence of nationalism, xenophobia and anti-Semitism in countries with established democracies, as well as in the former Eastern bloc, posed new challenges to the United Nations. In Africa, the rise of tribalism undermined the integrity of nations and led to widespread abuse of the most basic rights to life. In more than one region of the world, there has been a disturbing re-emergence of genocide in situations of armed conflict.

Social Work Principles

Human Rights condenses into two words the struggle for dignity and fundamental freedoms which allow the full development of human potential. Civil and political rights have to be accompanied by economic, social and cultural rights.

Social workers serve human development through adherence to the following basic principles:

i) Every human being has a unique value, which justifies moral consideration for that person.

ii) Each individual has the right to self-fulfilment to the extent that it does not encroach upon the same right of others, and has an obligation to contribute to the well-being of society.

iii) Each society, regardless of its form, should function to provide the maximum benefit for all of its members.

iv) Social workers have a commitment to principles of social justice.

v) Social workers have the responsibility to devote objective and disciplined knowledge and skill to work with individuals, groups, communities, and societies in their development and resolution of personal-societal conflicts and their consequences.

vi) Social workers are expected to provide the best possible assistance without unfair discrimination on the basis of both gender, age, disability, race, colour, language, religious or political beliefs, property, sexual orientation, status or social class.

vii) Social workers respect the basic human rights of individuals and groups as expressed in the United Nations Universal Declaration of Human Rights and other international conventions derived from that Declaration.

viii) Social workers pay regard to the principles of privacy, confidentiality and responsible use of information in their professional work. Social workers respect justified confidentiality even when their country's legislation is in conflict with this demand.

ix) Social workers are expected to work with their clients, working for the best interests of the clients but paying due regard to the interests of others involved. Clients are encouraged to participate as much as possible, and should be informed of the risks and likely benefits of proposed courses of action.

x) Social workers generally expect clients to take responsibility for determining courses of action affecting their lives. Compulsion which might be necessary to solve one party's problems at the expense of the interests of others involved should take place after careful explicit evaluation of the claims of the conflicting parties. Social workers should minimise the use of legal compulsion.

xi) Social workers make ethically justified decisions, and stand by them, paying due regard to The Ethics of Social Work - Principles and Standards adopted by the International Federation of Social Workers.

These principles, drawn from the experience of social workers in carrying out their responsibility to help people with individual and social problems, place a special responsibility on the social work profession to advance the cause of human rights throughout the world.

Role of Social Workers

Social workers deal with common human needs. They work to prevent or alleviate individual, group and community problems, and to improve the quality of life for all people. In doing so, they seek to uphold the rights of the individuals or groups with whom they are working.

The value base of social work with its emphasis on the unique worth of each individual has much in common with human rights theory. Social workers frequently operate in situations of conflict, and are required by their national codes of Ethics and in the international Ethical Principles and Standards to demonstrate respect for all regardless of their previous conduct. Their experience of the impact of social conditions on the capacity of individuals and communities to resolve difficulties means that they recognise that the full realisation of civil and political rights is inseparable from the enjoyment of economic, social and cultural rights. Policies of economic and social development have, therefore, a crucial part to play in securing the extension of human rights.

As a result of their particular role and responsibility in society, social workers are often the conscience of the community. Therefore, the value system, training and experience of social workers requires that they take professional responsibility for promoting human rights. Social workers need to work with other professions and non-governmental organisations in action on human rights issues. As advocates for change, they are often in the forefront of movements for change and thus are themselves subject to repression and abuse. The IFSW Human Rights Commission was established in 1988 to support social workers under threat for pursuing their professional responsibilities.

Policy Statement

Human rights are those fundamental entitlements that are considered to be necessary for developing each personality to the fullest. Violations of human rights are any arbitrary and selective actions that interfere with the full exercise of these fundamental entitlements.

The social work profession, through historical and empirical evidence, is convinced that the achievement of human rights for all people is a fundamental prerequisite for a caring world and the survival of the human race. It is only through the recognition and implementation of the basic concept of the inherent dignity and worth of each person that a secure and stable world can be achieved. Consequently, social workers believe that the attainment of basic human rights requires positive action by individuals, communities, nations and international groups, as well as a clear duty not to inhibit those rights.

The social work profession accepts its share of responsibility for working to oppose and eliminate all violations of human rights. Social workers must exercise this responsibility in their practice with individuals, groups and communities, in their roles as agency or organisational representatives and as citizens of a nation and the world.

IFSW, representing the social work profession internationally, proclaims the following human rights as a common standard and guide for the work of all professional social workers:

Life

The value of life is central to human rights work. Social workers have not only to resist violations of human rights which threaten or diminish the quality of life, but also actively to promote life enhancing and nurturing activities.

Physical and psychological well-being is an important aspect of the quality of life. The deterioration of the environment and the non-existence of curtailment of health programs threaten life.

Social workers assert the right of individuals and communities to have protection from preventable disease and disability.

Freedom and Liberty

All human beings are born free. The fundamental freedoms include the right to liberty, to freedom from slavery, to freedom from arbitrary arrest, torture, cruel inhuman or degrading treatment, and freedom of thought and speech.

Next to life itself, freedom and liberty are the most precious human values asserting the worth of human existence.

Equality and Non-Discrimination

The fundamental principle of equality is closely linked to principles of justice. Every person regardless of birth, gender, age, disability, race, colour, language, religious or political beliefs, property, sexual orientation, status or social class has a right to equal treatment and protection under the law.

Social workers have to ensure equal access to public services and social welfare provision in accordance with the resources of national and local governments, and have a particular responsibility to combat discrimination of any kind in their own practice.

Justice

Every person has a right to protection against arbitrary arrest or interference with privacy, and to equal protection under the law. Where laws have been violated, every person has a right to a prompt and fair trial by an objective judicial authority. Those convicted are entitled to humane treatment whose purpose is to secure the reform and social readaptation of the individual.

The impartial operation of the law is a crucial safeguard for the citizen in the administration of justice. Social justice, however, requires more than a legal system untainted by interference by the executive. It requires the satisfaction of basic human needs and the equitable distribution of resources. It requires universal access to health care and education, thus enabling the achievement of human potential. It underpins concepts of social development. In the pursuit of social justice workers may have to face conflict with powerful elite groups in any given society.

Solidarity

Every person whose fundamental freedoms are infringed has a right to support from fellow citizens. The concept of solidarity recognises the fraternity ideal of the French Revolution, and the importance of mutual support. Social workers give expression to this through the Human Rights Commission in relation to social workers whose political freedoms are infringed. In their daily practice they express solidarity with the poor and oppressed. Poverty, hunger, and homelessness are violations of human rights. Social workers stand with the disadvantaged in campaigning for social justice.

Social Responsibility

Social responsibility is the recognition that each of us has a responsibility to family, to community, to nation and to the world community to contribute personal talents, energy and commitment to the advancement of human rights. Those with intellectual and physical resources should utilise them to assist those less well equipped. Social work's engagement with the disadvantaged is a reflection of that responsibility. No person or collective body has the right to engage in any activity, including propaganda, to incite war, hostility, hatred, bigotry or violence, contrary to the institution and maintenance of human rights.

Peace and Non-Violence

Peace is more than the absence of organised conflict. It is the goal of achieving harmony with self and with others. Social workers are committed to the pursuit of non-violence. Their experience in conflict resolution teaches that mediation and arbitration are effective instruments to overcome seemingly irreconcilable differences. Non-violence does not mean passivity in the face of injustice. Social workers will resist and exercise non-violent pressure for change, but will not engage in acts of violence in the course of their professional activity. Social workers devote their energies to constructive efforts to achieve social justice.

The Environment

Humankind has trusteeship responsibility for the care of the planet. Environmental degradation poses a threat to life itself in some areas, and to the quality of life in many countries. False development models based on industrialisation, the unequal distribution of resources, excessive consumerism and ignorance of the pernicious consequences of pollution have all contributed to this global plight. Social workers need to work with community groups in tackling the consequences of environmental decline and destruction.

Key Terms

Ableism – This term refers to the belief in the superiority of able-bodied people over disabled people.

Aboriginal approach to social work – The development of an Aboriginal approach to social work practice should be consistent with four key principles. These principles are: (1) the recognition of a distinct Aboriginal worldview; (2) the development of Aboriginal consciousness regarding the impact of colonialism; (3) an emphasis on the importance of cultural knowledge and traditions; and (4) utilizing the concept of Aboriginal empowerment.

Aboriginal empowerment – In the context of social work, Aboriginal empowerment emphasizes the participation of community members in promoting self-determination and social change.

Aboriginal peoples – Individuals who have Native origins. It is a term commonly used to refer to Indians, Inuit and Métis in Canada. Aboriginal peoples have their own names for themselves in their respective languages: Anishnaabe, Inuit, Innu, Nuu-chah-nulth, and Métis.

Aboriginal political activism – A surge of Aboriginal political activism, beginning in the 1970s, has led to the development of several national organizations representing and uniting distinct constituent groups. Among these are: (1) the Assembly of First Nations, which represents status Indians who reside on Indian reserves across Canada; (2) the Inuit Tapirisat of Canada, representing Canada's Inuit population; (3) the Métis National Council; (4) the Congress of Aboriginal Peoples, representing off-reserve Aboriginal peoples; and (5) the Native Women's Association of Canada.

Aboriginal self-government – Quite simply, the concept expresses the desire of Aboriginal peoples to control their destiny. It precludes accountability to the provincial and federal governments in favour of accountability and responsibility to the Aboriginal peoples by their own Aboriginal leaders. Self-government is concerned with sovereignty in relation to the Canadian state – within it or outside it, depending on one's view.

Aboriginal worldview – While Aboriginal peoples do not have one single philosophy or worldview, one can draw upon the fundamental differences between Western Euro-Canadian and Aboriginal worldviews. For example, the concept of the circle captured in the Medicine Wheel illustrates the notion of balance prevalent in Aboriginal societies, in contrast to the typically linear models of cause and effect common in some Western societies.

Absolute poverty – A definition of poverty that looks at the minimum income required for physical survival.

Accessibility – One of five principles of Medicare in Canada. This means that there must be a wide range of services, accessible services and a reduction or elimination of user fees. Each province is required to provide health care with reasonable access, both financially and geographically. This applies to ward care in a hospital, free choice of a physician, reasonable compensation to physicians and adequate payments to hospitals.

Addiction – Addiction can be defined as a compulsive need for, or persistent use of, a substance known to be harmful.

AH-HAH! Method – An approach to popular education that aims to help people see how local problems are influenced by larger societal-level structures. It refers to the experience people have when they understand clearly something they knew only in a partial or confused way.

Ambiguity of social work – This refers to the dilemmas faced by social workers in the social work relationship. While social workers are helpers, they are also expected to enforce rules and regulations in the helping relationship with the client.

Anger-control theory – This theory focuses on the idea that men must be held accountable for their violent behaviour and learn to deal with and control their tempers, showing their feelings in more appropriate ways.

Anti-racist social work – Racism is the subordination of one group by another using arbitrary physical features such as skin colour. It can occur at the individual, institutional or societal levels in the form of attitudes, beliefs, policies or procedures. Anti-racist social work is an approach to practice that aggressively combats racism on all three levels.

Approaches to social work practice – The generalist approach and structural approach are common approaches to social work practice in Canada. A body of knowledge or theoretical base informs each approach to practice. Think of knowledge as a collection of beliefs and ideas. These take the form of concepts and propositions about reality. A theory then combines these concepts and propositions into a coherent picture of reality. Finally, a model or approach takes the theory and moulds it into a visual or metaphoric representation of the theory or theories.

Assessment and planning – The process of developing an understanding of the presenting problem and a plan of action. It will include different elements and emphasis depending on the perspective or approach of the social worker.

Assimilationist policies – The policy of the federal government towards Aboriginal people that attempted to deny and destroy Aboriginal life, culture and society in favour of integrating Canada's First Nations into the mainstream. The policy was pursued vigorously and viciously in the residential schools.

Average income deficiency – A measure of poverty that shows how much additional income would be required to raise an individual or household above Statistics Canada's Low-Income Cut-off.

Best interests approach – The "best interests" approach to child protection emphasizes the protection and well-being of the child, whereas the "least restrictive" approach emphasizes the least disruptive course of action that will leave the child with his or her family, if at all possible.

Bill C-23 – This Bill amends 68 federal statutes to provide same-sex couples with equal rights and responsibilities as heterosexual married couples. At the last minute the government introduced a change that excluded same-sex couples from the definition of "marriage."

Biological essentialism in sexual attraction – This approach assumes the origin of all sexual attraction and behaviour is innate and predetermined; a component of the person's biological endowment. It believes the homosexual is born, and professional treatment is required to ensure that the person does not act upon "deviant" sexual drives and desires.

Burnout – The term burnout refers to the anxiety resulting from increased workplace pressure and increased workloads. This type of stress occurs among social workers and others who are faced with increasing responsibility and less and less control over how the work is to be completed

Canada Assistance Plan – Federal legislation, passed in 1966 and considered by many as a keystone of the Canadian welfare state. The legislation required the federal government to fund half the cost of social programs undertaken by the provinces.

Canada Health and Social Transfer (CHST) – Federal legislation that combines federal funding for health, post-secondary education and welfare and transfers a designated amount of money based on population size to each province rather than transferring a percentage of actual costs. It replaced both the Canada Assistance Plan (CAP) and Established Program Financing (EPF).

Canadian Association of Schools of Social Work (CASSW) – A voluntary, national charitable association of university faculties, schools and departments offering professional education in social work at the undergraduate, graduate and post-graduate levels. Established in 1967, CASSW is the successor to the National Committee of Schools of Social Work, which, since 1948, had been the forum for programs offering professional education in social work.

Canadian Association of Social Workers (CASW) – Founded in 1926 to promote the profession of social work in Canada, to monitor employment conditions and to establish standards of practice within the profession. As a federation of the ten provincial and one territorial social work organizations, the Canadian Association of Social Workers (CASW) provides a national leadership role in strengthening and advancing the social work profession in Canada.

Canadian census – A full census of the Canadian population is taken every four years by Statistics Canada. The census is used to develop social policy. For the first time, the 2001 Canadian Census asked Canadians if they live in same-sex relationships.

Casework – In social work, casework refers to using systematic methods of investigation, assessment and decision making. It is often associated with a psycho-social or generalist approach to clinical practice.

Charity Organization Society – Social welfare agencies established in the latter part of the 1800s that utilized a "scientific charity" approach to studying the needs of individuals and families. The society was formed in London, England, in the 1860s by upper and professional men and women because of "urban chaos" and the indiscriminate giving of relief by uncontrolled charities. It differentiated between the deserving and undeserving poor, believing that indiscriminate material relief would cause pauperism.

Charter of Rights and Freedoms – The Canadian Constitution was patriated in 1982; that is, it was brought under Canadian control. The first section of the *Constitution Act*, the *Charter of Rights and Freedoms*, describes the fundamental individual and group rights of citizens, including freedom of religion, voting rights and equality rights. The government of Quebec did not endorse the act on the grounds that it failed to recognize Quebec's distinctness.

Child abuse – The physical, psychological, social, emotional and sexual maltreatment of a child whereby the survival, safety, self-esteem, growth and development of the person are endangered. Separate categories include: physical abuse, neglect, sexual abuse and emotional abuse.

Code of Ethics – A profession's set of standards concerning the ethical behavior of its members. All members are expected to be guided by this code in their professional activities. The CASW has a code of ethics, which is a set of principles to guide a social worker as he or she deals with issues arising in the workplace.

Colonialism – Political domination of one nation over another that is institutionalized in direct political administration by the colonial power, control of all economic relationships and a systematic attempt to transform the culture of the subject nation.

Coming out – "Coming out," the political act and strategy of gay and lesbian liberation of the 1970s, is now regarded as an important psycho-social developmental process. It has become the unique challenge for every gay man and lesbian, a task deemed necessary for self-acceptance and relationship development.

Community – A group of people having common ties or interests and/or living in the same locality or district. It may be a geographic community or a group of people with similar interests or problems.

Community health centres – In the 1970s, the federal government recommended the establishment of community health centres (CHCs) with the intention of providing primary care, health promotion and prevention services using salaried primary health care professionals. Studies have found that CHCs provide better primary care, decrease the costs of patient care and decrease hospitalization rates.

Community work – A social work method practised with communities. It involves six steps: entry, data collection and analysis, goal setting, action planning, action taking and termination.

Comprehensiveness – Each provincial medical insurance plan must cover insured services provided by hospitals, private medical practitioners and other related health care services provided on the request of a physician. This varies from province to province according to what services are listed as essential.

Confidentiality – The use of client records raises concerns about the confidentiality of sensitive information: what constitutes the ethical disclosure of information about a client? A social worker is obligated to follow the guidelines of the agency or organization employing them and obey legislation and association policy. The CASW *Code of Ethics* stipulates, at length, the requirements for collecting, recording, storing and accessibility of client records.

Consciousness-raising – The process by which an individual or members of a group become aware of and understand that other people share with them common experiences, that others too are restricted and damaged by certain practices, patterns of relations, beliefs, stereotypes, myths, expectations and social structures. It is the process by which people begin to understand the relationships between their own biographies, other people's biographies, history and the social infrastructure.

Contracting out – The practice of hiring private for-profit companies to implement specified public social welfare activities and deliver certain services in return for payment from public funds.

Cost containment – Medical care costs in Canada have been rising steadily because of the ageing of the Canadian population, the emphasis on curative and high technology medicine, the increasing demand for hospital services and for expensive equipment, and the increasing fees of medical personnel. Cost containment has become an area of major concern.

Court order – A directive from a child welfare court. Court order options include the placement of the child with some other person subject to the agency's provision, child welfare agency wardship, Crown wardship, or consecutive child welfare agency wardship and supervision order.

Criminal Code of Canada – Criminal law is distinguished from what is known as civil law. Criminal law governs actions and relationships that are deemed to harm society as a whole. These are defined in the Criminal Code of Canada.

Cultural competence – This model means that workers develop the ability to acknowledge different perceptions and experiences and incorporate these into practice applications. In other words, the worker must take this knowledge of the "other" culture and combine it with an analysis of how his or her own culture affects their social work interventions.

Culture – The generally shared knowledge, beliefs and values of members of society. Culture is conveyed from generation to generation through the process of socialization.

Cycle-of-violence theory – This theory seeks to explain what happens in individual relationships that causes violence against women in a three-step process: tension-building, acute battering and honeymoon period.

Demogrants – These are universal flat-rate payments made to individuals or households solely on the basis of demographic characteristics, such as number of children or age, rather than on the basis of proven need, as in the case of minimum income programs, or as in contributions in the case of social insurance.

Deserving poor – This refers to those who are deemed to be deserving of relief. This is a concept that historically underpinned charity relief and continues to influence income security provision today.

Diagnostic approach – In the diagnostic approach, the emphasis is on understanding the condition of the individual by reference to causal events in his or her early life. This approach requires a skilled worker who can diagnose the problem and establish and carry out a plan for treatment.

Digital divide – Most of the world's peoples do not have access to computers, the Internet and advanced communications technology. This problem is sometimes referred to as the "digital divide."

Direct social work – This involves working directly with people as individuals, in families or households and communities in a direct face-to-face way, i.e., in a counselling role.

Disability – Any restriction or lack (resulting from an impairment) of ability to perform an activity in the manner or within the range considered normal for a human being.

Disability organizations – Organizations that provide services to disabled people. For examples, see Chapter 12 on Social Work with Persons with Disabilities.

Disability rights organizations – The rise of disability rights organizations in Canada is rooted in the rise of the consumer movement, the civil rights movement, the peace movement, the gay rights movement and the women's movement of the late 1960s and the early 1970s. Disability rights activists attempted to redefine their social status. Rather than be labeled "defective or handicapped," they argued that they be seen as members of a minority group.

Discrimination – The unequal treatment of individuals on the basis of their personal characteristics, which may include age, sex, sexual orientation, ethnic or physical identity.

Disk list system – One gross example of the nature of state intervention in Inuit lives was the disk list system. As bureaucrats would not formally acknowledge the Inuktitut names for individuals, the disk list system assigned a numbered disk to each Inuk in order to identify them.

Duty to report – Not only child protection workers have a responsibility to report suspected instances of child abuse or neglect. Every member of society has a responsibility to report child abuse or neglect when there are reasonable grounds for believing a child may be in need of protection. People in professions that bring them into contact with children have a particular responsibility to ensure that young people are safe.

Early childhood development – This priority was identified and developed under the National Children's Agenda (NCA) document negotiated between provincial and federal governments in 1999-2000. In support of this initiative, the federal government has agreed to contribute $2.2 billion for early childhood development over five years, beginning in 2001-02. This initiative will provide better access to services such as pre-natal classes and screening, pre-school programs and child care, parent information and family support, and community supports.

Electronic advocacy – The process of using communication and information technologies to disseminate information and mobilize support from a large constituency to help influence decision-making processes.

Emotional abuse – Emotional attacks or omissions that cause, or could cause, serious emotional injury. This could include behaviour of parents or guardians who persistently do not take an interest in their child, for example, not talking to or hugging their child, and being chronically emotionally unavailable to their child. This could also include repeated threats, confinement, repeated exposure to violence, ongoing humiliation and ridicule, and fundamental attacks on a child's sense of self.

Employment equity – All Canadian provinces and the federal government have equal employment opportunity legislation in place, usually as part of their human rights codes. This legislation prohibits discrimination on the basis of race, age, religion, nationality and sex. Employment equity legislation, designed to help women's employment and promotion opportunities, was not introduced in Canada until the 1980s.

Employment Equity Act – The purpose of the *Employment Equity Act* of 1986 is to ensure equity in the workplace so that no one is denied access to employment for reasons unrelated to merit and skills.

Empowerment – The sense that people can create and take action on their own behalf to meet their physical, spiritual and psychological needs.

Equal-pay policies – During the 1950s and 1960s, every Canadian province enacted legislation requiring equal pay for similar or substantially similar work. During the 1970s both Quebec and the federal government introduced pay equity legislation that required equal pay for work of equal value (allowing comparisons between occupations). In the 1980s, most other jurisdictions followed suit, at least with respect to public sector employment.

Ethical dilemmas – In the course of their work, social workers are inevitably confronted with situations in which the policy and regulations of the agency conflict with what they, as experienced social workers, see as being in the best interests of their client. As well, the standards and ethics of the profession may be inconsistent with an agency's procedures and practices. Balancing one's beliefs, professional standards and agency rules can be difficult.

Ethnic group – A social group that has a common cultural tradition, common history and common sense of identity and exists as a subgroup in a larger society. The members of an ethnic group differ with regard to certain cultural characteristics from the other members of society.

Ethnicity – Ethnicity, from a Greek word meaning "people," refers to a group of people who share a common heritage, identity or origin. Isajiw defines an ethnic group as "an involuntary, community-type group of persons who share the same distinct culture or who are descendants of those who have shared a distinct culture and who identify with their ancestors, or their culture or group" (Isajiw 1999).

Ethnocentrism – An attitude that one's own culture, society, or group is inherently superior to all others. Ethnocentrism means an inability to appreciate others whose culture may include a different racial group, ethnic group, religion, morality, language, political system, economic system and so on. It also means an inability to see a common humanity and human condition facing all women and men in all cultures and societies beneath the surface variations in social and cultural traditions.

Eugenics movement – Over the years, thousands of people with disabilities (most often intellectual disabilities) were sterilized. This policy was in line with the now widely discredited eugenics movement, advocated by the Fascists in Nazi Germany among others, which was based on the notion that careful planning through proper breeding is the key to bettering society.

Evaluation/termination – The final step in the social work process, in which the client and the social worker have worked together to assist the client to achieve a resolution to the original problem.

Extra billing – Extra billing is an extra charge levied by the physician beyond the negotiated or scheduled rates set by the provinces.

Facilitating programs – Many changes, other than directly labour-related legislation, have been introduced to help put women on an equal footing with men in the Canadian labour market. Among other things, these include changes in divorce laws, policies against sexual harassment at work, expanded maternity leave provisions, policies to protect part-time and temporary workers and policies designed to ensure women have equal access to higher education.

Family or household groups – Any combination of two or more persons who are bound together over time by ties of mutual consent, birth and/or adoption/placement and who, together, assume responsibilities for variant combinations of some of the following: physical maintenance and care of group members; addition of new members through procreation or adoption; socialization of children; social control of members; production, consumption and distribution of goods and services; and affective nurturance – love. The definition of family in Canadian Family Law is extremely restrictive and does not recognize gay and lesbian couples.

Federalism – A system of government in which sovereignty is divided between a central government and several provincial or state governments.

Feminist social work practice – Many of the principles of feminist social work are similar to those of social work practice in general, such as the empowerment of the individual and examining society through a critical lens, egalitarian client-therapist relations and working at both the individual and social levels, although to varying degrees. As with other approaches to social work, feminist social work practice seeks to understand a client's situation by acquiring knowledge of the client's history, family and social relations, and cultural context. However, in analyzing individual problems and working out effective interventions, the feminist approach gives greater emphasis to the harmful role of patriarchal relations within the family and within the wider society.

Feminist theory – There are different definitions of feminism and numerous formulations and debates in feminist theory. There is, however a common core theory asserting that sex-role stereotypes and social structures perpetuate women's subordination.

Feminization of poverty – The number of women in poverty is increasing faster than that of men.

Food banks and feeding programs – With cutbacks in many income security programs, Canadians are increasingly resorting to food banks and feeding programs in order to survive.

Freudian thought – Freudian thought played an increasingly important role in social work in the 1920s. Social work shifted from a concern with the societal context to a concern with a person's psychological make-up as the source of problems.

Friendly visitors – People charged with doing home visits to determine if a person was deserving of charity or relief in the late 1800s and early 1900s. They provided "out-of-door relief" during the nineteenth century. Those who provided the early forms of relief were known as charity visitors. They were wealthy and it was hoped that their moral rectitude would rub off on the needy.

Functional approach – Attitude theories that emphasize that people develop and change their attitudes based on the degree to which they satisfy different psychological needs. To change an attitude, one must understand the underlying function that the attitude serves.

Gay and lesbian communities – Within Canada, as well as other parts of the world, the urban environment provided opportunities for political and social organizing and this fostered the development of identifiable gay and lesbian communities. They are an example of the social networks people developed in response to societal dynamics of oppression, prejudice and stigmatization.

Gender – The culturally specific set of characteristics that identifies the social behaviour of women and men and the relationship between them. Gender, therefore, refers not simply to women or men, but to the relationship between them and the way it is socially constructed. Because it is a relational term, gender must include women and men. Like the concepts of class, race and ethnicity, gender is an analytical tool for understanding social processes.

Geographic community – A geographic community is as defined by a specific neighbourhood, city district or local ward, with specific geographical boundaries.

Gerontological social work – Social work with older adults is often called gerontological social work. As the Canadian population ages, this field of practice is rapidly expanding. Twelve percent of Canada's current total population are seniors; by 2041, this will have risen to 23 percent. Practitioners in this field need specialized knowledge of health care issues, poverty, housing and mental health, including knowledge of the ageing process and the issues surrounding Alzheimer's disease. Since a large proportion of the elderly population are women, social work with older adults is often considered a women's issue.

Global social welfare – In this new era of globalization, the traditional concerns of social welfare practitioners in addressing the immediate needs of their clients will need to be broadened to include a concern with the issue of global human rights. Global social welfare refers to concern with justice, social regulation, social provision and redistribution between nations.

Globalization – The newest development in the expansion of global capitalism. It is a new manifestation of an old system of market liberalism, but occurring on an international rather than national level and marked by the expansion of the size and power of multinational corporations.

Great Depression – The largest downturn or economic depression in the economy in Canada took place in 1930s. It was characterized by deflation, which occurs when few people are buying products.

Group work – A social work method practised with groups of individuals. This method includes five steps: intake, assessment and case plan, group composition, intervention and termination.

Harm-reduction approach – Increasingly social workers in addiction treatment programs are taking a harm-reduction approach, instead of an abstinence approach to treatment. The harm-reduction approach seeks to minimize or reduce the adverse consequences of drug use.

Hate crimes – When people are the targets of violence solely because of who they are, or who they are thought to be, they are the victims of hate crimes. The most common targets of hate-motivated crime are Blacks, Jews and gays.

Healing lodges – Lodges that provide residential treatment or both treatment and lodging for people who become overwhelmed by social, emotional and spiritual problems. Approximately fifty treatment facilities currently provide Aboriginal residential healing. The Nechi Institute and Poundmaker's Lodge in Alberta are examples, providing healing and lodging for people dealing with addictions.

Health gap – Despite the availability of public health care across the country, there is a serious health gap between the rich and the poor in Canada. The rich are healthier than the middle class, who are in turn healthier than the poor. The well educated are healthier than the less educated, the employed are healthier than the unemployed and so on.

Heterosexism – A system of cultural beliefs, values and customs that exalts heterosexuality and denies, denigrates and stigmatizes any non-heterosexual form of behaviour or identity.

Holistic approach to health care – The holistic approach to health care involves taking into account not only the physical aspects of health, which have commonly been addressed by physicians, but also the social, cultural, mental and spiritual aspects of the person.

Holistic approach to healing – This means that the whole of the person and the situation is examined and acted upon.

Home care – Home care involves the provision of health-related care by one person to another in the client's home. Home care services generally include the provision of health services by two tiers of workers: professionals, such as social workers, physicians, nurses, physiotherapists, occupational therapists, speech therapists and dieticians, and unregulated workers, such as homemakers, personal support workers and personal care attendants.

Homophobia – Homophobia is a pervasive irrational fear of homosexuality. It includes the fear that heterosexuals have of many homosexual feelings within themselves, any overt mannerisms or actions that would suggest homosexuality and the resulting desire to suppress or stamp out homosexuality.

Human rights – Those rights that are inherent in our nature and without which we cannot live as human beings, based on the recognition of individual political and civil rights and collective cultural, social and economic rights.

Human rights codes – Codes of laws designed to protect and advance the rights of specific groups of people in society, such as minorities and women. For example, the 1980s brought major changes for the lesbian and gay community. During the later part of the decade, major legal changes were also gained, particularly the inclusion of "sexual orientation" in provincial human rights codes (rulings by the Supreme Court of Canada have ensured this inclusion in all provinces and territories).

Human rights commissions – All federal and provincial jurisdictions have legislated rights protection law and have created rights commissions to implement such policy. National human rights legislation in Canada began with the passage of the Canadian Bill of Rights in 1960. Later in that decade other provinces enacted similar legislation, and by 1975, all provinces in Canada had human rights codes.

Human rights legislation – National human rights legislation in Canada began with the passage of the Canadian Bill of Rights in 1960. Later in that decade other provinces enacted similar legislation, and by 1975, all provinces in Canada had human rights codes. The constitutional division of powers determines whether a rights violation complaint is heard at the federal or provincial levels. Grounds of discrimination vary slightly depending on the jurisdiction.

Ideology – A system of beliefs and values that explains society and prescribes the role of government.

Immigration policy – Ethnic and race relations in Canada have been heavily influenced by immigration policy. Prior to 1967, "Nationality" was one of the criteria used to qualify for admission to Canada, and Canadian immigration policy was undoubtedly Eurocentric. In 1967, new legislation introduced a point system, whereby prospective immigrants had to qualify based on such criteria as education, work experience, language fluency and age.

Income security – Income support in the form of demogrants, social insurance, Social Assistance, and income supplementation that can be unconditional or based on an income or needs test, or negative income tax.

Income supplementation – Programs that, as the name suggests, supplement income that is obtained elsewhere whether through paid employment or through other income security programs. These programs are not intended to be the primary source of income. Family Allowance (which was also a universal demogrant) and the National Child Benefit are examples of income supplementation programs.

Independent Living Movement (ILM) – The Independent Living Movement has been a key player in the struggle to achieve human rights legislation for people with disabilities. Originating in the United States during the early 1970s and introduced to Canada in 1979, the Movement has become a dominant force in disability rights activity in Canada. In addition to promoting disability rights, the ILM promotes the social oppression theory of disability.

Indian Act – Legislation that provides the Government of Canada with the legal framework of authority over Indians and lands reserved for Indians, as stated in the *Constitution Act*, 1867. The main purpose of the Act is to control and regulate Indian lives. An Indian is a person who is registered or entitled to be registered in the Indian Register (a centralized record).

Indian Agent – The *Indian Act* was, and still is, a piece of social legislation of very broad scope, which regulates and controls virtually every aspect of Native life. The so-called Indian Agent administered the Act in Aboriginal communities. These agents were to displace traditional Aboriginal leaders so as to institute a new way of living consistent with the intentions of the government. The Indian Agents had extraordinary administrative and discretionary powers. In order to ensure this, Clause 25 of the Act established the government's guardianship over Indian lands.

Indian problem – With the colonization of what would become known as Canada, the land's original inhabitants became "the Indian problem," and impediments to "civilization." Colonial representatives and, later, government officials devised various schemes to address the Indian problem, including land-cession treaties and assimilation policies.

Indirect social work – Social work of benefit to those in need, but the work is often with organizations that advocate, research, plan and implement social service and income security programs. Most often those who do indirect social work will be working with government, social service agencies or what are called advocacy or research groups, and organizations whose purpose is to advocate for and with people in need and conduct research.

In-home services – In-home services are provided to help a household or family members live together harmoniously in a secure and safe environment. The main categories of in-home services include family counselling services, parenting supports, child protection, in-home child care, homemaker services and family educational services.

Institutional view of social welfare – A view that emphasizes the preventive role of social welfare in modern industrial societies and sees the welfare of the individual as the responsibility of the social collective. The market will not, and cannot, meet the needs and aspirations of a people and, therefore, the optimal distribution of welfare can only be achieved by an acknowledgment that there is a significant role for a publicly funded and organized system of programs and institutions.

Institutionalization – Beginning in the mid-nineteenth century, the segregation, institutionalization and isolation of persons with disabilities became the common method for dealing with such people.

Intake – Intake is usually the first step taken by a worker when a client seeks help. Intake is a process whereby a request for service is made by or for a person, and it is then determined whether and what kind of service is to be provided. The social worker attempts to gather initial information from the client in order to determine what assistance is needed, and whether the agency and worker is the appropriate provider.

Inter-governmental organizations (IGOs) – International organizations that consider worldwide issues and relations between nations. Social workers are active in various international inter-governmental organizations (IGOs). The United Nations is the best known of these IGOs. Formed as World War II came to an end, the UN seeks to develop a framework of international law that will be followed by all nation states around the world.

Internalized homophobia – Today, social workers require, to be effective, a critical self- and social awareness about issues of sex, sexuality and sexual identity. They need to recognize their comfort level and feel accepting of and within their own sexual bodies, emotions and feelings. Internalized homophobia (attitudes that devalue same-sex relationships) needs to be acknowledged and challenged.

International community work – A common social work activity in developing countries is international community work. Social workers use community work to organize people to bring about major social change between nations, within nations, and between groups of people. They work through communities to achieve the fullest participation of people in transforming different aspects of their lives.

International Federation of Social Workers (IFSW) – The International Federation of Social Workers is a successor to the International Permanent Secretariat of Social Workers, which was founded in Paris in 1928. In 1950, the International Federation of Social Workers was created, with the goal of becoming an international organization of professional social workers. Today the IFSW represents over half a million social workers in fifty-five different counties. The IFSW seeks to promote social work as a profession, link social workers from around the world and promote the participation of social workers in social policy and planning.

Intervention – A "action" step in which a client provides the social worker with information and shares whatever progress has been made in attempting to resolve the problem.

Involuntary clients – Those who accept services because of a legal mandate, such as prisoners on parole, or children in care.

Keynesianism – Economic theory named after British economist John Maynard Keynes, which holds that economic efficiency and equity are compatible. Social spending helps economic recovery, enhances productivity and keeps the labour market flexible. Also called demand-side economics: if people are employed, they will spend money, the demand for products will increase, and the economy will improve.

Land-cession treaties – The desire by the government to obtain land held by Aboriginal peoples for the settlement of non-Aboriginal people was a primary goal for much of the policy directed towards Native peoples. Reserves were seen as a way to move

Indians into agriculturally-based communities, both to assimilate them and also to free-up vast tracks of land for non-Aboriginal settlement. Further to this end, numerous treaties were signed between Indians and colonial officials between 1670 and 1923. It is these land treaties (in many cases, the lack of them) that are currently in dispute across the country today.

Learning theory – The main idea in this theory is that violence is a behaviour learned in childhood. Boys learn that it is okay to be violent, and girls learn that it is okay to be on the receiving end of violence – that is what relationships are about. This theory holds that all children are socialized to accept violence in our society and that this, coupled with the different roles that boys and girls are socialized into, supports and perpetuates abuse. Children who witness violence in the home are much more likely to become abusers or be abused.

Least restrictive approach – The "least restrictive" approach to child protection emphasizes the least disruptive course of action that will leave the child with his or her family, if at all possible.

Low Income Cut-off (LICO) – According to Statistics Canada, those who spend more than 55 percent of their earnings on basic needs are living under the LICO. A household that spends 20 percent more than the average household spends on food, clothing and shelter is below the LICO or in "straightened circumstances." Although LICO is not put forth as an official poverty line, many analysts, including the United Nations, treat it as such. For example, the 2000 LICO for a family of four in a medium-sized city of 100,000-500,000 is $29,356. Some have called it a "relative necessities" approach.

Maternal feminism – This term generally refers to the notion that it is because of a woman's special roles as mother and homemaker that she has an obligation and a right to participate in the public sphere. Although they brought women into public life and social work, the early maternal feminists now tend to be viewed as being quite conservative, insofar as they supported more traditional conceptions of the family in which women were expected to stay in the home.

Means test – A test used in selective income security programs to determine eligibility based on the income of the prospective recipient. The benefit is reduced according the income level, and there is always a level at which no benefit is granted.

Medical model – The view that behavioral and emotional problems are analogous to physical diseases.

Medical social work practice – One of the chief settings for medical social work practice is the hospital. Almost every hospital in Canada has social workers in its departments, including emergency services, oncology, pediatrics, surgery, intensive care, rehabilitation, gerontology and orthopaedics.

Medicare – Today, Canada has a health care system that is funded by government insurance, but medical care itself is privately delivered by physicians who are self-employed or employed by physician-owned corporations. The system is an interlocking set of ten provincial and three territorial health insurance plans. Known as Medicare, the system provides access to universal, comprehensive coverage for hospital, in-patient and out-patient physician services.

Medicine Wheel – There are different Medicine Wheels and different interpretations of the components of the Medicine Wheel depending on the First Nation, and each will illuminate a variation on social work practice. Traditionally, many Aboriginal people have used some form of Medicine Wheel to underpin their approach to healing. The four directions of the wheel can help the social worker see which aspects of the problem being presented one should address.

Membership community – A membership community is defined by a sense of belonging to a specific group; for example, the gay and lesbian community, the black community, the Native community and so on.

Mental illness – A general term referring to psychological, emotional, or behavioral disorders as well to the view that these disorders are diseases of the mind.

Minimum income – Social Assistance is a minimum income program. It provide the bare minimum needed to survive.

Model of community development – The nature of community work differs depending on the perspective informing one's practice. A useful approach is Rothman's model of community development, which allows one to see the differences between the various forms of community development discussed and debated in Canada today.

Monetarism – An economic theory that asserts, among other things, that social spending stimulates inflation, undermines labour market flexibility and productivity, and distorts the work leisure trade-off.

Multiculturalism – In 1971, Canada became the first country to adopt multiculturalism as an official policy. The policy was aimed at a greater integration of Canadian society by providing diverse ethnic minority groups with a sense of belonging to Canada.

Needs test – A test used in selective income security programs to determine eligibility based on the income and the need of the prospective recipient. Eligibility criteria define need, which is then compared to the applicant's income.

Neglect – Sustained deprivation of food, clothing, hygiene, shelter and other needed care so as to cause, or potentially cause, physical, emotional, developmental or psychological harm.

New world order model of international social work – This approach has its origins in the idea that the present world order is not very democratic at all, but is controlled by a relatively small number of wealthy countries that manipulate the international system to their own advantage. Those who practice with this approach in mind are oriented more towards a fundamental rebuilding of the global cultural, social, political and economic structures.

Non-governmental organizations (NGOs) – NGOs are international organizations not directly linked to governments, allowing them more freedom in taking up important issues and bringing about effective change. NGOs tend to be small dynamic groups that work on a variety of issues depending on their particular political or philosophical stances.

North-South divide – The economic world divides, broadly speaking, along North-South lines, the so-called North-South divide, with the countries of the First World awash in relative affluence and those of the Third World, in abject squalor.

Out-of-home services – Out-of-home services are implemented when the home situation becomes unsuitable for the upbringing of a child. These services include foster care, adoption, day care centres, community supports (e.g., the Community Action Program for Children and Aboriginal Head Start), group homes, institutional care, parenting self-help and empowerment groups, and family housing assistance.

Overseas humanitarian programs – Churches and other religious groups and organizations have perhaps the most extensive variety of overseas humanitarian programs and frequently employ the services of social workers. These groups tend to operate in the poorer countries of Africa, Asia and Latin America.

Participatory action research (PAR) – A type of community work that refers to a process of research comprised of education, investigation and action directed at changing the structures that promote inequality and the structures that produce knowledge that perpetuates the current power structures.

Patriarchy literally means the "rule by the father" but, in a broader sense, it has come to mean the domination of society by men. Men are still the major stakeholders in Canadian society, men continue to be represented in higher numbers in positions of authority and male interests continue to take precedence over those of females.

Person with disabilities – The term describes a person whose physical or mental condition limits his or her ability to perform certain functions. Terms such as *cripple, defective, abnormal, handicapped, physically challenged* or *mentally challenged* have been applied to people who are disabled. The most acceptable terms are those that put the person first and not the disability: *people with disabilities, person with disability, person with intellectual disability* and so on. *Disabled person* is now also generally acceptable usage.

Personal tragedy theory of disability – The view that problems faced by disabled people are not the result of physical impairments alone, but also of the social and political inequality that exists between people with disabilities and able-bodied people.

Person-in-the-environment – A key aspect of effective social work practice is to go beyond "internal" (psychological) factors and examine the relationship between individuals and their environment. This person-in-the-environment approach is partly what distinguishes social work practice from other helping professions. These "environments" extend beyond the immediate family and include interactions with friends, neighbourhoods, schools, religious groups, laws and legislation, other agencies or organizations, places of employment and the economic system.

Physical abuse – Physical assaults such as hitting, kicking, biting, throwing, burning or poisoning that cause, or could cause, physical injury as well as behaviours or omissions that cause, or could cause, physical injury to a child.

Political economy – The economic outlook that believes that the operation of economic markets is tied to private concentrations of ownership of the productive enterprise and is essentially exploitative. Social spending is a right fought for by the working class. Some within this approach believe that social spending serves to prop up and justify the economic system. This is called the accumulation and legitimating functions of the welfare state.

Political rights model of disability – A theory of disability primarily concerned with broader social and political change. It contends that a comprehensive understanding of disability can only occur through examination of a social oppression theory of disability, along with the already predominant personal tragedy theory of disability.

Poor relief – The early English legislation, the Poor Law, required local parishes to provide relief to the deserving poor (those who were elderly, ill or disabled). Parishes were administrative districts organized by the Church of England. Each had a local council that was responsible for assistance to the poor, known as poor relief.

Portability – One of the five principles of the *Canada Health Act*. Health services must continue to be covered when residents move from one province to another. It is supposed to cover Canadians temporarily out of the country.

Post-modernism view about sexuality – The view that "difference" is personally mediated by life experience, recognizing that sex and sexuality are only one of many contested domains of living. Such factors as historical period, ethnicity, financial resources and opportunities all play a significant role in self-definition. The "homosexual-heterosexual dichotomy" is the result of scientific explanations of sexual expression that attempt to bring organization to a domain of human behaviour and experience viewed as threatening to a defined social order.

Poverty gap – Poverty rates do not show whether poor people are living in abject poverty or merely a few dollars below the poverty line. To determine this, we need to measure the poverty gap or how much additional income would be required to raise an individual or household above the LICO.

Power theory – A feminist-based theory explaining that wife abuse is a societal problem that occurs because of the power imbalance between men and women, specifically because of the dominance of men and men's roles. Wife abuse continues because there has been historical acceptance of abuse and of men's right to control women, even by force.

Praxis – A process that involves a combining and re-combining of actions into new ways of looking at things; a process of "action-reflection-action."

Prejudice – An adverse opinion that "pre-judges" entire groups based on incomplete and inaccurate information.

Pre-payment health plans – From 1880 to the 1950s, there were a variety of pre-payment health plans in place across Canada, sponsored by local governments, industries and volunteer agencies. These voluntary insurance plans did not cover all medical services, and they were available only to those who could afford to pay the premiums.

Preventive medicine – Provincial governments have begun to practice preventive medicine, using policies designed to anticipate and reduce the likelihood of illness or its worsening.

Private charities – The pre-industrial phase of the development of social work includes the period from the formation of Canada up to the 1890s. Private charities developed during this time, offering material relief and lessons in moral ethics. Many were explicitly associated with religious organizations, and it was religiously motivated individuals working through these organizations who became the early social workers.

Private social welfare – Social welfare programs funded by voluntary charitable contributions of individuals and private organizations, by fees people pay for the services they receive, or which are provided by funds spent by corporations to provide social welfare services for their employees.

Privately funded disability programs – Privately funded disability programs include programs that are provided through private insurance plans or through long-term disability plans as part of job benefits. These private income security programs are based on the amount of funding that the recipient has contributed directly to the plan, or funding which has been contributed to the plan on behalf of the recipient.

Privatization – The use of the private sector to provide social welfare services, often in addition to or instead of existing public services.

Problem-solving techniques – An approach to social work that breaks down every problem into component parts and develops objectives that must be met in order to solve the overall problem.

Professional associations – Today most Canadian social workers are members of public sector unions as well as members of professional associations. The associations represent social workers in issues pertaining to the development of the profession, the education of its members and in discussions of social issues and social policy. The unions represent them in the areas of pay or working conditions.

Public administration – Provincial health care plans must be publicly administered and operated on a non-profit basis, and are subject to public audit.

Public sector unions – Today most Canadian social workers are members of public sector unions. Indeed, they were part of the wider unionization of the public sector during the 1960s and 1970s, when, for the first time, public sector employees were permitted to join a union. The unions represent their members in the areas of pay or working conditions. The professional association and the union complement each other and both have mandates to act as voices for those they represent.

Public welfare – Public welfare refers to the provision of welfare services at the three levels of government: the federal or national government, the provincial and territorial governments and the regional and municipal governments.

Publicly funded disability programs – Publicly funded disability programs are programs covered by federal, provincial and municipal legislation. These programs include the Canada Pension Plan-Disability Pension (a federal program), and various provincial disability support programs.

Quintile income distribution – A quintile represents one-fifth (20 percent) of the total number of people being studied. If the Canadian population is divided into five sections (quintiles), Statistics Canada's studies suggest that the richest 20 percent get 44 percent of all income in Canada and the poorest 20 percent get only 5 percent of all income in Canada.

Race – Race is an arbitrary classification of human beings based on skin colour and other superficial physical characteristics. This classification, conceived in Europe in the colonial period, placed the populations of the world in a hierarchical order with white Europeans superior to all others. Modern biologists do not recognize "race" as a meaningful scientific category and recent human genome research is conclusive on this point.

Racism – Individual and institutionalized beliefs and practices that advocate that some "races" are inferior to others. The belief that one's racial group is somehow superior to other groups leads, with the aid of stereotypes, to discrimination and prejudice.

Reclaiming Aboriginal culture – A principle of Aboriginal social work that goes beyond regaining language, religion and folkways, in emphasizing an awareness of and reflection on common aspects of culture and identity. By examining Aboriginal history, culture and traditions and dispelling conventional views of Aboriginal reality flowing form colonialism, Aboriginal people can begin to see the structural causes of individual problems.

Rehabilitation – A goal-oriented and time-limited process aimed at providing an impaired person with the tools to change her or his own life, thus enabling him or her to reach optimal mental, physical, and/or social functioning. It can involve measures intended to compensate for a loss of function or a functional limitation (e.g., technical aids) and other measures intended to facilitate social adjustment or readjustment.

Relative poverty – A definition of poverty that looks at income in comparison to the income of other Canadians.

Residential school – This school system was used to remove Native children from Native homes and communities and restrict their culture and language. It separated children from their families and communities for up to years at a time. The purpose was to fulfil the assimilation policies of the federal government. Large numbers of Native children experienced emotional, physical and sexual abuse.

Residual view of social welfare – This view asserts that governments should play only a limited role in the distribution of social welfare. The state should step in only when normal sources of support fail and the individual is unable to help his/her self.

Rights of children – (p.97)

Risk assessment – In the area of child abuse, risk assessment refers to an educated prediction regarding the likelihood that a child will be maltreated based on a careful examination of pertinent data.

Rothman's model of community development – A useful approach to conceptualizing community development is a typology developed by Rothman, involving three components: locality development, social planning and social action. To these should be added a fourth: participatory action research.

Royal Commission on Aboriginal Peoples – The Final Report of 1996 brought together six years of research and public consultation on First Nations issues. This is the most extensive research to date and provides the basis for significant strides forward. Among the many issues discussed, the Report examines the need for Aboriginal people to heal from the consequences of domination, displacement and assimilation. The foundation for a renewed relationship, according to the Report, involves recognition of Aboriginal nations as political entities.

Scientific philanthropy – An historical approach that contributed to the rise of social work with the idea that charities should become organized in order to deal more systematically with the problem of poverty. It emerged from ideals of social reform and social progress, which were increasingly influenced by scientific methods and approaches.

Scoop – "The Scoop" refers to the massive removal of Aboriginal children from Native families and communities and their placement in non-Aboriginal foster and adoptive homes. This took place mostly in the 1960s.

Scrip system – The situation among the Métis in the late nineteenth and early twentieth centuries was unique. The Métis in western Canada could seek to become status Indians by aligning themselves to certain treaty areas or they could "take scrip." The scrip system entitled the bearer of a scrip certificate to either land or money; in exchange, the person who took scrip gave up all further claims to land. Although the scrip system offered to the Métis was different from the treaty-making process for Indians, the result was the same.

Selective programs – Target benefits aimed at those determined to be in need or eligible based on a means test (sometimes called an income test) or a needs test.

Self-help community – A self-help community consists of non-professional persons with similar problems or difficulties (e.g., those living with addiction, disability or unemployment, or coping with illness or the death of a loved one), who provide mutual support and exchange information.

Self-help or peer groups – The acquiring of information or the solving of one's problems, without the direct intervention of professionals or experts, through joining or forming a group comprised of others who have the same problem.

Settlement houses – A movement that began in the late 1800s in which the middle and upper classes lived with the poor and advocated for better social and working conditions. The purpose was to bring the educated middle class and even the charitable upper class or gentry to live among the urban poor in working class neighbourhoods.

Sex – This refers to the biological differences between women and men (see also "gender").

Sexism – Similar to the dynamics of racism. Males are believed to be superior to females and when this belief is put into action it leads to females being treated as objects, the last to be hired, first to be fired, and paid less for equal work.

Sexual abuse – Any sexual exploitation of a child whether consented to or not. It includes touching of a sexual nature or any behaviour of a sexual nature towards a child.

Sexual orientation – One's sexual attraction towards members of either one's own sex or the other sex.

Social change mandate – The social change mandate of social work means working in solidarity with those who are disadvantaged or excluded from society so as to eliminate the barriers, inequities and injustices that exist in society.

Social constructionism in relation to sexual attraction – In this approach sociocultural experience is given primacy in the construction of a homosexual identity and role. Social constructionism gave rise to perspectives of "choice" and "lifestyles," challenging the innate deterministic understanding of sexual orientation as advanced by essentialism.

Social development model of international social work – Social workers who hold to this approach seek primarily to address the immediate causes of human degradation, powerlessness and social inequality and to guide collective action towards the elimination of all forms of oppression, injustice and violence. They are concerned with the fuller participation of people at all levels of the political and economic systems of their countries and with fostering social, political and economic systems that are more humane, inclusive and participatory.

Social gospel movement – A movement that began in the 1880s and was directed towards a more socially oriented church among the Anglican, Methodist, Presbyterian and Congregationalist churches. It advocated for improved living and working conditions and basic social justice.

Social insurance – A type of income security program in which participants make regular payments into a fund from which they receive benefits if the risk covered by the insurance occurs. These programs follow the insurance principle of shared risk. Many contribute with the understanding that not all will necessarily need to access the benefits of the program.

Social oppression theory – In contrast to the personal tragedy theory of disability, the social oppression theory of disability argues that the problems faced by people with disabilities are not the result of physical impairments alone, but are the result of the social and political inequality that exists between disabled people and able-bodied people.

Social policies – The rules and regulations, the laws and other administrative directives, that set the framework for state social welfare activity.

Social programs – A detailed outline of state activity that follows and implements a specific social welfare policy. A social program outlines the funds to be spent and the purposes for which they will be spent.

Social security – This is sometimes used as a substitute for the term *social welfare* or *income security*. It is generally an American term, but has been also used by Canadian governments. For example, *Social Security in Canada*, published in 1994 by the federal government, uses the term to refer to both income security and social services, but the term *social welfare* is more widely accepted.

Social services – Non-monetary personal or community services provided by the state and non-profit organizations for members of the community, such as day care, housing, crisis intervention, and support groups for women experiencing abuse.

Social structures – This refers generally to wider social institutions, policies and systems in society, such as the economic system (capitalism, social class), the political system (democratic rights), family relations (patriarchy and gender inequality), ideologies and belief systems (religion, racism, ageism, ableism, homophobia) and so on.

Social survey research – Towards the end of the nineteenth century, social survey research was beginning to be used to highlight the extent of poverty and inequality in Canadian cities. Early studies by social researcher and reformers, such as J.J. Kelso in Toronto and J.S. Woodsworth in Winnipeg, contributed to an understanding of poverty and what to do about it. Royal Commissions also contributed to increased awareness and a growing interest in social service and social work.

Social Union Agreement of 1999 – The Social Union Agreement of 1999 between the Government of Canada and the provinces and territories is the umbrella under which governments will concentrate their efforts to renew and modernize Canadian social policy. So far, several social welfare initiatives have been established under this framework: the National Child Benefit, the national children's agenda for child care, and services for persons with disabilities.

Social welfare – This refers to how people, communities and institutions in a society take action to provide certain minimum standards and certain opportunities. It is generally about helping people face contingencies. Social welfare comprises a range of institutions and involves the provision of programs of income security and social services.

Social welfare model of international social work – The more conventional social welfare model of international work is based on the notion that basic social welfare services should be developed in all countries to meet basic human needs. Social workers following this model of international practice are mainly concerned with the satisfaction of basic social and material needs of people (e.g., minimal standards of living, access to at least basic health, education, and other essential social services).

Social work practice – Work, consisting of a series or process of interventive actions, that is of benefit to those in need, especially work undertaken by trained staff. It may consist of social work with individuals, group work or community work. Social work is an action-oriented field in which individual and social change play key parts.

Social work with individuals – Social work with individuals is directed towards helping individuals using counselling and other one-on-one methods.

Social worker roles – In performing their day-to-day work, a social worker is expected to be knowledgeable and skilful in a variety of roles. The role that is selected and applied should ideally be the role that is most effective with a particular client in particular circumstances.

Stages of group development – For successful group work intervention, it is important to know how to identify the stages of group development. The intervention tasks for group work will be quite different depending on the type of group (e.g., self-help or treatment), but the stages of group development will often be the same for each type of group. By identifying the group's stage of development, workers can better help the group meet its needs and goals.

Stereotype – A set of beliefs or perceptions of groups of people, or ideas held by a number of people, often not based on fact.

Suffragette movement – The suffragette movement campaigned for the right for all women to vote. The following are the years in which women's suffrage was obtained in a variety of countries: New Zealand (1893); Australia (1902); Finland (1906); Norway (1913); Denmark (1915); the Netherlands and the Soviet Union (1917); Canada and Luxembourg (1918); Austria, Czechoslovakia (now the Czech Republic and Slovakia), Germany, Poland, and Sweden (1919); Belgium (partial, 1919; full, 1948); Ecuador (1929); South Africa (1930); Brazil and Uruguay (1932); Turkey and Cuba (1934); France (1944); Italy and Japan (1946); China and Argentina (1947); South Korea and Israel (1948); Chile, India, and Indonesia (1949). Switzerland granted the franchise to women in 1971.

Suicide risk – This refers to the likelihood that a person will take their own life as a result of the social and psychological circumstances in which they find themselves. For example, the suicide risk levels of gays, lesbians and bisexuals is now an area of grave concern.

Sustainable development – Development that meets the needs of the present without compromising the ability of future generations to meet their own needs.

Systemic discrimination – The operating policies, structures and functions of an ongoing system of normative patterns that serve to subjugate, oppress and force the dependence of individuals or groups. This involves establishing and sanctioning unequal rights, goals and priorities and sanctioning inequality in status as well as access to goods and services.

Systems theory – This theory that is the foundation for the generalist approach to social work, an approach that assumes that the human being is made up of smaller subsystems, such as cells and organs, but that the human being is in turn part of larger systems, such as family and society.

Task groups – This term is used to signify any group in which the major purpose is neither intrinsically nor immediately linked to the needs of the members of the group. In task groups, the overriding purpose is to accomplish a mandate and complete the work for which the group was convened.

Therapy groups – Therapy groups consist of individuals who do not share a household together or have any kind of relationship with one another outside the group setting. They are people seeking individual assistance.

Third World – The Third World includes the countries of Central and South America, Africa, and Asia. The First World refers to the Western capitalist countries of America and Western Europe. The Second World refers to the old Soviet Union countries.

Transition houses – Transition houses are homes set up to respond to the needs of abused women and their children. Because of their success, the number of transition houses or shelters is growing.

Treatment groups – Treatment groups gather for the purpose of meeting the therapeutic objectives of the group members. Individuals work as a group to address problems that they experience personally. The three types of treatment groups are family or household groups, therapy groups and self-help or peer groups.

Two-tier health system – A two-tiered health system refers to one in which those who can pay the extra fee or who work for employers who have extended health benefits are more privileged than others.

Undeserving poor – Poor people designated as deserving are seen as being of good moral character and only temporarily out of luck due to no fault of their own. This is an historical concept that arose with the early Poor Laws but it still informs income security today.

Unemployment – Unemployment is an involuntary loss of wage income. Official unemployment, or those counted in the unemployment statistics, are those who cannot find paid employment and are actively looking for a job. If a person has given up the search for a job, they are not considered to be part of the labour force and are not included in the statistics.

Unemployment rate – The percentage of individuals who are actively looking for work and are able to work but do not have a job, i.e., the number of unemployed individuals, divided by the total number of people fifteen years of age and older who have a job or are actively looking for work expressed as a percentage.

Universal benefits – Universal benefits are available to everyone in a specific category, such as "people over age sixty-five" or "children," on the same terms and as a right of citizenship. The idea is that all persons regardless of income and financial situation are equally eligible to receive program benefits.

Universal public health care – Canadians have not always had ready access to quality health care. Prior to the late 1940s, access to health care was based solely on one's ability to pay. Universal public health care for everyone in Canada took over five decades to evolve.

Universality – Section 10 of the *Canada Health Act* requires that 100 percent of the insured persons of a province be entitled to the insured health services provided for by the plan on uniform terms and conditions.

User fees – A small extra fee above the scale charged directly to the patient for hospital and physician services.

Virtual community work – Today, the Internet makes it possible for community workers and activists to expand their networks by identifying and contacting people in other communities who have similar interests and concerns. This could be loosely referred to as a kind of virtual community work.

Visible minorities – Within the Canadian context, this term (widely used in government statistics) refers to individuals who can be visibly identified and perceived as belonging to a racial group other than those of European origin. For this reason, it is a somewhat contentious term.

Voluntary clients – People who have chosen to seek the services of a social worker.

Welfare state – A system whereby the state ostensibly undertakes to protect the health and well-being of its citizens, especially those in financial need.

Workfare – Work for a specific minimum number of work units (measured in hours or output) in a job that is designated or approved by the welfare authority to qualify for the basic welfare benefit. In Ontario it is the name for Social Assistance.

Index